COMPARATIVE TREATMENT
OF EATING DISORDERS

3

COMPARATIVE TREATMENT OF EATING DISORDERS

Edited by
Katherine Miller and J. Scott Mizes

FREE ASSOCIATION BOOKS / LONDON

First published in Great Britain 2000 by
Free Association Books
57 Warren Street, London W1T 5NR

ISBN 1–85343–528–7

Typeset in the United States of America
Printed in the European Union by
Antony Rowe Ltd, Chippenham, England

Katherine J. Miller, Ph.D., is the Director of Clinical Training in the Department of Psychology at the Philadelphia College of Osteopathic of Medicine (PCOM), where she has helped to develop the Psy.D. program in clinical psychology since its beginning in 1995. She received her doctorate in counseling psychology from Temple University in 1990. She completed her psychology internship at Michigan State University Counseling Center, where she began her work with people with eating disorders under the supervision of Dr. Imogen Bowers. She worked with women with eating disorders for three years at the Renfrew Center in Philadelphia, Pennsylvania, and subsequently worked as a psychologist at the Graduate Hospital Eating Disorders Program in inpatient, outpatient, residential, and day treatment settings. She taught at the Temple University Counseling Psychology Program for three years before moving to her current position at PCOM. She has published several articles and book chapters, including her research on childhood sexual abuse and eating disorders and on body image among college men and women of diverse racial/ethnic backgrounds.

J. Scott Mizes, Ph.D., is currently an Associate Professor in the Department of Behavioral Medicine and Psychiatry at the West Virginia University School of Medicine, where he provides services to eating disorder and anxiety disorder patients. He received his Ph.D. in clinical psychology from the University of Arkansas-Fayetteville in 1983. He completed his internship at the University of Alabama-Birmingham School of Medicine, and completed a postdoctoral fellowship in behavior therapy and behavioral medicine at Case Western Reserve University (CWRU) School of Medicine in Cleveland, Ohio. He was on the faculty at the CWRU-MetroHealth Medical Center campus until 1997, where he was Director of the Eating Disorders Clinic. He is a Diplomate in Clinical Psychology, American Board of Professional Psychology, and a Fellow of the Divisions of Clinical Psychology and Health Psychology of the American Psychological Association. He has published several research articles and chapters on eating disorders. A significant portion of his research has focused on the development and validation of the Mizes Anorectic Cognitions Questionnaire (MAC), which is designed to assess the characteristic cognitions found in persons with bulimia nervosa, anorexia nervosa, and binge eating disorder.

Contents

Contributors

Rachel Bryant-Waugh, Ph.D.
Department of Psychological
  Medicine
Great Ormond Street Hospital
  for Children
Great Ormond Street
London, Great Britain

Scott C. Bunce, Ph.D.
MCP Hahnemann School of
  Medicine
EPPI
3200 Henry Avenue
Philadelphia, PA

Scott J. Crow, M.D.
University of Minnesota
Department of Psychiatry
2450 Riverside Avenue South
Minneapolis, MN

Piero De Giacomo, M.D.
University of Bari
Department of Neurological
  and Psychiatry Science
Policlinic Hospital of Bari
Piazza Giulio Cesare, 11
70124 Bari, Italy

Jenny Zoler Dounchis
San Diego State University
SDSU/UCSD Joint Doctoral
  Program in Clinical Psy-
  chology
Center for Eating and Weight
  Disorders
6363 Alvarado Court, Suite 100
San Diego, CA

April Fallon, Ph.D.
MCP Hahnemann School of
  Medicine
EPPI
3200 Henry Avenue
Philadelphia, PA

David H. Gleaves, Ph.D.
Department of Psychology
Texas A&M University
College Station, TX

Carolyn Gralweski, Ph.D.
Adler School of Professional
  Psychology
65 East Wacker Place, Suite
  2100
Chicago, IL

Nancy Logue, Ph.D.
The Renfrew Center of Bucks
   County
90 West Afton Avenue
Yardley, PA

James E. Mitchell, M.D.
Neuropsychiatric Research Insti-
   tute
University of North Dakota
   School of Medicine and
   Health Sciences
Medical Education Center
Neuroscience Department
1919 North Elm Street
Fargo, ND

Susan B. Netemeyer, Ph.D.
Family Therapy Clinic
7913 Wrenwood Boulevard,
   Suite B
Baton Rouge, LA

Carol B. Peterson, Ph.D.
Eating Disorders Research Pro-
   gram
University of Minnesota
2701 University Avenue SE
Suite #206
Minneapolis, MN

Susan Sands, Ph.D.
1664 Solano Avenue
Berkley, CA

Antonietta Santoni Rugiu
Eating Disorders Center and
   Day Hospital
Policlinic Hospital of Bari
Piazza Giulio Cesare, 11
70124 Bari, Italy

**Ulrike Schmidt, Ph.D., M.Phil,
   MRCPsych**
Bethlem and Maudsley Eating
   Disorder Unit
Denmark Hill
London, Great Britain

Mary F. Schneider, Ph.D.
Adler School of Professional
   Psychology
65 East Wacker Place
Suite 2100
Chicago, IL

Stacey Summers
Department of Psychology
Philadelphia College of Osteo-
   pathic Medicine
4190 City Avenue, Suite 226
Philadelphia, PA

**Janet Treasure, Ph.D., MRCP,
   FRCPsych**
Bethlem and Maudsley Eating
   Disorder Unit and Institute
   of Psychiatry
Denmark Hill
London, Great Britain

Nicholas A. Troop, Ph.D., B.Sc.
Department of Psychology
University of Essex
Wivenhoe Park
Colchester
Great Britain

R. Robinson Welch, Ph.D.
SDSU/UCDS
Joint Doctoral Program in Psychology
6363 Alvarado Court, Suite 103
San Diego, CA

Denise Wilfley, Ph.D.
SDSU/UCDS
Joint Doctoral Program in Psychology
6363 Alvarado Court, Suite 103
San Diego, CA

Donald A. Williamson, Ph.D.
Pennington Biomedical Research Center
6400 Perkins Road
Baton Rouge, LA

Tara L. Williams, M.S.
Department of Psychology
Texas A&M University
College Station, TX

Stephen A. Wonderlich, Ph.D.
Neuropsychiatric Research Institute
University of North Dakota School of Medicine and Health Sciences
Medical Education Center
Neuroscience Department
1919 North Elm Street
Fargo, ND

Foreword

I thoroughly enjoyed this book, but that is not to say that I agreed with everything written herein. In fact, my pleasure in reading derived in large part from the fact that I was stimulated and not infrequently provoked by the various opinions of my colleagues. The format of this series on comparative treatments is the same for each volume. There is an introductory chapter, a case presentation followed by a list of questions and a number of chapters by an author or authors representing different theoretical orientations. In the case of the present volume on eating disorders, which has been ably edited by Katherine Miller and Scott Mizes, the result is a book that provides a rich compendium on approaches to the treatment of a patient with a longstanding eating disorder. As I read, I found myself agreeing strongly with some observations and passionately disagreeing with others. I also was educated and enlightened by some of the insights provided in the chapters. There is no better way, I think, to clarify one's own thinking and stimulate creativity than to be presented by a series of pieces that focus on the same problem and that differ widely on approaches to a solution. All clinicians that work with patients with eating disorders for any length of time develop a sense of humility about our ability to help patients resolve these frequently refractory problems. This volume provides the collective wisdom of a series of experts who have given substantial thought to helping patients with these complex, often frustrating and difficult to treat disorders.

The initial chapter by David Gleaves, Katherine Miller, Tara Williams, and Stacey Summers provides a scholarly review of the diagnosis, epidemiology, associated morbidity, etiology, and treatment of eating disorders and provides an excellent introduction to the field and to the subsequent chapters. There is also a comprehensive summary (Appendix A), which provides an integrated summary of the comparisons among treatments presented in the preceding chapters. I found it helpful to refer to this summary at numerous points as I was reading and thinking about similarities and differences among the treatment approaches.

In addition to the Appendix, the volume concludes with a chapter by Katherine Miller that summarizes and compares the treatment models presented in the chapters. Therefore, I'd like to suggest some questions that the reader might want to consider or think about while reading the book. Specifically, are there crosscutting components of all of the treatments? Are there general principles that underlie effective treatment for any problem, and for Kristen's eating disorder, in particular? How do the treatments differ, and what are the implications of these differences for effective treatment?

All of the treatments have a structure that reflects the treatment philosophy. The treatment sessions are of specified duration and sessions are scheduled according to an agreed-upon plan. The treatment itself has a specified duration (although the understanding may be that the overall length of the treatment is indeterminate). Each of the treatments has phases, which include a beginning (including assessment), middle (during which the bulk of the work is accomplished), and termination (used for review and planning, and for ending the therapeutic relationship). For each type of treatment, there is a requirement that the treating clinician will have received the appropriate level of training and an assumption (either implicit or explicit) that the therapist will monitor his or her adherence to the model. Finally, each approach has assessment tools that are consistent with the treatment model and that may be used to monitor the progress of treatment.

Moreover, all of the treatments have a conceptual framework that provides a guide for understanding the development of human problems, a "theory of illness" as it were, and specific strategies to solve them. All therapists need a philosophy that aids in conferring a sense of cohesiveness to the treatment and informing clinical interventions. Moreover, it is critical for patients or clients to feel that the clinician's approach meshes with their values and is appropriate for their problem. All individuals who seek treatment for serious difficulties need to feel that they have come to the right place and that the therapist is qualified to be of help. Thus the provision of hope, a therapeutic frame, and a plan of action are probably necessary components of any good treatment.

All of the approaches also emphasize that treatment is a collaborative venture in which the therapeutic relationship provides the context and means of building and refining a shared understanding of the problem and the strategies to effect change. In an effective treatment, the therapist and patient create a "shared language" that promotes understanding or insight on the part of the patient and movement toward mutually agreed-upon goals.

In summary, there are numerous commonalities among the approaches and perhaps all psychotherapeutic interventions. Recently, there has been an increasing emphasis on the need for evidence-based or scientifically supported treatments and the use of "brand name" interventions. One downside to this trend is that it will be impractical for clinicians to obtain adequate training to utilize the growing number of evidence-based interventions. Therefore, it will behoove us to attempt to identify the general principles that underlie any effective treatment and identify ways to promulgate this information. Therefore, I encourage readers to think about general principles of effective psychotherapy while reading this volume.

There are also significant differences among the therapeutic models. First, there is considerable variability in the structure of the treatments. For example, some of the models emphasize highly structured, short-term interventions and others emphasize open-ended approaches over a longer period of time. The treatments also differ in the level of activity of the therapist (directive vs. nondirective) and targets of the intervention (behaviors, thoughts, feelings, interpersonal or family interactions). Finally, the models differ considerably on assumptions about the necessary conditions for and mechanisms of change or lasting improvement.

The dramatic differences among treatments raise critical questions. Is there any treatment model that is poorly conceived or any intervention that is ineffective? Are there any strategies that are ill advised, or worse, harmful to patients? I have my opinions about these questions, and I suspect that readers will too. I think that it's appropriate for me to maintain neutrality in the context of this introduction. However, I will comment that some of the treatment approaches may be less feasible than other approaches, at least in locations where there are insurance limits on payment for eating disorders treatment. I'll also go on record to assert that any eating disorders treatment that does not provide adequate medical monitoring for low weight or purging patients is unacceptable and potentially dangerous. However, when it comes to philosophy of treatment, my opinions are likely to differ substantially from those with other orientations. It is incumbent upon each of us to work to demonstrate the utility and efficacy of our particular models of treatment.

I hope each reader will find reading this book to be as stimulating and valuable as I did. As noted, I expect that you will be provoked and stimulated, but that you also will be pleased and satisfied with what you will learn.

Marsha D. Marcus
Department of Psychiatry
University of Pittsburgh
School of Medicine
May 2000

Preface

Developing effective treatment methods is a collective process. Clinicians share new problems and their efforts to solve them—informally at first, in restaurants with close colleagues, later at professional conferences. Case studies and exploratory research appear in the literature. Therapists from different schools of thought try what they know best. Eventually paradigms of treatment evolve. Researchers abstract what may be curative factors and compare the efficacy of different treatment approaches. Nevertheless, clinicians are still motivated by the persons they treat, by the complexity of patients' lives and the stories they tell, to refine theory and improve methods of helping.

The first chapter provides an overview of the eating disorders, including their characteristics, prevalence and incidence, medical complications, theories of etiology, and course. A brief history of the treatment of the eating disorders follows, with a summary of controlled studies on psychological treatment methods and what research shows regarding pharmacological interventions.

Chapter 2 introduces the case of Kristen, a composite portrait of a patient whose character development and life story were informed by the therapy of hundreds of women seen by the writers of the case. The case will allow readers to think about their own ideas about Kristen's condition and situation and how they might embark on assessment and treatment. The questions that we asked of each contributor are listed in this chapter as well.

Chapters 3 through 11 are the heart of the book—examples of how expert therapists representing nine different theoretical perspectives would approach Kristen had she presented herself to them for treatment. Each chapter describes the author(s)' theories about treatment and the therapist's skills and attributes and demonstrates the kind of clinical thinking and planning they would do. There are sections on assessment, conceptualization, and treatment planning; essential qualities of the therapeutic relationship; and treatment implementation and outcome. These chapters offer windows into the practices of psychotherapy as it is practiced daily by therapists who have devoted much of their professional lives to eating disorders treatment. Some authors are major researchers in the field and most have academic affiliations; yet there is great variety among the settings in which they work, ranging from private practice to large tertiary care facilities.

We had anticipated that descriptions would show that "pure" theoretical stances had been modified by formerly competing viewpoints, but we were surprised by the extent of integrative thinking found among these authors. Some readers may focus more on the similarities among approaches while others may prefer to emphasize the differences. Nevertheless, readers will be able to learn a great deal about each approach and consider its usefulness. The final chapter of the book summarizes and compares the nine treatment models, with an accompanying chart in Appendix A.

We hope that this practical approach to clinical work will be useful to those currently practicing in the eating disorders field, to clinicians who are interested in exploring this specialty, and to students of psychology and other mental health professions. It is a variation on the traditional case study which demonstrates the clinical reasoning and application of theories by experienced eating disorder clinicians. This book offers the clinician an opportunity to compare different points of view about what is effective as related to the same case. We hope that this is a contribution to the ongoing conversation in the field about effective treatment for the eating disorders.

1

Eating Disorders: An Overview

David H. Gleaves, Katherine J. Miller,
Tara L. Williams, and Stacey A. Summers

The understanding of anorexia nervosa and bulimia nervosa put forth in this chapter provides a snapshot in time, a particular picture of the eating disorders provided by recent empirical studies and clinical experience. We will review the characteristics, prevalence and incidence, and medical complications of anorexia nervosa and bulimia nervosa. The multidetermined nature of eating disorder etiology will be outlined, including biological, sociocultural, and psychological factors, with a brief presentation of what is known about the course of the disorders. The last section provides an overview of the history of treatment for eating disorders, with findings of recent controlled outcome studies.

CHARACTERISTICS OF ANOREXIA NERVOSA AND BULIMIA NERVOSA

The eating disorders, anorexia and bulimia nervosa, are characterized by gross disturbances in eating behavior and highly characteristic extreme concerns about shape and weight (Fairburn & Cooper,

1996). In both disorders, self-esteem is influenced to a great degree by feelings and/or perceptions of body weight, size, and shape (American Psychiatric Association, 1994).

Anorexia Nervosa

According to the current Diagnostic and Statistical Manual of Mental Disorders (DSM-IV) (APA, 1994), the hallmark feature of anorexia nervosa is a "refusal to maintain body weight at or above a minimally normal weight for age and height" (p. 544). Significantly underweight is defined as less than 85% of that expected for an individual of particular height, although earlier editions of the DSM used a criteria of 75%. Individuals with anorexia can be underweight for two reasons: (1) in early adolescence they failed to gain weight when their height was increasing (Lask & Bryant-Waugh, 1997); or (2) in late adolescence they became underweight by engaging in dieting, exercise, or purgative strategies (Barlow & Durand, 1999; Walsh & Garner, 1997). Individuals with anorexia are underweight due to conscious efforts to avoid gaining weight, such as skipping meals and exercising excessively (Walsh & Garner, 1997; Davis et al., 1997), and often experience obsessional thoughts of thinness that motivate them towards extreme dieting practices (Williamson, Bentz, & Rabalais, 1998).

Anorexics, according to DSM-IV (APA, 1994) criteria, also have "intense fear of gaining weight or becoming fat, even though underweight" (p. 544). This fear may not necessarily be a fear of obesity, but rather, a fear that they will become "fatter" than they are right now. Paradoxically, this fear of fatness often intensifies as more weight is lost (APA, 1994; Walsh & Garner, 1997).

A "Disturbance in the way in which one's body weight or shape is experienced, undue influence of body weight of self evaluation, or denial of the seriousness of current low body weight" (APA, 1994, p. 545) is another aspect to anorexia nervosa. Individuals with anorexia may experience their bodies, or parts of their bodies, as being bigger than they actually are (Walsh & Garner, 1997; Schlundt & Johnson, 1990). However, this experience is most likely not an error in perception (perceptual body image), but is rather an error in judgment (attitudinal or affective body image), reflecting the strong negative thoughts and feelings that individuals with anorexia have about their bodies (Garfinkel, 1995; Williamson, 1996; Williamson, Cubic, & Gleaves, 1993). Anorexics may weigh or measure themselves frequently, and feel ashamed, embarrassed, or frustrated if they gain weight. However, weight loss is viewed as a great accomplishment and an illustration of self-control and self-discipline (APA, 1994; Walsh & Garner, 1997; Schlundt & Johnson, 1990).

The final diagnostic criterion for anorexia nervosa is amenorrhea, defined by DSM-IV as "the absence of at least three consecutive menstrual cycles." Menarche can be delayed by the onset of anorexia, or can cease due to the disorder (Walsh & Garner, 1997). Amenorrhea is due to the effects of starvation on the secretion of hormones by the pituitary gland, and is considered the physical index of the effects of starvation (APA, 1994; Barlow & Durand, 1999). However, not all women who are extremely emaciated experience amenorrhea and some women who are of normal weight or even above normal weight may experience menstrual irregularities or complete amenorrhea, which has led to questions being raised about whether or not it should be a diagnostic criterion of anorexia nervosa (Cassell & Gleaves, in press).

In addition to the core eating and body image–related psychopathology of anorexia nervosa, a variety of additional psychopathology has been described in the literature (Braun, Sunday, & Halmi, 1994; Herzog, D. B., Keller, M. B., Sacks, N. R., Yeh, C. J., & Lavori, 1992). Axis I problems include depression (Fornari, Kaplan, Sandberg, Mathews, & Skolnick et al., 1992; Herzog, Keller, Sacks et al., 1992; Strober & Katz, 1988), anxiety (Fornari et al., 1992; Herzog, Keller, Sacks et al., 1992), obsessive compulsive behavior (Kaye et al., 1992), posttraumatic stress disorder (Gleaves, Eberenz, & May, 1998), and substance use (Henzel, 1984; Holderness, Brooks-Gunn, & Warren, 1994; Zweben, 1987). Interpersonal and family problems (Steiger, Liquornik, Chapman, & Hussain, 1991) and personality disorders (Garner, Marcus, Halmi, & Loranger, 1989; Wonderlich, Swift, Slotnik, & Goodman, 1990), especially of the borderline type, are also common. Gleaves and Eberenz (1993) included all of the core and additional psychopathology in a factor analysis to develop a multidimensional model of anorexia. The dimensions were: (1) fasting and restrictive eating; (2) depression, anxiety, and negative self-image;

(3) bulimic behaviors; (4) fear of fatness/body image disturbance; and (5) impulsive behavior/post-trauma response" (p. 147).

Two subtypes of anorexia have been identified and are differentiated in the DSM-IV: restricting subtype, and binge-eating/purging subtype. Individuals with restricting subtype do not engage in binge-eating or purging behavior (vomiting, laxatives, diuretics, etc.); they are "successful self-starvers." Restricting anorexics are usually obsessional in thinking and may be more socially awkward and isolated than binge-eating/purging anorexics (Walsh & Garner, 1997). About half of diagnosed anorexics engage in bingeing and purging (Agras, 1987). Binge-eating/purging anorexics are regularly engaged in binge-eating and purging. These individuals usually have a history of higher weight or obesity, may be heavier, and often demonstrate impulsive behavior and thinking (DaCosta & Halmi, 1992; Garfinkel, 1995; Garner, Garfinkel, & O'Shaughnessy, 1985).

Bulimia Nervosa

Some researchers have suggested that anorexia and bulimia should be thought of as two manifestations of a single disorder with fear of weight gain as the primary criterion (Schlundt & Johnson, 1990). Although anorexia and bulimia do have in common body image disturbances and fear of weight gain or fatness, bulimics are usually of normal weight (Williamson, Cubic, & Gleaves, 1993). The clinical presentation of bulimia is different from that of anorexia nervosa (especially the restricting type) in several ways.

The first salient characteristic of bulimia nervosa is "recurrent episodes of binge eating." According to the DSM-IV (APA, 1994), in order to be diagnosed with bulimia, an individual must eat large amounts of food in a discrete period of time (two hours or less, an amount larger than would be eaten in a similar period under similar circumstances), and feel a lack of control over eating during the episodes (Garfinkel, 1995). The concept of a binge, however, is quite subjective. Eating binges (as described by some bulimic patients) may not be objectively large or unusual in time or circumstance (Walsh, 1993), but may rather be characterized by eating something that was simply unintended. In addition, it has been found that there is extreme variability among bulimics in the size of binges, some being large and some very small (Rossiter & Agras, 1990). Subjective and objective binges differ only with regard to the amount of food consumed (Niego, Pratt, & Agras, 1997). Thus, it may be the quality of the binge, rather than the quantity, that characterizes a person's binge eating (Garner, Shafer, & Rosen, 1992). In general, binges usually consist of dessert or snack foods, and are often triggered by hunger, feelings/mood states, or stressors (APA, 1994; Garfinkel, 1995; Schlundt & Johnson, 1990; Walsh & Garner, 1997).

The second salient feature of bulimia nervosa is that "recurrent inappropriate compensatory behaviors [are used] in order to prevent weight gain" (APA, 1994, p. 545). The most frequently used compensatory behavior is self-induced vomiting, employed by around 80% of bulimics (Schlundt & Johnson, 1990). Other methods include laxatives, diuretics, enemas, and thyroid medication (Mizes, 1985; Schlundt & Johnson, 1990; Walsh & Garner, 1997). Individuals engaging in these compensatory methods are classified as the purging type of bulimia nervosa. Purging bulimics have been found to exhibit more psychopathology than nonpurging bulimics (Willmuth, Leitenberg, Rosen, & Cado, 1988). However, other efforts may be made by bulimics to compensate for binge eating, including fasting and excessive exercise (Barlow & Durand, 1999; Walsh & Johnson, 1997). Bulimics engaging solely in these compensatory behaviors are classified as non-purging type (APA, 1994; Garfinkel, 1995). It is the pattern of binge eating followed by compensatory behaviors that characterizes bulimia nervosa and must, on average, occur at least twice a week for 3 months in order for bulimia nervosa to be diagnosed.

As in anorexia, there is a body image component to bulimia, and empirical research suggests that it may be equivalent to that found in anorexia nervosa (Williamson, Cubic, & Gleaves, 1993). The DSM (APA, 1994) notes that "self evaluation is unduly influenced by body shape and weight" (p. 550), and many researchers posit that compensatory methods of weight control are motivated by intense fear of weight gain and body image disturbances like those seen in anorexia nervosa (Garfinkel, 1995; Williamson, Bentz, & Rabalais, 1998). Bulimics, like anorexics, have self-esteem that is regulated by appearance, feel pressure to diet and lose weight, and feel distressed by weight gain (Barlow & Durand, 1999; Garfinkel, 1995; Schlundt & Johnson, 1990; Walsh & Garner, 1997).

As with anorexia nervosa, bulimia nervosa is also frequently associated with a variety of additional psychopathology (Williamson, 1990), including depression (Herzog et al., 1992), anxiety (Braun et al., 1994), substance abuse (Braun et al., 1994), and personality disorders (Braun et al., 1994; Holderness, Brooks-Gunn, & Warren, 1994). Researchers have also adopted multidimensional models to best account for the core and additional psychopathology of the disorder (Gleaves & Eberenz, 1995; Gleaves, Williamson, & Barker, 1993; Tobin, Johnson, Steinberg, Staats, & Dennis, 1991). Across several studies, the core dimensions that are most consistently found are: (1) bulimic behaviors (i.e., bingeing and purging); (2) restrictive eating; (3) body dissatisfaction/fear of fatness; (4) affective disturbance; and (5) personality disturbance. Some studies have found the latter two dimensions to be a single dimension.

PREVALENCE AND INCIDENCE OF ANOREXIA AND BULIMIA NERVOSA

Incidence rates of anorexia nervosa (per 100,000 per year) have been reported to range from .24 to 1.12 (Hsu, 1990). In mental health facilities since the 1970s, the incidence of reported anorexia cases has been about 5 per 100,000 of the total population per year. The average point prevalence for anorexia has been calculated as 280 per 100,000 young females (0.28%) (Garfinkel, 1995). For late adolescent and early adult women, the prevalence rates of anorexia have been found to range from 0.5% to 1%. Overall, the prevalence of anorexia is most likely less than 1%, but may be higher in specific populations (Schlundt & Johnson, 1990; Williamson, 1993).

The incidence of bulimia nervosa in mental health care has been reported to be 6 per 100,000 per year (Garfinkel, 1995). Estimates of prevalence in late adolescent and young adult females have ranged from 1% to 3% (Fairburn & Beglin, 1990; APA, 1994). Rates of prevalence of bulimia among females have been reported to be especially high in college populations (e.g., 12.5 to 18.5%) (Pope, Hudson, Yurgelun-Todd, & Hudson, 1984), with up to 19% of female students reporting some bulimic symptoms (Garfinkel, 1995). However, the prevalence of bulimia is less in older populations; Bushnell, Wells, Hornblow, Oakley-Browne, and Joyce (1990) found that among women 25 to 44, the prevalence was 2%, and 0.4% among women 45 to 64.

MEDICAL COMPLICATIONS OF THE EATING DISORDERS

Medical complications are common in eating disordered individuals and can even be life threatening. Such complications are due to the effects of starvation, vomiting, and the use of laxatives, diuretics, and other medications to enhance weight loss (Garner, 1997). Some physical problems are common to anorexia and bulimia nervosa. Individuals with both disorders are likely to have electrolyte imbalances due to dieting practices, which can lead to cardiac arrythmia or other cardiac dysfunction (Barlow & Durand, 1999). Fluid imbalances and edema can result in kidney or renal dysfunction (Brotman, Rigotti, & Herzog, 1985; Garner, 1997; Pomeroy, 1996). Furthermore, anorexics and bulimics are both at risk for cerebral atrophy (Touyz & Beumont, 1994), neurological abnormalities (Brotman et al., 1985; Garner, 1997), hypothalamic-pituitary-adrenal axis dysfunction (Devlin, Walsh, Katz, Roose, Linkie et al., 1989; Weiner, 1985), and abnormal thyroid functioning (Brotman et al., 1985; Spalter, Gwirtsman, Demitrack, & Gold, 1993). However, the physical consequences of each individual patient will depend on her extent of malnutrition and the maladaptive weight loss strategies chosen. Starvation, vomiting, laxatives, and diuretics each have unique medical complications.

Medical Complications of Starvation

The obvious effect of starvation on physical health is a decline in body weight and percentage of body fat. However, the effects of starvation on the body extend beyond weight loss. The first study of the effects of starvation on physical and mental functioning was conducted by Keys, Brozek, Henshel, Mickelsen, and Taylor (1950). These researchers found that the semi-starvation of a group of men had extreme physical effects that included: decreased body temperature, heartrate, respiration, and basal metabolic rate; gastrointestinal pain, dizziness, headaches, reduced strength, poor motor control, edema, hair loss, decreased tolerance for cold temperatures, and visual and auditory disturbances. Since this research, the effects of starvation in anorexic patients have been further studied and elaborated. Starvation results in reduced activity, lack of energy, and slower movement (Garner, 1997; Schlundt & Johnson, 1990). Starvation can cause cardiac abnormalities, possibly even mitral valve prolapse (Mitchell, Pomeroy, & Adson, 1997), as well as tachycardia, hypotension, ventricle arrhythmias, and cardiac failure (Brotman et al., 1985; Mizes, 1985; Sharp & Freeman, 1993). Menstrual dysfunction (including amenorrhea) and infertility may result from starvation (Barlow & Durand, 1999; Brotman et al., 1985; Garner, 1997). Starvation leads to hair loss and the development of lanugo hair (peach like fuzz) on the face and body (Barlow & Durand, 1999; Garner, 1997). In addition, starvation may cause anemia (Howard, Leggat, & Chaudhry, 1992), bone marrow suppression (Pomeroy, 1996), and increased risk for osteoporosis (especially if the anorexia occurs during critical developmental periods such as adolescence) leading to bone fractures (Sharp & Freeman, 1993). Starvation may also result in gingivitis and periodontal disease due to malnutrition (Pomeroy, 1996).

Medical Complications of Vomiting and Laxatives

Vomiting is frequently used by bulimics, despite its ineffectiveness as a long-term weight loss strategy (Garner, 1997). The medical complications resulting from self-induced vomiting are extensive, and some can be fatal. The most dangerous consequence of self-induced vomiting is electrolyte imbalance. Electrolytes (e.g., sodium, potassium, chloride, etc.) are essential for metabolic and cell functioning and, if abnormal, can lead to cardiac complications and sudden death (Brotman et al., 1985; Garner, 1997; Mizes, 1985; Pomeroy, 1996). Gastrointestinal problems, such as constipation, abdominal pain, bloating, and delayed gastric emptying may also result from frequent vomiting. In addition, erosive esophagitis, esophageal perforation, or esophageal strictures are potential problems (Brotman et al., 1985; Geliebter, Melton, McCray, Gallagher, Gage et al. 1992; Mizes, 1985; Pomeroy, 1996). Other physical risks include: aspiration of gastric contents, chemical or bacterial pneumonitis, and thoracic pressure forcing air into surrounding bodily tissues such as the head, neck, and chest (Pomeroy, 1996). Swollen salivary glands (Mizes, 1985; Sharp & Freeman, 1993) as well as erosion of tooth enamel (Brotman et al., 1985; McComb, 1993) may also result from self-induced vomiting. Lastly, vomiting may cause skin or conjunctival hemorrhages, in addition to bruises and callouses on the thumb and fingers (Pomeroy, 1996).

Ipecac is a drug that is used to induce vomiting and may be used by eating disordered individuals to aid them in self-induced vomiting. Ipecac has medical complications beyond those resulting from self-induced vomiting alone, such as cardiotoxicity leading to sudden death (Garner, 1997), cardiomyopathy, and skeletal muscle atrophy (Mitchell, Pomeroy, Seppala, & Huber, 1988). Ipecac is not eliminated from the body; thus it accumulates over time.

Laxatives are used by some anorexics and bulimics because they lead to temporary weight loss by depleting the body of fluids. However, laxatives are ineffective for long-term weight loss because the loss of fluid is soon offset by the body's normal homeostatic mechanisms (Garner, 1997). Laxatives, like vomiting, can lead to electrolyte imbalances, leading to cardiac dysfunction and possible death (Brotman et al., 1985). Laxatives also cause metabolic acidosis, dehydration, black discoloration of the colon, and colon dysfunction (Brotman et al., 1985; Pomeroy, 1996). It is possible that long-term use of laxatives can cause loss of normal peristolic function (Pomeroy, 1996), causing an individual to become dependent on laxatives for normal bowel movements (Schlundt & Johnson, 1990). Laxative abuse may also lead to urinary, kidney, and pancreatic dysfunction, as well as gastrointestinal bleeding.

Medical Complications of Diuretics and Diet Pills

Diuretics lead to perceived weight loss by inhibiting the renal reabsorption of electrolytes, which leads to a loss of sodium and body water, and mild dehydration (Schlundt & Johnson, 1990). In addition to the physical effects of dehydration, diuretics can cause electrolyte abnormalities, edema, and metabolic alkalosis, and may lead to idiopathic anemia, as well as a kidney disorder known as Psuedo-

Bartter's syndrome (Brotman et al., 1985; Pomeroy, 1996; Schlundt & Johnson, 1990).

Over-the-counter diet pills suppress appetite by stimulating the sympathetic nervous system (Schlundt & Johnson, 1990). Appetite suppression drugs may be very appealing to an eating disordered individual who is having difficulty adhering to restrictive eating patterns. The medical consequences of diet pills include: agitation, anxiety, hypertension, seizures, renal failure, neurological impairment, and cardiac arrythmia (Mitchell, Pomeroy, Seppala, & Huber, 1988; Pomeroy, 1996).

THE ETIOLOGY OF EATING DISORDERS

Although different theories of etiology have been proposed, few researchers or clinicians would take the position that eating disorders have a single or unitary cause. Just as their psychopathology is believed to be multidimensional, their etiology is assumed to involve multiple factors. Generally, these can be grouped into biological, psychological, and social factors leading to a combined biopsychosocial model of the etiology of these disorders (Johnson & Connors, 1987).

Biological Factors

Regarding biological variables, family studies suggest that eating disorders seem to run in families and may thus have a genetic component. In twin studies of bulimia (Kendler et al., 1991) and anorexia (Walters & Kendler, 1995) researchers used structured interviews to study the prevalence of the disorders among 2,163 female twins. For bulimia nervosa, there was a concordance rate of only .09 for dizygotic twins; the rate was .23 for identical twins. However, because adoption studies have not been conducted, sociocultural influences cannot be ruled out. Furthermore, if eating disorders are inherited, what exactly *is* being inherited is not clear. Earliest biological theories of the eating disorders focused on the possible role of the hypothalamus; lesions in the lateral hypothalamus and ventral medial hypothalamus were surmised to be associated with anorexia and bulimia, respectively. Early animal studies have not generalized to humans. More recent biological theories of bulimia nervosa propose disturbances in neurotransmitters, specifically serotonin (Goldbloom & Garfinkel, 1990; Jimerson, Wolfe, Metzger, Finkelstein, Cooper et al., 1997).

One biological theory, known as the affective variant hypothesis (Hinz & Williamson, 1987; Hudson, Pope, Jonas, & Yurgelin-Todd, 1983) is that eating disorders are a variation of an affective disorder. Support for this theory comes from four lines of evidence: (1) depression is often a prominent feature of patients with bulimia nervosa; (2) a high prevalence of affective illness has been found among family members of bulimics; (3) some bulimics respond favorably to antidepressant drugs; and (4) there is a similarity between bulimics and depressed patients in their response to the Dexamethasome Suppression Test (Wilson & Lindholm, 1987).

However, the propositions that follow from the affective variant hypotheses have not been supported (Swift, Andrews, & Barklage, 1986; Hinz & Williamson,1987). Studies have shown that only a minority of bulimics are depressed when they present for treatment. Only when the bulimic's entire life is considered are high rates truly found. It is common for most psychiatric patients to be depressed at some point in their life. The DST may reflect neuroendocrine abnormalities, but it is not generally regarded as diagnostic of depression. Controlled family studies have failed to yield positive results. Studies of antidepressant medications were found to be inconsistent, and it is generally considered illogical to draw etiological inferences from treatment (Hinz & Williamson, 1987).

For anorexia nervosa, another possible biological mechanism in the development or maintenance of the disorder is a possible dysregulation in the endogenous opioids (Marrazzi & Luby, 1986), leading the person to being "addicted" to the state of starvation. However, this mechanism would not explain how and why the individual began strictly dieting in the first place or explain the origin of the high fear of fatness. Furthermore, opioid antagonists have not been found to be successful in the treatment of anorexia.

In terms of overall conclusions that can be drawn regarding biological variables and eating disorders, Barlow and Durand (1999) reviewed the literature and concluded that there is no question that biological factors are active in the regulation of eating and that there is some degree of biological dysregulation (most likely in the neurotransmitter serotonin) associated with the eating disorders. However, the emerging consensus is that these neurobiological variables are a result of the starvation and the binge-purge cycle rather than a cause.

Thus, if eating disorders are inherited, what exactly is being inherited? Hsu (1991) speculated that it might be nonspecific personality traits (such as poor emotional stability and impulse control) that are inherited. The biological vulnerability might then interact with social or psychological factors to produce an eating disorder. Overall, despite a wealth of data on the physiology of eating disorders, the role that these factors play in the etiology of the disorders is still unclear (Weiner, 1985).

Socio-Cultural Factors

Socio-cultural factors are considered by many to play a major role (if not *the* most important role) in the etiology of eating disorders. In fact, many researchers regard anorexia and bulimia nervosa as culturally bound syndromes that cannot be understood outside of a cultural context. The socio-cultural factors considered to be related to the etiology of eating disorders are western society's preoccupation with thinness, dieting, and physical fitness (Sobal, 1995). We live in a culture in which physical appearance is extremely important. As Wilfley and Rodin (1995) wrote, "thinness in women has come to symbolize competence, success, control, and sexual attractiveness, while obesity represents laziness, self-indulgence, and a lack of will-power" (p. 78). Obesity is regarded not only as a health concern, but also a significant social stigma, especially among women.

Although some would argue that today's society has become obsessed with beauty and physical *perfection*, some writers (e.g., Wilfley & Rodin, 1995) would assert that it is not really physical perfection that has become the ideal but rather an *unnatural, unrealistic* body size ideal that is forcing young women to treat their bodies in an unnatural way. According to these authors, a healthy normal weight woman would have 22 to 25% body fat, whereas the current ideal is based on models who have 10 to 15% body fat (on average, with some significantly less). It can be demonstrated that many fashion models, as well as Playboy Centerfolds and Miss America contestants, would meet the body weight criterion for anorexia nervosa (Wilfley & Rodin, 1995; Wiseman, Gray, Mosimann, & Ahrens, 1992). Unfortunately, the problem is getting worse rather than better. Wiseman et al. (1992) demonstrated that the average body weight for Miss America contestants and Playboy centerfolds has steadily declined over the last few decades while the weight of the average American woman has steadily increased.

There is a wealth of data supporting the role of sociocultural factors in the etiology of eating disorders. Persistent attempts at weight reduction have reached epidemic proportions among young women in Western societies (Rodin, Silberstein, & Striegel-Moore, 1984; Rosen & Gross, 1987). Among college aged and adolescent women, dieting has been found to be more common than not dieting, with attempts to lose weight usually beginning at the age of 12 to 15 years (Schlundt & Johnson, 1990). There is also evidence that eating disorders as currently defined occur mainly in industrialized, developed countries and that they are rare outside Western societies and less affluent western societies. It has also been found that when persons immigrate from less to more industrialized countries, they are more likely to develop eating disorders (Wilfley & Rodin, 1995). Eating disorders are also becoming more common among countries (e.g., Spain) as they become more "westernized" or "Americanized" (Raich, Rosen, Deus, Pèrez, Requena et al., 1992).

A final factor supporting the role of sociocultural factors in the etiology of eating disorders is the great disparity in the prevalence or incidence of eating disorders between men and women, where women outnumber men approximately 10:1 (Wifley & Rodin, 1995). This disparity is greater by far than for most other psychiatric disorders. One could argue, of course, that a gender difference does not necessarily imply that the causal factor is sociocultural; it may imply a biological factor. In fact, there is evidence for biological differences in the way dieting affects serotonergic functioning (see above biological factors) in men versus women (Goodwin, Fairburn, & Cowen, 1987). However, there is ample evidence that the gender difference in the prevalence of eating disorders is largely explained by sociocultural factors. For one, there is a greater incidence of eating disorders among subgroups of males where there are pressures for thinness (e.g., male models, wrestlers, jockeys; Andersen, 1995; Wilfley &

Rodin, 1995). Second, body image studies (beginning with the classic study by Fallon & Rozen, 1985) consistently demonstrate that, on average, men are simply not dissatisfied with their body size while women are on average highly dissatisfied. In fact, if men are dissatisfied, they may actually want to be larger rather than thinner (Fallon & Rozen, 1985). Finally, when men are forced to diet as women with eating disorders do, the men develop many if not all of the symptoms of eating disorders (Keys et al., 1950). Thus, the biological potential to develop eating disorders may be there for men; they simply don't diet or have the extreme fears of weight gain that women do, most likely due to sociocultural differences and/or psychological differences, which will be discussed next.

Life Events

Katzman and Lee (1997) cite Asian populations with all of the symptoms of anorexia nervosa except the fear of fatness, and they have suggested a broader definition of the eating disorders which emphasizes powerlessness. In this formulation, food refusal is an attempt to free oneself from external control rather than a manifestation of the fear of fatness. Several lines of research indicate that family problems, trauma, and other difficult life events which could lead to feelings of powerlessness are risk factors for eating disorders. This research offers clues to why some who are not subject to cultural pressures for thinness may have eating disorders.

Welch, Doll, and Fairburn (1997) found in a community study that bulimic women had experienced significantly more negative life events in the year before onset of the eating disorder than a group matched for age and parental class, and that the stress was cumulative. These events included disruption from a major house move, change in family structure, physical illness, pregnancy, or sexual or physical abuse. Schmidt, Tiller, Blanchard, Andrews, and Treasure (1997) found that eating disordered patients had more major life difficulties than community controls, with stresses in close relationships the most common before onset. Another community study (Fairburn, Welch, Doll, Davies, & O'Connor, 1997) compared bulimics to healthy and psychiatric controls. Bulimics had experienced more parental depression, alcoholism, and drug abuse; parental arguments, criticism, underinvolvement, and high expectations; low parental contact; and more critical comments about shape, weight, or eating from their families. Other studies (see O'Kearney, 1996, for a review) have indicated that attachment problems are common in women with eating disorders, and family studies have shown significant differences in the quality of family relationship. For example, Humphrey (1988, 1989) found that parents of anorexics give mixed messages of nurturant affection and neglect of their daughters' needs for self-expression, as well as having high marital dissatisfaction. Bulimic families tend to have more conflict, hostility, mutual neglect, and rejection than other families (Humphrey, 1988, 1989; Wonderlich, Klein, & Council, 1996).

Van der Kolk (1996) writes that eating problems are one way that traumatized persons regulate the intolerable feelings and extreme physiological arousal of posttraumatic stress. Wonderlich, Brewerton, Jocic, Dansky, and Abbott (1997) published a rigorous literature review on childhood sexual abuse and eating disorders and concluded that childhood sexual abuse is a risk factor for bulimia nervosa. Other types of trauma that have been associated with eating disorders are refugee status (Ajdukovic & Ajducovic, 1993), acculturation (Dolan, 1991), and racism, poverty, and heterosexism (Thompson, 1994).

Psychological Factors

Behavioral and Cognitive Theories

There is no single generally accepted cognitive-behavioral theory for the etiology of anorexia or bulimia nervosa. Within this broad paradigm, investigators have differed in the degree to which they attribute symptoms to stress, anxiety, distorted patterns of thinking, habitual behavior, lack of assertiveness, poor labeling of internal states, relationship problems, and cravings associated with restrictive dieting, or the maintenance of a subnormal weight.

Anxiety due to the possibility of weight gain has received a large amount of attention and has been proposed to be the principle factor in more strictly behavioral models of bulimia nervosa (Mizes, 1985; Rosen & Leitenberg, 1982; Slade, 1982; Williamson, Kelley,

Davis, Ruggiero, & Veitia, 1985). According to this anxiety model of bulimia, binge eating produces anxiety about gaining weight, and purging is an act to lower this anxiety. The post-purge anxiety reduction is hypothesized to have a negative reinforcement effect which will increase the probability of further purges (Mizes, 1985). Purging is also seen as an outlet to further bingeing in that, if the ability to purge is taken away, the patient generally does not binge (Rosen & Leitenberg, 1982). The purging also eliminates nutrients from the body, which leads to biological deprivation and hunger which lead to more binge eating. The initial biological deprivation and hunger is usually brought on by dietary restraint. It has been concluded elsewhere (Clark & Palmer, 1983; Smead, 1984) that dieting *precedes* bingeing and eating disorders rather that the reverse.

The anxiety model for anorexia nervosa (Williamson, 1990) is basically a modification of that for bulimia nervosa, the difference being that the behavior that is reinforced is avoidance of food altogether, excessive exercise, or other behaviors that eliminate or avoid caloric intake. When the anorexic does eat, anxiety about gaining weight intensifies, which leads to intensified dieting.

Cognitive theories about eating disorder etiology are in line with cognitive theories of other emotional disorders (e.g., Beck, 1976). According to Fairburn (1997), cognitive distortions are the prominent core feature of both anorexia and bulimia nervosa. The cognitive distortions associated with eating disordered individuals and the role such distortions play in the symptomatology of the disorder have been well documented. Polivy, Herman, Olmsted, and Jazwinski (1984) described the rigid rules and dichotomous thinking style employed by most eating disordered individuals. In addition to the thinking errors associated with other emotional disorders such as depression and anxiety, persons with anorexia or bulimia nervosa are generally found to have a variety of irrational beliefs specifically related to food and diet (e.g., some foods automatically make you fat, regardless of the amount; one should never eat carbohydrate rich foods), purging (e.g., all food is purged by vomiting or using laxatives), binge-eating (e.g., I have no control after eating a forbidden food), and appearance (e.g., my worth as a person depends on my physical appearance; Rosen, 1987).

Cognitive behavioral models also place great emphasis on the role of dieting behavior in the etiology of anorexia and bulimia. Dieting is a major component of anorexia nervosa, restricting type, and is one of the diagnostic criteria. With bulimia nervosa, the connection between dieting and the disorder is more controversial (e.g., Anderson, 1998; Wilson, 1995). While almost all researchers and/or clinicians acknowledge that dieting plays some role in the etiology of the disorder, there is great disparity in terms of the degree to which researchers think it plays a role. Some conclude that dieting plays a major causal role in the etiology of the disorder (e.g., Polivy & Herman, 1985) while there are others who point to the fact that dieting and weight loss may have a number of positive rather than negative psychological effects (Wilson, 1995). The resolution of this controversy may require careful attention to how dieting is being defined (e.g., attempting to reduce calories versus actually doing it, and reducing calories to lose weight versus not gain weight), how one distinguishes between different types of dieting (e.g., starvation and fad diets versus healthy meal planning and lifestyle changes) and attention to dieting as an initiating factor versus a maintaining factor in bulimia nervosa (e.g., Lowe, Gleaves, & Eberenz, 1998).

Psychodynamic Theories

As with cognitive-behavioral theories, there is also not one generally accepted psychodynamic formulation for bulimia nervosa. The early psychodynamic/psychoanalytic literature generally did not differentiate between anorexia and bulimia, and bulimia was not regarded as a separate diagnostic entity. Accordingly, early theories did not differentiate between the disorders.

Although most psychoanalytic thinkers share a core set of assumptions and beliefs about eating disorders derived from Freud's theories, there are a number of contemporary variations in psychoanalytic theory, each of which is associated with a different conceptualization of eating disorders. Some emphasize ego processes, whereas others focus on the development of the personality through the psychosexual stages, and others on internal representations (Schlundt & Johnson, 1990).

Freud wrote very little about eating disorders. In what he did write, he attributed anorexia to traumatic childhood events mainly centered around childhood seduction and oral sex. The early psychoanalytic proposition equated eating behavior with sexual instinct. It was suggested that the adolescent is unable to meet the demands of mature genitality and regresses to a more primitive level, at which oral gratification is associated with sexual pleasure. Thus, anorexia is viewed as a defense against oral impregnation fantasies (and the anxiety generated by such fantasies), and bulimia is seen as an expression of unconscious desires for sexual gratification. This view was prominent during the 1940s and 1950s (Bruch, 1973).

The classic psychodynamic formulation of anorexia and bulimia has been extended to include aggression and guilt. A variety of possible meanings have been given to food and eating. According to Falstein, Feinstein, and Judas (1956), "Eating may be equated with gratification, impregnation, intercourse, performance, pleasing the mother, growing; or it may represent castrating, destroying, engulfing, killing, cannibalism. Food may symbolize the breast, the genitals, feces, poison, a parent, or a sibling" (p. 765).

With more modern psychoanalytic theories, conflicts are still thought to be very important, but the emphasis recently is not so much on sexual conflicts as it was with the earlier psychoanalytic theories. Now theorists acknowledge conflicts in many areas, and that sexuality may be only one small part of the disturbed personality. Bruch (1973) emphasized the mother-daughter conflict in the etiology of eating disorders. Early maternal deprivations are thought to produce defects in the child's ego and ambivalence toward the mother. Because of the poor relationship, the infant fails to develop a sense of effectiveness in mastering the demands of independent existence. Bruch also described the anorexic girl as the object of much family attention and control who is trapped by a need to please and a feeling of inadequacy. An extreme sense of ineffectiveness leads the anorexic to attempt a desperate bid for control and to express an individual identity at the time when it is appropriate (usually in adolescence) to begin the development of autonomy and individuation from parental influences. Control of the body through the intake of food is believed to be the only defense.

A similar theory was suggested by Goodsitt (1985) who viewed the fear of fat in anorexics and bulimics as an expression of a more generalized fear of losing control or falling apart. According to the theory, anorexics and bulimics are conceptualized as feeling passive, dependent, and helpless. Weight loss is again viewed as a desperate attempt to exert self-control in a world that is controlling and manipulative.

Another psychodynamic formulation, in which anorexia is explained in terms of object relations theory, was proposed by Palazzoli (1988). Using the concept of incorporation, she theorized that frustrating early experiences with the mother form the basis for negative introjection. The infant's body comes to represent the discomfort experienced in the maternal relationship and becomes symbolic of the bad object. The attempt to starve the body is thus an attempt to prevent the negatively introjected mother from overwhelming the child's ego.

Casper (1987) viewed anorexia as a form of paranoia in which the fears are projected into the body instead of into the outside world. The fears center around fatness but really represent the child's failed attempt at individuation. Thus, the eating disorder is viewed as the result of a failed attempt to properly separate from the parents (similar to that of Bruch).

Bulimic episodes have also been specifically described according to psychodynamic theory. The basic psychic mechanism is that of introjection through incorporation. The defense is employed symbolically through massive overeating to return to the security of the maternal breast. Anything that produces anxiety can lead to use of this defense to assure gratification through a primitive identification with the mother. Bulimia has been noted specifically as a defense against depression (Kornhaber, 1970).

Lerner (1983) analyzed bulimia nervosa from a psychoanalytic perspective and presented a formulation of a specific case based on Kohut's self-psychological viewpoint (Kohut & Wolf, 1992). A chaotic social history centering around a turbulent mother-daughter relationship resulted in a failure to develop a viable sense of self-worth which in turn undermined the production of self-other differentiation. The bulimic patient is seen as a dichotomy. The very well dressed, thin appearance that the bulimic patient presents to the world as a result of her overreliance on external structure and expectation is contrasted with the chaotic bingeing and purging that are a consequence of the failure to develop an adequate self structure. Food becomes symbolic of the failed mother-daughter relationship, and the voracious ingestion of food represents a desire to return to an early stage of complete symbiosis between mother and infant.

The binge-purge cycle represents a recurring quest for maternal need and gratification and the conflicts surrounding maternal rejection (Barth & Wurman, 1986).

COURSE OF THE DISORDERS

Age and Circumstances of Onset

Bulimia nervosa typically begins in late adolescence or early adulthood, although it may begin before the age of 10 or after the age of 40 (Hsu, 1990). Typically, after various reducing diets have been attempted, usually with little success, the individual begins binge eating. Either accidentally (e.g., following an illness), through reading about it, or through hearing a friend or coworker talk about it, the individual then becomes aware that self-induced vomiting or laxative use may be used to control weight (Cassell & Gleaves, in press).

The onset of anorexia nervosa, in the absence of binging and purging, is a bit more difficult to define. Some studies use the onset of severe dieting as the onset of the illness whereas others use the onset of amenorrhea or some specific weight criteria (Hsu, 1990). In an interesting study of 105 anorexics, Halmi, Casper, Eckert, Goldberg, and Davis (1979) found a bimodal distribution of age of onset with peaks at ages 14 and 18. The authors speculated that these were the ages when dependency issues were most challenged, corresponding with the beginning and the finishing of high school.

For both anorexia and bulimia nervosa, there is evidence that onset of the disorder is associated with environmental stressors. Strober (1984) found that commonly identified stressors were change in peer relations, arguments with or between parents, parental or personal illness, father's absence from home, and involvement with drugs. Other precipitating events that have been identified include leaving school or home, separation from a boyfriend, the first experience of sexual intercourse, and being raped (Lacey & Read, 1993).

Length, Severity, and Long-term Course

More is known about the long-term course of anorexia nervosa than about bulimia nervosa because the former has been recognized and studied for a longer period of time. Herzog, Rathner, and Vandereycken (1992) reviewed the literature on the long-term course of anorexia nervosa and reached several conclusions. The mortality rate was found to be approximately 1/2 to 1% per year (i.e., after 20 years, 10 to 20% of the patients will have died). About 40% of patients will achieve complete recovery. Between 7% and 40% of anorexics report episodes of bulimia during intermediate to long-term follow-up.

Long-term follow-up studies of bulimia nervosa have just been published in the past few years. Keller, Herzog, Lavori, Bradburn, and Mahoney (1992) followed 30 women over a period of up to 35 to 42 months. The authors reported extraordinarily high rates of relapse (e.g., a 63% cumulative risk of relapse by 78 weeks after recovery). Much more positive long-term follow-up (approximately 6 years) was reported by Fairburn and colleagues (Fairburn et al., 1995) who followed patients treated in three different forms of therapy. These authors concluded that the longer-term outcome of the disorder depends on the type of the original treatment. Patients who had been treated with behavior therapy did poorly at follow-up while those treated with cognitive behavior or interpersonal therapy had a better prognosis. It is a closer look at these various forms of therapy to which we turn next.

HISTORY OF THE TREATMENT OF ANOREXIA

The treatment of self-starvation, binge-eating, and purging has varied according to the current understanding of symptom constellations and etiology. This brief review of treatment may be augmented by reading the scholarly work of Blinder and Chao (1994), Bliss and Branch (1960), Brumberg (1988), Goldbloom (1997), Habermas (1989), Parry-Jones and Parry-Jones (1991), Russell (1997), Silverman (1997a, 1997b), and Stunkard (1993). In this section we will review the history of treatment for self-starvation and anorexia nervosa and some current research on modern treatments. Treatment and related research on bulimia nervosa will follow.

Early History of Treatment of Self-Starvation

Self-starvation was one of the ascetic religious practices in Europe in the Middle Ages, primarily by holy women, which signified that the woman was miraculously sustained by God and devoted to the ideals of suffering and service (Brumberg, 1988). Over time the miraculous nature of pious fasting, *anorexia mirabilis*, became suspect as fakery for personal notoriety and gain, as work of the devil, or as threats to scientific medicine. Investigations of *anorexia mirabilis* were made by clergymen, physicians, and officials, and the focus was on the accuracy of the reports, not on treatment. As piety waned, medical accounts gained ascendancy with the takeover of scientific medicine: by 1900 "food refusal was transformed from a legitimate act of personal piety into a symptom of disease" (Brumberg, 1988, p. 98).

Some (Blinder & Chao,1994; Silverman, 1997a) credit Richard Morton's 1689 account of "nervous consumption" with being the first *medical* description of anorexia nervosa, although others question that interpretation (Brumberg, 1988). Morton, physician in ordinary to the King of England, described food refusal by an 18-year-old girl for which he tried pharmacological interventions:

> . . . the outward application of Aromatick Bags made to the Region of the Stomach, and by Stomack-Plaisters, as also by the internal use of Bitter Medicines, Chalybeates, and Juleps made of Cephalick and Antihysterick Waters, sufficiently impregnated with Spirit of Salt Aromoniack, and Tincture of Castor, and other things of that Nature. (Bliss & Branch, 1960, p. 11)

The girl died. Morton tried similar remedies with a 16-year-old minister's son, but when he saw the treatment was not working, he sent the boy to the country, prescribing riding and asses' milk. Interestingly, the boy thus escaped the stress of his father's constant arrests for nonconformist religious beliefs, and he made at least some improvement (Bliss & Branch, 1960; Silverman, 1997a).

In 1859, William Chipley (Brumberg, 1988) reported similar symptoms associated with food refusal to be a form of sitomania, a disorder characterized by an intense fear of food included in American medical dictionaries. Some forms of sitomania included fear that one's food was poisoned or the idea that a higher power was telling the patient not to eat. However, Chipley defined a variant in which middle-class young women refused food to manipulate family and friends by gaining sympathy and power, and he as a Kentucky asylum superintendent recommended institutionalization for moral treatment and forced feeding.

Silverman (1992) credits Dr. Louis-Victor Marcé of Paris in 1860 with "perhaps the seminal report of the 19th century" (p. 9). Marcé described anorexic symptoms and behavior as a "hypochondriacal delirium" and recommended gradual refeeding and care of the patient by strangers outside of their family and acquaintances. Nevertheless, the credit for first describing what has come to be known as modern-day anorexia nervosa is often given to two prominent physicians, Sir William W. Gull and Charles Lasègue in 1873.

Sir William W. Gull, physician at Guy's Hospital and likely London's greatest clinician, first used the clinical term *anorexia nervosa* in 1873 (Silverman, 1997a). Due to his prominence in London's medical circles he propelled the concept of self-starvation into a disease unto itself (Brumberg, 1988; Garfinkle & Garner, 1982). Gull defined anorexia as an independent disease that stems from "a perversion of the ego" (Brumberg, 1988, p. 121). He believed that family relations and friends were not suited for attending to the anorectic patient. Although Gull did not require that all patients be isolated from the family entirely, he did believe that some type of moral authority from outside the home, such as a doctor or nurse, must intervene in order for treatment to be effective. Gull recommended that this moral authority should administer a diet of milk, cream, soup, eggs, fish, and chicken every 2 hours to the patient. Other physicians criticized Gull's treatment regime of feeding intervals, warm bed rest, and home nursing for avoiding extreme treatment interventions such as forced feeding and complete isolation (Brumberg, 1988).

Charles Lasègue, professor of clinical medicine in the Faculty of Medicine of Paris, published in the same year (1873) a similar description and called it *anorexia hysterique* (Blinder & Chao, 1994). He believed that the disease was a disturbance of the central nervous system which was localized in the gastric system and that its etiology lies in emotional stresses, related to romantic interests, intrafamilial conflict, or other frustrations (Brumberg, 1988). Lasègue paved the way for a family systems approach to the disease, contending that the family played a large part in maintaining the disease, and thus advocated the separation of the patient from his or her family in order for treatment to be efficacious. He believed that the physician should wait until the final stage of the disease before intervening as moral authority and expert, when the patient, at last overcome with anxiety and guilt regarding her current situation, would be most receptive to intervention (Brumberg, 1989). While Lasègue never detailed his treatment, he offered important observations about family struggles around the daughter's refusal to eat.

In Europe and America in the late nineteenth century, according to Brumberg (1988), few middle- and upper-class families were willing to put their young daughters into a public hospital, and even private hospitals and cottage hospitals were seldom used for anorectics before the turn of the century. General practitioners tried home remedies such as warm baths, massages, and stimulation of the appetite with appealing foods (Brumberg, 1988). Sometimes forced feeding was done at home, or stimulation with electrical shocks in the doctor's office. Yet others were sent to private medical facilities or on trips. Specialists or consultants, the most prestigious physicians, were called in for extreme cases.

Charcot was the first to recognize the pursuit of thinness as a factor in the development of anorexia nervosa, according to Habermas (1989). He discovered a pink ribbon around the waist of a young patient who described it as a warning against weight gain: "I prefer dying of hunger to becoming as big as mamma" (Habermas, 1989, p. 263). Charcot was very influential in French medical circles and advocated strict isolation from the family as a condition of treatment (Silverman, 1997b).

Treatment of Anorexia in the Early 1900s

The treatment of anorexia took a biological turn in 1914 when Simmonds published evidence that severe weight loss was due to pituitary insufficiency (Silverman, 1997a). Patients were given pituitary abstracts and implants, and psychosocial treatment went out of fashion. In the 1930s, evidence from both sides of the Atlantic brought the psychological nature of anorexia nervosa to the fore again.

Ryle (1936) reported that he told the anorexic patient and her parents separately that she would recover with enough nourishing food. He advocated "explanation, reassurance, distraction, and firm treatment of the starvation" (Silverman, 1997a) rather than using psychoanalytic methods or discussing motives. If the treatment did not work at home, he advocated a nursing home where the nurse would sit with the patient until her food was eaten, staying in bed and warm, with few visitors to upset her.

Farquharson and Hyland (1938) reported a case series of eight anorexics and their treatment at Toronto General Hospital. They worked on changing the patients' attitude toward food, using psychoeducation while in the hospital to overcome emaciation. They also worked on preventing relapse by helping the patient gain insight regarding possible inner conflicts. They took a thorough history, especially of the patient's relationships, and interviewed family and friends. Patients were also given occupational therapy to promote achievement and self-confidence. As others had reported earlier, drugs did not seem to help. A follow-up report on this group and others in 1966 showed that two-thirds of their 15 patients had made a good recovery.

A psychoanalytic viewpoint incorporating drive theory was published in 1940 by Waller, Kaufman, and Deutsch. The symptoms of anorexia nervosa were seen as a defense against guilt associated with fantasies stemming from fears of oral impregnation. This idea was part of a search in psychosomatic medicine for a specific set of psychodynamics associated with each disease entity (Minuchin, Rosman, & Baker, 1978). Ensuing psychoanalytic formulations did not lead to innovations in treatment *per se*, and psychoanalysis was not particularly successful with anorexic patients (Bruch, 1973).

Hilde Bruch, Arthur Crisp, and Gerald Russell

Hilde Bruch (1973) saw self-starvation as representing a struggle for autonomy, competence, control, and self-respect. She wrote, "The aim of therapy is to help them in developing a more competent, less painful, and less ineffective way of handling their problems"

(p. 336). Bruch evolved a "fact-finding" approach to psychotherapy in which she helped anorexics to gradually relabel their errors in thinking and misconceptions from faulty developmental experiences (1973). She observed that interpretation by the therapist tended to confirm the patient's sense of inadequacy, and that eliciting and clarifying the patient's inner feelings and experiences step by step was much more productive. Bruch's treatment often included hospitalization where activity programs, group therapy, art work, and milieu therapy were included. Bruch found that including the family was essential, sometimes in conjoint sessions but more often by individual family sessions. She helped parents find satisfaction in other parts of their lives so they could allow their daughter more autonomy. Although Bruch's thinking originated in psychoanalytic thought, her methods were a "springboard" for modern cognitive therapy for anorexia nervosa (Garner & Bemis, 1982).

Arthur Crisp (1967, 1980) promulgated a developmental model that focused on the anorexic's symptoms as a way of coping with the demands of psychological and physiological development. He observed that weight gain necessitates the patient's facing her fears about maturing, and in therapy he emphasized the development of alternative coping strategies.

Gerald Russell concurred with Bruch and Crisp that the morbid fear of fatness was central to the definition of anorexia nervosa (Silverman, 1997a). He recognized the self-perpetuating nature of anorexic symptoms and emphasized the importance of trained nursing staff in the treatment of the disorder. Russell (1979) also distinguished bulimia nervosa in its current form and saw binge-eating as evidence that the central psychopathology of eating disorders has changed.

Family Therapy Approaches to Anorexia Nervosa

As we have seen, early accounts of most physicians inferred that the parents of the anorectic patient were overly preoccupied with their daughter's progress. Families were seen as an impediment to effective treatment. With the rise of family systems theory in the 1960s and 1970s, researchers such as Selvini Palazzoli (Selvini, 1988) and Minuchin (Minuchin et al., 1978) began conceptualizing anorexia nervosa in the family system and using family interventions to effect change.

Minuchin et al. (1978) sought to influence transactions among family members in order to alter the family system. Restructuring boundaries and developing competency were two of the objectives to help the family honor autonomy as well as belonging. They worked on symptom remission with a combination of behavioral and family therapy techniques, raising the intensity of interactions by methods such as asking the parents to get the anorectic to eat during the first session. They reframed food refusal as a "fight for control" and challenged the family's enmeshment, overprotection, conflict avoidance, rigidity, and detouring of conflict.

Mara Selvini Palazzoli treated anorexics from an object relations viewpoint before joining Boscolo, Cecchin, and Prata at the Milan Center of Family Studies (Selvini, 1988). The Milan group evolved a conceptualization of anorexia nervosa as a pattern of communication disorders characterized by secret coalitions, mutual rejection of one another's messages, parental refusal to assume leadership, and blame shifting. Male and female co-therapy teams used therapeutic double binds, paradoxical prescriptions, and concrete directives to expose and counter hidden dynamics. This was a shift from explanatory techniques to an "implicit pedagogy of communication, in which therapists serve as models of nonrejecting communicative style while criticizing the communicative incongruities of the family by nonverbal means" (Selvini, 1988, p. 149). Of the 12 families treated with this method for 20 sessions or less, 9 had a successful outcome.

Family therapy methods have evolved further and are now researched at multiple sites. These methods still focus on issues of rigidity, loyalties, intergenerational triangulation, separation and individuation, enmeshment, overprotectiveness, and conflict resolution. The emphasis is not on placing blame on the anorectic's family but on identifying problematic functions within the family unit that hinder the patient from recovery. As eating disorders have come to be seen as multidetermined, family therapy has become incorporated as part of a multidimensional approach to treatment (Woodside & Shekter-Wolfson, 1991).

Randomized controlled trials of family therapy for anorexia nervosa following inpatient refeeding at the Maudsley Hospital in London demonstrated that family therapy was more efficacious than individual supportive therapy or focal psychodynamic psychotherapy, for patients who became anorexic at 18 years or younger and had anorexia for less than 3 years (Russell, Dare, Eisler, & Le Grange, 1992). Five-year follow-up (Eisler, Dare, Russell, Szmukler, Le Grange et al., 1997) indicated continued benefit of the treatments, with family therapy being more successful for anorexia nervosa of early onset and short history, and individual therapy being better for late onset patients. These studies found conjoint family therapy and family counseling (seeing parents and the identified patient separately) to be equally effective on the whole, although family counseling was sometimes more efficacious in families with very low or very high expressed emotion (Dare & Eisler, 1995).

Early Behavioral Therapies for Anorexia Nervosa

The earliest documented behavioral therapy for eating difficulties occurred in the ninth century. A Persian boy, son of the Khalifah of the Islamic empire, refused to eat or drink and rapidly lost weight, with secondary complications (Hajal, 1982). A court physician took a behavioral approach by giving him rewards for eating, and his weight and health were gradually restored.

Most early modern-day investigators have examined the effectiveness of behavior modification for anorexia nervosa (e.g., Agras, Barlow, Chapin, Abel, & Leitenberg, 1974; Bhanji & Thompson, 1974; Blinder, Freeman, & Stunkard, 1970; Halmi, Powers, & Cunningham, 1975). These types of programs generally lead to significant initial weight gain but have had difficulty demonstrating long-term success.

Inpatient programs that are strictly behavioral (operant), and harsh in their methods or implementation, have also been criticized as being possibly iatrogenic (e.g., Bruch, 1974, 1978; Garner, 1985; Goodsitt, 1985; Touyz, Beumont, & Dunn, 1987) because they may focus exclusively on weight restoration and eating behavior at the expense of other core aspects of the patient's psychopathology. Such programs may also be perceived by the patient as being overly controlling and disempowering, which replicates many of the environmental characteristics of their dysfunctional families.

More recently, a lenient, flexible approach to behavioral treatment of anorexia nervosa has been presented and found to lead to equivalent amounts of weight gain, relative to strict operant conditioning programs (Touyz, Beumont, Glaun, Phillips, & Cowin, 1984; Touyz, Beumont, & Dunn, 1987). The need to combine behavioral interventions with individual, group and family psychotherapy, cognitive restructuring, psychoeducation, pharmacotherapy, nutritional counseling, and body image therapy has also been emphasized (Hsu, 1990; Yager, 1988; Williamson, Cubic, & Fuller, 1992). Such an integrative approach appears to address many of the problems associated with a strictly behavioral program.

Recent Research on Treatment for Anorexia Nervosa

Very few well-designed and controlled treatment outcome studies of anorexia nervosa have been conducted. We found a total of five studies that used any type of control group (Channon, de Silva, Hemsley, & Perkins, 1989; Crisp, Norton, Gowers, Halek, Bowyer, et al., 1991; Gowers, Norton, Halek, & Crisp, 1994; Sohlberg, Rosmark, Norring, & Holmgren, 1987; Treasure, Todd, Brolly, Tiller, Nehmed et al., 1995), and most of these suffered from notable limitations. Channon et al. (1989), who compared behavioral and cognitive behavioral treatments, included only eight subjects per group. Not surprisingly, no group differences were found. Sohlberg et al. (1987) compared the outcome of 13 patients in a combined "eating control program" and psychoanalytically oriented psychotherapy with 13 who were treated "according to other principles" (p. 243) and a no treatment group. However, there were only three patients in the no treatment condition.

Perhaps the most methodologically sound study conducted was by Crisp et al. (1991) with 2-year follow-up reported by Gowers et al. (1994). They randomly assigned 90 anorexics to one of four treatment conditions: two outpatient, one inpatient, and one assessment only (no treatment). According to the authors, who used weight gain, return of menstruation, and improvements in social and sexual adjustment as the criteria for improvement, all three treatments were highly successful whereas the control group was largely unimproved. At 2-year follow-up (Gowers et al., 1994), 12 of 20 patients assigned to the outpatient individual and family treatment were classified as "well" or "nearly well." The main problem with this set of studies is that the treatments described were quite comprehensive, making it difficult to determine what the active ingredient(s) were. Perhaps the most important finding was that outpatient therapy was as effective as inpatient.

The number of controlled outcome studies is probably small because it is ethically dangerous to put persons who are physically at risk in a "no treatment" or wait-list control group. Crisp et al. (1991) actually noted that three patients died either while awaiting treatment or during the course of the study. However, there is clearly a need for more controlled research, and comparative studies (i.e., comparing two or more treatments or comparing a specialized treatment to a "treatment as usual" control group) may be the only ethical way of conducting such research.

HISTORY OF THE TREATMENT OF BULIMIA

Early Definition and Treatment of Bulimia

The definition of bulimia has varied greatly over the last 2 millennia, ranging from extreme appetite (from the Greek "ox-hunger") to syncope (temporary loss of consciousness due to fall in blood pressure; Bowman, 1998). Early treatments for ravenous hunger included antiphlogistics (blood letting, purgation, and low diet); internal administration of ice, crude mercury, mineral waters, iron filings, or acid; special diets high in fat and meat; and/or medicines, such as opium, testaceous powders made from pounded shells, ambergris, belladonna, chalybeate, brandy, and medicines having a warming effect on the stomach (Parry-Jones & Parry-Jones, 1991). Some early cases remitted when the patient was treated for worms or diabetes (Parry-Jones & Parry-Jones, 1991), or for hypoglycemia (Bowman, 1998).

An 1864 article in the *British Medical Journal* (Parry-Jones & Parry-Jones, 1991) reported that Guipon related "temporary bulimia" to psychological sources, primarily hysteria and depressed mood, and by 1900, a psychological component in bulimia was widely accepted (Parry-Jones & Parry-Jones, 1991). In the next hundred years, bulimia was seen usually in the context of anorexia nervosa or another psychological disorder (Russell, 1997). It was not until 1979, that the current syndrome of bulimia nervosa was formulated by Russell, including both binge-eating and compensatory behavior related to concern about body weight and shape. Three earlier case reports may also fulfill current criteria (Russell, 1997): Nadia seen by Janet in 1903, Patient D of Wulff in 1932, and Ellen West seen by Binswanger in 1944–1945.

Treatment approaches for bulimia nervosa have evolved side by side with treatment for anorexia nervosa in the last 20 years and will be described in their respective areas below.

Controlled Research on Bulimia Nervosa

Because of the scarcity of controlled research with anorexia, most of what we know about treatment of the disorder (some of which was described above and some of which will be reviewed below) is based on uncontrolled studies. The same cannot be said for bulimia nervosa, for which there have now been numerous controlled and/ or comparative outcome studies. The treatments that have received the most empirical research are behavioral therapy, cognitive behavioral therapy, and interpersonal psychotherapy.

Behavioral Therapy

Behavioral interventions attempt to alter environmental antecedents and consequences assumed to initiate and maintain the bingeing and purging. Self-monitoring is often used to identify these factors. Psychoeducation, meal planning, and attempts to get the client to reduce dietary restraint are also part of behavioral treatment approaches (Thackwray, Smith, Bodfish, & Meyers, 1993). Strictly behavioral programs do not include cognitive components that will be discussed below. Behavioral treatments sometime include exposure with response prevention (ERP) in which clients are exposed to and encouraged to eat "forbidden foods" but are then not allowed to purge. The ERP is based largely on the anxiety model of bulimia nervosa (e.g., Williamson, 1990), and the treatment is derived from treatments for obsessive compulsive disorder. Whether or not ERP is efficacious for the treatment of bulimia is a topic of some controversy. In fact, Agras, Schneider, Arnow, Raeburn, and Telch (1989) concluded that not only did ERP not enhance the effectiveness of behavioral treatments, but it actually detracted from the intervention (perhaps because the clients found it so aversive).

Cognitive Behavioral Therapy

Fairburn (1981) was the first to describe a combined cognitive behavioral package for treating bulimia nervosa patients. The program that he reported has two main phases. In the first phase, the main goal is to interrupt the cycle of overeating and vomiting by helping the patient to learn to control his/her food intake. The rationale of the treatment is discussed, with the emphasis being on gaining self-control. Patients are also advised of the dangers of self-induced vomiting and purgative abuse. The patient is then instructed to self-monitor her eating, including where and when the meal occurred and her mood associated with the meal. After the patient is monitoring regularly, she is instructed to restrict her eating to conventional meal times. In subsequent sessions, problems associated with the previous goals are discussed and ways of increasing control are presented. It is often worthwhile to encourage the patient to engage in activities that are incompatible with overeating (e.g., visiting friends, exercise) when she feels that self-control is low. At the end of each session, the patient sets very concrete and limited behavioral goals for the week. During this phase of the treatment, Fairburn (1981) recommends bringing the patient's family or friends into treatment if possible. This is done partially to bring the problem into the open, but also to examine the patient's environment at home so that it can be modified if possible.

In the second part of the treatment, self-monitoring continues and each session begins with a review of the previous week's eating. After the eating has somewhat normalized, it is necessary to identify the circumstances under which loss of control occurs. Usually the events or mood changes can be determined through self-monitoring. At this point, training in problem solving is used to help the patient find alternative responses to the problematic situations. At the same time, the patient is also helped to identify those thoughts and beliefs that are preventing behavior change. These are usually irrational concerns about body shape, weight, and nutrition. Traditional cognitive techniques are used to teach the patient to change maladaptive thoughts and attitudes (e.g., Beck, 1976; Ellis, 1975). During this part of the treatment, more traditional strategies are also employed, the most important of which is exposure. Patients are gradually exposed to their forbidden foods and shown that they can eat them without losing control or gaining large amounts of weight. Thus, their significance in the client's diet diminishes.

This basic approach has since been supported in several controlled outcome studies (see Fairburn, 1997, or a recent meta-analysis by Lewandowski, Gebing, Anthony, & O'Brien, 1997) and at present appears the most commonly reported treatment approach. In Lewandowski et al.'s meta-analysis, they concluded that "Overall, results suggest that the use of a cognitive-behavioral therapy will result in favorable treatment outcomes . . . " (p. 703).

Interpersonal Psychotherapy

Interpersonal psychotherapy (IPT) (Klerman & Weissman, 1993; Weissman & Markowitz, 1994) is a time-limited focal psychotherapy that was originally developed in the 1960s as a treatment for depression. The goal of IPT is to help clients identify and resolve problems in current interpersonal relationships. Since its development, IPT has been applied to a wide variety of problems other than depression, including bulimia nervosa (see Fairburn, 1997, for a discussion of the use of IPT with bulimia nervosa). The aspect of IPT that differs most significantly from behavioral and cognitive behavioral methods is that the former does not directly address eating behavior or attitudes regarding eating, weight, body image, et cetera. In terms of the empirical support for the use of IPT with bulimia nervosa, there have now been several studies supporting its effectiveness with the disorder. However, because these have all been comparative studies where IPT was compared to behavior therapy and/or cognitive-behavioral therapy, they will be discussed in the following section.

Comparing Behavioral, Cognitive-Behavioral, and Interpersonal Therapies for Bulimia Nervosa

As one would imagine, the therapies that have received the most empirical attention have been tested against one another. Thackwray et al. (1993) compared cognitive-behavioral and behavioral interventions along with an attention placebo condition. Although behavioral and cognitive behavioral therapies were more efficacious than the placebo condition and were roughly equivalent at posttreatment (100% and 92% respectively of participants were abstinent from bingeing and purging), the cognitive behavioral treatment showed a clear superiority over the strictly behavioral treatment at 6-month follow-up in that 69% of the participants in that condition were abstinent compared with 38% of those in the strictly behavioral treatment.

In a very important comparative study, Fairburn, Jones, Peveler, Hope, and O'Connor (1993) compared all three of the aforementioned empirically supported treatments (BT, CBT, and IPT). Consistent with standards for these approaches, the behavioral therapy focused only on changing eating behavior/habits, cognitive-behavioral therapy focused on changing both eating behavior and attitudes about weight and shape, and IPT focused on improving interpersonal relationships (without directly addressing eating behavior or attitudes about shape, weight, and eating). Consistent with the findings of Thackwray et al. (1993), at follow-up the persons in the cognitive-behavioral treatment were doing better (i.e., a 90% reduction in bingeing and purging, as well as changes in attitudes about weight and body shape) than those who received behavioral treatment. Interestingly, although cognitive-behavior therapy appeared slightly superior to interpersonal psychotherapy at posttreatment, the differences had disappeared at one-year follow-up. Fairburn et al. (1995) also followed the above-mentioned group along with those from another study and found that, even after 6 years, the persons in the cognitive-behavioral and interpersonal psychotherapies conditions had maintained their gains, and the two treatments appeared equally effective. This was a very important finding as it demonstrated that a treatment that did not directly address eating behavior and eating-related attitudes could be as effective as one that does.

PHARMACOLOGICAL INTERVENTIONS

Although the goal of this book is to describe different psychotherapeutic approaches to the treatment of eating disorders, it is important to note that a variety of pharmacological interventions are also frequently used to treat eating disorders either in addition to or instead of psychologically based treatments. With anorexia nervosa, a variety of drugs have been tried including neuroleptics, antidepressants, appetite stimulants, lithium, and opioid antagonists. To date, no medication has been shown to treat the core psychopathology of the disorder (Johnson, Tsoh, & Varnado, 1996). The use of medication, usually antidepressants, is most typically an attempt to treat the accompanying psychopathology such as depression or obsessive compulsive disorder.

The same cannot be said with regard to bulimia, for which several types of antidepressants have been found to be effective in reducing bingeing and purging behavior (Johnson et al., 1996; Walsh, 1991), and recent research suggests that for at least some antidepressants, the efficacy in treating bulimia nervosa is not simply secondary to its effect on depression (Goldstein, Wilson, Ascroft, & Al-Banna, 1999). Among the antidepressants, the more recently developed selective serotonin reuptake inhibitors (e.g., fluoxetine) seem to be the drugs of choice. This conclusion seems warranted for two reasons. First, the side effects are less than with tricyclic antidepressants and MAO inhibitors. Second, whereas earlier research with tricyclics demonstrated that they led to decreases in bingeing and purging but not body image, more recent research with SSRIs suggest that they may indeed have an effect of improved body satisfaction (Goldbloom & Olmsted, 1993).

The biggest limitation of pharmacological interventions is that their effectiveness may be short-lived. That is, the patient may relapse when taken off the drug, and currently there is a lack of evidence that the drugs remain effective over extended periods of time even when the patient remains on them (Walsh & Devlin, 1995).

CONCLUSION

The most useful nosological specification of the eating disorders is still in some question. Although the DSM-IV (APA, 1994) has brought some order and practicality to our working definitions, we can expect further development in this area. Recent developments include re-

search questioning whether bulimic anorexia should best be classified as a variant of anorexia versus lying on a continuum with bulimia
nervosa (Gleaves, Lowe, Green, Cororve, & Williams, in press). Based
on taxometric research, the overall continuum model of eating disorders (e.g., Scarano & Kalodner-Martin, 1994) has also been called
into question (Gleaves, Lowe, Snow, Green, & Murphy-Eberenz,
2000). Whether dimensional or categorical, multifaceted models
have been developed that integrate the variety of core and additional
psychopathology of both anorexia and bulimia nervosa.

Etiological models continue to emphasize biological, sociocultural, and psychological factors although, relative to other forms of
psychopathology, sociocultural factors may play a greater role. As
has been briefly described above and will be described in more detail
below, the particular psychological factors emphasized differ as a
function of theoretical orientation. Recent research also suggests
that eating disordered individuals are a more heterogeneous group
than first thought in terms of, for example, demographics, co-morbidity, family dynamics, personality, and even etiology. This heterogeneity needs to be taken into account when considering treatments
for anorexia and bulimia nervosa.

Regarding treatment, almost every possible approach has been
attempted for eating disorders, especially for anorexia nervosa because of its longer history and more obvious presentation. Current
research findings on eating disorders provide a good example of
the current state of psychotherapy research in general. Case studies
and observations in specialized treatment programs have been followed by increasingly sophisticated studies, culminating in some
controlled, randomized studies comparing manualized treatments,
with follow-up. Some studies address client variables (e.g., age of
the patient, age of onset), but little is known about how therapist
or psychotherapy process variables affect change.

Although we have briefly summarized different conceptualizations
and treatment approaches for eating disorders, the remainder of
the book will address in depth how clinicians from various theoretical
orientations conceptualize or formulate a specific eating disordered
individual and how this conceptualization and/or empirical research
inform treatment. The reader may want to examine common factors
across treatment methods as well as specific techniques, perspectives,

or approaches that distinguish the different comparative treatments. It is our hope that what follows in this book will be educational for clinicians of all theoretical orientations and at all levels of training. Although we have briefly reviewed which approaches currently have the most empirical support, our goal is not to argue for the superiority of any particular approach, but rather advance the field by sharing information so that treatment of all persons with eating disorders may evolve.

REFERENCES

Agras, W. S. (1987). *Eating disorders: Management of obesity, bulimia, and anorexia nervosa.* Elmsford, NY: Pergamon Press.

Agras, W. S., Barlow, D. H., Chapin, H. N., Abel, G. G., & Leitenberg, H. (1974). Behavior modification of anorexia nervosa. *Archives of General Psychiatry, 30,* 279–286.

Agras, W. S., Schneider, J. A., Arnow, B., Raeburn, S. D., & Telch, C. F. (1989). Cognitive-behavioural and response-prevention treatments for bulimia nervosa. *Journal of Consulting & Clinical Psychology, 57,* 215–221.

Ajdukovic, M., & Ajdukovic, D. (1993). Psychological well-being of refugee children. *Child Abuse & Neglect, 17,* 843–854.

American Psychiatric Association. (1994). *Diagnostic and statistical manual of mental disorders (4th ed.).* Washington, DC: Author.

Anderson, A. E. (1995). Eating disorders in males. In K. D. Brownell & C. G. Fairburn (Eds.), *Eating disorders and obesity: A comprehensive handbook* (pp. 177–182). New York: Guilford.

Barlow, D. H., & Durand, V. M. (1999). *Abnormal psychology: An integrative approach.* Pacific Grove, CA: Brooks/Cole.

Barth, D., & Wurman, V. (1986). Group therapy with bulimic women: A self-psychological approach. *International Journal of Eating Disorders, 5,* 735–745.

Beck, A. T. (1976). *Cognitive therapy and emotional disorders.* New York: International Universities Press.

Bhanji, S., & Thompson, J. (1974). Operant conditioning in the treatment of anorexia nervosa: A review and retrospective study of 11 cases. *British Journal of Psychiatry, 124,* 166–172.

Blinder, B. J., & Chao, K. H. (1994). Eating disorders: A historical perspective. In L. Alexander-Mott, D. Lumsden, D., & Barry (Eds.), *Understanding eating disorders: Anorexia nervosa, bulimia nervosa, and obesity* (pp. 3–35). Philadelphia, PA: Taylor & Francis.

Blinder, B. J., Freeman, D. M. A., & Stunkard, A. J. (1970). Behavior therapy of anorexia nervosa: Effectiveness of activity as a reinforcer of weight gain. *American Journal of Psychiatry, 126,* 1093–1098.

Bliss, E. L., & Branch, C. H. H. (1960). *Anorexia nervosa: Its history, psychology, and biology.* New York: Hoeber.

Bowman, M. L. (1998). Bulimia: From syncope to obsession. *Psychology of Addictive Behaviors, 12,* 83–92.

Braun, D. L., Sunday, S. R., & Halmi, K. A. (1994). Psychiatric comorbidity in patients with eating disorders. *Psychological Medicine, 24,* 859–867.

Brotman, A. W., Rigotti, N., & Herzog, D. H. (1985). Medical complications of eating disorders: Outpatient evaluation and management. *Comprehensive Psychiatry, 26,* 258–272.

Bruch, H. (1973). *Eating disorders: Obesity, anorexia nervosa, and the person within.* New York: Basic Books.

Bruch, H. (1974). Perils of behavior modification in the treatment of anorexia nervosa. *Journal of the American Medical Association, 230,* 1419–1422.

Bruch, H. (1978). Dangers of behavior modification in the treatment of anorexia nervosa. In B. Brady (Ed.), *Controversies in psychiatry.* Philadelphia: Saunders.

Brumberg, J. J. (1988). *Fasting girls: The history of anorexia nervosa.* Cambridge, MA: Harvard University Press.

Bushnell, J. A., Wells, J. E., Hornblow, A. R., Oakley-Browne, M. A., & Joyce, P. (1990). Prevalence of three bulimia syndromes in the general population. *Psychological Medicine, 20,* 671–680.

Casper, R. C. (1987). Psychotherapy in anorexia nervosa. In P. J. V. Beumont, G. D. Burrows, and R. C. Casper (Eds.), *Handbook of eating disorders—Part I: Anorexia and bulimia nervosa* (pp. 255–269). Amsterdam: Elsevier.

Cassell, D. K., & Gleaves, D. H. (in press). *The encyclopedia of obesity and eating disorders* (2nd ed.). New York: Facts on File.

Channon, S., de Silva, P., Hemsley, D., & Perkins, R. E. (1989). A controlled trial of cognitive behavioral and behavioral treatment of anorexia nervosa. *Behaviour Research and Therapy, 27,* 529–535.

Clark, M. O., & Palmer, R. L. (1983). Eating attitudes and neurotic symptoms in university students. *British Journal of Psychiatry, 142,* 299–304.

Crisp, A. H. (1967). The possible significance of some behavioral correlates of weight and carbohydrate intake. *Journal of Psychosomatic Research, 11,* 117–131.

Crisp, A. H. (1980). *Anorexia nervosa: Let me be.* London: Academic Press.

Crisp, A. H., Norton, K., Gowers, S., Halek, C., Bowyer, C., Yeldham, D., Levett, G., & Bhat, A. (1991). A controlled study of the effects of therapies aimed at adolescent and family psychopathology in anorexia nervosa. *British Journal of Psychiatry, 159*, 325–333.

DaCosta, M., & Halmi, K. A. (1992). Classifications of anorexia nervosa: Question of subtypes. *International Journal of Eating Disorders, 11*, 305–311.

Dare, C., & Eisler, I. (1995). Family therapy and eating disorders. In K. D. Brownell & C. G. Fairburn (Eds.), *Eating disorders and obesity: A comprehensive handbook* (pp. 318–323). New York: Guilford.

Davis, K. L., Katzman, D. K., Kaptein, S., Kirsh, C., Brewer, H., Kalmbach, K., Olmstead, M. P., Woodside, D. B., & Kaplan, A. S. (1997). The prevalence of high-level exercise in the eating disorders: Etiological implications. *Comprehensive Psychiatry, 38*, 321–326.

Devlin, M. J., Walsh, B. T., Katz, J. L., Roose, S. P., Linkie, D. M., Wright, L., Vande Wiele, R., & Glassman, A. H. (1989). Hypothalamic-pituitary-gonadal function in anorexia nervosa and bulimia. *Psychiatry Research, 28*, 11–24.

Dolan, B. (1991). Cross cultural aspects of anorexia nervosa and bulimia: A review. *International Journal of Eating Disorders, 10*, 67–79.

Eisler, I., Dare, C., Russell, G. F. M., Szmukler, G., Le Grange, D., & Dodge, E. (1997). Family and individual therapy in anorexia nervosa: A 5-year follow-up. *Archives of General Psychiatry, 54*, 1025–1030.

Ellis, A. (1975). *A new guide to rational living.* Englewood Cliffs, NJ: Prentice Hall.

Fairburn, C. G. (1981). A cognitive behavioural approach to the treatment of bulimia. *Psychological Medicine, 11*, 707–711.

Fairburn, C. G. (1997). Interpersonal psychotherapy for bulimia nervosa. In D. M. Garner & P. E. Garfinkel (Eds.), *Handbook of treatment for eating disorders* (2nd ed.) (pp. 278–294). New York: Guilford.

Fairburn, C. G., & Beglin, S. J. (1990). Studies of the epidemiology of bulimia nervosa. *American Journal of Psychiatry, 147*, 401–408.

Fairburn, C. G., & Cooper, P. J. (1996). Eating disorders. In K. Hawton, P. M. Salkovskis, J. Kirk, & D. M. Clark (Eds.), *Cognitive behaviour therapy for psychiatric problems: A practical guide.* New York: Oxford Medical Publications.

Fairburn, C. G., Jones, R., Peveler, R. C., Hope, R. A., & O'Conner, M. (1993). Psychotherapy and bulimia nervosa: Longer-term effects of interpersonal psychotherapy, behavior therapy, and cognitive behavior therapy. *Archives of General Psychiatry, 50*, 419–428.

Fairburn, C. G., Norman, P. A., Welch, S. L., O'Connor, M. E., Doll, H. A., & Peveler, R. C. (1995). A prospective study of outcome in bulimia nervosa and the long-term effects of three psychological treatments. *Archives of General Psychiatry, 52,* 304–312.

Fairburn, C. F., Welch, S. L., Doll, H. A., Davies, B. A., & O'Connor, M. E. (1997). Risk factors for bulimia nervosa. *Archives of General Psychiatry, 54,* 509–517.

Fallon, A. E., & Rozen, P. (1985). Sex differences in perceptions of desirable body size. *Journal of Abnormal Psychology, 94,* 102–105.

Falstein, E. I., Feinstein, S. C., & Judas, I. (1956). Anorexia nervosa in the male child. *American Journal of Orthopsychiatry, 26,* 751–772.

Farquharson, R. F., & Hyland, H. H. (1938). Anorexia nervosa: A metabolic disorder of psychologic origin. *Journal of the American Medical Association, 111,* 1085–1092.

Fornari, V., Kaplan, M., Sandberg, D. E., Mathews, M., Skolnick, N., & Katz, J. L. (1992). Depressive and anxiety disorders in anorexia nervosa and bulimia nervosa. *International Journal of Eating Disorders, 12,* 21–29.

Garfinkel, P. E. (1995). Classification and diagnosis of eating disorders. In K. D. Brownell & C. G. Fairburn (Eds.), *Eating disorders and obesity: A comprehensive handbook* (pp. 125–134). New York: Guilford.

Garfinkel, P. E., & Garner, D. M. (1982). *Anorexia nervosa: A multidimensional perspective.* New York: Brunner/Mazel.

Garner, D. M. (1985). Iatrogenesis in anorexia nervosa and bulimia nervosa. *International Journal of Eating Disorders, 4,* 701–726.

Garner, D. M. (1997). Psychoeducational principles in treatment. In D. M. Garner & P. E. Garfinkel (Eds.) *Handbook of treatment for eating disorders* (2nd ed.) (pp. 145–174). New York: Guilford.

Garner, D. M., & Bemis, K. M. (1982). A cognitive-behavioral approach to anorexia nervosa. *Cognitive Therapy & Research, 6,* 123–150.

Garner, D. M., Garfinkel, P. E., & O'Shaughnessy, M. (1985). The validity of the distinction between bulimics with and without anorexia nervosa. *American Journal of Psychiatry, 142,* 581–587.

Garner, A. F., Marcus, R. N., Halmi, K., & Loranger, A. W. (1989). DSM-III-R personality disorders in patients with eating disorders. *American Journal of Psychiatry, 146,* 1585–1591.

Garner, D. M., Shafer, C. L., & Rosen, L. W. (1992). Critical appraisal of the DSM-II-R diagnostic criteria for eating disorders. In S. R. Hopper, G. W. Hynd, & R. E. Mattison (Eds.), *Child psychopathology: Diagnostic criteria and clinical assessment.* Hillsdale, NJ: Erlbaum.

Geliebter, A., Melton, P. M., McCray, R. S., Gallagher, D. R., Gage, D., & Hashim, S. A. (1992). Gastric capacity, gastric emptying, and test-meal intake in normal and bulimic women. *American Journal of Clinical Nutrition, 56,* 656–661.

Gleaves, D. H., & Eberenz, K. (1993). The psychopathology of anorexia nervosa: A factor analytic investigation. *Journal of Psychopathology and Behavioral Assessment, 15,* 141–152.

Gleaves, D. H., Eberenz, K. P., & May, M. C. (1998). Scope and significance of posttraumatic symptomatology among women hospitalized for an eating disorders. *International Journal of Eating Disorders, 24,* 147–156.

Gleaves, D. H., Lowe, M. R., Green, B. A., Cororve, M. B., & Williams, T. L. (in press). Do Anorexia and Bulimia Nervosa Occur on a Continuum? A Taxometric Analysis. *Behavior Therapy.*

Gleaves, D. H., Lowe, M. R., Snow, A. C., Green, B. A., & Murphy-Eberenz, K. P. (2000). The continuity and discontinuity models of bulimia nervosa: A taxometric investigation. *Journal of Abnormal Psychology, 109,* 56–58.

Gleaves, D. H., Williamson, D. A., & Barker, S. E. (1993). Confirmatory factor analysis of a multidimensional model of bulimia nervosa. *Journal of Abnormal Psychology, 102,* 173–176.

Goldbloom, D. S. (1997). The early Canadian history of anorexia nervosa. *Canadian Journal of Psychiatry, 42,* 163–167.

Goldbloom, D. S., & Garfinkel, P. E. (1990). The serotonin hypothesis of bulimia nervosa: Theory and evidence. *Canadian Journal of Psychiatry, 35,* 741–744.

Goldbloom, D. S., & Olmsted, M. O. (1993). Psychotherapy of bulimia nervosa with fluoxetine: Assessment of clinically significant additional change. *American Journal of Psychiatry, 150,* 770–774.

Goldstein, D. J., Wilson, M. G., Ascroft, R. C., & Al-Banna, M. (1999). Effectiveness of fluoxetine therapy in bulimia nervosa regardless of comorbid depression. *International Journal of Eating Disorders, 25,* 19–27.

Goodsitt, A. (1985). Self psychology and the treatment of anorexia nervosa. In D. M. Garner & P. E. Garfinkel (Eds.), *Handbook of psychotherapy for anorexia nervosa & bulimia.* New York: Guilford.

Goodwin, G. M., Fairburn, C. G., & Cowen, P. J. (1987). Dieting changes serotonergic function in women, not men. Implications for the etiology of anorexia nervosa? *Psychological Medicine, 17,* 839–842.

Gowers, S., Norton, K., Halek, C., & Crisp, A. H. (1994). Outcome of outpatient psychotherapy in a random allocation treatment study of anorexia nervosa. *International Journal of Eating Disorders, 15,* 165–177.

Habermas, T. (1989). The psychiatric history of anorexia nervosa and bulimia nervosa: Weight concerns and bulimic symptoms in early case reports. *International Journal of Eating Disorders, 8,* 259–273.

Hajal, F. (1982). Psychological treatment of anorexia from the ninth century. In B. J. Blinder, B. F. Chaitin, & R. S. Goldstein (Eds.), *The eating disorders* (pp. 247–258). New York: PMA.

Halmi, K. A., Casper, R., Eckert, E. D., Goldberg, S. C., & Davis, J. M. (1979). Pretreatment indicators of outcome in anorexia nervosa. *British Journal of Psychiatry, 134,* 71–78.

Halmi, K. A., Powers, P., & Cunningham, S. (1975). Treatment of anorexia nervosa with behavior modification: Effectiveness of formula feeding and isolation. *Archives of General Psychiatry, 32,* 93–96.

Henzel, H. A. (1984). Diagnosing alcoholism in patients with anorexia nervosa. *American Journal of Drug and Alcohol Abuse, 10,* 461–466.

Herzog, D. B., Keller, M. B., Sacks, N. R., Yeh, C. J., & Lavori, P. W. (1992). Psychiatric comorbidity in treatment-seeking anorexics and bulimics. *Journal of the American Academy of Child and Adolescent Psychiatry, 31,* 810–818.

Herzog, W., Rathner, G., & Vandereycken, W. (1992). Long-term course of anorexia nervosa: A review of the literature. In W. Herzog, H. C. Deter, & W. Vandereycken (Eds.), *The course of eating disorders: Long-term follow-up studies of anorexia and bulimia nervosa* (pp. 15–29). New York: Springer-Verlag.

Hinz, L. D., & Williamson, D. A. (1987). Bulimia and depression: A review of the affective variant hypothesis. *Psychological Bulletin, 102,* 150–158.

Holderness, C. C., Brooks-Gunn, J., & Warren, M. P. (1994). Co-Morbidity of eating disorders and substance abuse: Review of the literature. *International Journal of Eating Disorders, 16,* 1–34.

Howard, M. R., Leggat, H. M., & Chaudhry, S. (1992). Haematological and immunological abnormalities in eating disorders. *British Journal of Hospital Medicine, 48,* 234–239.

Hsu, L. K. G. (1990). *Eating disorders.* New York: Guilford.

Hudson, J. I., Pope, H. G., Jonas, J. M., & Yurgelun-Todd (1983). Family history study of anorexia and bulimia. *British Journal of Psychiatry, 142,* 133–138.

Humphrey, L. L. (1988). Relationships within subtypes of anorexic, bulimic, and normal families. *Journal of the American Academy of Child and Adolescent Psychiatry, 27,* 544–551.

Humphrey, L. L. (1989). Observed family interactions among subtypes of eating disorders using structural analysis of social behavior. *Journal of Consulting & Clinical Psychology, 57,* 206–214.

Jimerson, D. C., Wolfe, B. E., Metzger, E. D., Finkelstein, D. M., Cooper, T. B., & Levine, J. M. (1997). Decreased serotonin function in bulimia nervosa. *Archives of General Psychiatry, 54,* 529–534.

Johnson, C., & Connors, M. E. (1987). *The etiology and treatment of bulimia nervosa: A biopsychosocial perspective.* New York: Basicbooks.

Johnson, W. G., Tsoh, J. Y., & Varnado, P. J. (1996). Eating disorders: Efficacy of pharmacological and psychological interventions. *Clinical Psychology Review, 16*, 457–478.

Katzman, M., & Lee, S. (1997). Beyond body image: The integration of feminist and transcultural theories in the understanding of self starvation. *International Journal of Eating Disorders, 22*, 385–394.

Kaye, W. H., Weltzin, E., Hsu, L. K. G., Bulik, C., McConaha, C., & Sobkiewicz, T. (1992). Patients with anorexia nervosa have elevated scores on the Yale-Brown Obsessive-Compulsive Scale. *International Journal of Eating disorders, 12*, 57–62.

Keller, M. B., Herzog, D. B., Lavori, P. W., Bradburn, I. S., & Mahoney, E. M. (1992). The naturalistic history of bulimia nervosa: Extraordinarily high rates of chronicity, relapse, recurrence, and psychosocial morbidity. *International Journal of Eating Disorders, 12*, 1–9.

Kendler, K. S., MacLean, C., Neale, M., Kessler, R., Heath, A., & Eaves, L. (1991). The genetic epidemiology of bulimianervosa. *American Journal of Psychiatry, 148*, 1627–1637.

Keys, A., Brozek, J., Henshel, A., Mickelsen, O., & Taylor, H. L. (1950). *The biology of human starvation* (2 vols.). Minneapolis: University of Minnesota Press.

Klerman, G. L., & Weisman, M. M. (Eds.) (1993). *New applications of interpersonal psychotherapy*. Washington, DC: American Psychiatric Press.

Kohut, H., & Wolf, E. S. (1992). The disorders of self and their treatment. In D. Capp & R. K. Fenn (Eds.), *Individualism reconsidered: Readings bearing on the endangered self in modern society, Volume 398* (pp. 315–3217). Princeton, NJ: Princeton Theological Seminary.

Kornhaber, A. (1970). The stuffing syndrome. *Psychosomatics, 1*, 580–584.

Lacey, J. H., & Read, T. R. C. (1993). Multi-impulsive bulimia: Description of an inpatient eclectic treatment programme and a pilot follow-up study of its efficacy. *Eating Disorders Review, 1*, 22–31.

Lask, B., & Bryant-Waugh, R. (1997). Prepubertal eating disorders. In D. M. Garner & P. E. Garfinkel (Eds.), *Handbook of treatment for eating disorders* (pp. 476–483). New York: Guilford.

Lerner, H. D. (1983). Contemporary psychoanalytic perspectives on gorgevomiting—a case illustration. *International Journal of Eating Disorders, 3*, 47–63.

Lewandowski, L. M., Gebing, T. A., Anthony, J. L., & O'Brien, W. H. (1997). Meta-analysis of cognitive-behavioral treatment studies for bulimia. *Clinical Psychology Review, 17*, 703–718.

Lowe, M. R., Gleaves, D. H., & Murphy-Eberenz, K. P. (1998). On the relation of dieting and bingeing in bulimia nervosa. *Journal of Abnormal Psychology, 107*, 263–271.

Marrazzi, M. A., & Luby, E. D. (1986). An autoaddiction model of chronic anorexia. *International Journal of Eating Disorders, 5,* 191–208.

McComb, R. J. (1993). Dental aspects of anorexia nervosa and bulimia nervosa. In A. S. Kaplan & P. E. Garfinkel (Eds.), *Medical issues and the eating disorders* (pp. 101–144). New York: Brunner/Mazel.

Minuchin, S., Rosman, B. L., & Baker, L. (1978). *Psychosomatic families: Anorexia nervosa in context.* Cambridge, MA: Harvard University Press.

Mitchell, J. E., Pomeroy, C., & Adson, D. E. (1997). Managing medical complications. In D. M. Garner & P. E. Garfinkel (Eds.), *Handbook of treatment for eating disorders* (2nd ed.) (pp. 383–393). New York: Guilford.

Mitchell, J. E., Pomeroy, C., Seppala, M., & Huber, M. (1988). A clinician's guide to the eating disorders medicine cabinet. *International Journal of Eating Disorders, 76,* 211–223.

Mizes, J. S. (1985). Bulimia: A review of its symptomotology and treatment. *Advances in Behavior Research and Therapy, 7,* 91–142.

Niego, S. H., Pratt, E. M., & Agras, W. S. (1997). Subjective or objective binge: Is the distinction valid? *International Journal of Eating Disorders, 22,* 291–298.

O'Kearney, R. (1996). Attachment disruption in anorexia nervosa and bulimia nervosa: A review of theory and empirical research. *International Journal of Eating Disorders, 20,* 115–127.

Palazzoli, M. S. (1988). Interpretation of anorexia nervosa by the object-relations theory. In M. S. Palazzoli and M. Selvini (Eds.), *The work of Mara Selvini Palazzoli* (pp. 155–166). Northvale, NJ: Jason Aronson.

Parry-Jones, B. A., & Parry-Jones, W. L. (1991). Bulimia: An archival review of its history in psychosomatic medicine. *International Journal of Eating Disorders, 10,* 129–143.

Polivy, J., & Herman, C. P. (1985). Dieting and binging: A causal analysis. *American Psychologist, 40,* 193–201.

Polivy, J., Herman, C. D., Olmsted, M. P., & Jazwinski, C. (1984). Restraint and binge eating. In R. C. Hawkins, W. J. Frenmouw, & D. F. Clement (Eds.), *The binge-purge syndrome: Diagnosis, treatment, and research* (pp. 104–122). New York: Springer.

Pomeroy, C. (1996). Anorexia nervosa, bulimia nervosa, and binge eating disorder: Assessment of physical status. In J. K. Thompson (Ed.), *Body image, eating disorders, and obesity* (pp. 177–203). Washington, DC: American Psychological Association.

Pope, H. G., Hudson, J. I., Yurgelun-Todd, D., & Hudson, M. (1984). Prevalence of anorexia nervosa and bulimia in three student populations. *International Journal of Eating Disorders, 3,* 45–54.

Raich, R. M., Rosen, J. C., Deus, J., Pèrez, O., Requena, A., & Gross, J. (1992). Eating disorder symptoms among adolescents in the United States and Spain: A comparative study. *International Journal of Eating Disorders, 11,* 63–72.

Rodin, J., Silberstein, L., & Striegel-Moore, R. (1984). Women and weight: A normative discontent. *Nebraska Symposium on Motivation*, 267–307.

Rosen, J. C. (1987). A review of behavioral treatments for bulimia-nervosa. *Behavior Modification, 11*, 464–486.

Rosen, J. C., & Gross, J. (1987). Prevalence of weight reducing and weight gaining in adolescent girls and boys. *Health Psychology, 6*, 131–147.

Rosen, J. C., & Leitenberg, H. (1982). Bulimia nervosa: Treatment with exposure and response prevention. *Behavior Therapy, 13*, 117–124.

Rossiter, E. M., & Agras, W. S. (1990). An empirical test of the DSM-III-R Definition of Binge. *International Journal of Eating Disorders, 9*, 513–518.

Russell, G. F. M. (1979). Bulimia nervosa: An ominous variant of anorexia nervosa. *Psychological Medicine, 9*, 429–448.

Russell, G. F. M. (1997). The history of bulimia nervosa. In D. M. Garner & P. E. Garfinkel (Eds.), *Handbook of treatment for eating disorders* (2nd ed.) (pp. 11–24). New York: Guilford.

Russell, G. F. M., Dare, C., Eisler, I., & Le Grange, P. D. F. (1992). In K. A. Halmi (Eds.), *Psychobiology and treatment of anorexia nervosa and bulimia nervosa* (pp. 237–261). Washington, DC: American Psychiatric Press.

Ryle, J. A. (1936). Anorexia nervosa. *Lancet, ii*, 893–899.

Scarano, G. M., & Kalodner-Martin, C. R. (1994). A description of the continuum of eating disorders: Implications for intervention and research. *Journal of Counseling and Development, 72*, 356–361.

Schlundt, D. G., & Johnson, W. G. (1990). *Eating disorders: Assessment and treatment.* Needham Heights, MA: Allyn and Bacon.

Schmidt, U. H., Tiller, J., Blanchard, M., Andrews, B., & Treasure, J. (1997). Is there a specific trauma precipitating anorexia nervosa? *Psychological Medicine, 27*, 523–530.

Selvini, M. (Ed.) (1988). *The work of Mara Selvini Palazzoli.* Northvale, NJ: Aronson.

Sharp, C. W., & Freeman, C. P. L. (1993). The medical complications of anorexia nervosa. *British Journal of Psychiatry, 162*, 452–462.

Silverman, J. A. (1992). Historical development. In K. A. Halmi (Ed.), *Psychobiology and treatment of anorexia nervosa and bulimia nervosa* (pp. 3–17). Washington, DC: American Psychiatric Press.

Silverman, J. A. (1997a). Anorexia nervosa: Historical perspective on treatment. In D. M. Garner & P. E. Garfinkel (Eds.), *Handbook of treatment for eating disorders* (2nd ed.) (pp. 3–10). New York: Guilford.

Silverman, J. A. (1997b). Charcot's comments on the therapeutic role of isolation in the treatment of anorexia nervosa. *International Journal of Eating Disorders, 21*, 295–298.

Slade, P. D. (1982). Towards a functional analysis of anorexia nervosa and bulimia nervosa. *British Journal of Clinical Psychology, 21*, 167–179.

Smead, V. S. (1984). Eating behaviors which may lead to perpetuate anorexia nervosa, bulimarexia, and bulimia. *Women & Therapy, 3*, 37–49.

Sobal, J. (1995). Social influences on body weight. In K. D. Brownell & C. G. Fairburn (Eds.), *Eating disorders and obesity: A comprehensive handbook* (pp. 73–77). New York: Guilford.

Sohlberg, S., Rosmark, B., Norring, C., & Holmgren, S. (1987). The year outcome in anorexia nervosa/bulimia: A controlled study of an eating control program combined with psychoanalytically oriented psychotherapy. *International Journal of Eating Disorders, 6,* 243–255.

Spalter, A. R., Gwirtsman, H. E., Demitrack, M. A., & Gold, P. W. (1993). Thyroid function in bulimia nervosa. *Biological Psychiatry, 33,* 408–414.

Steiger, H., Liquornick, K., Chapman, J., & Hussain, N. (1991). Personality and family disturbances in eating disorder patients: Comparison of "restrictors" and "bingers" to normal controls. *International Journal of Eating Disorders, 10,* 501–512.

Strober, M. (1984). Stressful life events associated with bulimia in anorexia nervosa: Empirical findings and theoretical speculations. *International Journal of Eating Disorders, 3,* 3–16.

Strober, M., & Katz, J. L. (1988). Depression in the eating disorders: A review and analysis of descriptive family and biological findings. In D. M. Garner & P. E. Garfinkel (Eds.), *Diagnostic issues in anorexia nervosa and bulimia nervosa* (pp. 80–111). New York: Brunner/Mazel.

Stunkard, A. J. (1993). A history of binge eating. In C. G. Fairburn & G. T. Wilson (Eds.), *Binge eating: Nature, assessment, and treatment* (pp. 15–34). New York: Guilford.

Swift, W. J., Andrews, D., & Barklage, N. E. (1986). The relationship between affective disorder and eating disorders: A review of the literature. *American Journal of Psychiatry, 143,* 290–299.

Thackwray, D. E., Smith, M., Bodfish, J. W, & Meyers, A. W. (1993). A comparison of behavioral and cognitive-behavioral interventions for bulimia nervosa. *Journal of Consulting and Clinical Psychology, 61,* 639–645.

Thompson, B. (1994). Food, bodies, and growing up female: Childhood lessons about culture, race, and class. In P. Fallon, M. A. Katzman, & S. C. Wooley (Eds.), *Feminist perspectives on eating disorders* (pp. 355–378). New York: Guilford Press.

Tobin, D. L., Johnson, C., Steinberg, S., Staats, M., & Dennis, A. B. (1991). Multifactorial assessment of bulimia nervosa. *Journal of Abnormal Psychology, 100,* 14–21.

Touyz, S. W., & Beumont, P. J. V. (1994). Neuropsychological assessments of patients with anorexia and bulimia nervosa. In S. Touyz, D. Byrne, & A. Gilandas (Eds.), *Neuropsychology in clinical practice* (pp. 305–326). New York: Academic Press.

Touyz, S. W., Beumont, P. J. V., & Dunn, S. M. (1987). Behavior therapy in the management of patients with anorexia nervosa: A lenient flexible approach. *Psychotherapy and Psychosomatics, 48,* 151–156.

Touyz, S. W., Beumont, P. J. V., Glaun, D., Phillips, T., & Cowin, I. (1984). A comparison of lenient and strict operant conditioning programs in refeeding patients with anorexia nervosa. *British Journal of Psychiatry, 144,* 517–520.

Treasure, J., Todd, G., Brolly, M., Tiller, J., Nehmed, A., & Denman, F. (1995). A pilot study of a randomized trial of cognitive analytical therapy vs educational behavioral therapy for adult anorexia nervosa. *Behaviour Research and Therapy, 33,* 363–367.

van der Kolk, B. (1996). The complexity of adaptation to trauma: Self-regulation, stimulus discrimination, and characterological development. In B. A. van der Kolk, A. C. McFarlane, & L. Weisaeth (Eds.), *Traumatic stress: The effects of overwhelming experience on mind, body, and society* (pp. 182–213). New York: Guilford Press.

Waller, J. V., Kaufman, M. R., & Deutsch, F. (1940). Anorexia nervosa: A psychosomatic entity. *Psychosomatic Medicine, 2,* 3–16.

Walsh, B. T. (1991). Psychopharmacologic treatment of bulimia nervosa. *Journal of Clinical Psychiatry, 52* (Suppl. 10), 34–38.

Walsh, B. T. (1993). Binge eating in bulimia nervosa. In C. G. Fairburn & G. T. Wilson (Eds.), *Binge eating: Nature, assessment, treatment* (pp. 37–49). New York: Guilford Press.

Walsh, B. T., & Devlin, M. J. (1995). Pharmacotherapy of bulimia and binge eating disorders. *Addictive Behaviors, 20,* 757–764.

Walsh, B. T., & Garner, D. M. (1997). Diagnostic issues. In D. M. Garner & P. E. Garfinkel (Eds.), *Handbook of treatment for eating disorders* (pp. 25–33). New York: Guilford.

Walters, E. E., & Kendler, K. S. (1995). Anorexia nervosa and anorexic-like syndromes in a population-based female twin sample. *American Journal of Psychiatry, 152,* 64–71.

Weiner, H. (1985). The physiology of eating disorders. *International Journal of Eating Disorders, 4,* 347–388.

Weismann, M. M., & Markowitz, J. C. (1994). Interpersonal psychotherapy: Current status. *Archives of General Psychiatry, 51,* 599–606.

Welch, S. L., Doll, H. D., & Fairburn, C. G. (1997). Life events and the onset of bulimia: A controlled study. *Psychological Medicine, 27,* 515–522.

Wilfley, D. E., & Rodin, J. (1995). Cultural influences on eating disorders. In K. D. Brownell & C. G. Fairburn (Eds.), *Eating disorders and obesity: A comprehensive handbook* (pp. 78–82). New York: Guilford.

Williamson, D. A. (1990). *Assessment of eating disorders.* New York: Pergamon Press.

Williamson, D. A. (1996). Body image disturbances in eating disorders: A form of cognitive bias? *Eating Disorders: The Journal of Treatment and Prevention, 4,* 47–58.

Williamson, D. A., Barker, S. E., & Norris, L. E. (1993). Etiology and management of eating disorders. In P. B. Sutker & H. E. Adams (Eds.), *Comprehensive handbook of psychopathology* (2nd ed., pp. 505–530). New York: Plenum Press.

Williamson, D. A., Bentz, B. G., & Rabalais, J. Y. (1998). Eating disorders. In T. Ollendick & M. Hersen (Eds.), *Handbook of child psychopathology* (3rd ed.) (pp. 291–305). New York: Plenum Press.

Williamson, D. A., Cubic, B. A., & Fuller, R. D. (1992). Eating disorders. In S. M. Turner, K. S. Calhoun, & H. E. Adams (Eds.), *Handbook of clinical behavior therapy* (pp. 355–371). New York: John Wiley & Sons.

Williamson, D. A., Cubic, B. A., & Gleaves, D. H. (1993). Equivalence of body image disturbance in anorexia and bulimia nervosa. *Journal of Abnormal Psychology, 102,* 177–180.

Williamson, D. A., Kelley, M. L., Davis, D. J., Ruggiero, L., & Veitia, M. C. (1985). The psychopathology of bulimia. *Advances in Behavior Research and Therapy, 7,* 163–172.

Willmuth, M. E., Leitenberg, H., Rosen, J. C., & Cado, S. (1988). A comparison of purging and nonpurging normal weight bulimics. *International Journal of Eating Disorders, 7,* 825–835.

Wilson, G. T. (1995). Psychological treatment of binge eating and bulimia nervosa. *Journal of Mental Health, 4,* 451–457.

Wilson, G. T., & Lindholm, L. (1987). Bulimia nervosa and depression. *International Journal of Eating Disorders, 6,* 725–732.

Wiseman, C. V., Gray, J. J., Mosimann, J. E., & Ahrens, A. H. (1992). Cultural expectations of thinness in women: An update. *International Journal of Eating Disorders, 11,* 85–89.

Wonderlich, S. A., Brewerton, T. D., Jocic, Z., Dansky, B. S., & Abbott, D. W. (1997). Relationship of childhood sexual abuse and eating disorders. *Journal of the American Academy of Child and Adolescent Psychiatry, 36,* 1107–1115.

Wonderlich, S. A., Klein, M. H., & Council, J. R. (1996). Relationship of social perceptions and self-concept in bulimia nervosa. *Journal of Consulting and Clinical Psychology, 64,* 1231–1237.

Wonderlich, S. A., Swift, W. J., Slotnick, H. B., & Goodman, S. (1990). DSM-III-R personality disorders in eating-disorder subtypes. *International Journal of Eating Disorders, 9,* 607–616.

Woodside, D. B., & Shekter-Wolfson, L. (Eds.) (1991). *Family approaches in treatment of eating disorders.* Washington, DC: American Psychiatric Press.

Yager, J. (1988). The treatment of eating disorders. *Journal of Clinical Psychiatry, 49,* 18–25.

Zweben, J. E. (1987). Eating disorders and substance abuse. *Journal of Psychoactive Drugs, 19,* 181–192.

2

The Case of Kristen

Katherine J. Miller and Nancy Logue

REFERRAL INFORMATION

Kristen O'Connell, age 26, was referred for evaluation by her primary care physician after her recent visit where she confessed that she had struggled with an eating disorder since her teens. She had concealed this during their initial meeting 2 years earlier when she had signed up with her company's managed care plan. She was doing better at that time, but now, in a relapse, she reports feeling tired all the time, occasional episodes of dizziness, great sensitivity to cold, and loss of concentration. She has been feeling so weak that she cannot work out for her usual hour or two each day. She is 5 feet 6 inches tall and weighs 110 pounds (Body Mass Index = 17.67), and her menses stopped 5 months ago.

Physical examination revealed swollen parotid glands, orthostatic hypotension, and dental enamel erosion. Kristen's lab tests showed dehydration, low potassium (3.0; normal range: 3.5–5.1) and magnesium (1.6; normal range: 1.7–2.2), with a BUN of 3.0 (normal range: 8.0–21.0) and creatinine of .6 (normal range: 0.7–1.2). She acknowledged purging by vomiting between 4 and 6 days per week, between 3 and 10 times per day.

Kristen asked for help now because she has a hard time getting up in the morning which has led to increasing lateness at work. Other problems at work have created a crisis situation in which she fears she may lose her job. The physician was not sure what level, type, or intensity of psychotherapeutic treatment would be appropriate, given the acuteness of the physical and psychological crisis. It is for this reason that he is referring Kristen for an expert opinion.

PRESENTING PROBLEMS

When she first saw her new therapist, Kristen discussed what brought her to ask for help at the present time. Kristen had agreed to the psychotherapy consultation due to the crisis in her career. She seemed far less concerned about the physical and emotional sequelae of the eating disorder. Kristen presented as both anxious and cheerful, speaking rapidly and wringing her hands but smiling as she described being terrified of losing her job.

The job problem arose during her second annual performance evaluation at the advertising company where she works as an account supervisor. Her formerly supportive supervisor had given her a mixed review: "Your creativity and productivity are outstanding," he said, "but I have gotten too many reports of conflicts between you and other staff members. People who get ahead in this company are team players." He cited behaviors such as criticizing an assistant in front of a client, being curt and demanding with coworkers, and taking on too much work instead of dividing it among the team members. She burst into tears on hearing this, and he wondered aloud whether she was under a lot of stress lately because he had noticed that she appeared to be losing weight. She promised to do better, but the very next week there was another crisis. A client changed his mind but denied it and blamed Kristen for "forgetting." She lost her temper and became sarcastic. The client became upset and walked out, and dropped his account with the company. Kristen was given a severe warning by her supervisor. She reflected, "It really wasn't my fault, but I don't know why I can't just slap on a smile like I used to."

Kristen was in a panic about losing her job. She described her eating disorder as worsening gradually over the past year, since the end of her one-year engagement to Joe. She finally realized after her recent confrontations at work that her eating disorder had escalated out of control.

Reluctantly, Kristen described her eating patterns. She currently skips breakfast, only drinking black coffee and she eats a "dieter's lunch" which consists of a salad, vegetable soup, or pretzels. All afternoon she snacks on hard candy at her desk. This continues into the evening as she works late, long after others have gone home. She gets takeout dinners nightly and eats in front of the television. Four to six nights a week she purges her dinner by vomiting, followed by binge-eating on doughnuts, chocolate cookies and cakes, and/or ice cream. This makes her feel miserably full and ashamed. Sometimes she continues the cycle of vomiting and binge-eating, while at other times she exercises late into the night, making it difficult to get up and get to work on time the next day. "I think about all the calories I'm burning when I exercise, and how thin and in control I'll feel when I lose a few pounds." On the weekends Kristen sometimes will binge and vomit up to 10 times a day.

Kristen is on the road 8 to 10 days a month for her job, and her eating is most out of control on these trips. Her job requires socializing with clients over dinner, where she feels temporarily in control by eating very little. Later she binges and purges alone.

Kristen had maintained a low normal weight of 120 pounds for about 4 years, and she described exercising an hour a day and purging only occasionally during this time. However, over the last year her restricting, binge-eating, and vomiting have increased markedly. She denied using laxatives or diuretics, and reported drinking alcohol socially but never using illegal drugs.

BACKGROUND

The historical information that Kristen revealed on an intake questionnaire and during her initial sessions is summarized here in chronological order.

Kristen related her family history in great detail but with little feeling. Kristen was the fourth child born to her parents, Charlotte and James. The oldest children, Bob, now 34, and Peter, 32, were followed by a daughter who was stillborn a year before Kristen's birth. Her parents married when both were young and separated when Kristen was in high school. They have engaged in a protracted divorce battle for several years.

Kristen's mother Charlotte came from an upper middle-class family with prominent social standing in the community. Kristen's maternal grandmother had been an exceptionally beautiful debutante and focused much of her energy on appearances. She married a physician, Kristen's grandfather, who worked long hours. He had a very busy social calendar as well, and served as a deacon in the Episcopal Church. Despite his frequent absence from the family, he was pleased to have a lot of money to indulge the women of the family. Kristen's maternal aunt Sissy, a sister 3 years older than Charlotte, was identified by popular consensus as "the beautiful one, just like her mother." Kristen's mother Charlotte, although also very attractive, was known as "the smart one." Their mother had favored Sissy during her childhood and young adulthood. For example, both parents were skeptical about Charlotte's marriage to an Irish Catholic car dealer from the working class. However, in recent years Sissy's marriage to a rich but abusive alcoholic has caused both embarrassment and stress. Kristen's grandparents frequently complain about Sissy's children being "out of control" and worry that they too, "like their father," will bring shame to the family.

Kristen's father James was the eldest of five children in an Irish Catholic family. His father died when he was 12, and his mother became a nurse's aide to support them. James took care of the younger children while his mother worked, and when he could, he made money doing odd jobs to contribute to family support. After high school, he went into the Army and served in the Korean War. After the war, he went to a state university where he met Charlotte. After a whirlwind romance, they married in their sophomore year over the reservations of both their families. When Charlotte became pregnant the following year, she and James both dropped out of college.

James worked two jobs to support Charlotte and their new son, Bob, and to save money for his dream of owning his own business. After the birth of their second son, Peter, James decided, against his wife's wishes, to take out a large loan to purchase a car dealership. He spent long hours at work, and he seemed to work even harder after their first daughter was stillborn.

At the time of Kristen's birth, the family's fortunes were beginning to improve. Kristen was healthy and had a sunny disposition. Her father's business was starting to succeed and he was able to take the family on vacations. Her mother continued to care for the home and children, taxiing everyone to lessons and athletic events. She also made time to resume her college career after Kristen started school. "Everything was great back then," Kristen said. "Daddy had made good, Mommy was back in school, and they were giving us the best of everything—dancing school, piano lessons, tennis camps. They used to joke about how we were all so perfect that we'd go to Ivy League schools and look down on our college dropout parents."

Abruptly, their luck changed. When Kristen was 8, a fire demolished her father's car dealership and created a devastating financial crisis. Her mother went to work at the dealership as a receptionist and bookkeeper while they rebuilt the family business. Kristen's maternal grandparents helped out by paying for one activity for each child. Kristen chose ballet and was the star of the town's dance studio. She had few friends, and after school she often went to her maternal grandmother's house where she spent many hours hearing stories about her grandmother's debutante days, discussing fashion magazines, and doing ballet exercises. "I hardly saw my parents back then, it seemed like, but I was their pride and joy. 'Look how well she's doing,' they'd tell all their friends. 'She gets As, she's a prima ballerina, so pretty, so polite, everybody loves her,' like that was all that mattered, like that meant everything was all right."

Over 4 years, the family business was rebuilt, and when Kristen was 12 her mother went to work for an accountant, while her father hired more specialized staff. When Kristen was a freshman in high school, her mother discovered that Kristen's father had been having an affair with his new bookkeeper, and she demanded a separation. James refused to move out, protesting that it didn't mean anything and that he would end the affair. But after several months of turmoil and sleeping in the guest room, he did leave.

Kristen handled these changes by working even harder. "I went all-out for everything—the school newspaper, the track team, even the homecoming court. I don't know how I did it!" A romance with the school's basketball star got her into a partying crowd. She got drunk with her friends, dieted and exercised to become even thinner than she was, and managed to juggle her 'A student' status with a popular place among her new friends. When her boyfriend dumped her for a girl who would "go all the way," she fell into a depression. "My so-called friends really tried to cheer me up at first, but they got impatient with me. They really didn't understand." Kristen started to stay home more and more, staying in her room and exercising late into the night.

A fainting spell in Kristen's junior year led to recognition of her anorexia by the school nurse, who called her parents. They were shocked and at first tried to talk Kristen into eating more, one or the other hovering over all her meals. Her mother felt guilty about not noticing that Kristen had gotten down to 105 pounds, nor that she skipped breakfast and dinner frequently, nor that her menstrual periods had ceased. She also blamed Kristen's father for ruining their family life. Kristen's father blamed her mother, but eventually they agreed that Kristen needed therapy. Through weekly individual and occasional family sessions, Kristen came to recognize some of the effects of her parents' warfare and her own anger and pain over the losses in her life. She saw a nutritionist a couple of times who showed her how to do meal planning, and she very slowly increased her food intake and started to gain weight. Her social life improved too as she developed a friendship with another achievement-oriented girl and had a few casual dating relationships. In her senior year, Kristen was able to eat at least two meals a day and gain enough weight to menstruate regularly, in part motivated by her desire to go to college. "I realized I had to get out of there, and college was the acceptable way. They wouldn't have let me go if I didn't gain weight, so I ate."

Kristen was accepted at several colleges and picked a major university about 2 hours from her home. Kristen arrived at the university with high hopes for a new life. She joined several campus organizations and became well-known for her school spirit and activity. Her parents continued to battle each other in court, and her brother Peter, who had lost his job because of his drinking, moved back home with their mother. Kristen's mother called her often with tearful updates on Peter's situation, looking for support. Kristen felt upset and overwhelmed after these calls. "How could I enjoy myself? My life was going too well—I had a new start, new friends, new everything, but they were still screwed up, fighting, driving each other crazy, and now Peter was messing up." She felt too ashamed of her distress to confide in any of her new friends.

Kristen became tense and avoided eye contact when describing a trauma in December of her sophomore year of college at age 19. She had found a home in an elite sorority where her beauty and accomplishments were valued. That fall, she got drunk at a sorority party and was raped by a senior from their brother fraternity. She was so embarrassed that she told no one, and while she minimized the event to herself, she gradually began to binge-eat to escape the violent memories and to comfort herself. Within a few months, she started to vomit periodically. "It was so depressing! Food took over my life again, but this time I was so out of control! I was disgusted with myself—I couldn't believe what was happening."

Kristen began avoiding parties and other events where she might see the rapist, and she had trouble concentrating on her work. After a year of deteriorating academic performance and increasing social isolation, she was confronted by her sorority sisters about her bulimia; she was then bingeing and vomiting daily. "It was so humiliating— even my best girlfriends were down on me." After a meeting with the dean and her parents, she was hospitalized.

Kristen spent 2 weeks in an eating disorders unit and returned to school against the advice of her treatment team. "I did go to the hospital, but I was not going to give up my semester after all my parents' battles over tuition." She had gained some control over her binge-eating, but she could only avoid vomiting after meals by physical activity or being in the presence of others. She struggled through the end of the term and made passing grades. " 'Forget those sorority girls,' I told myself and just focused on my work." Kristen took off the Spring term of her junior year and lived at home with her mother. She worked part-time in her father's business and took two courses at a community college. Kristen started outpatient therapy weekly with a new therapist, although she did not really like her. Kristen's therapy focused on coping with her parents' constantly putting her in the middle of their conflicts, and on doing less caretaking of her family. Kristen did not tell the therapist that she continued to binge and vomit about 3 times a week, though her weight (115 lbs.) and eating were relatively stable.

In the fall, Kristen returned to her university for her senior year and took extra courses so she could graduate with her class. She took pride in having "put her nose to the grindstone," and although her eating and social life were restricted, she went for weeks at a time without vomiting. After graduation, Kristen's grandmother encouraged her to move home and date other members of the country club, but instead, she entered a 2-year master's program in business administration (MBA) which combined work in a major corporation with intensive evening and weekend classes. "I did best when I was really busy, always on the go. I didn't worry that much about food, and I had a good excuse if friends wanted to go out—I always had homework, projects, presentations."

Kristen spoke of her final year in the MBA program with pride. In December, she met Joe, 8 years her senior, a regional sales manager in a company associated with her internship firm. She was charmed by his ease and sophistication and fell in love for the first time. He wined and dined her, and when they had been drinking she was able to overcome her fear of sexual relations. Kristen graduated with her MBA in May, magna cum laude, and landed a job in a prestigious advertising firm.

Joe proposed to Kristen under an August moon, the day after his divorce from his first wife was finalized. "I was thrilled! What a relief I thought it was going to be to get married without all that torture of dating that I heard the other women at work talking about." Kristen's parents joined in protesting this early commitment, to a man who was recently divorced, and in a compromise the wedding was set for 2 years later. At this point, Kristen had been so involved in her work and romance that her friendships remained superficial. "I decided not to have bridesmaids. Who would I choose? There was nobody, really."

Although Kristen herself was very busy in her new, high-pressure advertising job and had to travel a few times each month, she found it very difficult to tolerate her fiance's absence when he was on the road. She felt abandoned and increasingly mistrustful of him. Their relationship became strained with Kristen trying to be "good" and pleasing when they were together, exercising obsessively when she was alone. Throughout the next year, aware of the wedding drawing closer, Kristen became increasingly uncomfortable with Joe's drinking. When she expressed concern he became extremely angry and threatened to end the relationship. She redoubled her efforts to please him, cooking him gourmet meals, sending him special cards, wearing the body-revealing clothes he liked. "I kept thinking, 'He's unhappy, that's why he drinks; if I just pamper him, he'll feel better and won't need to drink.' " At the same time, Kristen began to lose weight slowly, about a pound each month.

One weekend, Kristen decided to fly to the city where he was working to surprise him and found him with another woman. She was devastated and immediately ended the engagement, feeling humiliated and betrayed. Kristen retreated into her work and her eating disorder. "I felt like such a failure. If I'd looked better, maybe Joe wouldn't have left me. I just wanted to be invisible, or disappear." Kristen suspected that her family was happy about her loss, and she distanced herself from them, even though they tried to be supportive. She spent long hours at her office and, in addition to increasingly severe dieting and exercise, she gradually began to binge and purge almost daily.

By the fall of her twenty-seventh year, Kristen was having difficulty with her job, her eating disorder was out of control, and her personal relationships were almost nonexistent. She finally decided to take the risk of revealing her problems to her physician and to accept the offer of help.

QUESTIONS FOR CONTRIBUTORS

All contributors were asked to comment on how they would treat Kristen, using the following questions as the format.

Questions for Contributors

We would like you to organize your response to the case of Kristen in the following manner. The total manuscript should be 30 pages at the maximum.

   I. **Treatment Model.** Please describe your treatment model in no more than three or four double-spaced pages.
   II. **The Therapist's Skills and Attributes.** Describe the clinical skills or personal attributes most essential to successful therapy in your approach (1 to 2 pages).

III. **The Case of Kristen.** It is important to the goals and mission of this volume that you answer *each* of the following questions regarding the enclosed case material. Please make your response to each question between one and three pages, for a total of 20 to 22 pages for this section.

A. *Assessment, Conceptualization, and Treatment Planning*

1. **Assessment.** What further information would you want to have to assist in structuring this patient's treatment? Are there specific assessment tools you would use? What would be the rationale for those tools?

2. **Therapeutic Goals.** What would be your therapeutic goals for this patient? What are the primary and secondary goals of therapy? What level of coping, adaptation, or function would you see this patient reaching as an immediate result of therapy? What would be the long-term outcome subsequent to the ending of the therapy? Please be as specific as possible.

3. **Timeline for Therapy.** What would be your timeline for therapy? What would be the frequency and duration of the sessions?

4. **Case Conceptualization.** What is your conceptualization of this patient's personality, behavior, affective state, cognitions, and functioning? Include the strengths of the patient that can be used in the therapy.

B. *The Therapeutic Relationship*

1. **The Therapeutic Bond.** What are the important considerations in the bond or affective relationship between therapist and client? Examples would include the development of trust, boundaries and limit-setting, self-disclosure, transference, and countertransference.

2. **Roles in the Therapeutic Relationship.** What are the appropriate roles of the therapist and the patient in your model of treatment, and what might you do to facilitate these roles? For example, what is the therapist's degree of directiveness and activity-level, and what is the therapist's role as an expert providing specific instruction? To what extent is the therapeutic relationship collaborative, and what are your expectations of the patient in her role?

C.   Treatment Implementation and Outcome

1. **Techniques and Methods of Working.** Are there specific or special techniques that you would implement in the therapy? If so, what would they be? What other professionals would you want to have collaborate with you on this case, and how would you work together? Would you want to involve significant others in the treatment? Would you use out-of-session work (homework) with this patient, and if so, what kind?

2. **Medical and Nutritional Issues.** How would you handle the medical and nutritional issues involved in the work with this client?

3. **Potential Pitfalls.** What potential pitfalls would you envision in this therapy? What would the difficulties be, and what would you envision to be the source(s) of the difficulties? Are there special cautions to be observed in working with this patient? Are there any particular resistances you would expect, and how would you deal with them?

4. **Termination and Relapse Prevention.** What would be the issues to be addressed in the termination process? How would termination and relapse prevention be structured?

5. **Mechanisms of Change.** What do you see as the hoped-for mechanisms of change for this patient, in order of relative importance?

3

Cognitive-Behavior Therapy

Donald A. Williamson and Susan B. Netemeyer

Cognitive-behavior therapy for eating disorders has its origins in the 1970s with behavioral approaches for anorexia nervosa (Agras, Barlow, Chapin, Abel, & Leitenberg, 1974) and the early 1980s with treatment methods developed by Fairburn (1981) and Rosen and Leitenberg (1982) for bulimia nervosa. These early treatment programs incorporated some of the behavioral techniques developed for obesity in the 1970s (Bellack & Williamson, 1982), but had the foresight to add treatment components related to fear of weight gain. Over the past 20 years, considerable progress has been made in refining these initial efforts (Williamson, Womble, & Zucker, 1998). Most important, cognitive-behavior therapists have established the efficacy of this approach in a large number of controlled investigations (Wilfley & Cohen, 1997). These controlled studies have focused primarily upon bulimia nervosa (Williamson, Womble et al., 1998).

Cognitive-behavior therapy is now considered to be the most strongly empirically supported treatment method for bulimia nervosa (Wilfley & Cohen, 1997). Cognitive-behavior therapy for anorexia nervosa has not been tested as extensively in controlled studies (Garner, Vitousek, & Pike, 1997). Cognitive-behavioral strategies used for bulimia nervosa have been modified for use with anorexia nervosa and are widely used. This chapter describes the basic methods of cognitive-behavior therapy and applies these concepts and methods to the case of Kristen.

TREATMENT MODEL

We approach all cases of eating disorders from the perspective of a continuum of care. This perspective assumes that intensity of treatment should be matched with severity of the eating disorder and related medical and psychiatric problems (Williamson, Duchmann, Barker, & Bruno, 1998). The continuum of care has four levels of care: (a) inpatient, (b) partial day hospital, (c) intensive outpatient therapy, and (d) outpatient therapy. Inpatient therapy involves hospital care on a 24-hour/day basis, and may include nasogastric tube feeding. Partial day hospital treatment generally begins with treatment on either 5 or 7 days per week, with treatment lasting 10 to 12 hours each day. Intensive outpatient therapy involves 3 to 5 days of treatment per week lasting 3 to 5 hours per day. Outpatient therapy may include group therapy 1 or 2 times per week and individual and/or family therapy once per week. As outlined by Williamson, Duchmann et al. (1998), severity of the illness determines the initial level of care which is assigned to a case, and progression through the levels of care is determined by the degree of improvement for each case. This approach to treatment has been found to be cost-effective, i.e., large numbers of patients can be treated in the partial day hospital or intensive outpatient programs that cost one-half to one-fourth the cost of inpatient treatment with the same degree of long-term efficacy. The specific treatment protocol that we employ has been described in detail by Williamson, Duchmann et al. (1998). The treatment approach is multidisciplinary, and includes cognitive-behavior therapy in individual, group, and family therapy. Pharmacotherapy, dietary, and medical interventions are incorporated into the treatment plan.

With regard to the cognitive-behavioral components of the treatment plan, it is presumed that fear of weight gain, overconcern with body size and shape, and body image disturbances are at the core of the eating disorder (Williamson, 1990). Treatment interventions are aimed at reducing fear of weight gain, etc., with the primary aim of modifying extreme methods for weight control, e.g., purging and restrictive eating. These treatment methods involve some type of exposure to the feared stimulus, i.e., feared foods or weight gain, via structured meal plans with the prevention of purging or through the process of gaining body weight. Also, binge eating is presumed to stem from dietary restraint (Williamson, 1990) or a disturbance of appetite (Blundell & Hill, 1993). Treatment procedures for binge eating emphasize eating three meals per day without purging and stimulus control over eating (Fairburn & Wilson, 1993). Cognitive components of treatment emphasize cognitive biases associated with overconcern with body size and overvalued ideas related to the value of thinness. Cognitive therapy is focused upon momentary automatic thoughts related to body and eating and to underlying core beliefs related to the person's sense of worthiness (Williamson, Womble et al., 1998).

THE THERAPIST'S SKILLS AND ATTRIBUTES

In our treatment model, each patient is assigned a case manager. The case manager assumes the role of primary therapist and generally follows the patient in therapy throughout all levels of care, unless there are practical problems which prevent this high degree of continuity of care, for example, long driving distances for outpatient therapy sessions or a previous therapeutic alliance with a professional who is not a member of our treatment team. As described in a later section, the case manager works closely with a multidisciplinary team to ensure comprehensive care. The case manager, in principle, can be either gender. For the case of Kristen, we would recommend a female therapist. Because of the sexual trauma that she experienced, we believe that rapport and trust in the therapist might be most easily accomplished with someone of the same gender.

We have found that it is very important that the therapist has been formally trained in the theories and techniques of cognitive-behavior therapy. Also, it is highly desirable that the therapist has at least 2 years of full-time experience with eating disorders. If the therapist has less than 2 years of experience, it is recommended that the therapist receive close supervision with a senior clinician with extensive experience in the treatment of eating disorders. Another important attribute is that the therapist should be a healthy model for the patient, i.e., the person should have very flexible eating habits, and should not express overconcern with his or her own body size/shape. The therapist must be very sensitive to the overvalued ideas of the patient and should systematically check with the patient to ensure that they have not misinterpreted some action of the therapist (Williamson, Muller, Reas, & Thaw, in press). Also, the therapist should have a good sense of "boundaries," that is, the extent to which they will assist the patient versus insist that the patient take responsibility for his or her own recovery. This issue is very complex and we believe can only be learned via experience and close supervision. Even for the very experienced clinician, it is quite useful to receive systematic feedback from the treatment team about how well they are managing this very sensitive and ongoing problem. Also, it is important for the therapist to have healthy and realistic attitudes regarding work and achievement. Most persons diagnosed with eating disorders were perfectionistic even before they developed an eating disorder. If they observe this same characteristic in their case manager, it is unlikely that they will seriously consider modifying this core belief. Finally, we believe that the therapist should have been well-trained in the philosophy of science so that he or she can maintain a high degree of objectivity and skepticism about the information that he or she gathers over the course of therapy. This same attitude enables the therapist to question therapeutic concepts and techniques which do not meet the criteria for meaningful scientific discourse.

THE CASE OF KRISTEN

Assessment, Conceptualization, and Treatment Planning

Assessment

Patients who are not in medical or psychiatric crises are evaluated in an outpatient assessment clinic for the purpose of diagnosis, case conceptualization, and treatment planning. Kristen would likely be assessed in this outpatient clinic assessment. The assessment is generally completed in a single session, which requires 3 to 4 hours. In this assessment, four types of evaluation are conducted: psychological, psychiatric, dietary, and body composition. Medical evaluation and laboratory studies are often ordered after the initial session, and the patient and her family are sometimes invited for one or more follow-up sessions if there is some ambivalence about acceptance of the recommendations of the assessment team.

In the psychological evaluation, the patient's history is obtained and a formal diagnostic interview is conducted using the Interview for Diagnosis of Eating Disorders, Fourth Version (IDED-IV) (Kutlesic, Williamson, Gleaves, Barbin, & Murphy-Eberenz, 1998). This semi-structured interview has been found to be a reliable and valid method for establishing an eating disorder diagnosis using the criteria established by the *Diagnostic and Statistical Manual for Mental Disorders, Fourth Edition* (DSM-IV) (American Psychiatric Association, 1994). We also administer the Eating Attitudes Test (Garner & Garfinkel, 1979), Bulimia Test-Revised (Thelen, Farmer, Wonderlich, & Smith, 1991), Beck Depression Inventory (Beck, Steer, & Garbin, 1988), the Structured Clinical Interview for the DSM-III-R (Spitzer, Williams, Gibbons, & First, 1990), and the Body Image Assessment (Williamson, Davis, Bennett, Goreczny, & Gleaves, 1989). These assessment methods have been found to be reliable and valid methods for measuring the severity of eating disorder symptoms and for establishing comorbid problems related to depression and personality disorders (Williamson, 1990). Given the history of Kristen, we would also interview her for a diagnosis of post-traumatic stress disorder (PTSD) and we suspect the presence of obsessive-compulsive personality disorder (OCPD) and Major Depression. For the purpose of further discussion, we will assume that additional interview data would be supportive of these secondary diagnoses and a primary diagnosis of anorexia nervosa, binge-purge subtype.

In the psychiatric evaluation, another opinion on diagnosis is determined and a family history of psychiatric problems is obtained. Also, evaluation of the biological versus psychosocial determinants of physical symptoms is conducted. Further evaluation of potential medical complications stems from this evaluation. In the case of Kristen, the findings of dehydration and electrolyte problems suggest the presence of such medical complications. Following a period of refeeding, these medical problems would be evaluated again. As a part of the psychiatric evaluation, a trial of medication for depression, obsessional thinking, and anxiety would be considered. If the patient had taken psychotropic medications before this evaluation, a history of the effectiveness of previous medications would be obtained.

The dietary assessment is conducted by a registered dietitian with extensive experience with eating disorders. This evaluation includes a dietary history, evaluation of current nutrient intake, and determination of a normal weight range (Williamson, Duchmann et al., 1998). If the patient is to be followed in an outpatient level of care, the patient is trained in self-monitoring of food intake and situational and emotional events surrounding eating and purging (Williamson, 1990). This information is incorporated into the early stages of treatment planning.

Body composition is measured using bioelectric impedance and skinfold measurement methods (Heymsfield, Allison, Heshka, & Pierson, 1995). Also, height and weight are converted into body mass index (BMI). The purpose of these assessment methods is to provide a valid estimate of body fat, lean body mass, and body fluids. Given the BMI of 17.67 that was reported for Kristen and the lengthy period of an inadequate nutrient intake, it is very likely that in addition to being dehydrated, her body fat and lean body mass are probably at very low and unhealthy levels.

Therapeutic Goals

The initial goals for Kristen would be consuming adequate nutrition to promote weight gain, eating three meals per day plus two snacks without purging or using other extreme methods to control body weight. Also, reduction of depression would be viewed as an important initial goal of therapy. Important long-term goals would be reduction of anxiety related to eating, modification of body image disturbances, and improvement of interpersonal trust. A final goal would be improvement of symptoms related to PTSD and OCPD.

Time Line for Therapy

Kristen would meet our criteria for admission to an inpatient level of care (Williamson, Duchmann et al., 1998), that is, she is significantly underweight with significant medical complications, and she is purging multiple times per day on most days of the week. We anticipate that she may require 2 to 3 weeks of inpatient treatment to stabilize her medical condition and to begin the process of refeeding. By the end of the inpatient phase of treatment, we would expect that she would be eating three meals and two snacks per day totaling at least 3,000 kcal/day without purging. We would expect that this level of nutrient intake would be very distressing to the patient and we would offer our support. Also, we would encourage her to face her fear of weight gain and we would assure her that the anxiety of eating more and gaining weight would eventually lessen in intensity over time. During the inpatient phase, it is likely that a trial of antidepressant medication would be initiated. Following the inpatient stage of treatment, Kristen would be discharged to the partial day hospital program, initially attending 7 days per week. We would anticipate that she would be at risk for purging when she went home at nights, and in response we would provide therapeutic support during the period immediately following the evening meal. We anticipate that Kristen would require 6 to 8 weeks of day hospital treatment. During the middle and latter parts of the day hospital stage of treatment, we would hope to reduce the number of days that she attended the program to 3 or 4 days per week. By the end of this stage of treatment, we would expect the initial goals of therapy to have been accomplished, that is, she would have gained about 10 to 15 lbs., would be eating three meals per day and two snacks without purging, and her depression would be improved. If her body weight was at a healthy level, the caloric prescription could be reduced to about 2,000 kcal/day. At this point, she could be discharged to intensive outpatient therapy, and would attend therapy from 3 to 5 hours per day on 3 to 5 days per week. Intensive outpatient therapy would be faded to once per week over the next 3 to 4 weeks. At the end of intensive outpatient therapy, Kristen would be discharged to outpatient therapy where she would be seen once per week by her primary therapist, i.e., the case manager who has conducted her therapy throughout the more intensive phase of therapy. Also, she would be scheduled to continue participation in an outpatient group therapy program, which she would have entered during the intensive outpatient therapy program. During outpatient therapy, problems related to PTSD and OCPD would be addressed more intensely than in previous stages of Kristen's therapy. Outpatient therapy would be faded over the next 6 to 12 months. It is likely that Kristen will need to be seen for periodic follow-up visits for several years after the conclusion of formal treatment. This continuum of care approach to therapy has the effect of fading out therapeutic support, while providing good continuity of care as the patient assumes a greater role in the process of recovery.

Case Conceptualization

As noted earlier, we have diagnosed Kristen with anorexia nervosa, major depression, PTSD, and OCPD. We conceptualize anorexia nervosa and depression to be primary clinical disorders with PTSD and OCPD as significant comorbid problems which have played an important etiological role in the development of the eating disorder and depression. We conceptualize the eating disorder to have been determined by a series of life stressors beginning at age 8 years (crisis in the family business) and continuing into adolescence (isolation from her parents and parental conflict ending in separation). We believe that if she had never developed overconcern with body size/ shape, she may have been at risk for depression, may have developed perfectionism, and that the date rape may still have occurred, but she would not have been likely to develop an eating disorder. The origins of concern with body size seem to stem from early exposure to social pressures that promoted thinness as a "secret to success." Her grandmother promoted some of these ideas and early participation in gymnastics probably served to strengthen these ideas so that they were eventually overvalued. These concerns and ideas persisted into high school where she began dieting and exercising to manage her body size and to reduce concerns about physical appearance which are quite normal during adolescence. The first episode of depression appears to have occurred during this period of her life. Dieting and exercise were used to reduce her anxiety about body and appearance and eventually, anorexia nervosa emerged from the interaction of habits, emotions, and overvalued ideas that led her to believe that control of eating and body size was the "secret to success" and the answer to her current life problems. We have found that this etiological history is quite common in restricting anorexia nervosa diagnosed during adolescence. In her junior year of high school, she received the first professional help for an eating disorder and depression, but as occurs all too often, this initial treatment was insufficient to achieve lasting changes in the cognitive, behavioral, and emotional bases of Kristen's problems. In her sophomore year of college, she experienced a date rape and this incident appears to have caused a second episode of depression, which was associated with the onset of binge eating. For the restricting anorexic patient, binge eating is the greatest fear, that is, losing control of eating which inevitably activates fear of weight gain and compensatory behavior to regain control and to prevent weight gain. Once Kristen began purging, it was as though she now had a "license to binge eat" without having to fear weight gain. It appears that Kristen went through periods of controlling binge eating, purging, and other extreme weight control habits throughout the next few years, but the concerns about body size and overvalued ideas about thinness and perfectionism persisted, making her at risk for another relapse. This relapse appears to have emerged from a series of life events ranging from the discovery of infidelity of her fiancé to the opportunity to secretly binge and purge in the travel associated with her job. All of these factors, combined with a final episode of depression, appear to have resulted in this latest effort to seek professional help for her problems. It is our impression that Kristen may now be ready for an effective trial of long-term therapy. Kristen's eating disorder and depression are now complicated by the failure of previous treatment and by PTSD, but we are confident that if she follows the treatment plan that she can now find the long road to recovery.

The Therapeutic Relationship

The Therapeutic Bond

Like other forms of psychotherapy, cognitive-behavioral therapy emphasizes the importance of the therapeutic relationship in contributing to patient change. Cognitive-behavioral therapists encourage patients to use rationality and intellect to change feelings and behavior by modifying faulty beliefs, while providing encouragement, support, and reassurance. They are also aware of interpersonal processes in psychopathology, and use the therapeutic relationship itself to understand and modify the patient's dysfunctional beliefs involving interpersonal relationships. Eating disordered patients like Kristen often have interpersonal difficulties, including problems with trust and intimacy which are likely to affect the therapeutic alliance. From a cognitive-behavioral viewpoint, the interpersonal difficulties are caused at least in part by dysfunctional schemata (cognitive structures that facilitate information processing) regarding interpersonal relationships which result from the patient's past experiences (i.e., with parents and significant others). The negative schemata are maintained by selective attention to information which is congruent with the faulty belief; therefore, the cognitive-behavioral therapist should consistently help the patient notice and process information within the therapeutic relationship which is inconsistent with the belief (i.e., positive relationship experiences). For example, based on her previous experiences it is likely that Kristen has the belief that positive, mutually fulfilling relationships are not possible and that to attempt them is to bring pain upon herself. She may, therefore, be quite reluctant to engage in a therapeutic relationship and expect that the therapist will somehow harm or reject her if she does. This expectation, which could be conceptualized as transference, may lead Kristen to test the therapist in terms of her trustworthiness and willingness to accept her.

Roles in the Therapeutic Relationship

Beck (1967) has referred to the therapeutic relationship in cognitive-behavioral therapy as one of "collaborative empiricism," in which the therapist and patient work together to gather evidence to identify, challenge, and replace the patient's irrational beliefs. The patient is viewed as a "scientist" who is able to make objective interpretations of events in the world, and the therapist actively engages the patient's participation in all phases of therapy. Since the relationship is one of collaboration, the therapist is constantly testing his or her hypotheses about the patient's difficulties and is open to changing them based on the patient's response to therapy. With persons diagnosed with eating disorders, it is especially important to clarify roles early in the therapeutic process. The patient may expect the therapist to "fix" her and may adopt a passive or even an antagonistic role. It is vital that the patient participate in her own recovery instead of viewing it as something she is being "forced" to do or as merely a means to get people to leave her alone. This problem is evident in Kristen's history and has likely contributed to her tendency to relapse under stress. It would be helpful to develop a written treatment contract with Kristen early in therapy. This contract would specify the expectations and responsibilities of both parties involved, and to revisit this issue as therapy progresses. She appears to be motivated by external factors to recover from her eating disorder at this time (i.e., her primary complaint is that the effects of the eating disorder and depression are interfering with her ability to work). Therefore, therapy would initially be aimed not only at establishing Kristen's trust in the therapist and therapy program, but to improve motivation. It may be helpful to have Kristen complete a "decision analysis form" (Pike, Loeb, & Vitousek, 1996), in which she would identify both positive and negative short- and long-term consequences of having an eating disorder versus not having an eating disorder. Another useful exercise involves asking the patient to draw a "pie chart" containing all the valued aspects of her life (e.g., family, school, work, etc.) with each aspect allotted an amount of space on the chart which corresponds with the desired amount of time she wishes to spend on it. The patient is then asked to modify this chart to include the amount of time she spends thinking about and engaging in habits which are motivated by fear of weight gain and drive for thinness. Most patients will realize that the eating disorder is currently taking up the majority of their time and energy and that the eating disorder is curtailing the time that can be devoted to all other valued activities and relationships in their lives.

Treatment Implementation and Outcome

Techniques and Methods of Working

As stated earlier, Kristen's treatment would initially be conducted on an inpatient basis and then gradually faded to outpatient therapy. An individualized treatment plan would be developed by a multidisciplinary treatment team, including (at a minimum) a psychiatrist, eating disorder therapist(s), and registered dietitian.

One goal of inpatient cognitive-behavioral therapy for eating disorders is to improve nutritional status through normalization of eating and discontinuation of purgative behaviors. Patients must be consistently given the message that "food is medicine" and that effective therapy cannot occur without improvement in eating and weight. Kristen's treatment plan would begin with the development of eating and weight goals. As stated earlier, one treatment goal would be to increase weight at the rate of about 1 to 2 pounds per week. She would initially be placed on a meal plan consisting of foods prescribed by the dietitian. As treatment progresses, she would be expected to assume increased responsibility for planning her own meals by participating in regular meal planning sessions. With the assistance of the dietitian, she would select foods for upcoming meals with the goal of meeting a prescribed number of dietary exchanges according to the American Dietetic Association/American Diabetic Association's dietary exchange program (1989). These sessions would also include nutritional education, including information about the physical and psychological effects of starvation and purging on the body (Keys, Brozek, Henschel, Michelsen, & Taylor, 1950). Meals would be initially monitored by a staff member who would record percentages eaten. As treatment progresses, Kristen would assume responsibility for self-monitoring her own food intake.

It is to be expected that Kristen's fear of fatness will be exacerbated by eating, causing an increase in anxiety especially around mealtimes. We have found that exposure (to eating) with response prevention (of purging) as described by Leitenberg, Gross, Peterson, and Rosen (1984) can reduce anxiety over the course of treatment through the process of extinction. The patient learns that although she feels quite anxious after eating, this anxiety can and will eventually subside without purging. Therefore, each meal and snack is viewed as having therapeutic value. Prevention of purging is accomplished through post-meal monitoring by a staff member. Kristen would be monitored after each meal and snack, for signs of purging. Since she has a history of using exercise to purge and to escape from negative affect, it would be especially important to monitor Kristen for even minor forms of exercise such as doing sit-ups, shaking arms or legs, or walking quickly. Although these forms of exercise burn a negligible amount of energy, we have found that they serve the same cognitive function as more intense forms of exercise, that is, the patient feels less anxious because she believes that she has compensated for food consumed, which negatively reinforces compulsive exercise and strengthens fear of weight gain. It would then be important to assist her in developing new, more adaptive ways to cope with negative feelings.

In addition to the initial treatment contract, daily and weekly behavioral contracting would be used to help Kristen establish goals. A typical goal might be "Following my meal plan every day" or "Practice relaxation before and after eating." Patients are encouraged to make small, concrete steps toward larger goals, since goals which are not met may be overwhelming and can result in feelings of failure and defeat. Praise from staff and other patients is an effective social reinforcer, and promotes Kristen's ability to notice and self-reinforce her own behavioral accomplishments.

A high degree of structure and consistency is important for inpatient treatment programs for eating disorders; any degree of ambiguity is often quite distressing to the patient. For example, Kristen would be weighed according to a predetermined protocol, that is, each morning after voiding while wearing pajamas or a hospital gown. Meals would be structured with standard portion sizes, eating times and place. Much of her free time would also be structured with homework and other assignments. These assignments increase the amount of time spent in therapeutic activities and reinforce the message that the patient must devote time and work to her own recovery process. An example of an assignment for Kristen would be to identify delay strategies and alternatives to binge eating to be put into practice when she returns home. Other assignments which might be helpful include: (1) journaling about thoughts and feelings (to be used in the cognitive restructuring part of therapy, described below) and (2) writing an "autobiography" which can help her begin to gain an understanding of the predisposing and precipitating factors which have brought her to the current point in her life.

The behavioral strategies described above are designed to facilitate normalization of Kristen's eating. However, they also increase her level of emotional discomfort (e.g., through eating and weight gain), which activates some of her fears about weight gain and makes them more accessible to intervention. The cognitive component of Kristen's therapy program would focus on helping her to understand how, because of her life experiences, she has developed "automatic thoughts" about eating and weight which are maladaptive to her health and happiness. These thoughts, which may occur without the patient's conscious awareness or attention (Williamson, Muller et al., in press), include such ideas as "my worth as a person depends upon my weight" and "Eating means being out of control." Kristen would be encouraged to become aware of these thoughts and the events which precipitate them through discussion and self-monitoring. Gradually, over the course of therapy, she would learn to recognize distorted thinking and to replace automatic thoughts with more realistic interpretations of life events related to food, body, and relationships. It appears that Kristen has developed a strong self-schema in which her identity is that of an eating disordered person; she has come to rely on the symptoms as a way to organize her life and to manage the stresses and conflicts that occur (Vitousek & Hollon, 1990). It would, therefore, be essential to assist her in developing alternate ways of coping with stress and, eventually, to discover a new identity which can be separated from the eating disorder. As stated earlier, cognitive restructuring should extend beyond thoughts about eating and weight to include more general maladaptive schemata and automatic thoughts about Kristen's general worth as a person, her ability to have healthy relationships with others, and her desire to be perfect at all times.

Body image therapy is an important component of cognitive-behavioral treatment of eating disorders. Rosen, Reiter, and Orosan (1995) and Cash (1997) have developed excellent treatment programs for body image dissatisfaction and preoccupation. These programs include: (1) education about the sociocultural, biological, and psychological factors which contribute to weight and body image disturbance; (2) cognitive restructuring of dysfunctional thoughts related to body image; and (3) behavioral exposure to distressing aspects of one's appearance. Elements of body image therapy would be incorporated into Kristen's treatment at all levels of care. We have found that during the more intense, earlier phases of treatment, anorexic patients do not benefit appreciably from body image therapy. We suspect that this problem may be due to a variety of factors: (1) the adverse cognitive effects of malnutrition may limit the amount of therapeutic information that is retained; (2) fear of weight gain is very strong, which causes the person to be very anxious when confronting body image disturbances; (3) thinness is so overvalued that alternative ideas promoting acceptance of a larger body size are considered to be unreasonable; and (4) body image concerns appear to be a core problem which persists long after significant behavioral changes have taken place. Given these observations, we have developed a 16-week outpatient program specifically for body image disturbances in recovering patients diagnosed with anorexia nervosa. This program includes many of the elements of treatment described by Rosen, Reiter et al. (1995) and Cash (1997), and adds exposure exercises that are designed to extinguish the negative emotional reactions to certain body areas. During outpatient therapy, after stabilization of eating and other emotional problems stemming from PTSD, Kristen would be referred to this outpatient body image treatment program for specialized treatment.

Kristen's treatment should involve her family since she is socially isolated and could easily "fall through the cracks" of treatment (i.e., after discharge from inpatient treatment) without family support. Her family also appears to have been the source of many of Kristen's ideas about the importance of maintaining a very thin, attractive appearance. It is likely that without engaging the family in her recovery (particularly by educating them about the causes of eating disorders and the recovery process), she will relapse or at least continue in the quasi-eating disordered state she has maintained since adolescence. However, since Kristen is now an adult and lives away from her parents, family therapy would not be a primary focus of treatment.

Finally, Kristen's treatment plan would include consideration of psychoactive medication, either during or after the refeeding process. Specifically, a serotonin-specific reuptake inhibitor (SSRI) would likely be effective in ameliorating her depressed mood and may also be effective in the pharmacological treatment of the eating disorder itself (Crow & Mitchell, 1996). A brief trial of a short-acting anxiolytic medication may help as well to manage intense anticipatory anxiety before meal times during the early stages of treatment (Williamson, Duchmann et al., 1998).

Medical and Nutritional Issues

Kristen is experiencing several physical complications which are probably secondary to her purgative behaviors and severely restrictive eating. She is dehydrated and has electrolyte disturbances, has episodes of dizziness, and is experiencing sensitivity to cold and orthostatic hypotension which are probably due to low blood pressure.

Rehydration and refeeding are necessary to improve her medical status, and an internist or family care physician should be consulted to monitor her during this process. Refeeding should begin slowly at first; for example, Kristen would be started at a meal plan consisting of 1,200 kcal/day and this caloric amount would be increased 200–300 kcal/day to a maximum of 3,000–3,500 kcals/day. Once refeeding has begun, she would be checked regularly for edema, fluid overload, and adequate gastric motility and bowel function. If these are found to be problematic, gastric motility agents and bulk fiber agents would be given on a scheduled basis. It would be important to inform Kristen that she may experience some discomfort when refeeding begins (e.g., bloating, constipation) but that these physical symptoms will abate with stabilization of body weight and nutrition. If she is unable or unwilling to consume the prescribed meal plan for several consecutive days, dietary supplementation would be considered. This decision is typically made in consultation with the entire treatment team and depends upon the weight status of the individual and the degree to which her medical status is compromised.

The treatment team should also be aware of other physical complications due to low body weight and body fat level. She is not currently menstruating and since she has a relatively long history of eating disturbance, she may be vulnerable to bone mineral density loss. A bone scan may be indicated and estrogen replacement and/or calcium supplementation might be considered. A dental consult may also be necessary, since Kristen is experiencing dental enamel erosion secondary to self-induced vomiting. Finally, a multivitamin/mineral supplement would also be considered.

Potential Pitfalls

Kristen's style of interacting with others, as well as her previous difficulties in treatment and with interpersonal relationships in general, suggest that the course of treatment may be marked by several potential problems. First, she does not seem to be particularly motivated for recovery from her anorexia except to the degree to which she can improve her functioning to be productive at work. She has participated in therapy previously at the insistence of her parents and others, but has never been sufficiently engaged in the process to fully recover. In fact, her eating has been continuously disturbed since her teens, and as stated above, she has come to depend upon disturbed patterns of eating, for example, restrictive eating and/or binge eating, as coping strategies for stress and negative emotions. She does not appear to fully acknowledge the seriousness of her condition now, although she has a number of physical symptoms. It is anticipated that one danger of treatment is that Kristen would take a "flight into health" in which she would do everything asked of her and would insist that she is better but would relapse quickly after discharge from inpatient treatment and would either disappear from treatment altogether or stay on the fringes where lasting therapeutic gains would never be made. She may also have the need to appear to be the "perfect patient" and would, therefore, deny experiencing common concerns while gaining weight, such as increased anxiety and labile body image disturbances. Consequently, these problems might not be adequately addressed in therapy. Another potential problem is related to Kristen's previous difficulties with interpersonal relationships. She is likely to be quite reluctant to invest in an emotional relationship with the therapist due to fears of abandonment, and consequently her therapy could become very superficial and merely intellectual. She might respond to the rationality and logic of cognitive therapy but would not be able to access and resolve the emotional distress associated with her underlying beliefs about the world (i.e., feelings of fear, anger, and disappointment).

Termination and Relapse Prevention

Patients and their family members often expect that they will be "cured" after inpatient treatment. It is important to help them view recovery from anorexia nervosa as a long, perhaps lifelong process. However, the therapist should also emphasize that the goal of therapy is not to solve every potential problem, but to learn skills to manage problems effectively in the future, that is, for the patient to become her "own therapist." We have found that gradual fading of therapeutic contact through the partial hospitalization program described earlier and 6 to 12 months of outpatient therapy is necessary to maintain treatment gains and to prevent relapses. Relapse prevention training should begin early in treatment. Patients are taught to identify and practice adaptive responses to high-risk situations. For example, Kristen would learn to identify ways to maintain control of eating (eating neither too much nor too little) while she is on business trips. Relapse prevention also includes learning and practicing active coping skills, and facilitating quick recovery from small slips or lapses (Marlatt & Gordon, 1985).

As stated earlier, a single case manager follows the patient throughout therapy. This person would become Kristen's primary outpatient therapist. It is expected that by this time Kristen will have established a trusting alliance with the therapist, and her disturbed patterns of eating will have stabilized so that she could profit from therapy for PTSD related to the rape she experienced in college. Body image therapy would be continued for an extended period of time, because dissatisfaction with body size often persists long after disturbed eating behaviors have changed. This dissatisfaction often stems from the anorexic patient's unreasonable expectations about thinness as an ideal body shape. As stated earlier, during the latter phases of outpatient therapy, Kristen would be referred to a specialized body image treatment program to address these concerns. Outpatient therapy would also focus on difficulties in interpersonal relationships and would continue to address core maladaptive beliefs which contribute to depression, feelings of unworthiness, and perfectionism. Outpatient therapeutic contact should also be faded gradually within a mutually agreed-upon time frame. It may be necessary to arrange periodic (e.g., once every few months) follow-up visits or calls and to make clear that the therapist is available if some unforeseen difficulty should occur that Kristen cannot manage on her own.

Mechanisms of Change

The initial change which must occur for treatment to be successful would be to improve Kristen's nutritional and psychological functioning through refeeding and weight gain. The cycle of dieting, binging, and purging that she has developed must also be broken through normalization of eating and prevention of purgative behaviors. A new, healthy way of eating and exercising should be learned and practiced. For lasting change, however, several other therapeutic goals must be accomplished. Automatic thoughts and distorted beliefs related to eating, fatness, and thinness must be identified, challenged, and replaced with more adaptive ones. Fear of fatness and drive for thinness must be substantially modified if lasting change is to occur. It is also important for Kristen to recognize situations which make her vulnerable to these thoughts and to learn and break the connections between distorted thinking, negative emotions, and disturbed patterns of eating. Ultimately, Kristen, in collaboration with the therapist, must challenge her underlying core beliefs about herself, other people, and the world. She must come to an understanding that although these beliefs once seemed quite reasonable and adaptive at an earlier stage of her life, they are no longer sensible and must be modified so that she can build better relationships and become a healthier, happier, and more complete person. Thus, cognitive-behavior therapy assumes that lasting change occurs at many levels, that is, behavioral, cognitive, and emotional. However, the primary mechanisms of lasting change are presumed to be cognitive. The person must alter overvalued ideas about the desirability of thinness and overcome fears related to weight gain. When these changes have been made, we have found most persons with eating disorders to follow a steady path of recovery.

REFERENCES

Agras, W. S., Barlow, D. H., Chapin, H. N., Abel, G. G., & Leitenberg, H. (1974). Behavior modification of anorexia nervosa. *Archives of General Psychiatry, 30,* 279–286.

American Dietetic Association/American Diabetes Association (1989). *Exchange lists for weight management.* Chicago/Alexandria, VA: Author.

American Psychiatric Association (1994). *Diagnostic and statistical manual of mental disorders* (fourth edition). Washington, DC: Author.

Beck, A. T. (1967). *Depression: Clinical, experimental, and theoretical aspects.* New York: Harper & Row.

Beck, A. T., Steer, R. A., & Garbin, D. W. (1988). Psychometric properties of the Beck Depression Inventory: Twenty-five years of evaluation. *Clinical Psychology Review, 8,* 77–100.

Bellack, A. S., & Williamson, D. A. (1982). Obesity and anorexia nervosa. In D. M. Doleys, R. L. Meredith, & A. R. Ciminero (Eds.), *Behavioral psychology in medicine: Assessment and treatment strategies* (pp. 295–316). New York: Plenum Publishing Corporation.

Blundell, J. E., & Hill, A. J. (1993). Binge eating: Psychobiological mechanisms. In C. G. Fairburn & G. T. Wilson (Eds.), *Binge eating: Nature, assessment, and treatment* (pp. 206–224). New York: Guilford Press.

Cash, T. F. (1997). *The body image workbook: An 8-step program for learning to like your looks.* Oakland, CA: New Harbinger Publications.

Crow, S. J., & Mitchell, J. E. (1996). Pharmacologic treatments for eating disorders. In J. K. Thompson (Ed.), *Body image, eating disorders, and obesity: An integrative guide for assessment and treatment* (pp. 345–360). Washington, DC: American Psychological Association.

Fairburn, C. G. (1981). A cognitive-behavioral approach to the treatment of bulimia. *Psychological Medicine, 11,* 707–711.

Fairburn, C. G., & Wilson, G. T. (1993). *Binge eating: Nature, assessment, and treatment.* New York: Guilford Press.

Garner, D. M., & Garfinkel, P. E. (1979). The Eating Attitudes Test: A index of the symptoms of anorexia nervosa. *Psychological Medicine, 9,* 273–279.

Garner, D. M., Vitousek, K. M., & Pike, K. M. (1997). Cognitive-behavioral therapy for anorexia nervosa. In D. M. Garner & P. E. Garfinkel (Eds.), *Handbook of treatment for eating disorders* (2nd ed.) (pp. 94–144). New York: The Guilford Press.

Heymsfield, S. B., Allison, D. B., Heshka, S., & Pierson, R. N. (1995). Assessment of human body composition. In D. B. Allison (Ed.), *Handbook of assessment methods for eating behaviors and weight-related problems* (pp. 515–560). Thousand Oaks, CA: Sage Publications.

Keys, A., Brozek, J., Henschel, A., Michelsen, O., & Taylor, H. L. (1950). *The biology of human starvation.* Minneapolis, MN: University of Minnesota Press.

Kutlesic, V., Williamson, D. A., Gleaves, D. H., Barbin, J. M., & Murphy-Eberenz, K. P. (1998). The Interview for the Diagnosis of Eating Disorders IV: Application to DSM-IV diagnostic criteria. *Psychological Assessment, 10,* 41–48.

Leitenberg, H., Gross, J., Peterson, J., & Rosen, J. C. (1984). Analysis of an anxiety model and the process of change during exposure and response prevention treatment of bulimia nervosa. *Behavior Therapy, 15,* 1–20.

Marlatt, G. A., & Gordon, J. R. (1985). *Relapse prevention: Maintenance strategies in the treatment of addictive behaviors.* New York: Guilford Press.

Pike, K. M, Loeb, K., & Vitousek, K. (1996). Cognitive behavioral therapy for anorexia nervosa and bulimia nervosa. In J. K. Thompson (Ed.), *Body image, eating disorders, and obesity: An integrative guide for assessment and treatment* (pp. 253–302). Washington, DC: American Psychological Association.

Rosen, J. C., & Leitenberg, H. (1982). Bulimia nervosa: Treatment with exposure and response prevention. *Behavior Therapy, 13,* 117–124.

Rosen, J. C., Reiter, J., & Orosan, P. (1995). Cognitive behavioral body image therapy for body dysmorphic disorder. *Journal of Consulting and Clinical Psychology, 63*, 263–269.

Spitzer, R. L., Williams, J. B. W., Gibbon, M., & First, M. B. (1990). *Structured Clinical Interview for DSM-II-R—Patient Edition (SCI-P), Version 1.0*. Washington, DC: American Psychiatric Press.

Thelen, M. H., Farmer, J., Wonderlich, S., & Smith, M. (1991). A revision of the Bulimia Test: The BULIT-R. *Psychological Assessment, 3*, 119–124.

Vitousek, K. B., & Hollon, S. D. (1990). The investigation of schematic content and processing in eating disorders. *Cognitive Therapy and Research, 14*, 191–214.

Wilfley, D. E., & Cohen, L. R. (1997). Psychological treatment of bulimia nervosa and binge eating disorder. *Psychopharmacology Bulletin, 33*, 437–454.

Williamson, D. A. (1990). *Assessment of eating disorders: Obesity, anorexia and bulimia nervosa*. New York: Plenum Press.

Williamson, D. A., Davis, C. J., Bennett, S. M., Goreczny, A. J., & Gleaves, D. H. (1989). Development of a simple procedure for assessing body image disturbances. *Behavioral Assessment, 11*, 433–446.

Williamson, D. A., Duchmann, E. G., Barker, S. E., & Bruno, R. M. (1998). Treatment manual for anorexia nervosa. In V. B. Van Hasselt & M. Hersen (Eds.), *Handbook of psychological treatment protocols for children and adolescents* (pp. 413–434). Hillsdale, NJ: Lawrence Erlbaum Associates, Inc.

Williamson, D. A., Muller, S. L., Reas, D. L., & Thaw, J. E. (in press). Cognitive bias in eating disorders: Implications for theory and treatment. *Behavior Modification*.

Williamson, D. A., Womble, L. G., & Zucker, N. L. (1998). Cognitive behavior therapy for eating disorders. In T. S. Watson & F. M. Gresham (Eds.), *Child behavior therapy: Ecological considerations in assessment, treatment, and education* (pp. 335–355). New York: Plenum Press.

4

The Psychoanalytic Perspective

April Fallon and Scott Bunce

TREATMENT MODEL

Kristen, described as intelligent, creative, productive, and beautiful, graduated magna cum laude from her MBA program. Currently employed with a prestigious firm, she is likely to be envied by those who take a casual glance at her life. What then would cause her to put her job, health, and very life at risk by gorging on high calorie foods, then forcing herself to vomit multiple times a day? It was this type of irrational behavior that led Sigmund Freud to formulate his psychoanalytic theory of the mind. He observed that some patients, despite a conscious effort to stop, continued to behave in ways that caused them great distress. Others acted in ways that were detrimental to their own well-being, yet appeared to be unaware or unconcerned with the problems they created for themselves. Unable to find any direct physical cause for the behaviors, Freud reasoned that the causes must be psychological in origin. Further, if the symptoms defied conscious control, he hypothesized that they must be maintained by an equally potent but unconscious psychological source. This simple but ingenious hypothesis foreshadowed what is now widely accepted in cognitive science; that there are important psychological functions that occur entirely outside the realm of conscious awareness that nevertheless influence ongoing thoughts, feelings, and behaviors (e.g., Shevrin & Dickman, 1980; Westen, 1990).

There is no single psychoanalytic theory that guides the conceptualization and treatment of bulimia. Rather, a constellation of theories, with at least four major schools of thought, constitutes the corpus of psychoanalytic thought. Pine (1988) labeled these the four psychologies of psychoanalysis: drive theory, ego psychology, object relations, and self psychology. Whereas the boundaries between these four schools of thought are fuzzy, each takes a somewhat different perspective on human psychological functioning and adds a unique contribution to our theoretical understanding of the human psyche and, consequently, to the clinical situation.

Despite this heterogeneity, several factors have been identified as prototypical of psychoanalytic approaches (e.g., Westen, 1990). First, psychoanalytic approaches are conative, that is, they focus on motivations, conceptualized as either conscious or unconscious drives, needs, wishes, or fears. Second, psychoanalytic theories hold as axiomatic the existence of a dynamic unconscious, that is, a person's behaviors and even their perceptions of reality are influenced by forces, either instinctual or learned, which are outside his or her conscious awareness. Third, psychoanalytic theories emphasize the importance of conflicting mental processes, the utilization of defenses and self-deception to make compromises between these competing mental processes, and belief that the compromises reached may be instantiated unconsciously. For example, a child might be angry with her mother for insisting she wear an "unhip" blouse. This creates a conflict because she has learned that expressing her anger results in a loss of mother's approval, whom she loves, as well as feeling like she is a "bad girl." Instead, she obediently wears the blouse, but accidentally and without *conscious* volition, spills grape juice on it at breakfast. This allows her to avoid wearing the blouse without risking her mother's disapproval. Fourth, psychoanalytic theories acknowledge the ongoing influence of interpersonal patterns learned in childhood. Finally, psychoanalytic theories give credence to the influence of sexual and aggressive motivations on thoughts, feelings and behaviors, which may be mediated at either the conscious or unconscious level.

Within a psychoanalytic framework, the restricting, bingeing, and purging behaviors that define bulimia are understood to be symptoms. Because psychoanalytic theory places an emphasis on understanding what motivates behavior, bulimic symptoms are conceptualized as being in the service of powerful needs or wishes that are not being met, or are being defended against. All symptoms are, by definition, maladaptive, because they cause distress and/or impairment. However, symptoms are thought to arise as a carefully constructed compromise between conflicting needs and demands (Brenner, 1982), and are thought to serve communicative, organizational, and/or reparative functions within the personality structure (Hamburg, 1989; Yarock, 1993). As such, patients have an ambivalent relationship with their symptoms. Although the symptoms are distressing, patients are loath to give them up because they serve some intrapsychic purpose and ward off more threatening psychological dangers. Symptoms serve a function within the personality structure, rendering them extremely resistant to change. As Freud observed, patients cannot simply give up distressing thoughts or behaviors, unless there is a set of behaviors put in place to serve that same function in the personality, but in a more adaptive way. This conception differs from the cognitive perspective, which typically sees symptoms as the result of maladaptive learning (e.g., Vitousek, 1996).

Symptoms are *overdetermined*, that is, each symptom results from the sum of many underlying causes (Waelder, 1936). Although symptom formation is often considered symbolic because it represents the underlying conflict, the symptoms may not make *logical* sense. Unconscious processes are not governed by the same rules that apply to conscious, secondary process thought, which is rational, logical, and linear. In primary process thought, objects may be classified together because they are the same color or the same shape, or because they serve the same function. This is why food and emotional nurturance can be equated in the unconscious, and how somatic pain can substitute for emotional pain. At the same time, bulimic symptoms are a final common behavioral pathway, and can reflect different underlying conflicts and compromises, resulting in considerable heterogeneity among bulimic patients (Fairburn, 1991; Wilson, Hogan & Mintz, 1983).

Psychoanalytic theory emphasizes the body, as well as sexuality, as central elements in the developing and adult psyches. Freud (1986, p. 26) stated that, after all "The ego is first and foremost a bodily ego." The world is perceived only through bodily sensations, sensations that are particularly crucial to our early development. Both the body and sexuality prove to have important dynamics among bulimics (Krueger, 1988). They fail to appropriately invest in their bodies, ignoring nutritional needs as well as other health-related concerns. Distortions and delusions about body shape suggest the body is poorly integrated into the sense of self. The physical and psychological aspects of sexuality play critical roles as body image and its relationship to the binge-purge cycle are inextricably woven into issues of sexual attractiveness and availability.

Finally, psychoanalytic theory focuses on the interpretation of the meaning of various symptoms to the bulimic; meaning can only be understood in the context of a learning history. This does not imply, however, that they have the *same* meaning for every individual. It is important to understand the bulimic patient's history, how she experienced herself, her wishes, and her needs in relation to other important people in her life. Only then will it become apparent what function the bulimic symptom is serving in her life.

Psychoanalytic Theories of Bulimia

Drive theory conceptualizes the individual in terms of instinctual motivational forces, or "drives." People are conceptualized as being pleasure seeking; other people are important to the individual only insofar as they satisfy drives or release instinctual tension. Conflicts arise when the individual's wishes are at odds with those of other people or the society at large. Psychic life is thought to be organized around managing these powerful conflicting wishes and fears. Classic drive theory focuses on the bingeing and purging symptoms as a compromise between the impulse or drive for libidinal gratification and the societal prohibitions against these gratifications. The wish for incestuous impregnation is the core of the early drive theories of anorexia, whereas bulimic activity has been conceptualized as an acting out of unconscious masturbatory fantasy (for a thorough review of this position, see Schwartz, 1988; Wilson et al., 1983).

Ego psychology departs from drive theory's notion that all psychic structure is essentially conflictual. Rather, the individual is conceptualized in terms of her capacities for adaptation, more or less mature defenses, and reality testing. These ego capacities develop slowly over time, and serve to help balance the intrapsychic world of motivations, affects, and fantasies in relation to the external world of reality demands. These developing capacities have the potential to be stunted or aberrant, resulting in "defects in the ego," such as an inability to tolerate or to regulate affects or impulses.

Bulimics are conceptualized as having impaired ego functions due to environmental insufficiencies, or an inability to utilize what the environment provides. Unable to regulate tension and anxiety states, the bulimic's internal affective states are experienced as intolerable, dangerous, and overwhelming. The inability to identify, articulate, and to modulate complex intrapsychic feelings states is a central feature in many psychoanalytic theories of bulimia. They have not developed the capacity to step back from a situation and reflectively analyze their own actions or reactions to the situation, which leaves them unable to effectively mediate between their impulses to act and the prohibitions against these actions (Yarock, 1993). This deficit results in the impulsivity often observed in bulimic women.

The bulimic symptom is a somatic and symbolic explosion of this tension, serving to defend against powerful urges or motivations (Friedman, 1985). To regulate the intolerable impulses of rage, shame, and sexuality, and the consequential guilt and self-deprecation, bulimics tend to rely on less mature defenses such as denial, repression, somatization, and dissociation (Demitrack, Putnam, Brewerton, Brandt, & Gold, 1990; see Moore & Fine, 1990, for definitions of unfamiliar terms.). The most intractable cases (which are often comorbid with borderline personality disorder) utilize the more primitive defenses of splitting, projective identification, and primitive idealization to neutralize these impulses. Within the personality organization, the binge/purge symptom has both protective and adaptive characteristics. It serves as a repository for or means of expressing the feelings of rage and shame that cannot be expressed or that have been dissociated. The bingeing and purging numbs the bulimic to the more critical but painful feeling states involved in relationships, allowing them to focus on the more tolerable physical sensations of eating and purging. By expressing the intolerable, the bulimic symptom allows the person to cope with relationships, school, or work.

The family environment sets the stage on which the intrapsychic dynamics are played out. The mothers of bulimic women are often perceived as inconsistent and unattuned to the needs of the child, a finding which has been confirmed in both observational and phenomenological studies (Humphrey, 1986; Humphrey, Apple, & Kirschenbaum, 1986; Wonderlich, Klein, & Council, 1996). Bulimic women often have a history of a seductive father-daughter relationship, resulting in early sexual overstimulation, if not outright abuse (Reich & Cierpka, 1998). The father's seductive kindness may be juxtaposed to impulsivity or occasional explosive outbursts, which leads to confusion among nurturance, sexuality, and aggression. The father is experienced as both a nurturing and an exciting object, making it difficult to differentiate needs for nurturance from sexual and aggressive needs, which prohibits mastery. In the environment of an unattuned mother, the "special attention" of the father figure may become a substitute for nurturance. This evokes a need to avoid the wish and threat of sexuality. Vomiting is a compromise between a symptom and a defense, a conscious act motivated by unconscious impulses and defenses. The gorging symptom is viewed as an aggressive incorporation of life-giving substances—a symbolic incorporation of a mother experienced as loath to relinquish nurturance. The subsequent vomiting is the symbolic rejection of the withholding mother, an expression of rage, allowing her to maintain control over what she is going to keep (Friedman, 1985). The symptom is not seen by the bulimic as expressing rage, but rather, tends to view it as evoking caregiving. As such, the compromise works; the bulimic does not fear losing the love of her parents by expressing rage, nor by destroying them in an act of rage. Guilt over sexual feelings and wishes, however, leads to avoidance of true sexual intimacy, and indeed from even fantasizing about it. Although bulimic women may have a history of promiscuity, this is typically an immature pseudosexuality. Without validation from men, these women often feel empty. Although they may present an overly compliant facade, this is usually a rigid and pseudo-mature persona, underneath which lies an enraged self; they often find partners who are attracted to these dynamics, and who are not psychologically healthy themselves.

According to object relations theory, humans are essentially "object-seeking," that is, sensual pleasure is secondary to the need for relatedness to other people. Object relations theory focuses on *repre-*

sentations that are based loosely on childhood experiences of the self in relationship to other people. The representations learned early in life influence the interpretation of new experiences; past experiences are brought to bear on the next similar encounter. These are not objective and veridical accounts of experiences with others, but memories of what is *experienced* by the child. This experience is an interaction between the motives and emotions active in the child at the time of the encounter and the environmental press.

Object relation theorists often focus on difficulties in the separation/individuation phase of development among bulimic patients (Friedman, 1985). Yarock (1993) characterizes the typical mother of a bulimic child as narcissistically vulnerable, with unmet dependency needs and unresolved separation/individuation issues. Typically, she is ambivalent about her own needs for nurturance, and generally derives little gratification from her relationship with her spouse. Under these circumstances, the mother turns to her daughter for unmet needs. The mother's relationship with her daughter tends to alternate between abandonment and intrusion; her emotional availability is consequently inconsistent and unpredictable. Although capable of giving love, these mothers can be experienced as controlling and demanding. They often have difficulty being in tune with their children's needs because they unconsciously require the child to be compliant, and fulfill their waffling needs for closeness and distance (e.g., Kanakis & Thelen, 1995). Obedience, conformity, submission, perfection, and what it means to be a "good girl" are dominant themes. Genuinely believing they are acting in their child's best interest, they overcontrol vital choices in their child's life—how they dress, how they look, how they act, where they go to school, who they socialize with, and so on. This parental overcontrol makes it very difficult for the child to negotiate the separation/individuation phase of development, to separate and form her own identity. To the eating disordered patient, the only domains she does control are her weight and the food she incorporates.

Under these circumstances, the child experiences herself as special, mother's needed caretaker and confidante. The bulimic typically experiences her mother as "overburdened," and she may prematurely separate from her mother and take on a pseudoindependent role to avoid being burdensome. Consequently, her own needs are experienced as too demanding to be tolerated and become a source of shame. This leads to a "basic fault" in her self-regulating capacities, leaving her with no ability to self-sooth or to self-regulate her affective and motivational states (Swift & Letven, 1984). The bulimic child is left with an unconscious hunger for the nurturing, soothing mother who can help her appropriately regulate her emotions and negotiate the separation/individuation phase of development. The normal, aggressive motivations that are typically used to facilitate separation from the mother are perceived as unacceptable. These aggressive needs must be split off or dissociated lest they be acted on, and are subsequently internalized as part of the "bad mother/bad self" schema. The bulimic child is caught, forced to deny her dependency needs on an overburdened mother while simultaneously being compelled to deny the anger she feels towards a narcissistically vulnerable mother. She is unable to complete the developmental task of separation-individuation because she must deny the anger that would allow her to develop psychological independence. The bulimic symptoms function as containers of those parts of the self that have been split off because they are unacceptable, e.g., her anger at being controlled. The symptoms also represent the reparative efforts of the psyche to bring into awareness the parts of the self that have been split off. They recapitulate the conflictual situation with the parents and simultaneously defend against it. Because the symptoms serve as both compromise and reparation in the face of this intolerable struggle, they often occur at times of anticipated or actual physical separation, such as when the adolescent attends college (Blos, 1967; Gonzalez, 1988; Yarock, 1993).

Self psychology focuses on self-definition in relation to important others, that is, the subjective experience of the self in relation to self-esteem, authenticity, a sense of agency, and of personal boundaries. See chapter 7 of this volume for further exposition of this perspective.

As the therapist focuses on the clinical phenomena of each case, there is likely to emerge a blending of the four domains of psychoanalysis within the patient's personality organization as she relates to the therapist (Pine, 1988; Yarock, 1993). One or another of these aspects will become central to the individual's pathology at a specific point in treatment, and this may vary over time. At one phase, conflict over expression of anger may be central, whereas at another, a focus

on issues of separation-individuation may be the most productive
level of analysis.

THE THERAPIST'S SKILLS AND ATTRIBUTES

Psychoanalytic treatment of a bulimic patient requires considerable
technical skill and experience. Competence in psychoanalytic psychotherapy requires a minimum equivalent of a 1- or 2-year postdoctoral program that includes a theoretical understanding, supervised therapy, and a personal psychoanalytic therapy experience.
In contrast, the psychoanalyst must graduate from an accredited
psychoanalytic training program, which typically includes 5 to 6 years
of course work, a personal psychoanalysis, and a minimum of three
completed supervised cases, requiring 8 to 12 years for completion.
Psychoanalysis allows a more in-depth approach to treatment, enabling the therapist not only to ameliorate bulimic symptomatology,
but also to pursue more basic intrapsychic alterations of the patient's
personality. The therapist's own personal treatment, an essential
component, enables a greater awareness of his or her own personality
and dynamics. Personal awareness is important in order to understand how the therapist's dynamics might interact with the patient's
dynamics and to fortify a sense of well-being so that if the therapist
experiences intense reactions (countertransference), he or she is
able to acknowledge them.

Both forms of treatment require a therapist who possesses: personal warmth to foster an atmosphere where patients can feel accepted and valued without feeling judged or controlled; the ability
to balance being genuine and truthful without feeling the necessity
to disclose personal information; empathy to accurately perceive
patients' multiple levels of communication, including suffering as
well as resistance to change; the patience to allow slow change; an
appreciation of the complexity of human nature; fortitude to tolerate
and contain intense, sometimes seemingly illogical, emotions and
projections from the patient (transference); the cognitive flexibility
and ingenuity to find ways to elicit self-exploration from patients who
appear to have little access to their inner life and little recognition of
their own conflicts, motivation, and defenses; and finally, the ability

to be involved with their patients without having his or her judgement distorted by the intensity of the interaction.

THE CASE OF KRISTEN

Assessment, Conceptualization, and Treatment Planning

Assessment

Many clinicians do not delineate the initial diagnostic evaluation from the psychoanalytic treatment itself, although there is variation on this issue. Regardless of whether assessment is formally separated from the commencement of treatment or not, the initial contact via telephone is conducted with an awareness of the crucial nature of the therapeutic relationship. Kristen's clinical vignette provides considerable information about her life history, details about her physical status, and the frequency of her bingeing and purging. However, assessing a patient for psychoanalytic treatment requires additional information. This information can be grouped into five categories: the quality of her interpersonal relationships (referred to as object relations); ego strength; capacity for introspection and awareness of feelings; concomitant symptomatology; and motivation for treatment.

Assessment, conceptualization, hypothesis testing, and reevaluation continue throughout the treatment process. The recollection of information, the symptom picture, and the patient's interest and ability to engage in the treatment process sometimes fluctuate considerably even in the first few sessions. Psychoanalytic assessment rarely uses a structured evaluation in which the therapist asks specific questions to "get the facts" of the case. Rather, the patient's presentation and defensive style, manner of relating to other people, ability to derive support from the therapist, and capacity to tolerate and use interpretations to gain insight are evaluated over several sessions through the patient's interactions with the therapist. If time is of the essence, assessment of motivations, typical defensive styles, and the quality of the patient's object relations can be augmented by a formal psychological test battery consisting of the WAIS-III, Rorschach, Thematic Apperception Test, and MMPI. Projective tests are essential when the patient is either unwilling or unable to provide accurate information. This feature may be particularly useful among bulimics, whose symptoms theoretically derive from unacceptable anger and disturbed relationships that they must keep out of awareness.

Object Relations.   From the case presentation we know the structure of Kristen's family and its members, that she had few friends, and only one serious heterosexual relationship. There is, however, relatively little information concerning the *quality* of her relationships with others, either in the past (with parents, grandparents, siblings, girlfriends, and boyfriends) or in the present (her fiancé, coworkers, boss, family, or friends). We are interested not only in her outward feelings and behavior toward others, but also in her internal representations of the important early relationships. What are her fears about these relationships? We know little about the quality of her intimate relationships. She mentions three heterosexual relationships (high school boyfriend, the fraternity brother who raped her, and her fiancé) all of which involved traumatic sexual interactions. A more detailed sexual history is essential. What is the role of these relationships in Kristen's life—does she trust and rely on them, or does she need them symbolically to fill her up and make her feel "whole"? Does she feel exploited by them or exploit them? Does she need to control or be controlled by them? How does she take positive and negative feedback from others? Are her relationships variable over short periods of time, changing from intense and emotionally charged to distant, or are they always distant? How do her relationships end? Can we detect similarities and patterns in her interactions with others past and present?

The assessment of Kristen's object relations is important not only because of its contribution to the development of the bulimic symptoms, but because the therapeutic relationship is the vehicle for change. The manner in which Kristen perceives and treats others will likely be recreated and projected onto the therapeutic relationship. The healthier her interpersonal relationships, the more quickly therapy will progress because she will have better ability to trust and to view the therapeutic relationship as collaborative, rather than one that she must control to avoid being controlled.

Introspection and Awareness of Feelings. Therapy proceeds most easily when patients have some ability to identify their affective states, access their inner life, and connect these thoughts and feelings to behavior, symptoms, and resulting external events. How aware is Kristen of her feelings toward herself and others? She expressed self-disgust, but does she experience anger, loss, fear, envy, guilt, et cetera? Does she recognize a relationship between her emotions toward herself and others (disgust, pride, anger) and her behavior (e.g., bingeing, purging)? Can she make any sense of the temporal connections between external events and her eating symptoms? Does she have the capacity to widen her sphere of awareness or increase her flexibility of response when offered explanations or interpretations of her behavior?

Ego Functioning Past and Present and Containment of the Drives. Ego functioning refers to the individual's ability to reality test, to make good judgments, to regulate emotion and impulses, to handle anxieties and environmental stressors in adaptive rather than maladaptive ways, and to maintain an even, accurate, and positive sense of self. These assessments can be made by exploring how Kristen handles daily anxieties, life pressures, and serious disappointments. How radically does her sense of self fluctuate with external events? What are the primary defenses she utilizes to contain her emotions and to maintain adequate self-esteem? How accurate is her ability to assess people and situations? Does she use her perceptions to make good judgments? For instance, in retrospect, was there any evidence that her fiancé was capable of infidelity, which might have motivated her impromptu flight to "surprise" him when she discovered his affair? Ego strength is critical because it determines the extent to which Kristen will be able to tolerate the exploration of her inner life and the concomitant awareness of painful emotions. The less ego strength Kristen has, the longer treatment will take to complete, because it will require a greater proportion of supportive or ego building techniques rather than interpretation (See Hollender & Ford, 1990, for a discussion of supportive techniques).

Other Symptomatology. Although the diagnosis of bulimia nervosa describes a circumscribed set of abnormal eating behaviors, they do not occur in isolation. Rather, they occur within a constellation of personality and developmental organizations. Common therapeutic issues encountered among bulimics include: low self-esteem, guilt, and depression; covert anger; interpersonal sensitivity, poor relationships with concomitant social isolation from peers; fear of loss of control; problems with impulsivity, including stealing, lying (Hall, Beresford, Wooley, Tice, & Hall, 1989; Hogan, 1983), delinquency, alcohol or substance abuse (including diuretics and laxatives); self-mutilation (e.g., Favazza, DeRosear, & Conterio, 1989; Garner & Rosen, 1994); and the sequelae of sexual assault (Herzog, Nussbaum, & Marmor, 1996; Vanderlinden & Vandereycken, 1997; Wonderlich, Wilsnack, Wilsnack, & Harris, 1996). In contrast to restricting anorectics, many bulimics present with an exaggerated emphasis on sexuality, appearance, and attractiveness, and sexual promiscuity is not uncommon. Consistent with Kristen's case, empirical evidence suggests that bulimics are likely to come from families that evidence more conflict, less structure and cohesion, and more psychiatric symptomatology than families of restricting anorectics or normal controls (e.g., Humphrey, Apple, & Kirschenbaum, 1986; Strober, 1982). Each of these factors has a complex network of meaning underlying them. Any comprehensive assessment, theory of etiology, or modality of treatment should address these associated syndromes.

The case material suggests that Kristen is likely to have other psychiatric symptomatology. In addition to a history of depression, she reports that her bulimic symptoms began soon after her rape in college. Kristen should be assessed for posttraumatic symptoms, that is, panic, anxiety, nightmares, et cetera. She does exhibit some shame about the rape, as she became anxious and avoided eye contact while describing the event. Kristen should also be evaluated for depression, suicidality, and the potential for other abuse.

A high prevalence of sexual abuse (30%–64%) has been documented in eating disordered women (Rorty & Yager, 1996), with only 50% of eating disordered patients having previously reported the abuse to anyone (Tice, Hall, Beresford, Quinones, & Hall, 1989). Abuse can have devastating effects on personality. Traumatized individuals often develop a victim's identity, desperately desiring the nurturance of relationships, but terrified by the potential for being exploited, abandoned, or betrayed (Herman, 1992). A secure, predictable environment allows a normative belief in an essentially "just world." This is compromised in an environment that allows abuse to occur (e.g., Janoff-Bulman, 1992). Traumatized individuals often fail to develop the capacity to identify and differentiate complex internal feeling states, leading to the inappropriate behavioral expression (acting out) of intolerable motivational and affective states that cannot be expressed in words.

Early abuse can result in a destruction of the systems of meaning by which a child understands the world (Rorty & Yager, 1996). A child that develops in an abusive environment must struggle to make sense of her reality; the environment that is the source of life-sustaining nurturance is simultaneously withholding and psychologically damaging. The learning process by which individuals make sense of the world is disrupted in the abused child. Frequently, the long-term sequelae of this type of assault on the developing self is personality pathology. Significant proportions of eating-disordered patients have personality disorders, with estimates ranging from 22% to 77% (Herzog et al., 1996). Borderline personality disorder, characterized by identity confusion, interpersonal and intrapsychic turmoil, internal emptiness, over- and undervaluation of others, self-mutilation, and self-destructiveness, is the most common Axis II diagnosis among bulimic groups (e.g., Herzog, Keller, Lavori, & Sacks, 1992; Rorty, Yager, & Rossotto, 1994). Although difficult to discern from the case material presented, Kristen should be assessed for traits indicative of personality or character pathology—particularly borderline or narcissistic characteristics.

Motivation for Treatment. Motivation for treatment depends on the ego strength of the patient, as well as her level of discomfort, desire for health, willingness to assume responsibility, and stamina to endure the emotional pain involved in uncovering the unconscious causes of her behavior. Because psychoanalytic therapy typically requires a significant time commitment, and does not necessarily lead to immediate symptom reduction, motivation for treatment is essential. Knowledge about Kristen's motivation can be inferred from the course of her two previous therapeutic treatments and, in particular, how they were terminated. Assessment of her response to frustrating life circumstances will also aid in the evaluation of her motivation. Another measure of Kristen's motivation for treatment is her willingness to make treatment a priority. Is she willing to devote time to therapy, to accept appointments that are less than ideal for her

schedule, and to keep appointments even when other life circumstances threaten to impinge on her treatment time?

Therapeutic Goals

The long-term goals of psychotherapy are the amalgamation of what
Kristen might like to accomplish and what the therapist may feel to
be optimal. Both the therapist and Kristen may agree that the relief
of emotional distress, reduction of bulimic symptoms, and the acquisition of solutions to deal with problems in her life, particularly at
work, would be desirable goals. The therapist is likely, however, to
be interested in more extensive goals, involving the alteration of
personality characteristics and interpersonal patterns of behavior
that interfere with Kristen's ability to experience pleasure, realize
her potential at work, and be involved in satisfying interpersonal
relationships. In order to accomplish these structural changes,
shorter-term goals and more specific long-term goals must be
achieved.

Short-Term Goals.   Mastering these goals would enable Kristin to
begin developing insight into her behavior, and allow her to work
on more extensive, long-term goals.

1. Development of a Therapeutic Alliance: The therapeutic alliance
is the working relationship that patients and their therapists develop
involving an understanding and acceptance of their mutual goals.
This includes: a hope that the therapy experience can aid the patient
in giving up her symptoms and improving her ability to function; a
trust that the therapist, together with the patient, can accomplish
this; and a willingness on the part of the patient to continue the
process, despite intense transferences. Patients such as Kristen often
have not had positive experiences with benevolent parental/author-
ity figures and consequently have a great deal of difficulty trusting
people. Developing a trusting therapeutic alliance is not only a means
by which other work can be accomplished, but also a critical part
of the therapeutic process itself. Through the process of developing
an alliance, Kristin can learn what it is like to be in a healthy,
trustworthy relationship with someone who is invested in her best interests.

2. Development of an Observing Ego: Developing an observing ego means helping Kristen develop the ability to observe herself—to become aware of her behavior, thoughts, and feelings as she is experiencing them. It involves learning to conceptualize and articulate an experience without the compulsory need to act on the feeling or thought. This skill is essential for Kristin to develop the ability to understand and regulate emotions and motivations, rather than to simply act on them. Kristen is currently expressing a conflict or need through action—bingeing and purging, but with little or no ability to articulate what those conflicts or needs might be, much less knowing how to fulfill them in a healthy way.

3. Awareness of Affective States: Related to the development of an observing ego, Kristen must learn to be aware of and label affective states (particularly anger). Bingeing and vomiting often occur in the context of an initially unidentifiable feeling state. Kristen must learn to identify these feelings, as well as the immediate precursors that precipitate bulimic episodes (i.e., affective states and external events). As she becomes more skilled in identifying her affective states, Kristen must connect her affective states to her intrapsychic life (fantasies, fleeting thoughts, dreams) and her behavior (including bulimic symptoms as well as other behavior). These abilities will allow Kristen to strengthen her conscious controls, facilitating her ability to tolerate and appropriately express a range of emotions (Provost, 1989).

4. Recognition of Consistent Patterns of Behavior That Are Incongruent with Her Goals: Kristin must develop an awareness of patterns of behavior that are inconsistent with her goals. For instance, she may recognize that, despite her desire for a relationship in which she is cared for and respected, the men that she has been involved with are not likely to meet these needs. As she becomes aware of her behavior patterns, Kristin can begin to make alternative choices, rather than acting on previously learned patterns of behavior that are overlearned and automatic, but no longer adaptive.

Long-Term Goals. Initially, only the therapist endorses many long-term goals. If Kristen were to obtain symptom relief or an attenuation of emotional distress, she might choose to leave treatment prior to achieving some of these goals.

1. Understanding the Multiple Functions That Bulimic Symptoms Serve: Bulimic symptomatology can have multiple and different etiologies for each patient. Although many bulimics have common conflicts, symptomatology itself is an external manifestation of an underlying conflict, need, or deficit that is determined by each patient's unique constellation of innate tendencies and environmental experiences. The therapist helps Kristen discern the multiple meanings and understand the functions that the bulimic symptoms serve for her in the context of her current situation and life history. For instance, in many cases the bulimic symptom serves as an expression of rage, disgust, or repulsion. The specific incidents and people who evoke the rage or disgust, however, may differ from case to case, or from time to time in a given case. In Kristen's case, her bulimic symptoms are likely linked to the rage and disgust she must feel in response to both the rape and her fiancé's betrayal. Her conflicts and inability to express her anger are likely to have other sources as well, for example, her parents' lack of emotional attunement and her father's affair.

2. Improvement of Self-Esteem: Analytic therapists do not consider top-down processes such as daily affirmations (i.e., thinking or saying good things about oneself) to be effective in improving self-esteem. Low self-esteem is not simply a "wrong cognition," else it would improve with the "correct information" that the patient is "a good or valued person." Patients with low self-esteem cannot seem to believe this because low self-esteem is the result of a lifetime of interactions with both an external and an intrapsychic environment. There are both valid and invalid reasons for feeling bad about the self, some of which are conscious, some of which are unconscious. A realistic exploration of these reasons in the presence of an empathic and nonjudgmental therapist is needed to help Kristen realistically evaluate her self-worth. Improvement in self-esteem develops through an experiential process of internalization. Kristen must come to accept and believe, at both a cognitive and an emotional level, that she is worthy of love and respect, and that she is valued because she can give love and be a productive and valuable member of society. This typically occurs only in the context of relationship, and, for Kristin, can occur through her relationship with her therapist.

3. An Increased Degree of Self-Differentiation: Kristen must discover (or rediscover) and assert her own needs and feelings, apart from those of her parents (or boyfriend). This assertion must be followed by a psychological separation from her parents and the establishment of a separate identity. Kristen must become self-reliant in her basic soothing functions, decide what her values are, and how she will live her life. These steps towards independence will function to attenuate her emotional emptiness and anxieties about being abandoned or rejected, and reduce her need to please others and to be perfect.

4. Amelioration of Bulimic Symptomatology and Improvement in Social Functioning.   As the preceding goals are achieved, Kristen will need help in developing a greater flexibility in her repertoire of responses when faced with thoughts and emotions that precipitate bulimic symptoms. Treatment is directed at the characterological aspects of her pathology, rather than simply at the presenting symptoms. As her insight deepens, Kristen is likely to experience a gradual attenuation of her bulimic symptoms, and to develop a greater appreciation of the interconnection between her bulimic symptoms and the other symptomatology she may be experiencing, with a concomitant improvement in social functioning.

Timeline for Therapy

Several factors affect the frequency and duration of psychoanalytic treatment including the severity of the case and the orientation of the therapist. Classic psychoanalysis involves a minimum of four to five sessions per week, during which the patient lies in a reclining position while the analyst sits behind the patient. The client is encouraged to maximize her attention on her own thoughts, feelings, and motivations, and to free-associate, that is, to say whatever comes to mind without censoring the content (e.g., Wilson, 1983).

By contrast, psychoanalytic psychotherapy is conducted face-to-face. Depending on the psychological resources of the client, psychoanalytic psychotherapy can range from very structured, focal, and time-limited treatments to unstructured, insight-oriented, and open-ended treatments (e.g., Crits-Christoph & Barber, 1991). Contrary to lay opinion, more intensive treatment is often recommended for clients with greater psychological resources because they can tolerate and consequently benefit from introspection, exploration of the unconscious determinants of their behavior, and the experience of working out their own solutions with the help of the therapist. Individuals with less ego strength and less mature defenses may initially need to focus on managing everyday stresses, which they often experience as overwhelming. They rely on the therapist for more direction, support, and structure to strengthen their healthy coping strategies. For example, Ms. A spends most of her sessions noticing and exploring her reactions to everyday interactions with others, as well as the distortions of others, including the therapist, while frequently exploring her conflicting feelings of desire for closer contact with her therapist juxtaposed to her fear of being controlled. In contrast, Ms. B experiences an intense and unresolvable fear that she is being controlled by the therapist, with no ability to recognize the symbolic quality of her reaction and no recognition of its parallels in her life outside therapy. Rather than exploring her inner psychological life, Ms. B needs considerable support and direction in deciding how to manage daily activities.

As symptoms are thought to stem from underlying conflicts and deficits, treatment is generally not considered complete until there is some resolution of these personality patterns.[1] Because treatment does not end with a cessation of the bulimic symptoms if unremitted anger, depression, posttraumatic symptoms, or interpersonal difficulties are still present, psychoanalytic therapy is generally considered long-term. Successful treatments can last a minimum of one year (Wilson et al., 1983), and may last 5 or more years. Whereas this may seem to be considerably longer than many other types of therapies offered, research suggests that bulimia is a chronic disorder characterized by multiple episodes of relapse and remission (Herzog et al., 1996), with significant symptomatology often present years

---

[1]Some therapists do, however, conduct psychoanalytically based focal psychotherapies, that may concentrate on ameliorating a certain deleterious pattern of behaviors through the resolution of the underlying conflicts or deficits, without a complete restructuring of the personality.

after the index episode. Psychoanalytic therapists attempt to work through the personality processes that maintain these symptoms, rarely accomplished in a short period of treatment.

Case Conceptualization

Although we are presented with many important *facts* about her case, several critical aspects of Kristen's intrapsychic life (detailed in the assessment section) essential for a psychoanalytic formulation of her case are absent. With more of this information, we could begin to formulate a psychoanalytic understanding of Kristen's personality structure, and the functions (i.e., organizing, communicative, reparative) that the bulimic symptoms serve within that structure. However, a working assumption of psychoanalytic theory is that Kristen may be unaware of, or unable to articulate, certain core features of her personality organization that lead to the development and onset of symptoms. For this reason, a psychoanalytic case conceptualization is developed over time, as some of these conflicts and deficits surface during therapy. Initially, Kristen may be either too defended against threatening information to allow it into consciousness, too developmentally immature or traumatized to articulate powerful feelings, or too ashamed to acknowledge information that may make her feel vulnerable. However, several aspects of Kristen's case *are* typical of bulimic women, and illustrative of the dynamics that psychoanalytically oriented therapists would wish to explore.

Children develop their intrapsychic models of reality, meaning, and value through the perceived experience of how their needs are met and responded to by the environment. For this reason, learning about the patient's early environment is important—both the actual facts (e.g., specific family traumas such as the fire that destroyed the business) and Kristen's perceived significant relationships (e.g., the availability of caretakers). Kristen was born into a family that emphasized beauty, competition, and perfection. She notes that her aunt, the favored child in her mother's family of origin, was valued for her beauty, whereas Kristen's mother, Charlotte, was known as the "smart one." Charlotte, however, did not attain this internalized ideal, dropping out of college when pregnant. Charlotte's failure to achieve her parents' expectations is likely to have had an impact on her self-esteem. Low self-esteem, in turn, may have affected her ability to mother, for example, to be attuned to her child's needs, to provide object constancy, and to derive gratification from being a good mother. Environmental circumstances such as the fire that destroyed the family business only intensified the emotional needs shared by Kristen and her family. Her parents' struggles and consequently her own were around themes of need, emptiness, consumption, greed, and satiety. There is a sense from Kristen's portrayal that there was never enough, whether it was money, emotional nurturance, or love. This type of deficit in nurturant parenting can leave a child feeling empty, ungratified, and unable to fully individuate, setting the stage for other pathological developments to occur (Mahler, Pine, & Bergman, 1975). We are aware of three ways that Kristen attempted to repair or manage her emotional emptiness—through academic or career achievement, through the use of relationships, and with food. When Kristen entered treatment, two of these (food and her fiancé) had failed to fulfill her emotional needs, and the third (her job) was in jeopardy.

The use of achievement to derive a sense of unique wholeness began when Kristen was quite young, and continued into her professional career. Indeed, Kristen was praised for her achievements and compliance ("politeness" and "straight A's"). To the extent that Charlotte saw Kristen as an extension of herself, she too gained self-esteem from Kristen's achievements (Miller, 1981). Despite both external and internal pressure to achieve, success in her early environment also meant to outperform her less accomplished parents, which carried with it the dangers of reawakening and aggravating the oedipal rivalry and exacerbating her mother's already suffering sense of self. The effect of the children's early success on their mother's self-esteem is reflected in the family myth that the children were "so perfect" that they would surpass and "look down on [their] college dropout parents." Kristen's attention to achievement for the glory of her parents meant that, to some degree, she had to quell her own initiatives and ignore her negative emotions. Furthermore, school achievement and professional success are not adequate substitutes for emotional needs.

A second way in which Kristen attempted to fill her emotional emptiness was through her relationships with others. Her concerns with emotional supply and nurturance are particularly evident in her heterosexual relationships. With her fiancé, she considered herself lucky to become engaged without having to date, presumably reducing her risk of rejection. Her hopes for emotional fulfillment were initially fueled by his lavish attentions. We also suspect that she did not relate to him as an equal partner, as she felt intense anxiety over abandonment, like an infant who would starve to death without her caretaker. When this relationship failed, she chose to focus on her own perceived shortcomings rather than confront her suspicions about his potential character flaws and risk discovering that he did not care about her in the way that she desired. This poor choice paralleled her experience in high school when a boyfriend rejected her because she refused to have sex with him. Kristen also appears to have difficulties with same sex relationships. She spent much of her free time in isolation, did not acknowledge any close friendships in her life, and could not even identify anyone she would wish to be her bridesmaid. We do not know *why* she avoided relationships, whether it was for fear of abandonment, rejection, ridicule, or some other reason. We do know that despite her mother's inability to provide adequate emotional sustenance, Kristen appears to have continued a close relationship with her, perhaps hoping to obtain this nurturance. Even in college she remained as her mother's confidante.

A third way in which Kristen attempted to fulfill her emotional needs was through the use of food. Bingeing is to be an extreme and voracious way of achieving emotional sustenance, but eventually results in weight gain. In a society that values thinness, unrestrained intake requires an antidote. Currently her eating habits are extremely restrictive during the day, as if her hunger is a reprehensible desire. When she is overwhelmed by her needs, the food she gorges on to satisfy and numb herself becomes a "poison" that she must work off through exercise, or regurgitate, lest it convert to ugliness and fat. The case material suggests that Kristen came to experience her own needs, whether hunger, emotional closeness, or sexual desires, as sources of humiliation and shame, and she began to deny her own physical needs. She did not allow herself to eat sufficient food to maintain her health as a teenager, felt guilty for experiencing happiness in college, and cannot allow herself to have sexual desires as a young adult, unless she is drinking.

There are other indicators that her symptoms are a source of shame, a common finding among bulimics (Sanftner, Barlow,

Marschall, & Tangney, 1995; Zerbe, 1995). She was "too ashamed" to confide in friends about her distress in college. Kristen did not tell her therapist that she continued to binge and purge about 3 times a week while in therapy. She concealed her bulimia from her primary care physician for 2 years, and, even now she is not seeking treatment for the bulimia *per se*, but because she fears losing her job. Indeed, 10% of patients at an eating disorders clinic who were also in psychotherapy elsewhere could not inform their therapist of their eating disorder because of their shame and guilt (Herzog, Franko, & Brotman, 1989).

In addition to denial, Kristen's use of several defenses is apparent from the record. Her tendency to use somatization is evident in her bulimic symptoms. She also tends to isolate affect, as she relates painful historical events such as affairs, divorces, and rapes with little emotion, suggesting that she has dissociated the affective component of these memories from the "facts." She also has a tendency to act out—a specific defense summoned to manage or obliterate anxiety. Bulimics (perhaps more than other eating disorders) often use action such as frenetic business, exercise, or bingeing and purging to fend off anxiety. Kristen uses alcohol to overcome social and sexual inhibitions, and frenzied activity and exercise to avoid thinking too much about painful emotions.

Her frenzied activities, and later, her bulimic behaviors, appear to act as distractions for Kristen, a way to avoid thinking about her tumultuous inner life. Lacking appropriate mechanisms to modulate intense emotions, bulimics often feel they may be overwhelmed by intolerable feelings and fear disintegration, "going crazy," or "having a nervous breakdown." There is evidence that Kristen is very angry, and unable to modulate her anger. Instead, Kristen relates to her anger much as the way she relates to her desire for food. She does not express the anger, holding it in until she becomes overwhelmed, at which time she erupts, "vomiting" anger in situations that are destructive to her career. This behavior may have its roots in an incomplete separation/individuation from her mother. Their incomplete individuation is exemplified by Kristen's acknowledgement that she was unable to allow herself to feel joy or contentment at college because her mother was unhappy. It is common for bulimic daughters to be unable to express the anger they feel towards a narcissistically vulnerable mother for fear of destroying her "fragile" mother, the relationship with her mother, or herself. It is the ability to express anger that allows the child to enter and complete the process of individuation (hence the prototype of the rebellious teenager). This process is often thwarted in bulimics. Incomplete separation-individuation can result in struggles around issues of control, and difficulty in forming new intimate relationships. Several aspects of Kristen's case suggest her bulimic symptoms are related to issues of control. Her restricting symptoms began at a time when many other aspects of her life were out of her control. She responded to this lack of control by focusing on the aspects of her life she *could* control—her grades and her weight. College was not the liberating experience she had envisioned, in part because her mother needed her as a confidante, but also because Kristen needed her mother's emotional support. This mutually symbiotic tie kept both of them focused on her mother's difficulties, rather than Kristen's need to individuate. The bulimic symptoms can be viewed as a symbolic reparation of her needs for emotional sustenance, individuation, and control. The binge allows her to symbolically take in emotional nurturance. The vomiting allows her to control, rather than be controlled, by her emotional needs, and she can purge herself of the unwanted or controlling aspects of the emotional sustenance. It allows her to keep what she wants, and reject all else. Kristen was continuously anxious about her fiancé's behavior because she could control neither his behavior nor his investment in her. Her inability to control her fiancé's emotional investment may re-create her struggle for emotional nurturance in her disengaged family of origin. Finally, her intense anger with her client at work appears to have erupted when she could not control his reaction to her work, and did not get the approval for her accomplishment that she sought.

In addition to Kristen's emotional hunger, her symptoms appear to be temporally linked to four separate sexual traumas. The first, her father's affair, coincided with the onset of her restricting behaviors (dieting and exercise) and striving for perfection. This affair, which led to a protracted battle between her parents that eventually ended in divorce, occurred at a time when her own romantic interests were surfacing. Although Kristen did not directly experience the sexual aspect of this trauma, the abandonment and betrayal transpired between the two people who were the source of her own internalized standards of sexual identity. It could be hypothesized that her restrictive behaviors may have been her attempt to deny or punish her desires for emotional fulfillment or it may have been an unconscious attempt to return to that prepubescent state and deny her own budding sexual desires. The second sexual trauma occurred the next year, when her boyfriend abandoned her because she would not have sex with him. She responded to this loss with depression, increased exercise, and isolation. The third sexual trauma occurred in college, when she was raped by a fraternity brother. Her bulimic symptoms began after the rape. Her own perception was that she began to binge to escape the violent memories of the rape. Dynamically, it could be construed that she was reenacting the violence of the rape through her bingeing and purging cycles. Although a more precise conceptual elaboration would require Kristen's further associations, there are a number of possible hypotheses about the symbolic meaning of the purging. Her violent efforts to rid herself of the contaminating food by vomiting can be seen as a symbolic expression of disgust, an effort to purge herself of the contaminating material and memories of the rape. The fourth sexual trauma was when she confirmed that her fiancé was cheating on her. Feeling humiliated and betrayed, over the next year her restrictive dieting and exercise increased, and her binge-purge cycle increased to a level that currently threatens her health, even her life.

Therapeutic Relationship

Entrance into treatment is often accompanied by reluctance and trepidation because bulimics fear feeling inadequate or dependent, and because they prefer to *act* (e.g., exercise, binge-purge) rather than to explore their intrapsychic life. This renders the initial phases of treatment particularly crucial (Reich & Cierpka, 1998). The therapist must remain respectful of the ambivalent relationship the patient has with her bulimic behavior and understand the function of the symptom for the patient to help her develop more adaptive ways to cope with conflicts. The therapeutic alliance is fostered by the therapist's empathy and by her ability to balance a knowledge of the complex, overdetermined nature of the symptoms with a compassion and urgency to relieve the patient's pain (Hamburg, 1989). Understanding, empathy, and commitment are conveyed through the therapist's ability to maintain a consistent presence and predictable style in the face of angry attacks, complaints, acting out, or withdrawal on Kristen's part. It is common for the patient to fear that she will be abandoned, rejected, or that she will destroy her relationships if she expresses her anger, or is less than perfect. To experience the therapist as consistent, empathic, and available, despite the expression of anger, disappointment, or need for the therapist, stimulates psychological growth. The strength of the therapeutic bond allows the collaborative exploration of the patient's psychopathology, despite her mistrust and fear of being controlled. The influence of the therapeutic relationship can be seen in Kristen's previous therapies. When she had a good relationship with her therapist, she improved as long as she continued therapy. When she did not like her therapist, she quickly discontinued treatment.

Boundaries are extremely important when topics of such intimate detail are discussed. An effort is made to confine treatment to the sessions and to minimize contact outside the sessions, including phone calls, letters, and chance meetings with the patient or her significant others. Whereas the therapist maintains a warm, genuine, and empathic stance, she exhibits limited personal self-disclosure, as it can interfere with the unfolding of the transference. The more "facts" Kristen knows about her therapist, the more Kristen's projections will be tainted by an independent reality, and the less the therapist will learn about her intrapsychic life.

Roles in the Therapeutic Relationship

The analytic method is typically nondirective, working with the current concerns of the patient. Therapists rarely structure sessions, make specific suggestions, or assign out-of-session homework. The therapist's activity level is somewhat determined by her style and the patient's level of functioning. Early in therapy, bulimics often have little to say, and so require the therapist to be more active than she might otherwise be. The therapist's nondirective stance, limited personal disclosure, and nonjudgmental attitude, coupled with active efforts to help patients understand the implications of their verbalizations, fosters the development of the transference. Transference can be defined as the displacement or projection of feelings, thoughts, or impulses that were experienced in previous interactions with other important figures in a patient's life onto their current interactions with individuals for whom these reactions do not realistically apply (e.g., Moore & Fine, 1990). The therapy gradually unfolds as a carefully crafted, interactive, and therapeutic "dance" between the therapist and patient. The interaction allows the patient to project distortions onto the therapist and the therapeutic situation that reenact the relationship dynamics, symptoms, and bulimic behavior, which are then identified, explored, and interpreted by the therapist. These distortions and reenactments may present in many ways, depending on the ego strength, psychodynamics, and particular symptom constellation of the patient. For example, the therapist's relative silence may be interpreted by some patients as being omniscient, benevolent, and noncontrolling. These patients may experience the therapy situation as soothing—permitting them to reduce tension and anxiety, utilize the therapist as an auxiliary ego to maintain a cohesive sense of self, and quell buried rage. Other patients may expect an active, care-taking therapist, and feel disappointed with the therapist's silences, experiencing the therapist as withholding or scorning. These patients may become accusatory and demanding, and engage in acting out behaviors (Oliner, 1988). The transference enactment in these two situations is the meaning given to the therapist's silence by the bulimics, which is based on their early experiences with parental figures.

Sometimes the entire interaction between the therapist and patient may symbolically reenact the bulimic symptomatology. The bulimic patient may act towards the therapist the same way as they act towards food (and other people in their lives). The patient's initial interaction with the therapist may be one of restraint and compliance. In this phase, the patient is likely to talk about superficial events involving minor problems and details, and hungrily seek advice from the therapist (a receptive "binge"). However, despite her eagerness, the patient perceives the observations from the therapist to be unhelpful or inconsistent with her view of herself and her interactions, so that she is unable to "digest" or make use of the therapist's observations. These ideas are likely to be rejected, much as she "vomits" unacceptable calories. In the session, "vomiting" could take the form of expressing uncontrolled anger at the therapist. Outside the session, it could take the form of acting out (increased bingeing and vomiting, intense arguments with others, alcohol or drug abuse, or suicidal behavior). These enactments serve to defend against an awareness of her internal (intrapsychic) experience, which is likely to include shame, rage, and emotional poverty.

The patient's transference often tugs at the therapist's sensitivities, evoking a counterreaction in the therapist termed *countertransference*. When recognized, countertransference can be used to understand how others may react to the patient, and provide opportunities for clarification that enable further progress. For example, an exacerbation of symptoms often serves a protective function, anesthetizing the patient against feelings that have surfaced, for example, rage or anxiety. It can also express the patient's desire to punish the therapist or demonstrate powerlessness. The therapist may in turn feel anger or helplessness. If the therapist acts on these feelings, it is likely to produce guilt and shame in the patient. However, if the therapist recognizes her role in this exchange, she can clarify the patient's reactions for her, point out their defensive function, and help the patient see how her actions might affect others. This recognition and understanding of the transference-countertransference interaction becomes the central focus of therapy.

Several countertransference reactions are common during therapy with bulimics. Many bulimics exhibit little introspection, defensively devalue the therapeutic relationship, and have a tendency to act out. It is tempting not to clarify or interpret these behaviors, but instead to simply "manage" the acting out with appropriate limit setting and a focus on the eating and purging. However, this focus should be kept to a minimum. Concentration on setting limits can place the therapist squarely in the controlling "parental" position and can interfere with the fostering of the therapeutic alliance. Often the bulimics' early experiences of being controlled by caretakers set the stage for the centrality of control and being controlled in the therapy session. Characteristic of many bulimic patients is their need to test the therapist—engaging the unsuspecting therapist in power struggles. The therapist's awareness of her own countertransference is helpful in withstanding the patient's attempts to get the therapist to respond in a manner that recreates the struggle with her omnipotent and controlling parent (Gonzalez, 1988). Rather, the therapist should strive to be experienced as an empathic person whose neutrality allows for distance between the controlling and the disengaged parent.

Conflicts and enactments within the therapeutic interaction can occur around superego conflicts.[2] This often occurs when a patient is doing something detrimental to her health or career, or is involved in a dangerous interpersonal encounter (e.g., impulsive sexuality, drug use). The therapist, in attempting to warn or even set limits with the patient, becomes the external representation of the controlling aspects of the superego. The patient, disowning her own superego, rebels, then becomes afraid of retaliation and disapproval and is likely to sullenly acquiesce (Reich & Cierpka, 1998). Sometimes the therapist is drawn into these enactments, feels "jerked around," and shows emotional involvement in the form of feeling overwhelmed, frustrated, or irritated. Recognition of the origins of these feelings can enable the therapist to help the patient reown those previously disowned parts of herself.

For those who treat many bulimics, it is often a relief to have what appears to be a compliant patient. However, this compliance may be an exhibition of what she perceives will appeal to the therapist. Bulimic women often develop a false self in which they attempt to reveal only what they believe is expected of them, either to further strengthen their ego integrity (Masterson, 1995), or because they fear disapproval and their resulting ego disintegration (Friedman, 1985). As therapists, our relief in not having to deal with a power struggle prevents us from recognizing that these women are presenting a false self. They present as if they are compliant and reflective, but offer little real self-revelation. Our response, after the initial relief (countertransference) may be to experience boredom and frustration with the lack of progress, and to be provoked into an attempt to "push" the patient to work. The patient may respond by distancing herself from the therapist (through anger or emotional disengagement) or assertively attempt to control the therapy.

Treatment Implementation and Outcome

Techniques and Methods of Working

In the initial phase of therapy, the therapist is attuned to fostering a working alliance, educating Kristen about the treatment process,

---

[2]The superego is that part of the individual that represents ideals and values, including morality, conscience, and societal and familial ideals and mores.

supporting the development of an observing ego, and encouraging active participation in the treatment process. It is essential to establish a therapeutic frame, which includes the particular "rules" of treatment and the structure of the sessions. The therapist articulates the mutually agreed upon goals of treatment and a statement of the treatment's underpinnings (a brief explanation of the dynamic meaning of symptoms). The therapist also explains the methods of working; for example, Kristen is encouraged to speak freely about whatever seems important to her. Also, as the analytic method would focus primarily on Kristen, significant others would not typically be included in treatment. Finally, the therapist should give an honest and hopeful statement about the viability of psychoanalytic therapy.

Several techniques would be used throughout Kristen's therapy, depending on her needs, abilities, and the course of therapy. These techniques, explained below, include *informative comments*, or clarifications, *the identification and articulation of feelings*, and *interpretations*, which serve to make the unconscious conscious. There are several levels of interpretation, and, depending on the particular interactions in the treatment process, the therapist might choose to interpret Kristen's defenses, her patterns of behavior, her resistance to treatment, or the transference.

Acclimation to the analytic and interpretive process is gradual. Kristen is encouraged to use her thoughts, associations, dreams, daydreams, and fantasies (thoughts not corroborated by current reality, though they may or may not be true) to understand her behavior: these are used to identify her affective states, to recognize the importance of fleeting thoughts and feelings she previously considered irrelevant, to discern basic conflictual issues, and eventually to discover and understand the transference relationship and its meaning in her life. The therapist helps Kristen elucidate her thinking by making occasional *informative comments*, that is, by asking informative and clarifying questions, and, at times, calling attention to what has not been said. These interventions are descriptive and do not venture beyond the immediate information that the patient presents (Hollender & Ford, 1990). The severity of the underlying psychopathology determines which of the other techniques are most therapeutic early in treatment. The use of more supportive techniques such as promotion of therapeutic optimism, reality testing, and problem solving are necessary in the initial phases for those with more severe psychopathology.

During the initial sessions, patients focus on their symptoms, the precipitating events, or the interpersonal circumstances bringing them to treatment. Exclusive attention to the details of the bulimic symptom is often considered a defense against exploring deeper and more threatening feelings. If Kristen continued to concentrate predominantly on her body and its products, her therapist would attempt to engage her curiosity in an exploration of her intrapsychic world and its conflicts. Given the case material, it is likely that Kristen's initial focus may center on her work situation, minimizing her bulimic symptoms to avoid the shame associated with her lack of control over them. In this case, the therapist would encourage the exploration of any thoughts and feelings Kristen may have had before, during, or after her bingeing and purging. The goal of this exploration is to help Kristen identify the thoughts and feelings associated with her binge/purge cycles (e.g., loneliness, emptiness, shame, and anger), and consequently to recognize that neither food nor her bulimic behaviors can provide the lasting relief she is seeking from her emotional distress.

Bulimic women are often cut off from an awareness of their feelings, and consequently lack the introspection necessary for progress in psychoanalytic treatment. They are vague in their descriptions of themselves, their significant relationships, and the important events in their lives, because they lack the ability to perceive and accept their own desires or motivations. To aid Kristen in the development of introspection, her therapist may highlight inconsistencies between her behavior and her goals. Kristen's increasing ability to experience and articulate anger, sadness, loneliness, and fear in the session, and to identify their relationship to her motivations, signal progress in therapy.

As Kristen develops the capacity to identify and articulate her thoughts and feelings, the therapist helps her to strike an adaptive balance between thinking and feeling. Any primary style of perceiving or interacting with the world that is either emotionally detached or affectively unbridled is likely to be maladaptive; Kristen is more likely to display emotional detachment with an occasional emotional outburst when she becomes overwhelmed. Identification and clarification of her feeling states will help Kristen to recognize her emotions early in the process, rather than denying, for instance, that someone is making her angry. This will allow her to make a conscious choice about how she wants to respond to the situation, rather than suddenly recognizing she is furious and exploding, as she did at work.

Bulimics typically are unaware of the behavior patterns that accompany their emotions. Kristen must recognize these patterns before she can begin to explore the meaning of her behaviors. As she explores her interactions in various life situations, she will begin to recognize that her reactions are influenced as much by her past experiences as by the demands of the current interactions. Because her responses are influenced by previously learned patterns that are operating outside of her conscious awareness, the conscious recognition of these patterns will allow Kristen more choice in her behavior rather than simply continuing to react in a fashion detrimental to her well-being.

In addition to making informative comments and helping Kristen identify and articulate feelings, the therapist interprets her resistance to treatment, the transference, and hypotheses about the origin of her conflicts. Interpretation is an informative statement conveyed to the patient based on the therapist's understanding of the patient's unconscious processes. It is designed to enhance the patient's self-knowledge by developing or expanding awareness of relationships or connections that had previously been unconscious, adaptively restructure their cognitive and affective experiences, and modify their behavior (Weiner, 1998). Timing is critical in making an interpretation. The therapist must gather sufficient evidence to support the hypotheses, and appreciate the patient's readiness to make use of the information (Hollender & Ford, 1990). A well-timed interpretation enables the patient to make further connections, as "An interpretation that fits is like a key that unlocks a storage chest, providing access to what is inside—first the objects on top and then those that are underneath" (Hollender & Ford, 1990, p. 87). Interpretation, clarification, and focus vary from session to session and from patient to patient, depending upon the material that the patient presents.

Progress in treatment is sporadic, in part because the anxiety produced by change may lead to resistance. Initially, self-accusations, a sense of shame, and possibly an exacerbation of her symptoms and/or anger at the therapist may follow the discussion of difficult material or even positive change. In response to these feelings, Kristen may display resistance—behavior that interferes with the treatment process and consequently with the development of self-understanding. Two forms of resistance are characteristic of bulimics, and likely to be important in the treatment of Kristen—acting out and superego resistance. The tendency to act out, for example, withdrawing, being less candid in the sessions, arriving late, or even missing sessions, must be interpreted. These nonverbal, action-oriented communications are viewed as attempts to repair a sense of self, or reenactments that are symbolic of conflicts, rather than being conceptualized as situations that require setting limits. As Kristen begins to experience more awareness of affects and comfort in sharing them, it will be important for the therapist to help her to explore both the accepted and previously rejected parts of her self.

As treatment progresses and Kristen gains some moments of pleasure, she is likely to experience superego resistance, which involves discomfort with feeling good or deserving. Many bulimics (and we suspect Kristen) have a perfectionistic streak that is accompanied by a harsh and critical self-evaluation when she compares her actions against her inner ideal. Abstinence from food is often symbolically equivalent to perfection, whereas bingeing and purging are equivalent to complete and utter inner badness, because only a "bad" person has wants, desires, or needs. Much of the early work in therapy may focus on this shame and the resulting self-flagellation (referred to as superego analysis). As this cycle of clarification, exploration, resistance, and interpretation continues, Kristen's motivations, or impulses, and her defenses against these impulses become central topics in the therapy. The therapist helps Kristen to understand how her motivations and her defenses against them, though largely unconscious, are manifested in thoughts, actions, and interactions with others. Making the "unacceptable" motives tolerable, and allowing the "unconscious" to become conscious, allows Kristen the ability to better choose how she would like to handle the situation.

Two motives will likely be important to the work with Kristen, sexuality and the "aggression" needed for separation/individuation. With each, an in-depth exploration using the above techniques will help Kristen to discover and articulate the symbolic relationship between her needs and desires and the resulting symptomatology in her current life outside the therapy session, in the transference, and, ideally, with her earliest relationships.

For bulimics, dealing with sexuality is often considered secondary to the exploration and resolution of early developmental difficulties (Casper, 1992; Bruch, 1985). Although sexuality may be brought to the forefront early in treatment because of sexual acting out, it is often initially quiescent, becoming central to the therapy only when the patient has developed an appreciation for the symbolic nature of intrapsychic life. Sexuality may play a critical role early in Kristen's case, as the development of her bulimic symptoms are contiguous with significant disappointments or traumas in sexual relationships.

Separation/individuation will become important in the therapy when Kristen's ego is strengthened by her newfound awareness and ability to predict her behavior, her recognition and acceptance of her negative affects, and her increasing ability to relinquish her perfectionism. As Kristen develops nascent preferences that are not based on her desire to please, nor on an angry rebellion against her parents and their values, she must give up her enmeshment with the parental introject (her mother) or more current parental representatives. This is likely to be experienced as a loss of both the qualities of the relationship as it is, and also aspects of the relationship she longed for, but never existed. Resolution often begins with either a total rejection of her family, her mother, and her attributes, or alternatively, a very controlled, limited interaction with her family to prevent being contaminated by their influence. The neutralization of hostility toward the parents and family is often pivotal in promoting the development of a separate identity. It is a sign of progress in treatment when the patient recognizes that she can share some of her mother's attributes without losing her own separate identity.

Transference interpretations, and helping Kristen to understand the implications of the interpretation (called "working through"), are often considered central to the permanent alleviation of symptomatology. Working through interpretations will help Kristen to use the treatment relationship experientially, to draw inferences about the distorted perceptions that occur in her interpersonal exchanges. Experiential knowledge is critical to this process. Experiential knowledge differs from strictly semantic or cognitive knowledge, just as the *experience* of happiness differs from reading about being happy in a book. It is the experiential knowledge that is gained in therapy that allows for personality changes, and this occurs through the transference. Transference interpretations are made when specific reactions to important early figures are reenacted in the session and are able to be scrutinized in the therapy environment, that is, when Kristen becomes aware that she is displacing onto the therapist, or other current relationships, reactions that belong to earlier relationships (Weiner, 1998).

Effective interpretation of the transference involves a sequence of steps which include: clarifying the reaction as a notable distortion not rooted in the current reality, exploring the origins and the implications of the distortion inside and outside the therapy, and understanding the way in which these distorted reactions apply to other interpersonal situations (Weiner, 1998). The timing of transference interpretations should occur when there is marked resistance to talking about the self. Even as treatment progresses, analysis of the transference and use of interpretations to obtain insight are less important than clarification of feelings in the treatment of more severe psychopathology (Swift & Letven, 1984). Transference analysis and insight become more prominent as the patient begins to appreciate the dynamic role of her symptoms. Analyses and interpretation of Kristen's faulty interactions occur in three realms—in her current life outside the therapy session (with her boss, parents, and fiancé), inside the session (e.g., in the transference), and in significant early relationships (e.g., mother, father, and siblings). For instance, Kristen may first notice that she makes a tremendous effort at work seeking the approval of her boss. When she does not experience his approval as forthcoming, she may experience anger, depression, and a loss of self-esteem. Somewhat later she may become aware that she maintains a very compliant demeanor in therapy, seeking the approval of her therapist. She again becomes dejected and irritable when she does not experience the therapist as appreciative of her efforts. Much later in treatment, she may recognize that these patterns with her boss and therapist parallel what she had wished for as a child, the interest and approval of her unavailable mother.

Medical and Nutritional Issues

Kristen's medical tests revealed extremely low potassium levels (hypokalemia), which put her at risk for cardiac arrhythmia, renal failure, and seizures. Her low BUN suggests she is dehydrated and is in danger of renal failure. These physiological conditions are likely secondary to her constant purging, rather than to low weight (Yager, 1990). As Kristen's case illustrates, it is important to have medical input even when treating normal weight bulimics; about 50% are likely to have an electrolyte imbalance secondary to repeated vomiting.

We prefer to discuss the case directly with the practitioner, particularly when there is medical management involved, to establish at what weight medical hospitalization will be required. Theoretical reasons recommend someone other than the primary therapist should monitor weight, intake, and eating behaviors, for example, a nurse or physician. Because the symptoms are used to avoid the conscious experience of the underlying psychological conflict, Kristen may be quite willing to talk at great lengths about her weight and eating habits to avoid talking about her conflicts in relationships, sexuality, anger, fear of dependency, fear of loss of identity, etcetera. Monitoring Kristen's eating and weight fosters the control dynamics that were problematic in her family of origin: without this responsibility, the therapist has the freedom to focus on the deeper psychological issues.

If psychotropic medications are necessary, the best success may be achieved with a dynamically minded psychiatrist. Although several antidepressants have shown promise in the amelioration of bulimic symptoms, compliance rates are poor, and dropout rates among bulimics are high (Lewis, 1995). Conflicts among bulimics tend to be organized around oral themes, that is, food, nurturance, dependency, and abandonment. Ingestion of an "effective" pill may elicit primitive fears of being dependent and being controlled by something outside of themselves (Lewis, 1995). Reactions to medications might parallel similar dynamics in their relationships. Their fear of dependency is warded off through a pseudoindependent stance, in which they reject the medication either because they do not want to rely on it, or because it is deemed unhelpful. Indeed, medication may be rejected precisely because it is effective (Lewis & Brisman, 1992). Symptom cessation before there is sufficient work on the psychological factors underlying the bulimia may leave the patient feeling controlled, vulnerable, or "not like the self she is used to" (Lewis, 1995). The psychiatrist must support the patient's continued therapeutic involvement.

Sometimes patients request the name of a nutritionist. Nutritionists can often be a valuable resource to patients. We prefer that the medical manager of the case provide the name of a nutritionist. Our experience suggests the request often has some meaning beyond the attainment of nutritional information. Further exploration often reveals their desire to have another person help them control their eating or represents their feelings of our incompetence.

Potential Pitfalls

Psychoanalytic treatment is dependent upon the development of a positive, honest, working relationship with the patient. Many analytic therapists acknowledge the difficulty in treating bulimics because of their mistrust of the therapist. This mistrust mirrors the same mistrust bulimics have of other significant people in their lives. In their desire to maintain some sense of autonomy, bulimics often withhold information and are deceitful and dishonest (Wilson, 1983; Bruch, 1978). Preferring action to words, they do not experience insight-oriented therapy as especially gratifying in terms of providing specific techniques and suggestions, and may terminate as a result. Many patients who come to psychoanalytic therapy after failed efforts at another form of treatment have an increased distrust and fear of being controlled because of these prior experiences (Stern, 1986). In addition, their lack of psychological-mindedness and limited abilities to introspect and free associate often extend the initial phases of therapy, which can prove a frustrating experience for both therapist and patient. As therapy does begin to progress, and painful material is uncovered, their lack of symbolic development can lead to acting out rather than verbal expression, further undermining treatment. As conflicts around dependence and sexuality emerge, their proclivity to act out may cause the symptom picture to grow worse. Therapists can become uncomfortable with the seeming lack of progress and consider abandoning the treatment. Instead, the therapist should be aware of these dynamics and interpret the acting out in the context of the emerging material.

There are also possibilities for strong countertransference, particularly around issues of control. The naive therapist is likely to become involved in a series of ongoing projective identifications that can damage the treatment if left unchecked. If the therapist is aware of these defensive maneuvers and can detoxify the projected elements, the treatment can be advanced in the process. Some bulimics, and Kristen could well be one of them, exhibit an initial pseudo-compliance to treatment, attempting to maintain a healthy sense of self by providing the therapist with what she believes the therapist is requesting of her (Masterson, 1995). This sometimes does not become evident for some period of time, and the neophyte therapist, experiencing frustration, may mistake this for controlling, manipulative, or withholding behavior, rather than the efforts of a closet narcissist to maintain adequate self-esteem.

Finally, as the patient is seemingly progressing, developing an independent sense of self, the therapist may mistake a defensive independence for true individuation. This pseudo-independence often masks a rebellion against the status quo. For Kristen, this may take the form of preferences or actions that are in direct opposition to important people in her life, although seeming on the surface to be "good decisions." One example might be to move to a distant city to accept a better job offer, even though her parents are opposed to the move. Thus, it is important to explore the process of reaching even good decisions.

Termination and Relapse Prevention

The ideal criteria for termination are the amelioration of specific symptoms, a substantial resolution of the transference, and the patient's development of the capacity for self-observation (Weiner, 1998). Patients, however, often wish to terminate treatment with the attenuation of their bulimic symptoms. As the patient's ability to express anger appears, the bulimic symptoms often subside (e.g., Lacey, 1992). However, the situational and relational determinants that give rise to the anger are newly emerging, and have not been worked through. Therapists typically make every effort to explore and work through the issues underlying the development and exacerbation of the symptomatology. If a patient pushes for termination, the therapist must weigh the likelihood that premature termination will precipitate the reemergence of bulimic symptomatology against the importance of the development of the patient's autonomy and the desire to avoid a power struggle. Under ideal circumstances, a mutually agreed upon date for termination is set well in advance.

This again allows for the opportunity to work on the separation/ individuation issues that are a core conflict for many bulimics.

In the termination phase, Kristen and her therapist will review and process the accomplishments of their work together. Important themes for bulimic patients include not achieving perfection, and the anger and disappointment that absolute support is not forthcoming either from their parents or their therapist. Many bulimics fear that they may be unable to maintain their independence and self-differentiation, and experience a regressive pull to "rejoin" the family when the therapist no longer provides ego support. Patients may also experience strong urges to engage in or a partial return of bulimic symptomatology. In our experience, many chronic bulimics cannot sustain the intense motivation for continued treatment after the amelioration of their bulimic symptoms. Breaks from therapy, or even termination, may be required to consolidate intrapsychic change as they master various aspects of individuation, with a necessary return to treatment to complete the process. It is critical that the bulimic does not perceive a return to treatment as a defeat or an irreparable assault to self-esteem. We emphasize that even though the patient has made important gains in therapy, stressful life events may precipitate the need for support, and that return to treatment may be the best course of action.

Mechanisms of Change

Psychoanalytic mechanisms of change include corrective emotional experiences, making the unconscious conscious, the acquisition of insight, and internalization. "The process of psychotherapy is designed not to impose change on the patient, but to create conditions within the context of the therapeutic relationship, which will allow changes to occur within the patient" (Waterhouse & Strupp, 1984). In the context of a "safe holding environment," the patient is able to begin to explore distressing emotional situations that they would not otherwise be able to tolerate. A safe holding environment is more complex than a confidential and nonjudgmental place to talk. Kristen must experience the therapist as interested, capable, and invested in her well-being. A safe holding environment is analogous to learning to swim with a good instructor. Although it may be frightening to be in the water, and the instructor cannot swim for the student, the instructor provides safety, a sense of security, and experienced guidance about learning to swim.

The critical aspect of a corrective emotional experience is that the therapist's attitude is different from that of other important people in Kristen's life. Rather than being criticized, made to feel guilty or selfish, Kristen's needs, fears, wishes, emotions, hopes, and dreams are listened to, tolerated, and responded to. Although not everything Kristen thinks, says, or does is right, the therapist always respects her, and her right to be the person she is. This allows the therapist to help her consider whether or not her actions and reactions are in her own best interest, and to accept parts of her personality she could not previously accept, without criticizing her as a person. The safe holding environment allows Kristen to explore previously unbearable emotional situations and learn to react to them differently (Alexander & French, 1946). Supported and protected by the therapist, Kristen, over the course of therapy, will create her own hierarchy of previously painful events to be explored, detoxified, and consequently tolerated. Within the therapeutic relationship, she may begin to develop new responses to old and new difficult problems. For instance, she will learn to deal with disappointments and the loss of important male figures in ways other than her bulimic behavior. She also will be able to accept her own anger and regulate her expression of these feelings without fearing retribution or worrying about destroying herself or others. This will allow her to be more sensitive to her feelings of anger, and to prevent the inappropriate expression of anger in ways that could cost Kristen her job.

Initial efforts in therapy would aid Kristen in developing an awareness of particular dysfunctional patterns of behavior (e.g., choice of boyfriends, interactions with authority, bingeing and purging behaviors, etc.). Psychoanalytic theory contends that much of Kristen's behavior or patterns of behavior are motivated by thoughts, feelings, fantasies, conflicts, and traumas that are outside of her awareness. Guided or free association, along with clarification and interpretation, are designed to enable her to better identify and understand what motivates her to engage in the identified behaviors or to make certain life choices. It is not necessary to fully understand the original trauma or conflicts. An understanding and analysis of the conflicts that are currently present in Kristen's life (but that may stem from some earlier trauma) can achieve the same awareness. Clarification and interpretation make her aware of the relationships among her thoughts, feelings, and behavior patterns that had previously been unconscious, so that Kristen can make more conscious and, therefore, more informed choices.

Internalization is a process by which an individual forms a dynamic schema that includes a concept of herself in relationship to another person. The schema is comprised of cognitive-affective memories that are formed during interactions with another person or the environment. These cognitive-affective memories link the person's motivations (wishes and fears) with mental representations about the other person, and how they will respond in a given situation. The quality of these representations will help determine which action tendencies will be chosen from among a repertoire of possible actions, that is, they serve to regulate interpersonal behavior. Kristen may have learned that if she expresses disappointment or anger with her mother, her mother will be extremely "wounded" and emotionally withdraw. This will leave Kristen without the love and nurturance she desires from her mother, with the added burden of feeling guilty and bad about herself for causing her mother so much emotional pain. Kristen may then be much less likely to express or even allow herself to experience negative emotions, even when appropriate, than a woman who believes that her pain will be responded to with concern and an attempt to address her needs.

Internalization is a two-step process. The first step involves the identification with or the "borrowing" of the therapist's good judgement to understand certain events or make decisions (Hollender & Ford, 1990). The patient initially relies heavily on what she believes the therapist might want her to say or do in a given situation, comparable to a child looking both ways before she crosses the street because those are the rules her parents have taught her. Kristen could begin to regulate her emotions, to be less self-critical, to handle unacceptable feelings, or to make choices based on what she believes the therapist would want for her. Gradually this identification becomes more internalized as she begins to develop a more clearly defined sense of self and to "own" those ways of thinking. She will "look both ways before crossing the street" not because those are the rules, but because she recognizes this as an important aspect of keeping herself safe and happy. As she interacts with the therapist over the course of therapy, Kristen will be given the opportunity to experience herself in a relationship with someone who responds to her with concern and empathy. These therapeutic interactions will allow Kristen to develop a sense of herself as a valuable person who deserves to be heard and treated with respect, and who has something to offer others in return.

REFERENCES

Alexander, F., & French, T.M. (1946). *Psychoanalytic therapy: Principles and application.* New York: Ronald Press.

Blos, P. (1967). The second individuation process of adolescence. *Psychoanalytic Study of the Child, 22,* 162–186.

Brenner, C. (1982). *The mind in conflict.* New York: IUP.

Bruch, H. (1978). The tyranny of fear. In K. Frank (Ed.), *The human dimension in psychoanalytic practice* (pp. 83–98). New York: Grune and Stratton.

Bruch, H. (1985). Four decades of eating disorders. In D. M. Garner & P. E. Garfinkel (Eds.), *Handbook of psychotherapy for anorexia nervosa & bulimia* (pp. 7–18). New York: Guilford Press.

Casper, R. C. (1992). Integration of psychodynamic concepts into psychotherapy. In K. Halmi (Ed.), *Psychology and treatment of anorexia nervosa and bulimia nervosa* (pp. 287–305). Washington, DC: American Psychiatric Press.

Crits-Christoph, P., & Barber, J. P. (1991). *Handbook of short-term dynamic psychotherapy.* New York: Basic Books.

Demitrack, M. A., Putnam, F. W., Brewerton, T. D., Brandt, H. A., & Gold, P. W. (1990). The relation of clinical variables to dissociative phenomena in eating disorders. *American Journal of Psychiatry, 147,* 1184–1188.

Fairburn, C. G. (1991). The heterogeneity of bulimia nervosa and its implications for treatment. *Journal of Psychosomatic Research, 35,* 3–9.

Favazza, A. R., DeRosear, L., & Conterio, K. (1989). Self-mutilation and eating disorders. *Suicide and Life-Threatening Behaviors, 19,* 352–361.

Freud, S. (1986). The ego and the id. *The standard edition of the complete psychological works of Sigmund Freud* (Volume 19, pp. 1–66). London: Hogarth Press and the Institute of Psychoanalysis. (Original work published 1923)

Friedman, M. S. (1985). Bulimia. *Women & Therapy, 4,* 63–69.

Garner, D. M., & Rosen, L. W. (1994). Eating disorders. In M. Hersen, R. T. Ammerman, & L. A. Sisson (Eds.), *Handbook of aggressive and destructive behaviors in psychiatric patients* (pp. 409–428). New York: Plenum Press.

Gonzalez, R. G. (1988). Bulimia and adolescence: Individual psychoanalytic treatment. In H. J. Schwartz (Ed.), *Bulimia: Psychoanalytic treatment and theory* (pp. 399–441). Madison: International Universities Press.

Hall, R. C. W., Beresford, T. P., Wooley, B., Tice, L., & Hall, A. K. (1989). Covert drug abuse in patients with eating disorders. *Psychiatric Medicine*, *7*, 247–255.

Hamburg, P. (1989). Bulimia: The construction of a symptom. *Journal of the American Academy of Psychoanalysis*, *17*, 131–140.

Herman, J. L. (1992). *Trauma and recovery*. New York: Basic Books.

Herzog, D. B., Franko, D., & Brotman, A. W. (1989). Integrating treatments for bulimia nervosa. *Journal of the American Academy of Psychoanalysis*, *17*, 141–150.

Herzog, D. B., Keller, M. B., Lavori, P. W., & Sacks (1992). The prevalence of personality disorders in 210 women with eating disorders. *Journal of Clinical Psychiatry*, *53*, 147.

Herzog, D. B., Nussbaum, K. M., & Marmor, A. K. (1996). Comorbidity and outcome in eating disorders. In J. Yager (Ed.), *The psychiatric clinics of North America: Eating disorders, vol 19* (pp. 843–859). Philadelphia: W. B. Saunders.

Hogan, C. C. (1983). Technical problems in psychoanalytic treatment. In C. P. Wilson, C. Hogan, & I. Mintz (Eds.), *The fear of being fat: The treatment of anorexia nervosa and bulimia* (pp. 197–215). New York: Jason Aronson.

Hollender, M., & Ford, C. (1990). *Dynamic psychotherapy*. Washington, DC: American Psychiatric Press.

Humphrey, L. L. (1986). Structural analysis of parent-child relationships in eating disorders. *Journal of Abnormal Psychology*, *95*, 395–402.

Humphrey, L. L., Apple, R. F., & Kirschenbaum, D. S. (1986). Differentiating bulimic-anorexic from normal families using interpersonal and behavioral observational systems. *Journal of Consulting & Clinical Psychology*, *54*, 190–195.

Janoff-Bulman, R. (1992). *Shattered assumptions*. New York: Macmillon.

Kanakis, D. M., & Thelen, M. H. (1995). Parental variables associated with bulimia nervosa. *Addictive Behaviors*, *20*, 491–500.

Krueger, D. W. (1988). Body self, psychological self, and bulimia: Developmental and clinical considerations. In H. J. Schwartz (Ed.), *Bulimia: Psychoanalytic treatment and theory* (pp. 55–72). Madison: International Universities Press.

Lacey, J. H. (1992). Long-term follow-up of bulimic patients treated in integrated behavioural and psychodynamic treatment programmes. In W. Herzog, H. C. Deter, & W. Vandereycken (Eds.), *The course of eating disorders: Long-term follow-up studies of anorexia and bulimia nervosa* (pp. 150–173). Berlin: Springer-Verlag.

Lewis, O. (1995). Psychological factors affecting pharmacologic compliance. In M. A. Riddle (Ed.), *Pediatric psychopharmacology I, 4*, 15–22.

Lewis, O., & Brisman, J. (1992). Medication and bulimia: Binge/purge dynamics and the "helpful" pill. *International Journal of Eating Disorders, 12*, 327–331.

Mahler, M., Pine, F., & Bergman, A. (1975). *The psychological birth of the human infant.* Basic Books.

Masterson, J. (1995). Paradise lost-bulimia, a closet narcissistic personality disorder: A developmental, self and object relations approach. In R. C. Marohn & S. C. Feinstein (Eds.), *Adolescent psychiatry: Developmental and clinical studies, vol. 20* (pp. 253–266). NJ: Analytic Press.

Miller, A. (1981). *Prisoners of childhood.* New York: Basic Books.

Moore, B. E., & Fine, B. D. (1990). *Psychoanalytic terms and concepts.* New Haven: American Psychoanalytic Association & Yale University Press.

Oliner, M. O. (1988). Anal components in overeating. In H. J. Schwartz (Ed.), *Bulimia: Psychoanalytic treatment and theory* (pp. 227–253). Madison: International Universities Press.

Pine, F. (1988). The four psychologies of psychoanalysis and their place in clinical work. *Journal of the American Psychoanalytic Association, 36*, 571–596.

Provost, J. A. (1989). Eating disorders in college students. *Psychiatric Medicine, 7*, 47–58.

Reich, G., & Cierpka, M. (1998). Identity conflicts in bulimia nervosa: Psychodynamic patterns and psychoanalytic treatment. *Psychoanalytic Inquiry, 18*, 383–402.

Rorty, M., & Yager, J. (1996). Histories of childhood trauma and complex post-traumatic sequelae in women with eating disorders. In J. Yager (Ed.), *The psychiatric clinics of North America: Eating disorders, Vol. 19* (pp. 773–791). Philadelphia: W. B. Saunders.

Rorty, M., Yager, J., & Rossotto, E. (1994). Childhood sexual, physical, and psychological abuse and their relationship to comorbid psychopathology in bulimia nervosa. *International Journal of Eating Disorders, 16*, 317.

Sanftner, J. L., Barlow, D. H., Marschall, D. E., & Tangney, J. P. (1995). The relation of shame and guilt to eating disorder symptomatology. *Journal of Social and Clinical Psychology, 14*, 315–324.

Schwartz, H. J. (1988). Bulimia: Psychoanalytic perspectives. In H. J. Schwartz (Ed.), *Bulimia: Psychoanalytic treatment and theory* (pp. 31–53). Madison: International Universities Press.

Shevrin, H., & Dickman, S. (1980). The psychological unconscious: A necessary assumption of all psychological theory? *American Psychologist, 35*, 421–434.

Stern, S. (1986). The dynamics of clinical management in the treatment of anorexia nervosa and bulimia: An organizing theory. *International Journal of Eating Disorders, 5*, 233–254.

Strober, M. (1982). The significance of bulimia in juvenile anorexia nervosa: An exploration of possible etiologic factors. *International Journal of Eating Disorders, 1,* 28–43.

Swift, W. J., & Letven, R. (1984). Clinical experience, bulimia and the basic fault: A psychoanalytic interpretation of the bingeing-vomiting syndrome. *Journal of the American Academy of Child Psychiatry, 23,* 489–497.

Tice, L., Hall, R. C. W., Beresford, T. P., Quinones, J., & Hall, A. K. (1989). Sexual abuse in patients with eating disorders. *Psychiatric Medicine, 7,* 257–267.

Vitousek, K. (1996). The current status of cognitive-behavioral models of anorexia nervosa and bulimia nervosa. In P. M. Salkovskis (Ed.), *Frontiers of cognitive therapy* (pp. 383–418). New York: Guilford Press.

Waelder, R. (1936). The principle of multiple function. *Psychoanalytic Quarterly, 5,* 45–62.

Waterhouse, G. J., & Strupp, H. (1984). The patient-therapist relationship: Research from the psychodynamic perspective. *Clinical Psychology Review, 4,* 77–92.

Weiner, I. (1998). *Principles of psychotherapy.* New York: John Wiley & Sons, Inc.

Westen, D. (1990). Psychoanalytic approaches to personality. In L.A. Pervin (Ed.), *Handbook of personality: Theory and research* (pp. 21–65). New York: Guilford Press.

Wilson, C. P. (1983). Contrasts in the analysis of bulimic and abstaining anorexics. In C. P. Wilson, C. Hogan, & I. Mintz (Eds.), *The fear of being fat: The treatment of anorexia nervosa and bulimia* (pp. 169–193). New York: Jason Aronson.

Wilson, C. P., Hogan, C., & Mintz, I. (1983). *The fear of being fat: The treatment of anorexia nervosa and bulimia.* New York: Jason Aronson.

Vanderlinden, J., & Vandereycken, W. (1997). *Trauma, dissociation, and impulse dyscontrol in eating disorders.* Bristol, PA: Brunner/Mazel.

Wonderlich, S., Klein, M. H., & Council, J. R. (1996). Relationship of social perceptions and self-concept in bulimia nervosa. *Journal of Consulting & Clinical Psychology, 64,* 1231–1237.

Wonderlich, S. A., Wilsnack, R. W., Wilsnack, S. C., & Harris, T. R. (1996). Childhood sexual abuse and bulimic behavior in a nationally representative sample. *American Journal of Public Health, 86,* 1082–1086.

Yager, J. (1990). Eating disorders. In A. Stoudemire (Ed.), *Clinical psychiatry for medical students* (pp. 315–330). Philadelphia: Lippincott.

Yarock, S. R. (1993). Understanding chronic bulimia: A four psychologies approach. *American Journal of Psychoanalysis, 53,* 3–17.

Zerbe, K. J. (1995). The emerging sexual self of the patient with an eating disorder: Implications for treatment. *Eating Disorders: The Journal of Treatment and Prevention, 3,* 197–215.

5

Interpersonal Psychotherapy

Denise E. Wilfley, Jennifer Zoler Dounchis, and R. Robinson Welch

TREATMENT MODEL

Empirical Basis of Interpersonal Psychotherapy

It is not uncommon for patients who have undergone interpersonal therapy (IPT) to state that this treatment has not only helped them recover from their eating disorder, but has also changed their lives. IPT has demonstrated efficacy for the treatment of several disorders, including nonpsychotic major depression (e.g., Elkin, Shea, Watkins, Imber, Sotsky et al., 1989), dysthymia (Markowitz, 1994; Markowitz, 1998), bipolar mood disorder (Ehlers, Frank, & Kupfer, 1988; Frank, 1991b), bulimia nervosa (BN) (Agras, Walsh, Wilson, & Fairburn, 1999; Fairburn, Jones, Peveler, Carr, Solomon et al., 1991; Fairburn, Jones, Peveler, Hope, & O'Connor, 1993; Fairburn, Norman, Welch, & O'Connor, 1995), and binge eating disorder (Wilfley, et al., 1993; Wilfley, 1999). IPT also has been studied in various populations including the elderly (Mossey, Knott, Higgins, & Talerico, 1996), adolescents (Moreau, Mufson, Weissman, & Klerman, 1991; Mufson, Moreau, Weissman, & Klerman, 1993; Mufson, Moreau, Weissman, & Wickramaratne, 1994), couples (Foley, Rounsaville, Weissman, Sholomskas, & Chevron, 1989), and patients with comorbid medical conditions (e.g., human immunodeficiency virus; Elkin et al., 1989; Markowitz et al., 1998; for review, see Swartz & Markowitz, 1998), and its efficacy for PTSD, social phobia, chronic somatization (Scott & Ikkos, 1996), borderline personality disorder (Angus & Gillies, 1994), and anorexia nervosa (AN) (McKenzie et al., 1999) is currently under investigation. Not surprisingly, IPT has been translated into several languages, and modified for groups (Wilfley et al., 1993), long-term treatment (Frank, 1991a), telephone intervention, and self-help (Weissman, 1995). No studies have yet examined the efficacy of IPT for the treatment of AN; however, recent findings supporting its use with BN and binge eating disorder suggest that such studies of IPT are warranted for AN as well. This case example is presented to illustrate the potential utility of IPT for AN and to stimulate research.

History of Interpersonal Psychotherapy

IPT was initially formulated not as a novel therapy, but as an attempt to represent the current practice of psychotherapy for depression (Klerman & Weissman, 1993). IPT was manualized by Klerman, Weissman, Rounsaville, and Chevron (1984) to be used in a treatment trial of depressed outpatients participating in weekly, time-limited therapy. This treatment is based on the assumption that depression is intimately related to disturbances in social functioning that may be associated with the onset and/or maintenance of the disorder (Frank & Spanier, 1995). IPT moves through three defined phases (i.e., initial, middle, final), each of which is associated with specific strategies and tasks for the therapist and patient (Klerman, Weissman, Rounsaville, & Chevron, 1984). Its well-defined treatment techniques and therapeutic stance are aimed at resolving problems within four social domains: grief, interpersonal role disputes, role transitions, and interpersonal deficits.

IPT's foundations lay in part in the work of Adolf Meyer, who considered psychopathology a result of maladaptive adjustment to the social environment (Meyer, 1957). Building upon Meyer's work, Harry Stack Sullivan (1953) believed that people cannot be understood in isolation from their interpersonal relationships. In his theory, Sullivan posited that people have "relatively enduring patterns of recurrent interpersonal situations" which can either foster self-esteem or result in hopelessness, anxiety, and psychopathology. IPT is also associated with the work of John Bowlby (1982), originator of attachment theory, who acknowledged the importance of early attachment on subsequent interpersonal relationships and psychopathology. In sum, IPT is derived from theory in which interpersonal function is recognized as a critical component of psychological adjustment and well-being.

Interpersonal Psychotherapy for the Treatment of Eating Disorders

Christopher Fairburn and colleagues modified IPT for the treatment of BN (Fairburn, Kirk, O'Connor, & Cooper, 1986; Fairburn et al., 1991), the aim of which is to reduce binge eating and inappropriate compensatory behavior by helping patients identify the link between problematic eating behavior and current social problems. In addition, Wilfley, Frank, Welch, Spurrell, and Rounsaville (1998) adapted IPT for binge eating disorder as well as for a group format.

IPT for the treatment of eating disorders is based on the interrelation between interpersonal functioning, low self-esteem, negative mood, and eating behaviors (see Figure 5.1). This model does not assume that interpersonal problems cause eating disorders, but that eating problems may have become and continue to serve as a maladaptive solution to interpersonal difficulties (Fairburn, 1993; Wilfley et al., 1998). Given the interpersonal milieu in which dysfunction occurs, improving current social roles and adapting to interpersonal situations are presumed to be necessary for treatment effectiveness. Whereas IPT for depression focuses on identifying and treating interpersonal *precipitants* of the depressive episode, IPT for eating disorders focuses on identifying and altering the interpersonal context in which the eating problem has been *developed* and *maintained*.

INTERPERSONAL PROBLEMS

↓

LOW SELF-ESTEEM
DYSPHORIA

↓

FOOD USED TO COPE WITH NEGATIVE FEELINGS

↓

BINGE EATING
EXCESSIVE RESTRAINT

FIGURE 5.1   Model of symptom maintenance.

THE THERAPIST'S SKILLS AND ATTRIBUTES

Therapist Background and Credentials

Psychotherapists should have familiarity with the eating disorder as well as with IPT. A professional degree with at least 2 years of prior psychotherapy experience are prerequisites to ensure therapists meet standards of clinical competence (Klerman et al., 1984). Theory and specifics of IPT can be obtained from Klerman and colleagues' book for the treatment of depression (1984), and training workshops or courses can provide further details about treatment implementation. Interested therapists are advised to videotape their cases and receive supervision, and those interested in providing IPT for research protocols to be certified by an IPT expert (Markowitz, 1998).

Present Orientation

IPT therapists maintain a present orientation, focusing on current interpersonal patterns and life situations. Onset of the eating disturbance and assessment of past relationships are used to provide a context through which immediate social functioning is better understood.

Intensive Interpersonal Focus

The hypothesized active ingredient of IPT is maintaining an intensive focus on the interpersonal context of a patient's life. Rather than reviewing cognitions or inner conflict associated with eating, themes are drawn relating relationship difficulties to symptom exacerbation (Frank & Spanier, 1995). Interpersonal goals are derived from specified problem areas and are formulated within the first three sessions. Meetings should not pass without reference to these goals, as they are unique and require specific and directive interventions by the therapist. Indeed, research on IPT maintenance treatment for recurrent depression has demonstrated that the therapist's ability to maintain focus on interpersonal themes is associated with less relapse (Frank, 1991a). In session, unfocused conversations are redirected to central themes of treatment, and abstract and vague discussions are minimized in order to maintain focus. Therapists avoid asking questions that elicit general or passive responses, such as general inquiries about the patient's week. Instead, questions such as "What would you like to work on today?" are asked to provide a more directed focus for the patient (Wilfley, 1993).

Patient Responsibility

Although the therapist's main task is to ensure the patient remains focused on the problem area, the patient is encouraged to take responsibility for the direction of therapy. Descriptive phrases such as "moving forward on your goals," and "noting progress" are used to encourage patients to be accountable for their treatment while reminding them that changing interpersonal patterns requires attention and persistence.

Patient Advocate

The therapist serves in an active role as patient advocate. He or she helps the patient feel comfortable by phrasing comments positively in order to foster a safe and supportive working environment. In addition, the therapist conveys a hopeful stance (Weissman & Markowitz, 1998) and optimistic attitude about the patient's ability to recover. Confrontations and clarifications are offered in a descriptive rather than interpretive manner, and feedback is provided about areas that patients can change.

Case Formulation

In order for the treatment to be impactful, both the patient and therapist must be convinced of the connection between interpersonal and eating disturbances. The therapist's ability to rapidly discern patterns in interpersonal relationships, amalgamate events with the onset and maintenance of the disorder, and formulate goals are crucial to the time-limited nature of this therapy (Markowitz & Swartz, 1997).

THE CASE OF KRISTEN

Assessment, Conceptualization, and Treatment Planning

Assessment

Additional ratings of current eating disorder psychopathology, alcohol use, interpersonal relationships, and mood can identify valuable information for treating the presenting case.

1. Eating Disorders Assessment. The Eating Disorder Examination (Fairburn & Cooper, 1993) is an investigator-based interview designed to assess the main behavioral and attitudinal aspects of eating disorders. This interview provides a detailed assessment of the degree of dietary restraint, the key behaviors of binge eating and inappropriate compensatory purging, and concerns about thinness, weight, and eating.

2. Alcohol Assessment. The Structured Clinical Interview for the DSM-IV (Ventura, Liberman, Green, Shaner, & Mintz, 1998) is helpful to assess current and lifetime alcohol abuse or dependence.

Modeled from the criteria of the DSM-IV (American Psychiatric Association, 1994), this widely used measure consists of structured questions from which the interviewer can determine whether diagnostic criteria have been met. If Kristen meets criteria for a diagnosis of current alcohol dependence, she will be encouraged to seek treatment for this prior to engaging in a focal psychotherapy such as IPT.

3. Interpersonal Measures. Three interpersonal measures are useful for the present case. The Inventory of Interpersonal Problems (IIP) (Horowitz, Rosenberg, Baer, Ureno, & Villasenor, 1988) measures type and extent of interpersonal problems. In this measure, assertive, sociable, intimate, submissive, responsible, controlling, and overall aspects of interaction are examined, and interpersonal problems are assessed along the axes of affiliation and control. The IIP has been shown to successfully discriminate psychiatric and normal populations and measure change, and is correlated with therapist ratings of patient behaviors (Horowitz et al., 1988). The Social Adjustment Scale (Weissman & Bothwell, 1976) is a measure of social behavior that has been widely used to assess actual interpersonal functioning. This instrument calculates scores for different role areas (e.g., Kristen's family, or work) and is sensitive to change resulting from psychotherapy. Finally, the UCLA Loneliness Scale-Revised (Russell, Peplau, & Cutrona, 1980), that measures perceptions of loneliness or inadequacy in social relationships, can be used to determine the degree of current interpersonal deficits.

4. Mood Measures. Several measures of psychological distress, tapping associated features of Kristen's eating disorder, are recommended. The Beck Depression Inventory (Beck, Ward, Mendelson, & Mock, 1961) is a self-report instrument that measures severity of depression and is sensitive to change. The Symptom Checklist-90-R (Derogatis, 1983) is a self-report measure assessing a wide range of psychiatric symptoms and global severity. The Emotional Eating Scale (Arnow, Kenardy, & Agras, 1995) assesses the urge to cope with negative affect by eating. This measure provides a list of emotions which cluster into anger/frustration, anxiety, and depression subscales and has been shown to provide an assessment of antecedents to binge eating for clinical populations (Arnow, Kenardy, & Agras,

1992). Finally, the Rosenberg Self-Esteem Scale, a widely used measure, provides an indication of general self-esteem (Rosenberg, 1979).

5. Interpersonal Inventory. The Interpersonal Inventory is a detailed review of significant relationships, making the link explicit between difficulties in interpersonal functioning and presence of eating problems. The importance of this aspect of treatment cannot be overemphasized, as understanding this connection makes treatment salient, and therefore, powerful. The Interpersonal Inventory also explores the interpersonal precipitants to disordered eating behaviors and interpersonal functioning both prior to and after the development of the disorder. Four content areas covered include the development of further disturbed eating behaviors and pathology (e.g., Kristen's binge-eating and purging), the nature of her relationships and whether her expectations for them were fulfilled, events or life circumstances, and evidence of depression or low self-esteem (Fairburn, 1998).

The Interpersonal Inventory can be charted on a timeline (see Table 5.1; Fairburn, 1993). The Interpersonal Inventory is begun after reviewing Kristen's current symptoms of eating psychopathology, examining the circumstances in which her maladaptive eating behaviors are performed (i.e., when and how often she binges and purges, the amount of calories she consumes, when she is likely to restrict, and her level of physical activity), and obtaining a history of her symptoms. A review of the very first instance of Kristen's disordered eating behavior (i.e., serious dieting in junior high school) in context of her interpersonal functioning at the time serves as a frame through which to move chronologically forward. Given that the early development of her eating disorder most likely interfered with her ability to attain milestones of social development, the relationship between her problematic eating behavior and interpersonal problems during adolescence should be assessed. The discussion continues through time until more recent eating behaviors and interpersonal functioning have been reviewed.

By focusing on the interpersonal context coinciding with changes in Kristen's eating behavior, hypotheses about the specific nature of her interpersonal problems are generated. Specifically, events causing Kristen to become more isolated (e.g., family trouble with

TABLE 5.1   Kristen's Timeline

Age	Weight/ eating problem	Relationships	Events/ circumstances	Mood
8		Few friends, spends little time with parents, discusses fashion with grandmother	Family financial crisis, begins ballet	
12			Parents busy rebuilding business	
14			Father having affair and mother demands separation, takes on many school activities	
	Diets, exercises, thinner	Romance with basketball star, drinking with friends		
	Diets, exercises late in the night	Boyfriend dumps her because she won't "go all the way," "so-called friends" try to cheer her up but become impatient, withdraws from others		Fell into depression
16	Fainting spell, AN diagnosed by school nurse, 105 lb.	Friendship with an achievement-oriented girl, a few casual dating relationships	Weekly individual and family therapy	Anger over parents, pain over losses
18	Eats two meals a day, enough weight gain to menstruate		Accepted into college, parents fighting in court, brother loses job due to drinking	

TABLE 5.1 (continued)

Age	Weight/ eating problem	Relationships	Events/ circumstances	Mood
19	Begins binge eating, vomiting within few months	Joined sorority, did not tell anyone about the rape	Raped while drunk	Depressed, embarrassed, shameful
20	Binges and vomits daily, confronted by sorority about vomiting	Avoids parties where she may see the rapist, increased social isolation	Deteriorating grades, hospitalized for 2 weeks	
	Avoids vomiting after meals by engaging in physical activities or being around people	Forgot about sorority sisters		
21	Binges and purges but does not tell therapist, 115 lb.		Takes semester off, moves in with mother, works for father, weekly individual therapy	
22	Restricts eating	Social life is restricted	Returns to college, taking extra courses	
23	Worries less about food due to busy schedule, purging only occasionally, 120 lb.		Begins 2-year Masters Program	
24	Conceals eating disorder	Meets Joe, friendships remain superficial	Signs up for health care	Feels abandoned, mistrustful

(continued)

TABLE 5.1   (continued)

Age	Weight/ eating problem	Relationships	Events/ circumstances	Mood
25	Eating disorder returns, begins losing 1 lb. a month, exercises obsessively	Expresses concerns to Joe about his drinking, engaged to Joe, decides not to have bridesmaids because there was no one to choose		
		Ends engagement with Joe	Catches Joe with another woman, retreats back to work	
26	Menses stop, confesses having eating disorder since teens, purges and vomits 4–6 days/wk 3–10 times/day, dental enamel erosion, dizziness, sensitivity to cold, loss of concentration, weakness, 110 lb.	Conflict between staff	Crisis in career, told she's not a team player	Upset with evaluation, cries at work
	Feels temporarily in control by eating very little, later binges and purges alone	Socializing with clients over dinner	On the road 8–10 times a month for job	Socially anxious, avoidant

TABLE 5.1   (continued)

Age	Weight/ eating problem	Relationships	Events/ circumstances	Mood
	Eating disorder gradually worsening, skips breakfast, light lunch, snacks on candy, takeout for dinner		Negative performance evaluation due to conflicts with staff, warning from supervisor	Panic about losing job
	Awareness that eating disorder has escalated out of control	No friends or social life, confrontations at work, unable to ask for help		

her brother, the rape, and her split from Joe) emerge as precipitants to her maladaptive eating, and her continued isolation emerges as critical to its maintenance.

Therapeutic Goals

Identification of Interpersonal Problem Areas

As specified by Klerman and colleagues (1984), IPT treatment goals evolve around four main interpersonal problem areas (see Table 5.2)[1] that are associated with the onset and/or maintenance of the eating disorder. These include *grief* over the loss of a person or a relationship; *interpersonal role disputes* with a spouse, lover, children, family members, friends, or coworkers; *role transitions* such as leaving a job or one's home, going away to school, divorce, other economic or family changes; and *interpersonal deficits* or ineffective social skills resulting in loneliness and social isolation.

---

[1]Cases in which there are multiple problem areas require focusing on the area most closely related to the onset and maintenance of the eating problem. If time permits in the course of therapy, work can also be done on the second problem area.

TABLE 5.2   Interpersonal Problem Areas

Main problem area	Description	IPT strategies
Grief	• Pathological grief stemming from fears of being unable to tolerate the painful affect associated with the loss	• Facilitate the mourning process • Help the patient re-establish interest in relationships to substitute for what has been lost
Interpersonal role disputes	• Disputes with partner, children, or other family members or coworkers	• Identify the dispute • Choose a plan of action • Modify expectations and faulty communication to bring about a satisfactory resolution
Role transitions	• Economic or family change: children leaving for college, new job, divorce, retirement, parent's caretaker	• Mourn and accept the loss of the old role • Restore self-esteem by developing a sense of mastery regarding the demands of new roles
Interpersonal deficits	• A long-standing history of social isolation, low self-esteem, loneliness, and an inability to form or maintain intimate relationships	• Reduce the patient's social isolation • Encourage the formation of new relationships

Goal Formulation

After the problem area is defined, individualized goals are the means through which a problem area is addressed. Provided in a written form, goals guide day-to-day work, serving as a treatment contract that is specific to the problem area. For an interpersonal problem area of *grief,* goals serve to facilitate the mourning process and help patients reestablish relationships. For *interpersonal role disputes,* goals aim to identify the dispute and modify expectations and communication. For *role transitions,* they assist patients to mourn and accept the loss of the old role while restoring self-esteem. As in the present case of *interpersonal deficits,* patients who are generally socially isolated or in chronically unfulfilling relationships are assigned goals aimed at reducing isolation and encouraging formation of emotionally intimate friendships.

Timeline for Therapy

The typical course of individual IPT lasts 12 to 20 sessions (Fairburn, 1998; Klerman & Weissman, 1993), and group treatment is standardized for 16 to 20 (Wilfley et al., 1993; Wilfley et al., 1998). Treatment progresses through three stages: the initial phase of identifying the problem area in significant relationships, the middle phase of working on the target problem area, and the late phase of consolidating work and preparing patients for future work on their own.

Case Conceptualization

Because social isolation and chronically unfulfilling relationships are involved in the onset and maintenance of Kristen's disordered eating behavior and attitudes, she is assigned the problem area of interpersonal deficits. Kristen's goals provide concrete prescriptions for change (Wilfley et al., 1998), linking her binge eating and food restriction to difficulties sustaining meaningful interpersonal relationships. Rather than considering painful episodes in Kristen's life (e.g., her parents' separation and her rape) as separate issues, her therapist gathers detailed information about the interpersonal context in which these occurred (Mufson & Moreau, 1998), and integrates this into an understanding of her interpersonal problem area.

In order to alter maladaptive patterns in her relationships, Kristen's work focuses on three goals (see Table 5.3). As her first goal, Kristen begins trying to identify her feelings. For years, she has used food as a way to disconnect. By examining this process, Kristen begins to intervene in her bingeing, purging, excessively exercising, and restricting. Secondly, by beginning to take in feedback about how she is coming across, Kristen becomes more comfortable in social interactions, feels better about herself, and is less likely to use food to manage interpersonal situations. Third, by actively making new social networks, Kristen feels less loneliness, isolation, and a decreased desire to turn to food or restraint to comfort herself or feel in control. In summary, by working on these goals, Kristen begins to change her problematic relationship patterns and thereby improve her eating disorder.

TABLE 5.3   Kristen's Goals

1.   During our meeting, you shared that you often use food at night and on the weekends as a way to feel less lonely. We know that many individuals who struggle with bingeing and purging use food as a way to comfort themselves because food is calming and soothing. Although this helps you to feel better temporarily, you end up cutting off important feelings which continue driving this cycle. The more you can let yourself experience your feelings without using food to cut them off, the less likely you will need food as a way to manage.

GOAL: In order for you to recover you will need to begin identifying the feelings that come up for you at these times. Since you are so used to automatically tuning your feelings out, you will need to work on slowing this process down. Stop and ask yourself, "What am I feeling? What's going on?" This may be difficult at first, but by actively working on identifying your feelings in our sessions as well as in your outside life, you will be less likely to use food to drown your feelings out.

2.   Although you report people have always regarded you as competent and achieving, you mentioned several times that you often feel scared and inadequate during interactions, and use food restriction as a way to stay "in control." You mentioned that you had used alcohol in a similar way to manage the anxiety of interacting with others. We know that food and alcohol can act in similar ways, numbing your emotions—including those of stress, conflict, and feeling bad about yourself. However, relying on these means to get through social situations has instead led you to feeling demoralized and out of control.

GOAL: In order to feel more confident in social situations, you will need to get feedback as to how you're coming across. Begin with our sessions and with your family by allowing yourself to accept feedback without challenging it (e.g., if your mother compliments you, try not to push it away just because "she loves you" so it doesn't count. If working with a client goes well, ask which aspects were helpful, and take in the feedback. If a coworker says you're acting moody, try to listen and see if that's actually the way you're feeling. Maybe you haven't eaten very much that day and were unaware of how it was affecting you.) In turn, trusting the feelings of others will allow you to feel more self-confident because you are allowing them to validate your worth and your own feelings. As you feel more trusting toward others as well as toward yourself, your relationships (including those with your family and at work) will improve.

3.   As we discussed, another area you wanted to begin working on is developing more social support. You mentioned that you find yourself bingeing and purging at times when you feel alone in the world. One reason that it may have been difficult for you is that you have always focused on achieving (through ballet, track, at college, and during business school) and not necessarily allowed yourself time to spend with others in non-goal oriented activities. Allowing yourself to get close to others means making the time to reach out to others, and allowing for them to be able to reach out to you.

TABLE 5.3 (continued)

GOAL: Use our sessions to discuss new ways to connect with others. Pushing yourself to talk about this will help you connect in your outside life. As you begin making connections with people in your outside life, share how your efforts are progressing. In turn, as you get your eating under control, you will feel better about yourself and more open for relationships with others.

Kristen's Progress Through Treatment

Initial Phase. The initial phase of treatment, approximately sessions one to five, is devoted to a detailed examination of a patient's interpersonal history. In order to systematically review these areas, the use of a checklist is suggested (see Table 5.4). Problem areas associated with the onset and maintenance of symptoms are identified, and a set of interpersonal goals to guide the therapeutic work is formulated (Klerman et al., 1984). The initial phase is begun by discussing Kristen's eating disorder symptoms, giving the syndrome a name, and providing Kristen with information about the prevalence and characteristics of binge-eating/purging anorexia.

Next, Kristen is placed in the "sick role," an important aspect of recovery aimed at giving her permission and the responsibility to take better care of herself. An inherent characteristic of eating disorder pathology encompasses a focus on the external aspects of oneself (e.g., judging oneself based on shape, weight, or ability to be very restrictive) to the exclusion of caring of oneself in the context of relationships. Because Kristen's consuming concern about body weight causes her to neglect many aspects of her needs, assigning her the sick role helps her to take responsibility for her own self-care. Kristen next is asked if she has had any prior psychological symptoms and treatment. After reviewing expectations about therapy from the perspectives of her and her therapist, Kristen is oriented to the model.

During the next step of this phase, the Interpersonal Inventory is conducted to place the eating disorder within an interpersonal context (Mufson & Moreau, 1998). This is a major aim of this phase, and devoting several sessions to the Interpersonal Inventory helps Kristen make the connection between eating problems and her in-

TABLE 5.4   Checklist for Initial Phase of Treatment

___ Discuss chief complaint and eating disorder symptoms.

___ Obtain history of symptoms.

___ Place Kristen in the sick role.

___ Establish whether or not there is a history of prior treatments for the eating disorder or other psychiatric problems.

___ Assess Kristen's expectations about psychotherapy.

___ Reassure Kristen about positive prognosis.

___ Explain IPT and its basic assumptions.

___ Complete an Interpersonal Inventory (detailed review of important relationships).

   I. review her *past* interpersonal functioning (e.g., family, school, social).

  II. examine her *current* interpersonal functioning (e.g., family, work, social).

 III. identify the interpersonal precipitants of episodes of binge eating, exercising, and dietary restraint.

___ Translate binge eating/purging and symptoms of restriction into interpersonal context.

___ Explain IPT techniques.

___ Contract for administrative details (i.e., length of sessions, frequency, duration of treatment, appointment times).

___ Provide feedback to Kristen regarding general understanding of her interpersonal difficulties via IPT problem area (i.e., define *interpersonal deficits*— loneliness and social isolation).

___ Collaborate on a contract regarding the treatment goals.

___ Explain tasks in working toward treatment goals.

ability to have meaningful relationships. In doing so, the major interpersonal problem area forming the basis of Kristen's current difficulties is identified, and Kristen is assigned the problem area of interpersonal deficits. The remainder of this phase is devoted to reaching a consensus about these goals and collaboratively identifying the specific steps Kristen needs to take in order to make concrete prescriptions for change. Through the process of developing this explicit treatment contract, Kristen is prepared for her work during treatment.

Middle Phase.   During the middle or work phase of sessions 6 to 15, work is directed to the goals specific to the problem area. Typically in IPT, if the problem area is *grief,* fears of being unable to tolerate the painful affect of grieving are explored, and circumstances either enabling or preventing opportunities for grieving are reviewed. For the problem area of *interpersonal role disputes*, work is done to resolve the nonreciprocal relationships and unfulfilled expectations by renegotiation and practice resolving disagreements. For the problem area of *role transitions*, work consists of guiding the patient through the phase without the use of restraint or binge eating in order to manage the associated negative affect. As in the present case of *interpersonal deficits*, focus is on the formation of new relationships.

In order to make changes, Kristen is encouraged to practice outside of session. Reviewing difficult social interactions that have come up over the week, focusing on the therapeutic relationship as a model for addressing problems she has in initiating and sustaining relationships, and examining repetitive patterns in relationships are all useful strategies to recreate and modify Kristen's social world (Klerman et al., 1984). Accordingly, as Kristen progresses in treatment, focus shifts toward events occurring outside the session (Mufson & Moreau, 1998). Interactions which occurred during the week are analyzed and helpful recommendations provided. Reviewing incidents in which Kristen feels isolated can help identify the social behaviors leading to these incidents and prevent them from reoccurring. Feedback from her therapist about observed changes in her functioning helps to build her self-esteem (Mufson & Moreau, 1998). Of note, when Kristen raises issues about eating, weight, or shape, attention is directed to how this issue fits within the context of her interpersonal problem area.

Final Phase. Although termination is addressed during the first phase of treatment and mentioned occasionally during the work phase, it takes a more primary focus during the final phase. Sessions 16 to 20, the late, final, or termination phase of treatment, is a time for review and consolidation. As such, the final phase serves dual purposes (Mufson & Moreau, 1998). The first aim of this phase is to help Kristen transition away from her therapeutic relationship. Given the painful endings of important relationships in her life (e.g., her parents' marriage, her high school romance, and her engagement to Joe), the impact of this termination needs to be considered from the perspective of her interpersonal problem area. Kristen is educated that the end of treatment is a time for grieving, and encouraged to identify associated emotions. The second aim is to foster Kristen's feelings of accomplishment and competence to prepare her to work on her own (Mufson & Moreau, 1998). Pointing out the skills and strategies she has learned, the goals she has met, and recalling Kristen's systems of support motivates her to continue working on her problem area. Outlining goals for Kristen's remaining work, identifying areas of anticipated future difficulty, and recognizing warning signs are all an important part of formulating plans for continued work after the treatment itself has ended. Given the chronic nature of Kristen's eating disorder and the need for vigilance to assure her weight becomes restored, she and her therapist may discuss her having one booster session a month for 8 months following her 20 weekly sessions. At the end of this year, her eating disorder is reevaluated with the aim of ending treatment.

The Therapeutic Relationship

The Therapeutic Bond

The supportive yet strong working alliance of IPT is conveyed through a genuine regard for the patient and respect for the relationship. This establishes a safe environment for Kristen to receive feedback about how she is coming across, experiment with new interaction styles, and experience a relationship in which she feels held in high esteem. Establishing early alliance with Kristen is especially important if she feels conflicted about seeking treatment, given a continuing desire to restrict and maintain a low weight (Pike & Wilfley, 1996).

Roles in the Therapeutic Relationship

The therapeutic relationship of IPT enacts a social microcosm in which the therapist highlights dysfunctional interpersonal patterns in the session and relates them to similar patterns in the patient's social life. Thus, IPT therapists are in a unique position as therapeutic consultants, skillful at using their knowledge to encourage patients to make changes in their social lives. The nature of this relationship is qualitatively different from that of the reciprocal sharing and support of friendship or the reenactment of primary relationships as seen in transference (Klerman et al., 1984). Neither distant, passive, nor interpretative, the therapist is in an interpersonal relationship with Kristen, working collaboratively based on agreed upon goals.

Treatment Implementation and Outcome

Techniques and Methods of Working

Specific techniques are frequently used during IPT sessions (Klerman et al., 1984).

Encouragement of Affect.   Difficulty identifying feelings is very common among those who binge and purge. Accordingly, the more aware Kristen is about her feelings (e.g., boredom or loneliness at night), the less likely she uses food as a way to manage them. When she begins to binge eat or feel out-of-control, Kristen can stop to check in with herself. Both in session and during the week are appropriate times for Kristen to try to identify feelings as they come up, in the moment. By distinguishing her feelings, Kristen can address the original cause of the problem rather than ignoring it, and therefore exercise a more appropriate solution (e.g., calling a friend or making plans to go out).

Communication Analysis.   Helping patients to communicate more effectively is an important aim of IPT, and Kristen's relationship with her therapist serves as an important model of her behavior in other relationships. Common communication difficulties are identified by pointing out ambiguous or mixed communication, asking Kristen for clarification, and requesting that she seek feedback from important people in her life. Drawing attention to inconsistencies between verbal and nonverbal behavior helps Kristen pinpoint underlying discrepancies between her affect and action. During her session, communication is studied by examining her descriptions of deep loneliness and hurt, and disconnection from others. Her style of remaining detached (formed by growing up with very little attention from her parents after their business was destroyed) has made it difficult for her to develop solid, intimate connections with others. Over the years, focusing on food has been a way for Kristen to distract herself from the emptiness she feels in her relationships. In order to feel closer and have more intimate relationships, she needs to learn the importance of being able to share with others. Identifying one or two people from whom she can get feedback assists her. Asking for feedback about how she is coming across pushes her to share and trust, while others share with her. Although she may feel she is putting herself at great risk, she soon finds herself developing bonds of intimacy. As her relationships improve, she finds it less necessary to turn to food.

Clarification.   Clarification is a technique that helps Kristen become more aware of what she is communicating (Klerman et al., 1984). Asking Kristen to repeat or rephrase unusual wording and calling attention to contradictions and inconsistencies between affective expression and verbal discussion (Klerman et al., 1984) helps her to become aware of her feelings and attend to her style of interaction.

Exploratory Techniques.   Exploratory techniques are used to gather additional information about Kristen's current functioning and can take many forms (Klerman et al., 1984). The use of open-ended, general questions to gather information and guide discussion is especially helpful during the initial phase of treatment as well as during the beginning of each subsequent session to determine how Kristen is progressing on her goals. These can be followed by more specific questions designed to examine hypotheses and gain clarity about details during the session.

Medical and Nutritional Issues

Inseparable from the health risks associated with AN, potential effects of starvation on mental status may compromise Kristen's ability to benefit from psychotherapy (Garner & Bemis, 1985). Kristen's therapist consults weekly with a treatment team, consisting of an internist and dietitian, to review her medical status. Although issues of weight are not addressed directly during IPT sessions, Kristen and her therapist need to come to an agreement that she is to be accountable for her medical condition. From her present 82.7% of recommended weight for height, Kristen is required to reach and stay at 90% (Garner, Vitousek, & Pike, 1997) in order to continue in therapy. If her condition worsens, her medical treatment will take priority over her psychological treatment.

Potential Pitfalls

Problem: Kristen has difficulty identifying her emotions. *Intervention:* This is likely to occur during the initial phase of treatment when Kristen is still attempting to control her feelings through the use of restraint, bingeing, and purging. Failure to identify her feelings is problematic, as Kristen will be unable to recognize the connection between her feeling and her use of food. In first working to identify feelings as they occur, Kristen may wish to entertain various hypotheses about what she could be feeling and examine the events that may have led up to her current state. Further checking in with herself throughout the day is helpful for Kristen to become more aware of times when she is feeling bad (e.g., lonely, frustrated) and to help her to get support from others in the moment rather than restricting or later turning to food for comfort.

Problem: In becoming aware of her emotions, Kristen fears being overpowered by them. *Intervention:* For years, Kristen has felt incapable of handling her emotions and has instead relied on hard work and food to get her through difficult situations. Kristen needs to be taught to view her emotions in a more positive light by learning that emotions provide important information by signaling things we need to express. In addition, it is helpful for Kristen to learn that although *having* feelings can be painful, the *feelings* themselves do not hurt us. By giving herself the opportunity to sit with uncomfortable feelings, she recognizes where they were coming from and finds out what it is that she can do—beyond her normal but ineffective means of escape—to feel better. The most important adaptive means of coping is connecting with family and others on a day-to-day basis. Not only does this help Kristen feel less backlogged with emotion but, by sharing with others rather than keeping them emotionally distant, people feel closer to her. Although breaking these patterns is difficult, doing so allows Kristen to feel more in control of herself as well as of her eating.

Problem: Kristen is not working on her goals. *Intervention:* There are several possible reasons for this potential stumbling block. First, Kristen may be resistant to change due to the fear that giving up severe restriction, bingeing, and purging as methods of coping leaves her with no means of managing her emotions. It is probable that her self-esteem has been derived from her ability to restrict, and Kristen fears that if she is no longer thin, she will not be liked. For this reason, Kristen should begin to get support from friends and family as soon as possible, as this leads her to feel less likely to need food for these purposes. Thus, she is not giving up the use of food to control her feelings, but finding the use of restraint and food unnecessary.

Alternatively, Kristen may not be working on her goals directly because she is focusing instead on other aspects of her relationships. Because of her work, her relationships may be improving and she may be already feeling better about herself. However, caution should be noted. The key to improving her eating disorder is for Kristen directly to work on her actual goals. Although she may be making strides in her overall well-being, without doing work on her goals, she is not addressing the relationship difficulties which lead to and maintain her dysfunctional eating, and her eating disorder will not remit. Kristen can be redirected to working on her goals in session, and discussions can take place for ways in which she can continue working on her goals during the week.

Problem: Forgetting to work on her goals. *Intervention:* It is important to examine Kristen's expectations about therapy and remind her of the active nature of this treatment. In order to improve, Kristen needs to make changes through daily hard work on her goals. As she begins to do this, difficult tasks such as checking in with her feelings or sitting with her emotions require less effort.

Problem: Kristen wishes to focus directly on issues regarding eating and weight. *Intervention:* This scenario is more likely to occur during the initial sessions of therapy if Kristen fails to recognize the connection between her relationships with others and her eating. Assisting

Kristen to identify and discuss how she is feeling in moments when she is likely to restrict or binge allows her to appreciate the impact of people on her mood, and subsequently on her eating.

Problem: Kristen fails to recognize that her severe restraint is a problem. *Intervention:* It is expected that Kristen be more motivated to gain control over bingeing and purging than to eliminate her excessive dietary restraint. Instead of directly challenging her continuing desire to diet, attention needs to be focused on the interpersonal context associated with the times in which she has the desire to severely restrict. As Kristen becomes in touch with her feelings, she begins to identify ways to feel less anxious in the presence of others.

Problem: Traumatic feelings about Kristen's rape resurface. *Intervention:* As Kristen begins to identify her feelings, she may find herself aware of very painful emotions arising from her rape. Kristen's attempts at cutting off feelings have perpetuated her binge-purge cycle. In order to recover from this past trauma and from her eating disorder, Kristen should be encouraged to share her feelings as they come up in session as well as with family members she trusts. By allowing her feelings to resurface while getting the support she needs, Kristen is able to process her feelings instead of trying to keep them covered. Furthermore, making connections with others assists Kristen in recognizing the importance of support.

Problem: Kristen feels unable to reach out to anyone. *Intervention:* Given the very limited friendships she has had throughout her life, it is understandable that Kristen is skeptical of developing mutually beneficial relationships. Individuals with AN often feel mistrustful of others, which derives from their not having well-integrated attachments to others or a secure sense of self (Casper, 1982). To address this, Kristen's recovery starts by her developing a secure relationship with her therapist. By building this relationship, reestablishing her former connections, and working to meet new people, Kristen can begin to form a new social network for herself and establish an identity that is separate from the disorder.

Problem: Kristen requests to prolong treatment. *Intervention:* Preparation for the end of treatment and addressing fears of termination is an essential part of treatment. Illustrating the link between the endings of past relationships in her life (i.e., that of her parents, her high school boyfriend, and her engagement to Joe) and her present fear of termination assists Kristen to recognize the many painful feelings she associates with loss. Encouragement of her expression of these feelings provides Kristen the opportunity to learn to grieve for the loss of these relationships rather than use food as a means of coping. Finally, Kristen's independence can be encouraged by helping her to identify the changes she has made on her own, and successes she has had in solving interpersonal difficulties. Rather than delaying termination, the expectation can be set that although she is not a "finished product," she is ready to apply her skills to new interpersonal challenges.

Termination and Relapse Prevention

Termination itself is an integral part of the course of IPT. Therapeutic interventions directed at the interpersonal context of the eating disorder facilitate Kristen's recovery from her acute episode and possibly have preventative effects against relapse and recurrence (Klerman et al., 1984). However, in addition to carefully planning for termination, it is important that Kristen and her therapist be able to work collaboratively to identify need for future treatment. As mentioned earlier, if Kristen's weight is not yet stabilized and her therapist feels she needs more concentrated work before terminating the treatment and beginning the booster sessions, their weekly meetings could be extended. Longer term treatment may be appropriate for patients with long histories of interpersonal problems (Mufson & Moreau, 1998) and a severe course of eating disorders. However, these instances should be seen as distinct from those in which patients do not wish to terminate but have the tools to continue on their own. Finally, if at termination Kristen desires more treatment, this issue is related to the aloneness Kristen had formerly worked to cover with food. Kristen is encouraged to explore these feelings of aloneness and continue her present work on her own for a few weeks, at the end of which her progress is reassessed (Mufson & Moreau, 1998).

Mechanisms of Change

Hypothesized Time Course. As predicted by the hypothesized time course of treatment (see Figure 5.2), improvements in Kristen's interpersonal functioning increase her self-esteem, subsequently resulting in decreased binge eating, decreased dietary restraint, and improved attitudes toward eating, shape, and weight (Fairburn, 1993). Thus, by drawing a connection between unhealthy eating patterns and problems in her interpersonal functioning, Kristen's insight into using food as a means of coping decrease food's efficacy in reducing her interpersonal distress. Furthermore, through work on her interpersonal problem area, Kristen learns to become more effective in handling the interpersonal distress. And, with improved social functioning and increased self-esteem, it is posited that Kristen is less likely to use binge eating and restraint as means of coping, and becomes less preoccupied with food and her body.

Hypothesized Mechanisms. The actual manner in which IPT for eating disorders functions is yet unknown (Wilfley et al., 1998). However, Fairburn (1998) has posited that the process of change begins with the patient having increased feelings of efficacy as a result of changing long-term interpersonal problems. This is achieved through an insistent focus on resolving interpersonal problems within the patient's life. With reductions in interpersonal stressors, decreases in binge eating are likely. Similarly, improvements in mood and self-esteem may decrease dieting, weight, and shape concerns. Finally, increases in social interaction may decrease feel-

**IMPROVED INTERPERSONAL FUNCTIONING
INCREASED SELF-ESTEEM**

↓

DECREASED BINGE EATING

↓

**DECREASED DIETARY RESTRAINT
IMPROVED ATTITUDES TOWARD EATING, SHAPE, & WEIGHT**

FIGURE 5.2   Hypothesized time course of treatment.

ings of isolation and loneliness, thus preventing the cycle from perpetuating. In summary, symptoms are reduced by focusing on the interpersonal problem most associated with the onset and/or maintenance of the disordered eating.

In the present case example, Kristen's bulimic and anorexic features suggest that the mechanisms of IPT may be similar. Indeed, as soon as she begins reconnecting with her family, it is posited that Kristen begins to erode the wall of isolation she has built, and excessive restraint and bingeing and purging no longer are her only solace. As she begins to feel better about her communication and examines how she is coming across, Kristen feels fewer interpersonal stressors, resulting in less bingeing and purging, and less excessive restraint with clients at work. Within a few months, Kristen already feels better about herself in relationship to others, and is less likely to judge herself based on her body or ability to control her intake of food. Finally, the effects of termination from treatment are buffered by Kristen's having formed a budding network of people to whom she feels connected and derives a growing sense of fulfillment.

In summary, as presented in this case example, IPT for the treatment of eating disorders is based on the assumption that eating disorders are intimately related to disturbances in social functioning. The aim of treatment is to reduce eating disorder symptoms by addressing interpersonal problems associated with the onset and maintenance of the disorder. IPT involves three well-defined phases of treatment, specific therapeutic techniques, and a therapeutic stance aimed at resolving current problems within four social domains.

Although no research has yet been conducted examining the use of IPT for the treatment of AN, many features of IPT appear especially advantageous for its use with this difficult to treat population. First, given the insidious nature of AN, intervening through the establishment of social support rather than more directly challenging restriction is especially helpful for patients resistant to the idea of giving up this aspect of their lives. Rather than setting out to *take away* present means of coping and also removing the patient's source of pride (i.e., thinness), the aim of IPT is to *replace* this with an alternative source from which the patient can derive self-esteem (i.e., improved social functioning). Second, current knowledge about AN points to the fact that it is often an all-consuming disorder to which patients attend at the exclusion of many other aspects of their lives. As Kristen's disorder has left her with a history of problematic attachments in her relationships (Pike & Wilfley, 1996), the bond of trust, collaboration, and advocacy between her and her therapist is especially important in allaying the suspicion and mistrust common to anorexics who are receiving treatment. Third, as the early development of Kristen's eating disorder most likely interfered with her ability to attain milestones of social development, making changes in her interpersonal functioning results in significant improvements in not only her eating disorder psychopathology, but in her general functioning.

The short-term and focused nature of IPT is consistent with the aims of health care delivery systems to limit costs and maximize delivery. IPT for the treatment of BN and binge eating disorder has resulted in significant improvements (Agras et al., 1999; Wilfley, 1999) as well as good maintenance of change (Fairburn, Jones, Peveler, Hope, & O'Connor, 1993; Fairburn, Norman, Welch, & O'Connor, 1995). In a similar manner, perhaps future research will support the efficacy of individual as well as group IPT for the treatment of AN either as a stand-alone, combination, or maintenance treatment.

REFERENCES

Agras, W. S., Walsh, B. T., Wilson, G. T., & Fairburn, C. G. (1999, April). *A multisite comparison of cognitive behaviour therapy and interpersonal psychotherapy in the treatment of bulimia nervosa.* Session presented at the meeting of the 4th International Conference on Eating Disorders, London.

American Psychiatric Association (1994). *Diagnostic and statistical manual of mental disorders* (4th ed.). Washington, DC: American Psychiatric Association.

Angus, L., & Gillies, L. A. (1994). Counselling the borderline client: An interpersonal approach. *Canadian Journal of Counselling, 28*(1), 69–82.

Arnow, B., Kenardy, J., & Agras, W. S. (1992). Binge eating among the obese: A descriptive study. *Journal of Behavioral Medicine, 15*, 155–170.

Arnow, B., Kenardy, J., & Agras, W. S. (1995). The Emotional Eating Scale: The development of a measure to assess coping with negative affect by eating. *International Journal of Eating Disorders, 18*, 79–90.

Beck, A. T., Ward, C. H., Mendelson, M., & Mock, J. (1961). An inventory for measuring depression. *Archives of General Psychiatry, 4*, 561–571.

Bowlby, J. (1982). *Attachment and loss: Vol. 1. Attachment* (2nd ed.). New York: Basic Books.

Casper, R. C. (1982). Treatment principles in anorexia nervosa. *Adolescent Psychiatry, 10,* 86–100.

Derogatis, L. R. (1983). *The SCL-90-R: Administration manual-II for the revised version.* Towson, MD: Clinical Psychometric Research.

Ehlers, C. L., Frank, E., & Kupfer, D. J. (1988). Social zeitgebers and biological rhythms. *Archives of General Psychiatry, 45*(10), 948–952.

Elkin, I., Shea, M. T., Watkins, J. T., Imber, S. D., Sotsky, S. M., Collins, J. F., Glass, D. R., Pilkonis, P. A., Leber, W. R., & Docherty, J. P. (1989). National Institute of Mental Health Treatment of Depression Collaborative Research Program: General effectiveness of treatments. *Archives of General Psychiatry, 46*(11), 971–982.

Fairburn, C. G. (1993). Interpersonal psychotherapy for bulimia nervosa. In G. L. Klerman & M. M. Weissman (Eds.), *New applications of interpersonal psychotherapy* (pp. 353–378). Washington, DC: American Psychiatric Press.

Fairburn, C. G. (1998). Interpersonal psychotherapy for bulimia nervosa. In J. C. Markowitz (Ed.), *Interpersonal psychotherapy* (pp. 99–128). Washington, DC: American Psychiatric Press.

Fairburn, C. G., & Cooper, Z. (1993). The Eating Disorder Examination (12th edition). In C. F. Fairburn & G. T. Wilson (Eds.), *Binge eating: Nature, assessment, and treatment.* (pp. 317–360). New York: The Guilford Press.

Fairburn, C. G., Jones, R., Peveler, R. C., Carr, S. J., Solomon, R. A., O'Connor, M. E., Burton, J., & Hope, R. A. (1991). Three psychological treatments for bulimia nervosa: A comparative trial. *Archives of General Psychiatry, 48*(5), 463–469.

Fairburn, C. G., Jones, R., Peveler, R. C., Hope, R. A., & O'Connor, M. (1993). Psychotherapy and bulimia nervosa. Longer-term effects of interpersonal psychotherapy, behavior therapy, and cognitive behavior therapy. *Archives of General Psychiatry, 50,* 419–428.

Fairburn, C. G., Kirk, J., O'Connor, M., & Cooper, P. J. (1986). A comparison of two psychological treatments for bulimia nervosa. *Behaviour Research & Therapy, 24*(6), 629–643.

Fairburn, C. G., Norman, P. A., Welch, S. L., & O'Connor, M. E. (1995). A prospective study of outcome in bulimia nervosa and the long-term effects of three psychological treatments. *Archives of General Psychiatry, 52*(4), 304–312.

Foley, S. H., Rounsaville, B. J., Weissman, M. M., Sholomskas, D., & Chevron, E. (1989). Individual versus conjoint interpersonal psychotherapy for depressed patients with marital disputes. *International Journal of Family Psychiatry, 10,* 29–42.

Frank, E. (1991a). Interpersonal psychotherapy as a maintenance treatment for patients with recurrent depression. *Psychotherapy, 28*(2), 259–266.

Frank, E. (1991b). *Biological order and bipolar disorder.* Paper presented at the meeting of the America Psychosomatic Society, Santa Fe, NM.

Frank, E., & Spanier, C. (1995). Interpersonal psychotherapy for depression: Overview, clinical efficacy, and future directions. *Clinical Psychology: Science & Practice, 2*(4), 349–369.

Garner, D. M., & Bemis, K. M. (1985). Cognitive therapy for anorexia nervosa. In D. M. Garner & P. E. Garfinkel (Eds.), *Handbook of psychotherapy for anorexia nervosa and bulimia* (pp. 107–146). New York: Guilford Press.

Garner, D. M., Vitousek, K. M., & Pike, K. M. (1997). Cognitive-behavioral therapy for anorexia nervosa. In D. M. Garner & P. E. Garfinkel (Eds.), *Handbook of treatment for eating disorders* (pp. 94–144). New York: Guilford Press.

Horowitz, L. M., Rosenberg, S. E., Baer, B. A., Ureno, G., & Villasenor, V. S. (1988). Inventory of interpersonal problems: Psychometric properties and clinical applications. *Journal of Consulting & Clinical Psychology, 56*(6), 885–892.

Klerman, G. L., & Weissman, M. M. (1993). Interpersonal psychotherapy for depression: Background and concepts. In G. L. Klerman & M. M. Weissman (Eds.), *New applications of interpersonal psychotherapy* (pp. 3–50). New York: American Psychiatric Press, Inc.

Klerman, G. L., Weissman, M. M., Rounsaville, B. J., & Chevron, E. S. (1984). *Interpersonal psychotherapy of depression.* New York: Basic Books.

Markowitz, J. C. (1994). Psychotherapy of dysthymia. *American Journal of Psychiatry, 151*(8), 1114–1121.

Markowitz, J. C. (1998). *Interpersonal psychotherapy for dysthymic disorder.* Washington, DC: American Psychiatric Press.

Markowitz, J. C., Kocsis, J. H., Fishman, B., Spielman, L. A., Jacobsberg, L. B., Frances, A. J., Klerman, G. L., & Perry, S. W. (1998). Treatment of depressive symptoms in human immunodeficiency virus-positive patients. *Archives of General Psychiatry, 55*(5), 452–457.

Markowitz, J. C., & Swartz, H. A. (1997). Case formulation in interpersonal psychotherapy of depression. In T. D. Eells (Ed.), *Handbook of psychotherapy case formulation* (pp. 192–222). New York: Guilford Press.

McKenzie, J., McIntosh, V. V., Jordan, J., Joyce, P., Carter, F., Luty, S., & Bulik, C. (1999, April). *Interpersonal psychotherapy for anorexia nervosa.* Session presented at the 4th International Conference on Eating Disorders, London.

Meyer, A. (1957). *Psychobiology: A science of man.* Springfield, IL: Charles C. Thomas.

Moreau, D., Mufson, L., Weissman, M. M., & Klerman, G. L. (1991). Interpersonal psychotherapy for adolescent depression: Description of modification and preliminary application. *Journal of the American Academy of Child & Adolescent Psychiatry, 30*(4), 642–651.

Mossey, J. M., Knott, K. A., Higgins, M., & Talerico, K. (1996). Effectiveness of a psychosocial intervention, interpersonal counseling, for subdysthymic depression in medically ill elderly. *Journals of Gerontology, 51*(4), M172–M178.

Mufson, L., & Moreau, D. (1998). Interpersonal psychotherapy for adolescent depression. In J.C. Markowitz (Ed.), *Interpersonal psychotherapy* (pp. 35–66). Washington, DC: American Psychiatric Press.

Mufson, L., Moreau, D., Weissman, M. M., & Klerman, G. L. (1993). *Interpersonal therapy for depressed adolescents.* New York: Guilford Press.

Mufson, L., Moreau, D., Weissman, M. M., & Wickramaratne, P. (1994). Modification of interpersonal psychotherapy with depressed adolescents (IPT-A): Phase I and II studies. *Journal of the American Academy of Child & Adolescent Psychiatry, 33*(5), 695–705.

Pike, K. M., & Wilfley, D. E. (1996). The changing context of treatment. In L. Smolak, M.P. Levine, & R. Striegel-Moore (Eds.), *The developmental psychopathology of eating disorders* (pp. 365–397). Mahway, NJ: Lawrence Erlbaum Associates, Inc.

Rosenberg, M. (1979). *Conceiving the self.* New York: Basic Books.

Russell, D., Peplau, L. A., & Cutrona, C. E. (1980). The revised UCLA Loneliness Scale: Concurrent and discriminant validity evidence. *Journal of Personality & Social Psychology, 39*(3), 472–480.

Scott, J., & Ikkos, G. (1996). *A pilot study of interpersonal psychotherapy for the treatment of chronic somatization in primary care.* Paper presented at the First Congress of the World Council of Psychotherapy, Vienna, Austria.

Sullivan, H. S. (1953). *The interpersonal theory of psychiatry.* New York: W.W. Norton.

Swartz, H. A., & Markowitz, J. C. (1998). Interpersonal psychotherapy for the treatment of depression in HIV-positive men and women. In J. C. Markowitz (Ed.), *Interpersonal psychotherapy* (pp. 129–155). Washington, DC: American Psychiatric Press.

Ventura, J., Liberman, R. P., Green, M. F., Shaner, A., & Mintz, J. (1998). Training and quality assurance with Structured Clinical Interview for DSM-IV (SCID-I/P). *Psychiatry Research, 79,* 163–173.

Weissman, M. M. (1995). *IPT mastering depression: A patient's guide to interpersonal psychotherapy.* New York: Graywind Publications Incorporated.

Weissman, M. M., & Bothwell, S. (1976). Assessment of social adjustment by patient self-report. *Archives of General Psychiatry, 33,* 1111–1115.

Weissman, M. M., & Markowitz, J. C. (1998). An overview of interpersonal psychotherapy. In J.C. Markowitz (Ed.), *Interpersonal psychotherapy* (pp. 1–33). Washington, DC: American Psychiatric Press.

Wilfley, D. E. (1993). *Interpersonal psychotherapy adapted for group (IPT-G) and for the treatment of binge eating disorder: Therapist manual.* Unpublished manuscript.

Wilfley, D. E. (1999, April). Treatment of binge eating disorder: Research findings and clinical applications. In B. T. Walsh (Chair), *Integrating research and clinical practice.* Plenary session presented at the meeting of the 4th International Conference on Eating Disorders, London.

Wilfley, D. E., Agras, W. S., Telch, C. F., Rossiter, E. M., Schneider, J. A., Cole, A. G., Sifford, L. A., & Raeburn, S. D. (1993). Group cognitive-behavioral therapy and group interpersonal psychotherapy for the non-purging bulimic individual: A controlled comparison. *Journal of Consulting & Clinical Psychology, 61*(2), 296–305.

Wilfley, D. E., Frank, M. A., Welch, R., Spurrell, E. B., & Rounsaville, B. J. (1998). Adapting interpersonal psychotherapy to a group format (IPT-G) for binge eating disorder: A model for adapting empirically-validated treatments. *Psychotherapy Research, 8*(4), 379–391.

6

Developmental-Systemic-Feminist Therapy

Rachel Bryant-Waugh

TREATMENT MODEL

This chapter describes an approach to treatment that is based on the integration of three separate theoretical influences: developmental psychology; systems theory and its application to therapy; and feminist ideology. Briefly, the relevant features of each of these major influences are as follows.

Developmental Psychology

Developmental psychology is concerned with exploring all aspects of human psychological development and change, encompassing changes in behavior, cognitions, and emotions throughout life (Berryman, Hargreaves, Herbert, & Taylor, 1991). It makes attempts to observe, study, and understand the processes underlying psychological development and change, common patterns, and also common problems in development. The occurrence of psychological problems in an individual can be understood by an exploration of that individual's responses to change and any external factors that may have contributed towards shaping those responses.

Bowlby and Erikson are examples of well-known developmental theorists. Bowlby studied the importance of "attachment" to a primary caregiver during infancy, and proposed that "failures" in the attachment process can have profound and lasting effects for emotional, social, and cognitive development (Bowlby, 1951). Although many of his conclusions are contentious, there can be no doubt that Bowlby's work has been highly influential in terms of understanding the importance of the very early mother-child bond for the capacity to form strong and satisfying relationships later in life. Likewise, Erikson's model of the different stages of human development, with characteristic goals to be achieved and hurdles to be overcome within each stage, has had a strong influence on understanding the development of psychological problems (Erikson, 1965). Difficulties in mastering specific developmental tasks in childhood may have long-lasting implications for the process of identity formation and the ability to form intimate relationships.

In the context of this chapter, the influence of developmental psychology is manifest by an exploration of the individual's developmental history and by an analysis of past patterns of response to developmental pressures and change.

Systems Theory

The application of systems theory to therapy is most clearly set out in the general literature on the theory and practice of family therapy. Systems theory is a general theory that focuses on the organization of parts into wholes (von Bertalanffy, 1968). This theory has been adapted and applied to the practice of addressing an individual's problems within the naturally occurring "system" of the family. Amongst others, Bowen (1978) expanded on the application of systems theory to therapy and refers to the family as a "combination of emotional and relationship systems." Very simply, through the adoption of a systemic approach, the clinician will attempt to understand the development and maintenance of problems in one individual in the context of the family members' interrelationships and situation. In practice, this involves viewing and arriving at an understanding of an individual within his or her social context, understanding the person in the context of interactions and relationships. A systemic approach to understanding problems forms a logical link with a developmental orientation.

Feminist Ideology

Feminism is often a problematic term, used to cover a wide range of political, socio-cultural, and ideological views. In the context of setting out the theoretical bases for developmental-systemic-feminist oriented therapy, feminist ideology encompasses the belief in a right to basic equality between men and women, with women's experiences, views, and responses to the demands of their lives being considered valid and of importance. A focus on the "oppression of women" and the embattled language and socio-political activity that goes with this is less relevant or central to the therapeutic approach described in this chapter. Important feminist principles incorporated here are the emphasis on collaboration and support; the minimization of power differentials (here between client and therapist); and the recognition that many women who present for treatment do not view themselves as having a right to negotiate relationships on equal terms. Feminism in this sense involves accepting differences (gender-related or otherwise) and celebrating them, not being directive or prescriptive in terms of how women or men should or should not think or act. It involves placing an emphasis on personal responsibility for health and well-being, and more importantly on supporting and facilitating women to make their own choices about their lives. This process can be difficult but is underpinned by the feminist principle of having an equal right to make such choices. Enhancing autonomy and self-worth, empowering, building on existing strengths and confidences, and working against the development of a sense of weakness and failure will be characteristic features of therapy arising from an embracement of basic feminist ideology. It should be noted that "feminist" principles in this sense can be relevant irrespective of the gender of the client and/or therapist.

These three main influences are individually wide-ranging and complex, but the integration of the fundamental starting points of each can provide a clear and coherent framework for therapy. The treatment model central to this chapter rests on a synthesis of these three theoretical influences. The type of therapy described is broadly nondirective, not reliant on the use of highly specific interventions, but nevertheless structured and consistent. The model represents a means by which problems can be conceptualized, assessed, and addressed, as well as providing a template for the nature and quality of therapist-client interactions.

The integration of underlying theoretical influences in the practice of developmental-systemic-feminist therapy is clearly demonstrated by the collaborative process of carrying out a functional analysis and arriving at a formulation of what the client brings to therapy. This consists of a thorough assessment eliciting as much detail as possible in the form of chronological events, emotional responses, social and family circumstances, and personal cognitive style. The development of problematic behaviors, thought patterns, and emotions are put together and made sense of in a personal context. Important aspects of the process of conducting the functional analysis are the establishment of a collaborative relationship between therapist and client; the validation of the client's behavioral and emotional responses; and the identification of key factors that may be maintaining the difficulty that brings the client to therapy (or understanding the factors that may be inhibiting the client from moving forward). Often these maintaining or perpetuating factors will be most amenable to intervention.

THE THERAPIST'S SKILLS AND ATTRIBUTES

The therapist whose work is based on this particular combination of developmental, systemic, and feminist thinking needs above all else to have the ability to listen without censorship. It is important to hear everything the client says as potentially relevant, to listen to her story without arriving at conclusions before she has finished. For most of us, the process of training in a particular treatment modality or theoretical model leads us to be selective in attending to and processing the information our clients bring to us. We all have a tendency to piece items of information together because they fit a pattern with which we are familiar; indeed, in the application of some treatment modalities it is right that we should do this.

However, the therapist working within a developmental-systemic-feminist framework will be alert to comments that are glossed over, will be prepared to question further for clarification, and will accept the client's own perception and emotional responses as valid. The therapist should check with the client to be sure to obtain an accurate picture or understanding of what has been discussed. The therapeutic style is based on person-centered principles of genuineness, empathy, and respect.

The therapist will also need to have a knowledge of key developmental stages and tasks and an ability to consider the potentially different impact of events and situations both at different developmental stages and in different individuals. For example, a mother's hospitalization could be expected to have a different impact on a 3-year-old compared to a 13-year-old. The impact on the 3-year-old will differ according to a number of other factors relating to the child's situation, for example, whether there are two parents, other siblings, the hospitalization was planned and the child prepared for it, the mother has been away from the child before, etcetera. The consideration of events and situations, and the impact they may have, in a developmental context must be accompanied by an openness to accept that different individuals respond to things in different ways, and that this response may be determined both by internal (e.g., character traits) and external factors.

Because the style of the therapy is collaborative, the therapist will need to be sensitive to and willing to address any power differential that may creep into the therapist-client relationship. Therapy proceeds through coworking, addressing difficulties together, and not because the therapist has the power or the knowledge to "make the client better." The therapist will need to reinforce the nature of this relationship by openly considering what she can do to assist the client in the process of addressing her own difficulties. In this context, the therapist must be able to extract the client's strengths and to build on these. An ability to positively reframe past situations and the client's response to difficulties is very important.

Lastly, the therapist will ideally have an ability to be creative and spontaneous. Most therapists have this naturally within them, but often lack the confidence to apply this aspect of themselves to the therapeutic process. Because the tasks of the therapy will be largely client led, it is very important to be able to work with client priorities.

Where the therapist feels very strongly that other issues need to be addressed in the interests of the client's health and safety, there will need to be a firmness and a willingness to negotiate in terms of therapeutic objectives. Such therapist insistence on putting certain items on the agenda should be understood as working towards enhancing individual responsibility. In addition, it often provides the client with an opportunity to practice negotiating skills in a safe relationship.

THE CASE OF KRISTEN

Assessment, Conceptualization, and Treatment Planning

Assessment

Assessment forms a crucial part of treatment, and involves, as has already been described, the taking of a detailed history. Further, to what we already know about Kristen, the following could provide important information or enable the material already available to be put together more easily to inform therapy:

1. *General mental state examination and risk assessment:* This should ideally be carried out with all clients who present for help with an eating disorder. We have observed that Kristen recounts her life history with little feeling, we know that her concentration is poor, and we know that she has had a tendency to "use" alcohol. It will be important to determine whether Kristen is currently depressed, and whether there are any other appropriate comorbid diagnoses. Also, we will need to clarify Kristen's current level of risk particularly in terms of self-harm (past and present), drug and alcohol use, etcetera.

2. The use of *two parallel time lines*, one documenting key life events and the other documenting weight history, eating difficulties, and the intensity of weight and shape concerns. This can allow the development of the eating difficulties and related body dissatisfaction, weight and shape concerns to be placed in the context of events, situations, and developmental stages in Kristen's life. It can

also serve as a good starting point for beginning to identify with Kristen relevant issues and/or themes to address in therapy.

3. *A meeting with Kristen and one or more of her family members* (possibly her mother and/or brothers: the choice would depend on who Kristen identified as most relevant). It is often helpful, where possible, to meet adult clients with eating disorders with one or more members of their family of origin. The client will clearly need to be in full agreement with this. Many of the issues the person with the eating disorder is struggling with will have their basis in earlier experiences and in difficulties negotiating developmental tasks. Current problems in relationships, with self-esteem, with assertiveness and self-preservation skills usually have well-established roots, and in this respect, Kristen seems no exception. Arranging a meeting as part of the assessment process with one or more parents or siblings can be useful in helping the client reconnect earlier experiences and responses with current "dysfunctional" coping strategies when faced with difficult or distressing situations. The therapist can also benefit by obtaining a wider view of developmental and systemic factors necessary to arrive at a better understanding of why and how the client has developed and maintained "unhelpful" responses. In some cases, relationships with family members may have broken down or a meeting with family members may not be possible for some other reason. This need not hinder therapy as the aim is not necessarily to focus on or repair family-of-origin relationships in therapy, but to assist the client in understanding her own logic behind her responses and to use this understanding as a basis for the process of moving forward.

4. *Administration of the Eating Disorder Examination* (Fairburn & Cooper, 1993) will identify in detail the nature and extent of Kristen's difficulties related to eating and weight and shape concerns. This is an "investigator based," standardized interview measure of the specific psychopathology of eating disorders. Its administration allows an assessment of disturbances in eating behavior and characteristic attitudes around food, eating, weight, and shape. The Eating Disorder Examination can assist in the clarification of a diagnosis, but also in identifying possible areas for intervention. Its use serves to ensure that a thorough assessment has been made of cognitions and behaviors specific to the eating disorder.

5. *A "cost-benefit" analysis*—a separate assessment of Kristen's readiness to change, identifying what might be lost and need replacing, what the risks would be for Kristen in giving up her eating disorder. This is related to the functional analysis and the exploration of the maintaining factors, the positive payoffs. Without openly acknowledging that there are "benefits" associated with the eating disorder and seeking to replace these via other less self-destructive means, the chances of successfully leaving the eating disorder behind will be limited.

Therapeutic Goals

Therapeutic goals will be generated as part of the collaborative process between the therapist and Kristen. To a large extent, the precise nature of these goals will be determined by Kristen. Goals do not necessarily have to relate specifically to the eating disorder. The therapist's role is to guide, inform where appropriate, and encourage Kristen to identify realistically attainable goals. In this case, there is a whole range of issues that Kristen might identify as areas for work: reducing her vomiting; developing a plan for identifying and managing stress at work; addressing guilty feelings around her stillborn sister; dealing with the effects of the rape; etcetera. We know that she has already worked on some issues during previous therapy, and the therapist may wish to check whether these areas remain problematic. The therapist and Kristen would then make an agreement as to which goals are to be addressed during the proposed duration of therapy (see next section).

Kristen has agreed to come to therapy because of the crisis in her career. She comes putting work-related problems higher on her list of priorities than the wish to address the physical or emotional aspects of her eating disorder. This order of priorities should be acknowledged and accepted, but the therapist may wish to make clear to Kristen that in the process of their joint evaluation of the development and maintenance of Kristen's current difficulties, other priorities may emerge. These will then be reviewed together, alongside Kristen's originally stated priority to focus on her work difficulties, before agreeing on the specific therapeutic goals to be addressed.

This process does not stop the therapist from highlighting goals which might not come spontaneously from the client. For the therapist, in Kristen's case, "bottom line" goals might be to encourage her to achieve some improvement in her current very poor physical state and to help her stay out of the hospital. In addition there will usually be a number of more general goals of therapy, for instance, to achieve some enhancement in Kristen's sense of autonomy and ability to establish positive personal relationships, and to help her derive some pleasure and satisfaction in some aspects of her life. A main aim of this type of therapy is to help the client become more aware and in control of her emotional and behavioral responses to situations, and to encourage her to find alternative coping mechanisms.

It is difficult to predict the course and outcome of therapy from the outset given the extent to which the goals addressed in therapy are dependent on client input. However, Kristen's presentation suggests a number of possible avenues, and most therapists would embark upon the process of working with her with some optimism. The specific changes in terms of coping and day-to-day functioning achieved at the end of therapy would be related to the particular goals that had been discussed and agreed on between Kristen and her therapist.

Timeline for Therapy

This type of therapy is time limited, delivered in blocks of sessions, each ending with a review session. The total number of sessions is not determined at the start of therapy but can be adapted to suit the individual client's needs. Blocks of sessions are interspersed with breaks from therapy to allow time for reflection and consolidation. This fits in with the aim of enhancing autonomy, self-reliance, and responsibility for self. It is important to avoid the development of a dependent relationship on the therapist as this is against the aims and ethos of the therapy. A typical therapy package might look something like this:

Stage 1

- Assessment sessions (minimum of two, spread over 4–5 hours)
- 2-week break

Stage 2

- 5–6 weekly sessions of 1 hour
- Review session
- One-month break

Stage 3

- 5–6 sessions (usually weekly) of 1 hour
- Review session
- One-month break

Stage 4

- 5–6 hour-long sessions (usually every 2 weeks)
- Review session

Stage 5

- Support group and/or 3-monthly individual support sessions
- Two 3-monthly follow-up sessions

This whole package (stages 1 to 5) will in most cases span approximately 12 to 18 months, to include two assessment sessions, around 18 individual therapy sessions, three review sessions, and five individual support sessions.

Case Conceptualization

It is essential in the formulation of the difficulties that Kristen brings to therapy to focus on her strengths as a way forward. We know that Kristen works hard, can be committed and determined, and from the background information she gives we get a sense of a tremendous perceived pressure to live up to expectations. Kristen seems to have played the role of receptacle for her parents' wishes and aspirations. This role has been increasingly impossible to fulfill given her parents' protracted battling with each other, her mother's need for support in dealing with Kristen's brother Peter, and Kristen's growing conflict between her tentative sense of her own needs and wishes and the effect that the expression of these has on those closest to her. She has been perceived as the "good" grandchild by a powerful maternal grandmother. Kristen indicates that she has acquired a need to do things right, not to displease, and to be good at all she does.

In terms of personality traits, we know that Kristen is accommodating to others and has a tendency to minimize the importance of her own needs. She glosses over or minimizes her own distress and difficulty, and has a tendency to be self-critical and self-doubting. Her general behavior seems to conform to an all-or-nothing pattern—she has a tendency to either throw herself into something full-time (e.g., studying, partying) or to withdraw. If she cannot be good, pleasing, and successful, it is as if she cannot continue in relationships. This all-or-nothing thinking is also evident in her presenting crisis in terms of her work, which she experiences as catastrophic. She works in advertising, a highly stressful environment, and is experiencing increasing conflict at work that she is not managing well. Her old coping strategy of "slapping on a smile" does not seem as available to her as a solution as it has in the past. At presentations, she is highly anxious, confused, out of control with her eating behavior, and failing to keep on top of her work commitments.

The Therapeutic Relationship

The Therapeutic Bond

The therapeutic relationship is characterized by respect and acceptance. Although Kristen is attending the sessions because she needs help with her problems, it is made clear that the therapist's role is to help her address her own difficulties by working together, rather than by the therapist having the answers. The relationship is not one where dependence is encouraged; the constant focus is on enhancing Kristen's sense of autonomy and self-reliance. In this context, self-disclosure on the part of the therapist is not appropriate. The relationship must also be characterized by trust and reliability. Kristen and the therapist will make a clear agreement about times and dates to meet. This negotiation is done at the start of each block of treatment. There will not be endless flexibility on the part of the therapist, but where possible, particularly difficult times for Kristen would, of course, be avoided. Once agreed, the time is Kristen's time, and she will be encouraged to take responsibility for using it.

Over-flexibility on the part of the therapist can give the message that the eating disorder, and other difficulties that Kristen may bring, are not particularly important, and that it is acceptable for attempts to address these to take second place to other priorities and demands.

The therapeutic relationship is therefore one with clear boundaries. The boundaries are present in terms of practical arrangements but also in the nature of the therapist-client interaction. Part of the function of the therapy is to enhance a sense of positive separateness in the client, and the availability of the therapist to the client will have clear limits. The therapist is available to Kristen at the prearranged times, and in the event of crises in between sessions she will be encouraged to use a number of strategies that will have been discussed in advance. These may include the use of written material prepared by the therapist and Kristen together, accessing her own social support network or, if necessary, accessing other emergency services.

It is in many cases clear that past experiences or habitual patterns of behavior may impinge on the therapeutic relationship. This can happen both in terms of how the client relates to the therapist, but also in terms of the responses the client's behavior and presentation evoke in the therapist. Such a situation can be openly acknowledged and discussed, bringing transference and countertransference issues deliberately into the dialogue, again to further the process of self-understanding in the client.

Roles in the Therapeutic Relationship

The roles of the therapist and Kristen in this model of treatment are those of collaborators, with a shared focus. This is a role that some clients seeking therapy initially feel uncomfortable with or unable to accept. In order to facilitate this way of working, the therapist will need to explicitly set out the basic tenets upon which the working relationship is based. The therapist will rarely issue instructions, but will inform, reflect, and advise where appropriate. The two members of the dyad bring different perspectives and knowledge to the shared task of addressing Kristen's difficulties. The therapist's expectations of Kristen will be that once she has agreed to enter into an agreement to meet regularly to work on personal issues, she will do precisely that. The "work" that the client is able to take on will be tremendously variable, and is expected to change during the course of the therapeutic process. The therapist will be able to adapt her own expectations of the client according to what is manageable at any one time. It is possible, in clients who have lost an ability to take care of themselves, for the therapist to be directive in matters concerning health and safety. It should be made clear that the therapist will act in this way for a period of time until the client feels more able to accept some of the responsibility for making her own choices.

Treatment Implementation and Outcome

Techniques and Methods of Working

There is in theory a wide range of possible techniques and types of intervention that can be used in therapy. The main tasks of the therapist and client are fourfold: to explore, to understand, to accept, and to experiment. It is appropriate to use whatever strategies and techniques might assist in accomplishing these four steps. In practice, certain types of techniques will lend themselves more to one of these steps than another. For example, in the exploration stages, the use of genograms, life journeys, and diaries may all help in structuring the process of gathering together relevant pieces of the person's life story, past and current. Understanding and accepting can be worked on through reflective listening, art therapy, psychoeducation, cognitive analytic techniques (Ryle, 1990), and many more. These tasks center around identifying and making personal sense of behavioral and emotional responses, and enabling the client to accept and tolerate different aspects of their experience. The experimental task is one where alternative responses can be explored, and again, there is a range of different possible interventions including cognitive behavioral, problem solving, and solution focused strategies. Out-of-session work would always be encouraged but not necessarily in the form of a formal homework task.

The therapist should always work with at least one other colleague (see section on medical and nutritional issues below), but may also work with additional colleagues as appropriate. For example, in Kristen's case, depending on her identified goals for treatment, some relaxation sessions with a colleague may prove beneficial. One or more sessions with a dietitian around gradually adjusting her diet in a way that seems manageable may also be indicated. We know that she has a set eating pattern regarding food intake, avoiding eating during the day and ending with evening binges. A dietitian may be able to help Kristen plan to adjust the pattern and content of her diet in small, acceptable steps. Kristen may also wish to involve significant others in her therapy, in which case it may be appropriate to involve a colleague as co-therapist, or to separately address a specific relationship or family issue with the relevant others present.

Clearly, access to such colleagues will very much depend on the setting within which the therapist is working, with a multidisciplinary team offering most potential for a wider range of types of input. Where a number of colleagues are involved, it goes without saying that communication must be open, clear, and complete, and that all members of the team must share the same treatment ethos. In reality, the specific combination of techniques and approaches used with any one client will be individually tailored and will reflect individual differences in communication style and psychological functioning. The main structure and the broad tasks of therapy, however, are fixed.

Using the therapy schedule outlined above, Kristen's sessions with the therapist might proceed along the following lines: The assessment sessions (spread over a minimum of two attendances in consecutive weeks) will tend to be longer than subsequent therapy sessions. Some people are unable to tolerate lengthy sessions, and in these cases it may be better to have a number of shorter sessions. Additional aims at this stage are to clarify what has prompted Kristen to seek therapy at this particular time, the route by which the referral has come, and Kristen's expectations of or wishes for therapy. The therapist should inform her of the general aims and style of working, and must make clear if there are any particular circumstances where the therapist would feel unable to continue with outpatient therapy, for example, weight or potassium levels dropping below a certain level. These assessment sessions should also be used to conduct the mental state examination and risk assessment, to draw up the time lines, and to conduct the Eating Disorder Examination. (See Assessment sections 1, 2, and 4 above.) Finally, Kristen should be asked about any existing support in terms of relationships with friends, colleagues, or family members. She should be encouraged to let at least one other person know that she is entering therapy, and where possible to draw on support that might be available outside the sessions. The therapist needs to assess the extent of any external support available as this may influence the final choice of issues to be worked on. In general, between 4 and 5 hours over two or more attendances should suffice to cover this material.

Following this there will be a 2-week break. In some instances, a client may disclose particularly distressing or previously undisclosed events during the assessment sessions. If this is followed by a break, it can be very difficult for individuals who may worry that they should not have spoken about the things that they did. The therapist has a responsibility to ensure that Kristen is aware in advance that there will be a 2-week break, and to take immediate action if she considers that Kristen's safety may be endangered through self-harm or suicidal thoughts and actions subsequent to any disclosures. While this will be a rare occurrence, it is nevertheless essential that the therapist is aware of the potential impact of recounting one's life story. It can often be helpful to have some prearranged telephone contact during this 2-week period.

Kristen's task during this break is to look at her copies of the two time lines, to reflect whether anything has been omitted, and to begin the process of thinking about the relationship between the two. During this period the therapist will send Kristen a letter setting out a proposed initial formulation of her current difficulties based on their discussions. Kristen is invited to change or rewrite anything that does not seem right. The formulation will include reference to developmental issues and systemic context.

During the initial block of sessions, Kristen and the therapist will explore further the personal relevance of events on the time lines, begin to develop a list of priorities to work on (suggestions can be made by both), and conduct the assessment of motivation and readiness to change, identifying the benefits and losses of changing the eating disorder behaviors. (See Assessment section 5 above.) If a meeting is to take place with one or more family members this should occur within this initial block. Kristen's weight at presentation is low, and if she continues to lose weight during this period, she should be reminded that it is her responsibility to keep her weight at least stable, and offered support and advice to enable her to do this. It is important that discussions around food and diet are not allowed to take up too much of the session.

In the subsequent review session, Kristen and the therapist review and revise the initial formulation of her difficulties and construct a list of priorities for further work. These priorities may or may not be related to weight, eating, or weight control strategies, but in Kristen's case they probably would continue to include a focus on restoring her physical health. The formulation will include the importance of earlier experiences on the development of Kristen's personal style and will be amended to be expressed in her own words. It will offer a means for understanding the development and maintenance of her eating disorder, and will aim to identify major perpetuating factors. Kristen can be helped to understand why she may have adopted the coping strategies that she has, but also that there may be alternative, less self-destructive strategies. The process of understanding these links is in itself empowering, as current difficulties are seen as related to personal logic, which can be reconsidered and redirected, and as attempts to resolve or alleviate problems rather than as an illness or a failure to manage life stresses.

A 1-month break follows this review session. Here again, the aim is to allow Kristen to reflect on what she and the therapist have discussed so far. It is often helpful at this stage, having addressed the issues of motivation and readiness for change, and having clarified the nature and extent of the eating disturbance, to give clients, where appropriate, a self-help guide to read and try. Through this the therapist's aim of enhancing client self-reliance and personal control can be furthered. For people with bulimia nervosa and binge-eating behaviors, books by Schmidt and Treasure (1993), Fairburn (1995), and Cooper (1993) are recommended. For those with anorexia nervosa, there is less evidence that self-help books are effective, but Crisp, Joughin, Halek, and Bowyer (1996) and Treasure (1997) are good examples of straightforward texts offering information and suggestions. As in the previous break, the therapist will need to use her clinical judgment regarding support. Wherever possible Kristen should be encouraged to use her own support networks. However, some contact by telephone or letter may be appropriate.

By the start of the second block of sessions, Kristen and the therapist will already have done quite a lot of work, and in many cases the client will already report a change in her behaviors, even though these may not have been an explicit focus for intervention. However, the formal business of this part of the therapy is to work on one or more of the agreed priorities. It is acceptable to work on one at a time, or more than one simultaneously. This will depend on Kristen's and the therapist's appraisal of the nature and difficulty of the task. This stage requires the greatest degree of versatility on the part of the therapist, who will ideally feel comfortable using a range of different therapeutic techniques and interventions. The priorities identified may vary considerably, and as has been suggested in Kristen's case might, for example, include reducing her vomiting; finding alternative ways of identifying and dealing with stressful situations at work; working on the impact of her experience of being raped; addressing her guilty feelings around her stillborn sister. The therapist's role is to guide her to an issue or a task that can realistically be addressed in an agreed time frame. The above examples would require the therapist and the client to work together in different ways. The key point here is that there is an assumption that enabling someone to successfully deal with something they have hitherto been struggling with, will have a "knock-on effect," in that they will be more likely to rely on growing self-confidence and self-reliance in continuing to address difficulties. The work with the therapist is, therefore, seen as a starting point rather than as a solution to all problems.

The second review session is for an evaluation of progress with regard to any goals that have been worked on, to identify particular hindrances or sticking points that may need more attention, and to identify positive changes. This is followed by a further 1-month break to reflect upon and consolidate progress, and to begin to work towards achieving goals without the therapist's more direct input.

If necessary Kristen might be offered a further 5 to 6 sessions. Sessions can now usually be more widely spaced. This block of sessions begins with a review of progress, motivation to continue to work with the therapist, and the putting together of a proposed agenda for the remaining meetings. Again, the therapist's use of interventions and techniques will tend to depend on the agreed focus for work. During this stage, the therapist will continually reinforce Kristen's attempts to understand and alter her responses, even if she is not always successful in achieving her goals. It is almost always possible to identify strengths and successes, however small, that should be made explicit. The final review session marks the end of the more "intensive" individual input. Kristen and the therapist will jointly make a decision on how to proceed from this point. Typically this might be to invite her to join a support group or to continue for monthly individual support sessions for a period of 3 months or so. It is quite possible that there may still be large and relevant pieces of work that have not been addressed in therapy. By this stage, Kirsten may be able to continue to work on such issues herself, and the review session can be used to identify which these might be. Following group attendance or the monthly support sessions, there should ideally be at least two 3-month follow-up sessions.

Medical and Nutritional Issues

Kristen is low weight, with a BMI of just over 17 and a half. She is not eating well and is engaging in excessive exercising and self-induced vomiting. Physically she is very unwell due to the conse-quences of these behaviors. Psychologically she is struggling, with poor concentration, low energy, and possibly some depression. Her physical ill-health and psychological state are likely to be adversely affecting each other.

In addition, Kristen has had an eating disorder since her teens, with past and current amennorhoea. This will likely increase her risk for osteoporosis and it might be advisable to arrange for a bone scan. The results of such an investigation not only allow for a more complete consideration of Kristen's current and future health needs, but can also act as a powerful motivator for the client to attempt to change behaviors. We know that Kristen has evidence of other longer term consequences of her eating disorder in the form of dental enamel erosion. There may well be other effects that require investi-gation.

Depending on the professional background of the therapist, it may be necessary to arrange and agree on who will be providing medical backup care. It is strongly recommended that this should be done in all cases where the therapist is nonmedically trained. In most situations this can be the client's family physician. In Kristen's case, the therapist should clearly and objectively explain the potential dangers of Kristen's behaviors and inform her of the associated need to monitor her physical well-being. She should be made aware of her lab test results, and their significance should be explained.

Kristen should be told that the therapist will need to work both in collaboration with her and her primary care physician, and check that this is acceptable. If not, an alternative source for medical backup should be sought. Kristen will need to visit her physician on a regular basis for blood tests in view of her vomiting, and for physical checks. The therapist's responsibility is to ensure that Kristen is informed and understands the reason for this, and to encourage her to take responsibility for arranging to visit her physician. In clients where weight loss is an issue, there should also be a clear agreement about who (other than the client) will monitor weight. Some clients prefer to be weighed by a nurse at their physician's clinic, whereas others may prefer the therapist to do this. Agreements regarding the monitoring of the client's physical state should be made early on, and will be related to the therapeutic goal of encouraging the client to achieve some improvement in her physical well-being.

Potential Pitfalls

In Kristen's case, as in any other, there may be a number of potential pitfalls. Unforeseen situations or events not uncommonly alter or influence the direction of therapy. The treatment model set out in this chapter, because of its flexibility and responsiveness to what the client brings, should be able to accommodate many unpredicted events. The therapist's task as ever is to look for the positives and to work on the client's strengths. In Kristen's case, predictable difficulties might arise from her ambivalence about attending. She might find it difficult to commit herself because to attend would (and should) mean that she would have to take time off work. She comes fearing that she may lose her job because of her recent performance, which is causing her to panic. She will inevitably be in a dilemma, recognizing that she is not functioning well at work, but frightened of jeopardizing her career. This is potentially a real problem, and it may take Kristen some time to work out how to manage the intolerable anxiety and stress with which she struggles. The therapist may need to be prepared to support Kristen through this, before being able to begin to address the tasks of therapy. Without Kristen's commitment to attending, it will be difficult to make any progress.

A further potential problem, related to the perceived need to hold on to the work situation, is the fact that Kristen has just split up from her partner. She has lost a core personal relationship, is worried about losing her job, and may initially not feel able to lose her eating disorder as well. The two other areas of loss will almost inevitably increase her reliance on her eating disorder. This will need to be acknowledged and explored, with Kristen being able to see and trust that there may be other ways to manage her current difficulties.

Termination and Relapse Prevention

In this model of treatment, termination is not identified as a separate stage of therapy, and the term itself is alien to the style and ethos of the relationship. From the start, the therapist will have worked together with the client to bring out and build on the client's own strengths and inner resources. The therapist is the catalyst and facilitator, whose function is to begin or restart with the client a personal process of development that has been inhibited or become stuck. The relationship itself, and the negotiations, discussions, and work conducted within the relationship, are part of this developmental process. Development is a process of change and growth, with a forward orientation. The notion of termination implies a punctuation, an end. The therapeutic relationship here is seen as a beginning, with the physical presence of the therapist becoming less and less central. From the start of the therapy, the client's sense of autonomy and self-reliance is actively promoted, with the breaks between blocks of sessions and the reduction in frequency of sessions consistent with this aim. The therapist and client together consider and plan the extent of support required following the more intensive stage of therapy, and this can be adapted to suit the individual concerned. Access to a support group over a longer period of time can promote relapse prevention.

Placing some responsibility on the client to assess her own support needs, and continually encouraging her to seek out and obtain support from sources other than the therapist, makes the process of termination of therapy less potent. Of course, it may be difficult for clients and therapists to part, and some sadness or anxiety may be entirely appropriate. However, personal development and empowerment have characterized the relationship, and the work completed in therapy will hopefully continue to be of relevance and use to the client without the need to continue to have direct contact with the therapist.

Mechanisms of Change

So for Kristen, what are the hoped for changes? That she will gain a better understanding of how and why she has developed a particular pattern of responses to conflict, stress, and difficult emotions. That she will be able to reflect on and accept these responses as valid but not unchangeable. That she will discover a capacity in herself to make personal choices that will enhance her sense of well-being, satisfaction, and enjoyment in life. It would be hoped that this would translate into a minimization or cessation of the self-destructive behaviors associated with the eating disorder, with consequent improvement in physical health, and a reduction in the characteristic unaccepting and self-undermining cognitions evident at presentation. The precise mechanisms of change will depend on Kristen's own inner resources, and the strength and vitality of her character. The collaborative process of exploring, understanding, reframing and accepting, and experimenting will hopefully have been a positive, affirmative experience that will enable Kristen to continue to develop and flourish with self-respect and self-acceptance.

ACKNOWLEDGMENT

I would like to thank all my colleagues at the Juniper Centre Eating Disorders Team in Southampton, UK, who have influenced the development of my own thinking and practice, and whose commitment and creativity are, I hope, reflected in this chapter.

REFERENCES

Berryman, J. C., Hargreaves, D., Herbert, M., & Taylor, A. (1991). *Developmental psychology and you*. London: British Psychological Society and Routledge.

Bowen, M. (Ed.). (1978). *Family therapy in clinical practice.* New York: Jason Aronson.

Bowlby, J. (1951). *Maternal care and mental health.* Geneva: World Health Organization. Monograph Series 179.

Cooper, P. J. (1993). *Bulimia nervosa and binge-eating: A self-help guide using cognitive behavioural techniques.* London: Robinson Publishing.

Crisp, A. H., Joughin, N., Halek, C., & Bowyer, C. (1996). *Anorexia nervosa: The wish to change* (2nd ed.). Hove: Psychology Press.

Erikson, E. H. (1965). *Childhood and society.* Harmondsworth: Penguin.

Fairburn, C. (1995). *Overcoming binge eating.* Hove: Psychology Press.

Fairburn, C., & Cooper, Z. (1993). The eating disorder examination (12th ed.). In C. Fairburn & G. T. Wilson (Eds.), *Binge eating: Nature, assessment and treatment* (pp. 317–360). New York: Guilford Press.

Ryle, A. (1990). *Cognitive-analytic therapy: Active participation in change.* Chichester: Wiley.

Schmidt, U., & Treasure, J. (1993). *Getting better bit(e) by bit(e): A survival kit for sufferers of bulimia nervosa and binge eating disorders.* Hove: Psychology Press.

Treasure, J. (1997). *Anorexia nervosa: A survival guide for families, friends, and sufferers.* Hove: Psychology Press.

von Bertalanffy, L. (1968). *General systems theory: Foundations, development, application.* New York: Braziller.

7

Self Psychology Therapy

Susan H. Sands

TREATMENT MODEL

Self psychology is a psychoanalytic theory and, as such, shares with other psychoanalytic theories a belief in intensive, long-term treatment focused on the patient's underlying dynamics as manifested in the transference relationship. The emphasis is on the patient's inner world, not her symptoms nor her external activities. What distinguishes self psychological from other psychoanalytic treatment models can best be discussed in terms of three major concepts: (1) the empathic/introspective stance; (2) the centrality of self experience; and (3) the concept of selfobject experience and selfobject transference (Kohut, 1959, 1971, 1977, 1984; Kohut & Wolf, 1978).

In his earliest paper on self psychology, Heinz Kohut (1959) introduced the "empathic/introspective stance" as the methodology of his new psychology, and, over the past 4 decades, it has remained the cornerstone of self psychological treatment. Empathy is a "tool"—the only tool we have for gathering psychological data about the internal subjective experiences of other people. When we assume the empathic vantage point, we attempt to think and feel ourselves into the inner life of another (Kohut, 1984). Indeed, the empathic introspective stance defines the content and limits of the field of psychoanalytic inquiry (Kohut, 1959). (I will have more to say about empathic responsiveness in the next section.)

A second defining characteristic of self psychology is the centrality of self experience—as opposed to the instinctual drives emphasized by classical analytic theory (Kohut, 1977). A self psychologist focuses on the state of the patient's "self" and seeks to understand which experiences disrupt and which restore or enhance the integrity of her self experience. Two particular dimensions of self experience are critical: *cohesiveness* (versus fragmentation) and *vitality* (versus depletion). In assessing the patient's self-cohesion, we look at how "together" or "solid" as opposed to "fragmented" or "shaky" the patient feels. In tracking the patient's sense of vitality, we try to get a sense of how "energized" or "alive," versus "depleted" or "dead," she feels. We watch for the impact of our therapeutic interventions on the patient's experience of self. For example, does the patient seem stronger and more consolidated following an interpretation, or does she become more depressed or dissociated?

The concept of *selfobject* is a third major feature of self psychology theory and perhaps its most original contribution. Selfobject functions are those which maintain or restore the cohesiveness and vitality of self experience. Kohut first became aware of the need for selfobject functions when he discovered that a certain group of patients, those with narcissistic personality disorders, developed certain characteristic transferences to him. In these transferences, Kohut was experienced as part of the patient's self—that is, he was experienced as supplying functions which were vitally needed by the patient to maintain a sense of self cohesion and vitality. Kohut (1971) first called these transferences "narcissistic transferences" and later (1977) renamed them *selfobject transferences*. The first two selfobject transferences he discovered were termed the *mirror transference*—in which the patient's early needs for confirmation and admiration are mobilized vis-a-vis the therapist—and the *idealizing transference*—in which the patient experiences the need to merge with the calmness and power of an idealized other. Kohut (1984) later added another selfobject transference, the *alterego* or *twinship* transference, in which the patient experiences the need to be "the same as" or "like" the other. Since then, other selfobject needs (and transferences) have been identified, which limited space does not allow me to enumerate.

According to self psychology theory, the self develops through the empathic responsiveness of the caregiving environment—what has come to be known as the selfobject environment (Kohut, 1971, 1977, 1984). The need for others to provide selfobject functions remains throughout life: selfobject responsiveness is as crucial for our emotional life as oxygen is for our physiological life. The developmental push in self psychology is not toward complete autonomy but, rather, toward more *mature* selfobject connections. If all goes well in one's development, one's selfobject needs become less urgent and less absolute, and there is a widening arc of persons and activities to which one can turn to restore one's emotional balance. Indeed, late in his life, Kohut (1984) defined health as the "efficient use of selfobjects."

The basis of self psychological treatment is the working through of the *selfobject transferences*. A selfobject transference is one in which the patient's early, developmental needs for selfobject responsiveness, which have been split off and retained in archaic form due to environmental failure, are remobilized and experienced in relation to the therapist. In a selfobject transference, the therapist is experienced as the longed-for object, a "new" object, as it were, as opposed to an "old," traumatogenic object (Stolorow, Brandchaft, & Atwood, 1987). Self psychology, while never denying the existence of the repetitive transference, has focused much, much more on the developmental, selfobject dimension. It is particularly through disruptions in the empathic connection between therapist and patient—when the patient feels hurt or misunderstood by the therapist—that we can learn the most about the patient's particular selfobject transference.

According to self psychology theory, psychopathology is caused by repeated empathic failures by the child's caregivers to which the child adapts and maladapts. When the child's normal developmental needs and longings are not recognized and responded to (usually because they somehow threaten the caregivers' narcissistic equilibrium), the child is forced to wall off these needs and longings. Development is arrested, and structural deficits ensue. Because of these defects in the internal structures that maintain self-cohesion, self-esteem, vitality, and temporal stability, the child becomes prone to states of fragmentation and depletion. In short, a self disorder develops—with symptoms such as low self-esteem, inability to regulate tension, rage-proneness, shame proneness, depression, hypochondriasis, and excessive needs for admiring or soothing responses from the environment. Addictions (including eating disorders), sexualizations, and other compulsive activities may then be seized upon as emergency measures to strengthen a fragmented and/or depleted self.

The goal of treatment, therefore, is the rehabilitation and strengthening of the self through the patient's acknowledging, accepting, and finally integrating the unfulfilled selfobject needs of childhood (Wolf, 1988). Rather than infantile wishes to be renounced, the childhood longings are seen as legitimate developmental needs which deserve expression and transformation within the therapeutic process.

How does all this apply to eating disorders? I view most eating disorders as self disorders (Sands, 1989; 1991)—that is, disorders which develop due to pervasive disturbance in the empathic interplay between the growing child and the caregiving environment and which are characterized by an inability to maintain the integrity of one's self experience. At some crucial point in development, the child invents a new, restitutive system by which disordered eating patterns, rather than people, are turned to meet selfobject needs, because previous attempts with caregivers have brought disappointment or frustration (Gehrie, 1990; Geist, 1985; Goodsitt, 1985; Kohut, 1977, 1987). Food is, of course, a particularly compelling selfobject substitute, since it is developmentally a first bridge between self and other—the first medium for the transmission of soothing and comfort. By turning to food, the individual tries to circumvent the need for human responsiveness and avoid further disappointment and shame.

The problem with the new restitutive system organized around food or other substances is that it does not "work," because the selfobject functions it provides, while often seductively powerful in the moment, are only temporary. These functions cannot be taken in and transformed into self-structure through the gradual transmuting internalization process. The eating disordered individual remains dependent on using an external agent or action to fill in for missing internal structure. The first goal of treatment, therefore, must be to encourage the patient, through our understanding of her hopes and fears, to give human beings another chance. Once the patient can experience, explore, and understand her longings in relation to another human being, the therapist, rather than to food or eating rituals, she can begin to make her needs and longings and "appetites" her own.

THE THERAPIST'S SKILLS AND ATTRIBUTES

As discussed above, the empathic vantage point is the cornerstone of self psychological technique. The capacity to empathize deeply with our patients is seen as the most crucial therapist skill. According to Stolorow et al. (1987), when we assume the empathic vantage point, we comprehend the experience of others from a perspective that is within, rather than outside of, the patient's own subjective frame of reference. Empathy has to do with the ability to put ourselves in another's shoes. Kohut (1959) offers the example of a very tall man with whom we can empathize only if we imagine ourselves in his shoes, having to, for example, bow our heads as we come through a doorway. As self psychological practitioners, we are trained in how to feel our way into another's experience—in how to be empathically attuned to or how to empathically resonate with another's subjective reality. Empathic inquiry allows the therapist to be tuned in to how it feels to be the *subject* rather than the *target* of the patient's needs, and it thus lends a more collaborative, less adversarial quality to the therapeutic exchange.

Because the concept of empathy is often misunderstood and therefore misused, I would like to point out what empathy isn't. Being empathic is not behaving compliantly or colluding with the patient's behavior; nor is it identifying with the patient's experience, nor being "nice," nor humoring the patient. Nor is it projection: it is not how I would feel if I were in his shoes; it is about understanding how *he* feels in his shoes. The only test of whether one is successfully being empathic is an empirical one: one is in empathic connection with the patient if the therapeutic work continues to deepen.

Of course, other therapist skills and attributes must also come into play. Once the therapist has empathically grasped the patient's experience, the therapist needs to have the intellectual acumen, theoretical understanding, clinical experience, verbal skill, sensitivity, and tact to be able to formulate interpretations which allow the patient to feel deeply understood. These interpretations must be "experience-near" (Kohut, 1959) as opposed to "experience-distant"—that is, they must speak the language of the patient rather than being formulated in abstract or theory-driven language which does not resonate with the patient's subjective experience. Self psychologists are not encouraged to be "neutral," in the sense of distant or "objective" or uninvolved, but, rather, to be warm, friendly, and human and to use the "deepest layers" of their psyches (Kohut, 1977) to resonate with their patients' experience.

THE CASE OF KRISTEN

Assessment, Conceptualization, and Treatment Planning

Assessment

In general, I would want Kristen's story to unfold in a natural way. Much can be learned about the patient's inner world—her deepest fears, longings, dreams, humiliations, etcetera—by observing the ways that the patient herself chooses to reveal herself to us. Having said this, however, I would be curious to learn more about certain areas of Kristen's life. I would be interested in getting a more thorough account of any family history of eating disorder, Kristen's own eating disorder history, weight history, dieting behavior, as well as a more detailed description of her bingeing and purging rituals, internal ideation regarding food, and body image. Because of the high coincidence of eating disorders and depression, I would particularly want to know about depressive illness in close family relatives. I would want to know more about the extent of Kristen's depression and particularly whether she has any suicidal ideation. Moreover, because of the high coincidence of eating disorders and sexual abuse, I would inquire (not right away but at some point) about childhood sexual abuse or sexual inappropriateness—particularly given Kristen's severely bulimic response to the rape at age 19, which could suggest a triggering of earlier sexual trauma.

I would not typically use any assessment tools. If I were particularly puzzled by the diagnostic picture—for example, if I suspected some kind of organicity—I might refer out for psychological testing. I use my knowledge of the various assessment tools—particularly those scales measuring severity of eating disorder, depression, or dissociation—mainly as useful guides for me to use in exploring the patient's subjective experience.

The particular kind of assessment that flows directly from a self psychological approach is an ongoing evaluation of the state of Kristen's self experience. As suggested above, I would be observing Kristen's sense of self, as manifested in her thinking, affect, and behavior, in terms of the degree of its cohesiveness (versus fragmentation) and the degree of vitality (versus depletion). I would also be observing whether she seems to be passing through various self states and how flexible or rigid the boundaries between these self states might be. I would be asking whether there is a selfobject transference and, if so, what? Through my interactions with her, I would try to get a sense of how easily Kristen's sense of self cohesion and vitality is disrupted and how she responds to misunderstandings, slights, or insults—that is, how easily she becomes narcissistically injured. Concomitantly, I would be observing how quickly she can "regroup" and restore her sense of self cohesion and/or vitality and how well she can work with me in "repairing" a rupture in the therapeutic bond. It is particularly through these empathic ruptures—that is, the ways in which the patient feels emotionally injured and retraumatized by the therapist—that I can learn the most about Kristen's specific selfobject needs. All this would give me a sense of the solidity of Kristen's self-organization—in other words, whether she could be thought of as having a mild, moderate, or severe self disorder.

I would also want to know whether Kristen moves into alternative self states while she is bingeing or purging or exercising. Does she sense herself to be in a distinct "bulimic self state" with its own feelings, needs, perceptions, and behaviors (Sands, 1991)? Are there certain affect states which are particularly intolerable and disruptive and which lead her to use eating behaviors to regulate herself? How are the bingeing and purging rituals experienced? For example, is the food unconsciously regarded as an idealized and omnipotent selfobject providing strength and comfort, or does it seem to be used in a more punishing way, or does it help her to dissociate and "numb out" painful affect states? Through these kinds of questions, I would try to get more of a sense of what functions Kristen's eating disorder is serving in maintaining and restoring her emotional equilibrium.

Therapeutic Goals

From a self psychological point of view, the treatment of the eating disorder would be viewed as simply one part of the treatment of Kristen's self disorder. I would not be looking only for symptomatic change but for underlying structural change as well. The primary and overarching goal of therapy, as mentioned earlier, is the strengthening of the patient's self through the patient's acknowledging, accepting, and finally integrating the unfulfilled selfobject longings of childhood.

The consolidation of Kristen's self experience will lead to a number of secondary goals—that is, new psychological skills—such as an increased ability to regulate her tension and affect states, maintain her sense of self-esteem, vitality, ambition, agency, inspiration, and continuity in time and space, and to have meaningful and mutual relationships. With the strengthening of her self and increased ability to regulate her emotional stability, we should expect to see a decrease (though certainly not a steady one) in her need for her eating disorder.

Given Kristen's considerable abilities, talents, and strengths and current desperation and desire for help, I can imagine a good prognosis for her. But I would not presume to chart her course for her. More specific behavioral goals must be decided upon (or, rather, groped toward) by Kristen herself, because, if they are not really "hers," she will somehow defeat them. How far she can go towards health will depend not only on Kristen's strengths and abilities to make good use of the therapeutic relationship, be honest about herself, and persevere during difficult times; it will also depend upon my ability to develop a solid, trusting, working relationship with her, to interpret her fears and protective strategies, to tolerate experiencing in myself her intolerable affects, and to allow a full selfobject transference to develop. Without having experienced a therapeutic relationship with Kristen, it is impossible for me to predict how well we could work together. For these reasons, long-term outcome is hard to even speculate about at this time.

Timeline for Therapy

I could not visualize a timeline for therapy, knowing as little as I do about Kristen's inner world. Even after coming to know Kristen better, I would still want to keep the timeline open, since it is impossible to accurately predict how her underlying psychopathology or the transference relationship will unfold. Given Kristen's level of distress and the severity of her eating disorder, I would want to see her as frequently as possible—ideally 3 times per week. The frequency, of course, would depend on Kristen's interest and availability; she appears to have the financial resources. I could speculate that she will not initially be open to coming in multiple times a week because of her pressing and enduring need to appear successful, "normal," and without need and that she will become open to the idea of greater frequency only after she has done much work on her fears of needing and depending on me.

Case Conceptualization

Kristen presents in a way typical for many patients who have self disorders combined with eating disorders—anxious but smiling and seemingly impervious to her physical and psychological needs and desires. She is aware of anxiety but not distinct feelings. She knows very little about her actual wishes or "appetites." Most of her energy goes toward creating an appearance of perfection; her genuine emotional and physical needs and desires are disowned. With an omnipotent disregard for her limitations, she takes on too much work at her job and is unable to share the workload, and she gets in trouble with coworkers and clients because she is as critical and demanding with them as she is with herself.

Kristen's symptoms are all attempts by the patient *to rid herself of the experience of need for others.* This particular personality organization has been referred to as a "vertical split" by Kohut (1971, 1977), which is similar to what Winnicott (1965) called "false self." Because Kristen's normal developmental needs for comfort, protection, admiration, and other selfobject responsiveness were not adequately responded to early on, they have been repressed and disavowed, and a vertically split-off, grandiose, omnipotent sector of her personality has developed (in compliance with her caretakers' wishes) to defend against the emptiness and bereftness she feels due to the segregation of her genuine longings. She is locked in an omnipotent, closed system, invested in her own self-sufficiency and perfection rather than in other people. The eating disorder helps maintain her self-sufficiency. Her eating disorder can thus be conceptualized as a "selfobject substitute" (Kohut, 1977). Food is a reliable selfobject over which she has omnipotent control.

The omnipotent defense makes a virtue out of necessity. No one was there to help, so Kristen did it for herself. Kristen's parents ignored her needs as a child, and, today, she still has no social support system. In an insidious role reversal, Kristen was asked to provide selfobject functions for her caretakers—that is, to be a selfobject rather than a self—as can be deduced from her mother's calling Kristen repeatedly regarding her brother's crises.

Kristen is consciously identified with the vertically split-off grandiose sector of her personality—the false, pleasing, perfectionistic self which has grown up in compliance with the narcissistic needs of her parents. At the same time, she can express through her bulimic symptomatology the disavowed, archaic developmental longings which are at odds with her ordinary self experience (Sands, 1991). Her eating disorder expresses (as well as defends against) her unacceptable "rebel needs."

Her eating disorder therefore needs to be conceptualized not simply as a symptom, but as the behavioral component of a whole sector of self experience—a separate self state with its own set of needs, feelings, perceptions, identity, and behavior (Sands, 1991). As Kristen's therapist, it is crucial that I recognize the healthy needs and longings embedded in her bulimic symptomatology. If I fail to show Kristen that I recognize the value of her bulimic self state, I will lose her, for Kristen unconsciously recognizes that her bulimic part is her salvation as well as her downfall and will fiercely defend it.

I would also like to point to the *relational* functions of her particular personality organization. When Kristen goes to herself to soothe herself all by herself, she is, in addition to trying to mute her anxiety, also trying to regulate and maintain relationship by "dissociatively cleansing" (Sands, 1994) herself of any needs or affects which might offend others. When Kristen as a child turned to autonomous comfort strategies, her caretakers were "excused" from being asked to meet her needs and failing, and Kristen was protected from her disappointment and rage at their failure to respond (as well as her own fears of destroying them). Kristen was saying, in essence, "Since I don't have needs, you are not failing to meet them." Her caretakers were shored up and preserved as idealizable—enough in her mind to provide some modicum of selfobject responsiveness.

I would view Kristen as having a moderately severe self disorder. The case material shows she has serious problems with affect regulation and self-esteem regulation and that she turns to her eating disorders—both bulimia and restriction—for help in calming herself in times of crisis or other narcissistic vulnerability. She did not have powerful idealized figures with whom she could merge and receive comfort and thereby, over time, internalize self-soothing functions.

She clearly also has serious deficits along the mirroring line of development. Her normal developmental needs to be recognized and admired were not adequately responded to by her parents. The extent of her parents' neglect is highlighted by their "not noticing" Kristen's substantial weight loss during her junior year in high school or that she was skipping breakfast and dinner. As in so many families of patients with eating disorders, it appears that her parents mirrored her more for a pleasing, successful, and false self presentation than for who she uniquely was. There seems to have been a predominant focus on appearances in Kristen's family (and her mother's family). Kristen, because of her natural endowments, was able to gratify her parents with her beauty, "politeness," and accomplishments—ballet, newspaper, track team, homecoming court. (The plight of Kristen's brother, Peter, reveals what happens to those who are not pleasing. He is considered to have brought shame to the family.) Kristen's parents' mirroring of a *fragment* of herself—her appearance and accomplishments—is itself fragmentation-producing (Kohut, 1971). Moreover, the distorted mirroring of little girls' exhibitionism in the broader culture, particularly the selective focus on physical appearance and sexual attractiveness, can encourage females like Kristen to use the body as a central pathway for expressing exhibitionistic concerns later on (Sands, 1989).

Kristen's trauma is the trauma of betrayal. Indeed, psychic trauma has been defined by Brothers (1995) as the betrayal of trust in the selfobject relationships on which selfhood depends. An event is traumatic when its *meaning* is such that it so shatters selfobject fantasies that self-restitution is impossible. A number of events in Kristen's life fall into this category: her father's business being destroyed by a fire when Kristen was 8 years old (while not the father's fault, it still undermines his strong, idealized status in her young psyche); the revelation of her father's affair when she was a freshman in high school; the rape by a senior in her sorority's "brother" fraternity at age 19, and, finally, her discovery of her fiancé's affair. It goes without saying that Kristen's discovery of Joe's having an affair is made even more traumatic by the fact that her father did the same a decade earlier, an event which catalyzed the breakup of the family. In all these cases, someone who was seen as trustworthy is proved otherwise, Kristen's selfobject fantasies are shattered, and the bottom falls out. Kristen responds to the first two betrayals—the destruction of her father's business and his affair—by working harder and becoming more successful in the world; in short, she turns to herself (her grandiose self-sufficiency) and away from her family to empower and shore up her weakened self. According to Brothers (1995), she increases trust in herself. In the second two instances of traumatic betrayal, increasing her successful performance in the world is not enough, and she turns to her eating disorder with a vengeance. She needs a more powerful and readily available way to regulate her overwhelming affect and fragmenting self experience.

I would add that I think Kristen is suffering from a great deal of "survivor guilt"—a problem for so many patients with eating disorders (Friedman, 1985). Since survivor guilt is not a uniquely self psychological concept, I will discuss it only briefly. The most obvious factor is the stillbirth of an older sister 1 year before Kristen's birth. In addition, Kristen appears to have been the most talented and successful member of the family. Her brother, Peter, "messes up"; her father loses his business and destroys the family by having an affair; her mother has given up social prominence and a college career to marry a man of a lower social class; her parents are constantly battling and cannot resolve their difficulties. Kristen may unconsciously feel that she has "too much," that her success has hurt the family, and that she can maintain her loyalty and connection to the members of her family only by unconsciously "messing up" in some way.

Kristen has many strengths. She is blessed with native intelligence, physical attractiveness, and many talents, including dancing, music, and sports. In addition, she is capable of high functioning—hard work, competence, mastery, persistence, creativity, and productivity.

She appears to have many social skills and to be capable of at least superficial social acceptance and popularity. These strengths should serve her well in the therapeutic process, which takes a great deal of hard work and persistence.

The Therapeutic Relationship

The Therapeutic Bond

The therapeutic bond is viewed as the primary vehicle of change in self psychology theory. It is via the working through of the selfobject transference or transferences that structural change occurs. The healing process will begin when Kristen starts to remobilize her sequestered, early developmental needs and longings within the transference relationship. Her relational needs, which have existed only in rudimentary, "potential" form, can then become articulated, developed, and experienced fully in relation to me as the wished-for object. This process cannot begin, of course, until some semblance of safety and trust has been established, and Kristen can dare to hope that her most vulnerable, early need states can finally be brought into relationship. Her longings will be alternately experienced and resisted, and it is this wrenching conflict around approaching the early relational needs which accounts for much of the most difficult work in self psychological treatment. If Kristen's selfobject longing are carefully understood and interpreted within the therapeutic relationship, they will over time become integrated into her central self experience.

An important aspect of transference analysis is the analysis of disruptions of the "empathic bond" between therapist and patient. This process has been conceptualized in self psychological theory as the "disruption-restoration process" (Kohut, 1971, 1977, Wolf, 1988). The process begins with my empathic immersion in Kristen's subjective experience. My empathic understanding and "optimal responsiveness" (Bacal, 1985) create trust and safety, and an empathic bond develops between us. At the same time, I need to be interpreting Kristen's anxieties about revealing her selfobject longings—for fear that she will receive the same traumatizing responses she got as a child. This fear is known in self psychology as the "fear of retraumatization." Through my empathizing with and interpreting Kristen's needs and fears, a selfobject transference slowly develops. My job is to *not interfere* with the unfolding of the transference but, rather, to let myself be experienced as a selfobject providing vitally needed functions. At some point, usually sooner rather than later, I will not respond optimally to Kristen (from Kristen's point of view), Kristen will feel injured, and the empathic bond between us will become disrupted. This is often called an "empathic break." Kristen will regress to more archaic modes of functioning; there may be an upsurge of symptoms, undoubtedly an intensification of her eating disorder. At this point, it will be my responsibility to recognize that I have disrupted Kristen's equilibrium, and together she and I will seek to understand the specifics of the interaction which disrupted her—what I said or did, the meaning of the events, and what they trigger from her past. I must also take responsibility for my part in the disruption, not in a guilty or apologetic way, but simply with a genuine acknowledgment of my contribution. The therapist's taking responsibility—an all-too-infrequent occurrence in classical psychoanalysis—typically and quite dramatically leads to increased trust and respect for the therapist. In this way—sometimes after a long time and much discussion—the empathic bond is "repaired," leading in turn to a deeper unfolding of the selfobject transference.

It is my belief (Sands, 1991) that many patients with addictive behaviors such as eating disorders have a more difficult time developing a selfobject transference than those without addictive disorders. Because their archaic selfobject needs have not only been repressed or split off but have been *detoured* into nonhuman addictive strategies, they are less available to fuel a selfobject transference. Their transference is to the addictive activity rather than to a human being. What this means, in my opinion, is that Kristen will probably have to first experience and understand her early, unmet needs vis-a-vis her transference to the food and process of eating and then, only later, begin to shift her selfobject transference from the food or eating behaviors onto me. (I will have more to say about this process in the next section.)

I think most self psychologists would agree that self disclosure should be kept to a minimum. Like any psychoanalytic practitioner, I believe that therapist self-disclosure too often provides relief for the therapist, not the patient, and can actually get in the way of the patient's inner exploration by urging the patient to attend to the therapist's experience. On the other hand, I believe there are certain times when it would be a serious mistake to *not* self disclose. One example would be if I found myself acting out my countertransference with Kristen in a destructive fashion, and I needed to take responsibility for my mistake. Another would be if we became engaged in an enactment, and I sensed a great deal of unconscious mutual influence, and I chose to disclose the nature of my own experience in the hopes that it could illuminate an important but unexplored realm of her experience.

It is the therapist's job to keep firm boundaries in order to maintain a strong "container" for the analytic work. Kristen's experience is of being out of control of her feelings; she feels unbounded and uncontained and is desperately seeking to regulate herself through bingeing and purging. My firm boundaries, reliability, and accurate empathy create the safety and containment which make possible the unfolding of the selfobject transference which, in turn, allows her to regress, and come to know the disowned parts of herself and, eventually, to develop new psychological skills. If Kristen's actions became harmful or dangerous for her, for me, or for someone else, I might decide that limit-setting would be the most empathic response. Limit-setting can be a crucial part of providing appropriate containment.

Roles in the Therapeutic Relationship

As already discussed, the central role of the therapist is that of empathic inquiry. The therapist's empathic activity may for conceptual purposes be broken down into two different activities— understanding and explaining (Ornstein & Ornstein, 1985) —although in actual practice they are intermixed. Understanding describes "staying with" the patient's experience without trying to make sense of it, while explaining pertains to the placing of the understanding into an interpretive, developmental-genetic context.

In working with Kristen, I will need to remain "neutral" enough to allow her to utilize me as a transference figure—that is, one who can provide the kind of selfobject experiences she needs. (The selfobject dimension is but one pole of the transference, of course; the other pole is the repetitive transference, in which I am experienced as a traumatogenic object from the past; Stolorow et al., 1987.) As discussed earlier, it is also part of my role to be warm, human, and interpersonally responsive. The extent of my activity will depend, of course, on Kristen's particular needs, the phase of treatment, etcetera. I think the only expectation I would have of Kristen in her role of patient is for her to try to say whatever comes to mind, observe certain boundaries, and to try to be honest.

Self psychology therapy is essentially a collaborative process, in which patient and therapist work together to illuminate and transform the patient's subjective universe. I see therapeutic "truth" not as something which is uncovered but something that is "articulated" (Stolorow et al., 1987) by patient and therapist together. I will be constantly testing my understanding of Kristen's communication by playing it back, then correcting or fine-tuning it. Is it like this? I will ask. No? Then like this? Oh, I see, more like this. And so on. In this way, Kristen and I will negotiate an understanding of her life narrative.

Self psychological treatment is also an intersubjective process. Patient and therapist are locked in a system of "reciprocal, mutual influence" (Stolorow et al., 1987), in which each constantly affects and is affected by the other. Kristen and I are both full participants in and cocreators of the unfolding transference/countertransference drama which illuminates Kristen's inner experience. I need to keep open a space inside myself in which to "receive" and process Kristen's unformulated affective communications so that Kristen can feel "understood from the inside out" (Sands, 1997). At the same time, I must constantly monitor myself in an attempt to keep my own personal reactions from intruding inappropriately. Such monitoring, however, cannot prevent the kind of profound mutual influence and mixed-upness of patient and therapist which is inevitable in any in-depth psychotherapeutic process. If I do find myself "taken over" by something in Kristen's experience, I will first try to understand it in myself, which may involve getting professional consultation. I may also need to talk about it with Kristen and try to sort it out as best we can, knowing that enactments are often the most powerful routes into crucial, but not yet consciously known, internal domains.

The roles of patient and therapist can thus be described as both symmetrical and asymmetrical. They are symmetrical in that both are adults worthy of respect and consideration, engaged in a collaborative, intersubjective process; they are asymmetrical in that it is the patient's subjectivity, not the therapist's, that is the focus of the work.

Treatment Implementation and Outcome

Techniques and Methods of Working

My basic "technique" in working with Kristen would be standard psychoanalytic technique. As discussed above, Kristen's job is to say what comes to mind, and my job is to empathize with and interpret her communications. The specifics of how I would respond therapeutically are different for every patient, because I am responding to the unique inner world of each patient. In working with a patient with an eating disorder, like Kristen, I do not primarily think of myself working with an "eating-disordered patient" but, rather, with a total human being who happens to have an eating disorder as a primary symptom.

Having said this, I would now like to discuss the ways in which my treatment with Kristen *would* differ slightly due to the fact that she has a serious eating disorder. Most obviously, I would insist on working closely with her internist, so that I feel reassured that her physical health is safeguarded and I can spend my time focusing on her psychological issues. I might also choose to work with a nutritionist. (I will have more to say about the medical and nutritional issues in the next section.) It is unlikely that I would want to involve significant others in Kristen's treatment, since the consistency and inviolability of the therapeutic container is of paramount concern in my model of treatment. As discussed earlier, the safety of the empathic connection is what makes possible the mobilization of and working through of the selfobject transferences.

I do not give homework, because I prefer to keep the work "in the room," within the container of the therapeutic bond, and because it conflicts with my role as one who understand and explains. If I were to give Kristen homework, I would be moving into a more didactic role, and the transference implications would be enormous. I would be setting up a situation in which Kristen, by doing or not doing her homework, would either be complying with or defying me. While this dilemma could certainly be interpreted, it would also distract us from our primary therapeutic endeavor, which is the illumination and transformation of Kristen's subjective world. On the other hand, having myself been trained in cognitive behavioral treatment, I will often share certain useful behavioral ideas in a very low-key and nondirective way. For example, I might tell Kristen that some people find it useful to keep eating records so that they can learn more about their bingeing and purging routines and what precedes and follows them. Or I might share what research on eating disorders (and famine) has shown about how eating normal, regular meals interrupts the deprivation/binge cycle: I might tell her that the best defense against binge eating is to eat. After sharing this kind of information, I would then leave it up to Kristen to decide how to use it.

As discussed above, it is my belief (Sands, 1991) that patients with eating disorders have a more difficult time developing a selfobject transference than many other patients, which means that I would work with Kristen using a slightly modified theoretical framework and slightly modified technique. The archaic selfobject needs of the eating disordered patient—like those of other patients with addictive problems—are not only repressed or split off; they have been *detoured* into disordered eating behaviors and thus are less available to fuel a selfobject transference. I believe this is one reason why patients with eating disorders are so often described anecdotally by clinicians as less "accessible" than other patients. The initial "transference" of patients with eating disorders is to the food or eating activity; the therapist is not looked to as a transference figure. The patient's walled-off, early developmental needs can thus remain sequestered indefinitely if the therapist does not know what to look for or how to respond when they first appear. What this means is that there is often *another step* in the treatment of patients with eating disorders: the patient must first understand her "transference" to the food and process of eating; then, only secondarily can she move her selfobject transference from the food or eating activity onto the therapist. I will now discuss this process in more detail.

Kristen must first come to understand how her deepest selfobject longings—for soothing, admiration, etc.—have been split off into what she subjectively experiences as a separate "bulimic self state" (Sands, 1991) and how the eating disordered symptomatology in some way expresses and fulfills these needs as well as defends against them. In short, she needs to recognize how her early, unmet needs are being experienced through her transference to the food and binge/purge process. How does such recognition come about? How does this more needy domain of self make its way into the therapeutic dialogue when it is being expressed primarily through the bulimia? Clearly, it cannot simply be talked about as a theoretical possibility. Kristen must somehow bring the *state itself* into the room where I can empathize with it more directly (Sands, 1991). I will not, for example, get very far asking Kristen to comment generally on her eating behavior, because, from her non-bulimic state, she probably can't or won't. She needs to keep her self-sufficient, perfectionistic self state separate from her more needy, messy one. I could ask her directly if she's aware of being in a different state or of being "somewhere else" when she's bingeing or purging or obsessing about eating or not eating. I might do better, however, to ask her if she can remember what it was like for her last night at 10:30 PM when she was bingeing or purging and to try to recall, in as much detail as she can, all her thoughts, feelings, sensations, and actions. Perhaps, during such a telling, I will sense the electricity in the room of a new, vulnerable presence; I will very gently comment that she seems different right now and ask her to tell me about the state she is experiencing; Kristen may then be able to simultaneously feel her way into the bulimic part and use her observing self to communicate what the bulimic self state is feeling.

The highly paradoxical intentionality of the bulimic self state makes it complicated both to approach and to engage (Sands, 1991). On the one hand, Kristen probably experiences her bulimic self state as negative and "not me" because it is self-destructive and out-of-control, almost involuntary. On the other hand, she unconsciously regards the bulimic sector as intensely positive, the only "true" part of her, because its actions are for her, not for her parents or anyone else. The bulimic behavior is thus both an assertion of self *and* a punishment for it. It is essential that I let Kristin know that I can appreciate the self-affirming as well as the self-destructive intentions of the bulimic part of her and that I communicate a kind of reverence for this secret, sacred part. It is crucial that I recognize the healthy, albeit distorted, attempts of the bulimic part of the patient to express her true longings. I think one of the most serious and common technical errors made by therapists treating eating disorders is to join with the patient in seeing the eating disorder as pathological and in trying to get rid of it before its meaning is fully understood.

Only after Kristen has understood her selfobject "transference" to the eating disorder can she begin to move her transference from the food or eating behaviors onto me—a move described by Kohut in one of his seminars (1987) as the addictive person's becoming addicted to the psychotherapist and by Ulman and Paul (1989) as the selfobject functions of substances becoming "intersubjectively absorbed" within the selfobject transference fantasies until these functions can be internalized by the patient herself.

I must emphasize that I am not advocating the imposition of a particular, systematic technique upon the patient. I would never, for example, suggest to Kristen that she has a hidden self, or ask to speak to her bulimic self. Rather, I would expect that Kristen's revelation of the "shy tendrils" (Kohut, 1971) of the needy self will usually be painstakingly slow and will only come about after I have interpreted again and again her fears of retraumatization and assured her that I can truly understand and even respect her bulimic adaptation.

Medical and Nutritional Issues

Given Kristen's abnormal electrolytes, dizziness, weakness, loss of concentration, and amenorrhea, I would want to have Kristen evaluated immediately by the internist with whom I work closely who specializes in eating disorders and whose opinion I trust completely. I would follow his opinion regarding how often Kristen needed to be monitored medically. If I judged Kristen's primary care physician to be competent to oversee treatment of an eating disorder, I would work closely with him or her. In addition, Kristen's loss of concentration and trouble getting up in the morning would alert me to possible depression, and I would want Kristen to have a psychiatric workup and to consider antidepressants.

In considering whether I would want to send her to a nutritionist, I would consider two issues. I would want to get a sense of how knowledgeable Kristen already is about the importance of good nutrition. Does she know how to take care of herself nutritionally? What has been her nutritional history? Secondly, I would want to get a sense of how "scared" she is of food. Does she need someone like a nutritionist to instruct and reassure her about how many calories she can eat without gaining weight, how much exercise she needs to offset a certain caloric intake, etcetera? My decision to refer her to a nutritionist would also depend on Kristen's openness to the idea. On the other hand, I would not be so flexible regarding the evaluation by the internist. I would insist she see the internist I work with whether she were open to the idea or not. Of course, if Kristen protested that she were afraid to see the internist, I would try to facilitate the referral by working with her around her fears. I would, however, make seeing an internist regularly a condition of ongoing treatment.

Potential Pitfalls

Because Kristen is invested in maintaining her eating disorder as a means of not needing other people, my model of therapy will necessarily pose a challenging and anxiety-producing situation for her. Any symptom reduction or exposure of her true inner yearnings will feel dangerous and disorganizing. (Recall that she kept her bingeing and purging hidden from her college therapist.) Because her developmental needs were so ignored or distorted by her parents, she now automatically experiences them as threatening and alienating to others. Herein lies the greatest anguish for patients with her personality organization. That which is most fervently yearned for—whether it be empathy, soothing, nurturance, admiration, or whatever—is also that which is most desperately feared. Understandably, the revelation of her hidden needs and fantasies will be slow and excruciating and marked by great heroism. Moreover, once the needs and longings begin to be felt in all their rawness, Kristen will then have to deal with the pain and frustration of reconciling these new felt parts of the self with the realities of the shocking deprivations of the past as well as the never completely gratifying realities of the present and future (Sands, 1994).

The biggest potential pitfall, therefore, is that Kristen might not be able to tolerate analytic therapy. If she cannot, she has other options like cognitive-behavioral therapy, which she might find more palatable. Whether she is able to stay with long-term intensive, analytic therapy will depend in large part, of course, on my ability to interpret her fears of exposing and recovering sequestered parts of her self. My task is a delicate one: to acknowledge Kristen's relational needs, while not shaming, exposing, or "disarming" her to such an extent that she feels there is no recourse but to leave treatment.

Termination and Relapse Prevention

I see termination mainly as a continuation of therapy. When the time comes and our mutual appraisal of Kristen's progress suggests she is ready to stop therapy, I will want to agree with her on a termination date some months in the future. During the termination period, it will be my job to keep termination issues in our awareness. By watching Kristen's material for references to termination, I can highlight these issues and help her explore and work through them. In this way, the termination process affords opportunities to deal with material which may not have come up before. For example, I can imagine that Kristen's leaving might bring up echoes of her father's leaving when she was in high school or the more recent breakup with Joe or all the ways that she has never really been able to say good-bye and feel loss fully. Moreover, having a termination date can lend a certain "pressure" to get the remaining work done which may be very beneficial.

From my model, the best relapse prevention is good therapy—that is, therapy in which Kristen's issues are worked through as much as possible.

Mechanisms of Change

I can separate out four mechanisms of change offered either explicitly or implicitly by self psychology over the years which, in their most simplified form, can be called forms of (1) internalization, (2) resumption of development, (3) desomatization, and (4) integration.

Kohut (1971, 1977, 1984) most explicitly conceptualized the "transmuting internalization process" as the means by which people change. In order for transmuting internalization to occur, Kohut believed, there must already be an empathic connection between therapist and patient, and the patient must be experiencing the therapist as providing certain crucial selfobject functions. Then, inevitably, the therapist fails in a non-traumatic way to respond to the patient's needs. Such an incremental failure on the part of the therapist can lead to "optimal frustration," because it allows the patient to do for herself what had been done for her. In that moment, the patient internalizes some of the therapist's selfobject functions and builds a bit of self structure, so that, for example, Kristen, in the absence of my soothing response, could become more able to soothe herself. In this manner, Kristen would slowly, incrementally, internalize my regulatory functions and build them into her own psychic structure. It should be pointed out that the therapist or even the therapist's functions are not incorporated whole. Rather, the therapist's functions are internalized and transmuted in the way protein is taken into the human body (Kohut, 1971)—that is, broken up into its constituents and then put back together again by the patient as her own, individual "protein."

More recently, self psychologists like Beebe and Lachmann (1988), who are heavily influenced by infant research, have conceptualized the internalization process as the internalization of "ongoing regulations," ongoing expectable patterns of repeated interactions. In other words, the "doing is the making." They are looking not at content but, rather, at the process itself: the minute ways in which my attempts to regulate Kristen (and Kristen to regulate me) are internalized and become part of Kristen's internal repertoire.

A second model of change running through all of Kohut's and later self psychological writing but not so explicitly labeled as such by Kohut relies on an even simpler mechanism than that of internalization. This model suggests that empathic understanding serves as a facilitating medium reinstating self developmental processes (Stolorow et al., 1987). In the fertile soil of empathic responsiveness, Kristen can resume her growth at the point where it was arrested earlier in her life.

Third, we can also expect that a *desomaticizing process* (Brickman, 1992) will be going on concurrently. Because Kristen's affect has been somatized, she requires affect attunement to help her separate affect from soma through affect articulation, affect differentiation, affect containment, and, finally, affect integration. My ability to "translate" the affective communications emanating from Kristen's soma (via her eating disorder, distorted body image, etc.) can raise them to a verbal, symbolic level, leading eventually to the crystallization of distinct feelings and to the differentiation of body self from psychological self, increasing the experiential territory covered by "mind" (Stolorow & Atwood, 1992).

A final model of change which runs through self psychology like a red thread is an *integration* model. According to this model, it is the empathic responsiveness of the therapist which allows disowned domains of the self to become recognized, understood, and slowly integrated into the patient's central self structure. It is to this mechanism of change that I have referred most frequently in this chapter in discussing how Kristen's needy, "bulimic self state" can be brought more into her usual self experience. It is my empathic stance which will allow Kristen to bring her walled-off early longings into the room. As Kristen experiences my recognition and understanding of her different need and affect states, she too will experience increased empathy for and acceptance of all of them (Sands, 1994). My ability to contain and "hold" Kristen's disowned parts of herself simultaneously will eventually allow her to bring them together in one central consciousness and to, quite simply, feel more like herself.

REFERENCES

Bacal, H. (1985). Optimal responsiveness and the therapeutic process. In A. Goldberg (Ed.), *Progress in Self Psychology: Vol. 1* (pp. 202–227). New York: Guilford Press.

Beebe, B., & Lachmann, F. (1988). The contribution of mother-infant mutual influence to the origins of self and object representations. *Psychoanalytic Psychology, 5*, 305–337.

Brickman, B. (1992). The desomaticizing selfobject transference: A case report. In A. Goldberg (Ed.), *Progress in Self Psychology: Vol. 8*. Hillsdale, NJ: The Analytic Press.

Brothers, D. (1995). *Falling backwards. An exploration of trust and self-experience.* New York: Norton.

Friedman, M. (1985). Survivor guilt in the pathogenesis of anorexia nervosa. *Psychiatry, 48*, 25–39.

Gehrie, M. (1990). Eating disorders and adaptation in crisis: An hypothesis. *Review of Psychiatry, 9*.

Geist, R. (1985). Therapeutic dilemmas in the treatment of anorexia nervosa: A self-psychological perspective. *Contemporary Psychotherapy Review, 2*, 115–142.

Goodsitt, A. (1985). Self psychology and the treatment of anorexia nervosa. In Garner & Garfinkel (Ed.), *Handbook of psychotherapy for anorexia nervosa and bulimia* (pp. 55–82). New York: Guilford Press.

Kohut, H. (1959). Empathy, introspection, and psychoanalysis. In P. Ornstein (Ed.), *The Search for the Self: Vol. 1* (pp. 205–232). Madison, CT: International Universities Press.

Kohut, H. (1971). *The Analysis of the Self.* New York: International Universities Press.

Kohut, H. (1977). *The Restoration of the self.* New York: International Universities Press.

Kohut, H. (1984). *How Does Analysis Cure?* Hillsdale, NJ: The Analytic Press.

Kohut, H. (1987). The addictive need for an admiring other in the regulation of self-esteem. In M. Elson (Ed.), *The Kohut seminars on self psychology and psychotherapy with adolescents and young adults* (pp. 113–132). New York: Norton.

Kohut, H., & Wolf, E. (1978). Disorders of the self and their treatment: An outline. *International Journal of Psycho-Analysis, 59,* 413–425.

Ornstein, P., & Ornstein, A. (1985). Clinical understanding and explaining: The empathic vantage point. In A. Goldberg (Ed.), *Progress in Self Psychology, Vol. 1* (pp. 43–61). New York: Guilford Press.

Sands, S. (1989). Female development and eating disorders: A self psychological perspective. In A. Goldberg (Ed.), *Progress in Self Psychology. Vol. 5* (pp. 75–104). New York: Analytic Press.

Sands, S. (1991). Bulimia, dissociation and empathy: a self-psychological view. In C. Johnson (Ed.), *Psychodynamic treatment of anorexia nervosa and bulimia* (pp. 34–50). New York: Guilford.

Sands, S. (1994). What is dissociated? *Dissociation, 7*(3), 145–152.

Sands, S. (1997). Self psychology and projective identification: Whither do they meet? *Psychoanalytic Dialogues, 7*(5), 651–668.

Stolorow, R., & Atwood, G. (1992). *Contexts of being.* Hillsdale, NJ: Analytic Press.

Stolorow, R., Brandchaft, B., & Atwood, G. (1987). *Psychoanalytic treatment: An intersubjective approach.* Hillsdale, NJ: Analytic Press.

Ulman, R., & Paul, H. (1989). A self-psychological theory and approach to treating substance abuse disorders: The "intersubjective absorption" hypothesis. In A. Goldberg (Ed.), *Progress in self psychology: Vol. 5* (pp. 121–142). Hillsdale, NJ: Analytic Press.

Winnicott, D. W. (1965). *The maturational processes and the facilitating environment: Studies in the theory of emotional development.* New York: International Universities Press.

Wolf, E. (1988). *Treating the self.* New York: Guilford Press.

8

An Adlerian Approach

Carolyn Gralewski and Mary F. Schneider

TREATMENT MODEL

Adlerian Psychotherapy (Individual Psychology) is as much a philosophy of life as it is a model of therapy. Developed by Alfred Adler, the theory views the individual as a socially embedded, creative, responsible being who is in the process of becoming—that is, in the process of moving toward subjectively created goals. Three tenets form the foundation of Adlerian thought. The sociological tenet holds that all behavior is social; the teleological construct contends that all behavior is purposeful and goal oriented; and the analytic component holds that subjectively held beliefs form the basis for movement (Adler, 1998, 1931).

Adler understood the sociological implications of the family constellation, viewing the family as the child's first society and socialization agent. For Adler, the individual's socialization begins at birth as the child finds a place, a way to belong with others, in the family constellation. Adler held that mental health was social interest, that is, belonging in that world that is useful versus ego-oriented. The individual develops ways to belong through interactions with parents and siblings which are based on the family values. Family values, consciously and unconsciously, are modeled and shaped by parents.

They form the context and quality of the family interactions as well as influence life-long interaction patterns and roles of family members. Siblings play a major role in the socialization process. Adler was the first to identify birth order and sibling competition as patterns and roles that hold life-long social implications. In sibling interactions, children develop and refine conclusions about how they secure a social place and engage in social behavior (Adler, 1998, 1927).

For Adlerians, parenting is a privilege and a social responsibility. It is the first step toward encouraging and teaching children how to belong to society in personally meaningful and socially valuable ways. Instead of confining his theory to university or medical settings, Adler took his ideas directly to parents and educators. He realized that psychotherapy provided proactive insights that belonged to the parents and teachers actively engaged in forming the child's social interest.

The term teleological means goal oriented. For Adlerians, life is a process of becoming—a movement toward mastery in the basic life task areas. In contrast to deterministic models, Adlerians hold that movement is purposeful and goal oriented. Individuals make choices, consciously or unconsciously,which are purposeful, that is, which reflect the individual's subjective beliefs about how they might belong—how they might find a place of value in the basic life task areas. Individuals are challenged to demonstrate healthy social interest within the life tasks.

Adler specifically named three life tasks: "society, work, and sex" (Mosak, 1995). Dreikurs and Mosak (1967) identified two other life tasks which were implied in Adler's writings—the spiritual life task and the task of self-understanding. In the social task, the healthy individual benefits from belonging to communities as well as contributes to the welfare of communities. In the work task, the healthy individual benefits from the work talents of others and is challenged to contribute to society through the identification and development of his or her unique talents. The sexual life task involves healthy cooperation and collaboration between the sexes. The spiritual life task entails making meaning of the universe, of a higher power, or God. The task of self-understanding is the task of learning how to develop and care for the evolving self.

For Adlerians, authentic social interest is the ability to function and collaborate, bringing the individual's unique contributions to the life task areas. This movement rests on self-understanding, encourages creativity, introduces choice, and entails personal and social responsibility. Developmental experiences, family values, and internalized beliefs influence the way the individual moves toward or avoids the challenges of the life tasks. Individuals with poorly developed social interest engage in movement on the ego-oriented or off-task end of the movement continuum. Instead of dealing with the life task, these individuals often avoid the life task or demand that the task bend to meet their egocentric goals.

The analytic tenet of the theory places Adlerian Psychology solidly in the cognitive camp and declares "cognitive organization" as the key to understanding the individual (Mosak, 1995). Adlerians hold that through the socialization process spearheaded in the family constellation and its social contexts, the individual develops a set of basic, subjectively held convictions. These convictions or beliefs cluster in four areas and are beliefs about the self, the self-ideal, the nature of reality, and the methods of movement open to the individual. Adlerians hold that these basic beliefs form the core of the individual's unique lifestyle. Personal change results from understanding the lifestyle, creatively challenging mistaken beliefs, and courageously following or developing preferred beliefs and methods of movement.

This narrative perspective extends itself to the creative work of therapeutic change. The Adlerian therapist believes that the responsibility for the solutions to the client's challenges rests with the client. For the therapist, this problem solving involves helping the client sort through competing values, speculate on possible movement, commit to specific values, and take the creative leap of translating these values into action. Like a novel in progress, there is no absolute path, only a range of possible choices. Adlerian therapists believe that authentic value-based movements provide the most satisfying range of choices out of which individuals construct life movement.

Adlerians view therapy as a process that awakens the client to personal point of view and to the notion that life may be constructed based on creative choice. Viewing the process with a narrative lens, Adlerian therapy has three fundamental stages (Schneider & Stone, 1998). In the first stage of therapy, the reflective stage, client and therapist engage in active reflection on the client's life story. In the second stage of therapy, the re-creative stage, client and therapist challenge the lifestyle material—edit the self-narrative—and harvest alternative values and choices. In the final stage of therapy, the creative constructive stage, client and therapist work to establish patterns that support and normalize the client's chosen values.

In the initial reflective stage, the eating disordered client often presents as externally controlled by forces she does not understand. Therapeutically, the goal during this phase of therapy is to help the client make sense of her personal story and to discover the lifestyle patterns that have influenced her feelings, beliefs, and actions. During this phase, Adlerian therapists devote several treatment sessions to the Life Style Assessment (Shulman & Mosak, 1988). The Life Style is an autobiographical process in a semistructured interview format. Through this process, the client formulates perspective, tells personal story, identifies patterns, forms conclusions, and assigns meaning to early family and socialization experiences. It is within this context of the client's Life Style that the therapist situates the challenges associated with the eating disorder. From an Adlerian perspective, the eating disorder functions as a sideshow—wasting creative energy that could fuel more personally rewarding values.

During the reflective phase, the eating disordered client resists hearing her own internal point of view. Often she discovers that she has been attempting to "perfectly" conform to external social standards and the process of hearing her own voice can be unsettling. The therapist must resist the temptation to assign meaning for the client as a way out of the client's confusion. The therapist must encourage the client to slowly form meaning, to draw simple conclusions. The therapist encourages the use of journal work and supportive relationships to validate, express, record, and normalize these new understandings. Systemic work may be introduced at this stage, but only when the client is comfortable enough to voice rather than to swallow the personal point of view. Care is taken that the systemic support strengthens the client's therapeutic progress rather than deepen old, self-defeating feelings, beliefs, and behavior.

In the reconstructive phase of therapy, the emphasis is on reorientation through insight and reframing. The therapist stimulates a climate of "interpretation culminating in insight" (Mosak, 1995). Once the client has begun to establish her point of view, therapist and client begin to edit old patterns of behavior. The client begins to see possible alternative stories and values which might have been more personally expressive and more potentially satisfying. This is where the client gains insight into the effects of the beliefs that fueled the eating disorder. This phase of therapy cannot be rushed with eating disordered clients. Gradually, obsessive and perfectionistic tendencies can be drafted into the service of overlearning new patterns which will serve to guide, soothe, and encourage the client as the client begins to contemplate future choices based on a more internal locus of control.

In the creative, constructive stage of therapy, the therapist and client are challenged to anchor the beliefs, patterns, and relationships that support the client's growing internal locus of control. It is common at this point to make new and more satisfying choices in each of the life task areas: new friends, new aspects of work, new perspectives on intimate relationships. For the eating disordered client, the challenge is to simplify and prevent perfectionism from creeping back into the point of view. As with affective disorders, the eating disordered client is encouraged to focus simply on the current day and current task. At this stage, eating disordered clients greatly benefit from self-help groups in which they may build a sense of social interest—caring for others who struggle with similar life issues. Systemic work at this stage is helpful for family members and friends who may need to understand and adapt to the client's shifting sense of self.

THERAPIST'S SKILLS AND ATTRIBUTES

We assume a set of fundamental skills: the ability to build rapport, a capacity for empathy, self-awareness in interpersonal interaction, personal maturity, and open mindedness. Beyond these baseline abilities, this section addresses some of the skills and attributes specific to Adlerian Therapy.

Well-developed listening skills are essential baseline tools in Adlerian therapy. Adlerians rely on reflective listening as an orientation device—a skill that marks out for both therapist and client the client's points of view (meanings) and shifts in point of view.

Reflective skills gain an additional layer of importance in family therapy where the therapist's reflective voice lends the power of consideration to points of view. Simply by repeating a family member's point of view, the therapist opens a topic for group conversation—that is, places the theme on the table for consideration. This type of reflective focusing encourages circularity and generates family members' divergent, creative points of view. These perspectives often result in the family solving the "problem" with the use of their own cognitive resources.

Life Style Assessment skills are a core and unique Adlerian therapeutic skill. The Life Style provides guiding lines regarding the client's movement. Adlerian therapists receive training and supervision in the Life Style processes. Such training is offered at the Adler School of Professional Psychology in Chicago and Adlerian training centers throughout North America. The Life Style Assessment introduces clients to the narrative perspective. The ability of the Adlerian therapist to think narratively is a core therapeutic skill.

For the Adlerian therapist this narrative focus requires a good memory for story and narrative detail, a delight in the client's own linguistic metaphors, and an ability to situate the "current problem" within the context of the narrative material of the Life Style. The Adlerian therapist develops the ability to stay oriented to the client's point of view while developing questions and interventions that help challenge and shift the limitations of the client's perspective.

Adlerians favor the use of questions in the therapeutic process. Questions are used Socratically, to help the client think through possible challenges and choices. The use of questions range from a Colombo-esque wondering (where the therapist has established ideas about the outcome of the questions) to questions which baffle the therapist as well as the client. This acceptance of wondering (sitting with questions) opens the therapeutic process to conversations with others.

The Adlerian emphasis on social embeddedness and the life tasks of love, work, and friendship implies that Adlerian therapy is systemic in nature. The systemic focus, grounded in family therapy course work, encourages the consideration and often participation of key figures in the client's life. Adlerian therapists extend their effectiveness by developing skills in conducting systemic and group work.

Finally, Adlerian therapists welcome collaboration with other professionals and embrace the use of peer supervision and consultation.

THE CASE OF KRISTEN

Assessment, Conceptualization, and Treatment Planning

Assessment

Initial psychological assessment, for Kristen, would be helpful in securing Kristen's safety and formulating treatment plans that support restabilization. Later, during a more creatively constructive phase of therapy, vocational testing may be helpful in encouraging Kristen to identify and claim her personal talents, skill, and abilities.

After the therapist conducts a careful inquiry regarding suicidal thoughts and behavior and secures medical team collaboration, the lifestyle assessment process could begin. In tandem with these information gathering sessions, Kristen would be asked to complete the Millon Clinical Multiaxial Inventory-III (Millon, Millon, & Davis, 1994) to assess the presence and intensity of DSM Axis II disorders.

As an initial step in the therapy process, Adlerians conduct a lifestyle assessment. Adler held that the "life style of any individual was a singular pattern of thinking, feeling, and acting that was unique to that individual and represented the context (Zusammenhang) in which all specific manifestations had to be considered" (Shulman & Mosak, 1988, p. 1). The lifestyle functions as a "guiding line" (Adler, 1998, 1931)—a set of convictions or beliefs that serve as a personal compass organizing the individual's movement and choice.

The Life Style assessment is a structured autobiographical interview designed to identify the client's preferred patterns of movement. The client forms these patterns or rules out of life experiences. The patterns consist of subjective convictions regarding perceived reality ("what is"), convictions regarding the perceived ideal ("what should be"), and convictions regarding methods of movement toward subjective goals (Shulman & Mosak, 1988, p. 12). There is a "soft-determinism" (Shulman & Mosak, 1988, p. 4) to these lifestyle beliefs, because they translate into life patterns that organize, direct, offer meaning, guide, predict, and also limit the client's field of possibilities. These patterns help the individual problem solve, make meaning of life, protect the self, find social value, create, and develop the self.

The lifestyle patterns regarding reality ("what is") include the client's beliefs about the self-concept, the client's image of the world (how does it work?), and the client's "Weltbild," the sense of relationship between himself or herself and others (Shulman & Mosak, 1988). The lifestyle patterns regarding the ideal ("what should be") encompass the client's ethical beliefs, moral judgments, and convictions about what life should be, "The Ideal World" (Shulman & Mosak, 1988). The lifestyle, which Adlerians believe is established by age 5 (Shulman & Mosak, 1988), develops as the individual draws conscious or unconscious conclusions as a result of lived experiences. Because these conclusions are drawn at a developmentally young age, they are subject to cognitive limitations which include simplification, overgeneralization, exaggeration, and misperception. These mistakes in logic, found in the lifestyle, are called basic mistakes (Dreikurs, 1989, 1935). The lived experiences are the narrative soup which the child consumes during the formulation of the lifestyle convictions. The child picks and chooses experience from this soup which is a mix of genetic influences, cultural and ecological factors, and family constellation influences. The Life Style assessment is conducted using the Life Style Inventory (Mosak & Shulman, 1988) and yields a narrative summary with four major sections: Summary of Family Constellation; Summary of Early Recollections; Interfering Attitudes, Beliefs, Behaviors; and Assets and Strengths. Information on the use the inventory is found in *A Manual for Life Style Assessment* (Shulman & Mosak, 1988) and *Life Style: A Workbook* (Schneider & Mosak, 1993). The Life Style Inventory (LSI) itself is an in-depth structured interview consisting of sets of questions in each of the following categories: Sibling Constellation, Sibling Groupings, Shared Traits and/or Interests, Sibling Ratings, Childhood Physical Developments, Elementary School Information, Childhood Meaning Given to Life, Childhood Gender and Sexual Information, Childhood Social Relationships, Parental Relationships During Subject's Childhood, Nature of Parents' Relationship, Family Information (cultural, socioeconomic, value, ethnicity, religion), Additional Parental Figures, Adult Models, and Early Recollection.

For the purpose of the LSI, clients are asked to provide six to eight early memories. Adler used early memories as a projective technique to determine the client's guidelines for movement. "Without memories it would be impossible to exercise any precautions for the future. They are not fortuitous phenomena but speak clearly the language of encouragement and warning. There are no indifferent or nonsensical recollections . . . " (Adler, 1998, 1927, pp. 40–41). The early memories are viewed as vignettes which capture the guiding lines of the client's preferred movement (Shulman & Mosak, 1988). Adlerians believe that early recollections are creative constructions of the mind—narrative pictures of the guiding patterns—pictures that hold clients, beliefs, and lines of movement. Early memories yield information regarding lines of movement and fundamental beliefs. Early recollections are a valuable tool throughout therapy for examining values, challenging beliefs, and developing new values.

Therapeutic Goals

From an Adlerian perspective, therapeutic goals would center on systemic, teleological, and analytic dimensions of functioning in each of the life task areas. The primary goals relate to Kristen's eating disorder, which is the core around which she organizes her experience. Secondary goals include the resolution of sexual trauma and family issues.

While Kristen is motivated to entertain therapy because she is troubled about the effect of the disorder on her ability to work, from an Adlerian perspective she is fearful that her most reliable method of anxiety reduction and belonging—work—is threatened by the disorder. She cannot see that every life task is threatened—not only by the disorder, but by Kristen's blind focus on achievement.

From the systemic or social perspective, treatment goals for Kristen include the development of more balanced social interactions, that is, the establishment of a sense of belonging in social contexts with the ability to display appropriate assertiveness as well as the ability to balance her own needs and expectations with the needs of others. Kristen would be encouraged to join groups that would benefit from her unique talents. Kristen will need to move away from social isolation and establish social connections and friendships.

From the teleological perspective, Kristen must come to identify and revise her self-defeating goals of superiority, control, and perfection. She needs to become aware of the purposes served by the eating disorder and the goals which underlie her self-destructive behavior. She must then engage in deliberate, thoughtful decision making regarding how she will revise her life choices and goals.

A great deal of effort will be required to address her functioning from the analytic perspective. The analytic aspects of treatment are primary in treating the client with an eating disorder. A strong emphasis will be placed on improving Kristen's ability to identify and manage feeling states. Rather than allowing internal feeling states to determine behavior and trigger unhealthy eating disordered behavior, Kristen must become more capable of identifying and labeling internal states and utilizing a problem solving approach to find healthy ways to self-soothe, self-calm, regulate, and express emotion and distress.

Along with increased awareness of feeling states, Kristen needs to become more aware of her thinking. She needs to revise her beliefs regarding her self-worth and self-value. She needs to confront her perfectionistic ideas and expectations and find the "courage to be imperfect." Her thinking must become more realistic and balanced. Ideals must be redefined so that healthier feminine role models and values can replace self-destructive, perfectionistic ones.

Timeline for Therapy

Given the complexity of eating disorders in general and Kristen's case in particular, the therapeutic timeline will be lengthy. The expectation is that ongoing, rather intensive work will be necessary for 1 1/2 to 2 years. The initial work will focus on the eating disorder, but eventually addressing the trauma experience will also be necessary. The therapist working with such complexity must be willing to be flexible in the therapeutic timeline and revise it as the pace of the client's progress demands. During the first phase of therapy, it may be necessary to schedule multiple sessions (two to three) on a weekly basis. Initial sessions may also need to be longer in duration than the traditional 50-minute psychotherapy hour as much needs to be accomplished during this period of stabilization. Sessions that run 1 1/2 hours may allow adequate time for psychoeducation, collaborative planning with Kristen for managing her life between sessions, and assisting Kristen in letting go of defensiveness and resistance. As the therapist and Kristen determine that she is functioning on a more thoughtful, balanced, and effective level between sessions, the decision to decrease the frequency and duration of sessions can be made. The option to again increase frequency and/ or duration of sessions during times of increased challenge or stress should be left open. Treatment of eating disorders must involve flexibility on the part of the therapist and client in terms of timelines and scheduling so that relapse can be caught early.

If hospitalization becomes necessary, the structure and scheduling of intervention shifts. If Kristen were to begin her treatment with hospitalization, transition to outpatient work would need to be effectively addressed. The introduction of various therapeutic treatment modalities will need to be decided in a collaborative team manner. It is expected, however, that during the course of Kristen's treatment, individual therapy, systemic therapy, and medical management will be the ongoing cornerstone of treatment. Eating disorder support group involvement will be the next therapeutic piece to be added when Kristen is ready. Termination will be gradual, over at least a 6-month time period. Family and individual therapy sessions will be phased out with Kristen continuing in group work for an additional 6- to 8-month time frame or longer should she find group work helpful in sustaining recovery.

Case Conceptualization

Adlerians begin case conceptualization with a consideration of the lifestyle material. The lifestyle assessment synthesizes the client's subjective experiences, beliefs, convictions, and memories into summary statements regarding the nature of the client's *Family Constellation*, the cognitive beliefs demonstrated in the *Early Recollections*, basic *Interfering Attitudes, Beliefs, and Behavior*, and basic *Assets and Strengths*. This summary material, assembled by the therapist in collaboration with the client, provides a cognitive map which illustrates the client's basic beliefs and lifestyle strategies. This functional map provides the therapist with a set of understandings that allow the therapist to predict and strategize regarding the client's movement. The lifestyle provides the therapist with cognitive and affective understanding which facilitates and deepens empathy and allows the therapist to view life from the client's perspective.

The *Family Constellation* is the arena in which the individual learns basic values, how to establish a place of significance with others, and how to interact with others: Kristen's case study provides skeletal information regarding the sibling constellation. We know that Kristen is the youngest of four, with two much older brothers and a sister (born dead) who was a year older than Kristen. As the youngest child, with significant years between Kristen and the next oldest siblings, Kristen may feel socially isolated. She may feel ambitious to duplicate or surpass the achievements of her brothers. Kristen may live in a family dominated by male values and aspirations—especially when it comes to being successful in the life task of work. Since a space of 6 or more years often produces an "only child" effect, Kristen may feel like an only child who is overparented by four adults. She may have highly developed beliefs and attitudes regarding self-reliance and independence. She may find sharing a challenge and she may lack the social skill strategies for satisfactory group involvement. If Kristen assumes the position of "failed youngest," she may experience discouragement and resort to dependent behavior (Shulman & Mosak, 1988).

The lifestyle assessment would go into depth regarding Kristen's perceptions of the sibship through rating on 60 some traits. In addition, other questions pertinent to case study conceptualization would include: How does she perceive each brother? What is the nature of her alliance/attachment with each brother? With whom does she share values? With whom does she compete? What are the gender roles? What is her perception of her family's reaction to the loss of her sister? What meaning does she make of her birth following a year after her sister's? Are there family stories about Kristen's birth? Kristen's responses to the life style questions regarding sibship would help define beliefs Kristen has about finding her place in the family. The competition in sibling relationships for parental recognition provides a striving that can result in the development of diverse talents (when parents recognize and encourage individual talents), dangerous rivalry (when parents recognize only a limited path of significance), or discouragement (when parents ignore or disparage a child's unique identity). Kristen and her brothers may be following the family work ethic. We suspect that Kristen's parents were so focused and anxious regarding work, that little time was devoted to recognizing Kristen's unique talents. We do not know if this same pattern was present during her brothers' developmental years.

The family values adopted by Kristen appear to be a striving to maintain social status, preoccupation with work achievement, focus on material success, belief in the value of external appearances, reliance on highly developed critical skills, desire for control, and emotional distance. Both of Kristen's parents came from families who relied on the work ethic. Kristen's father modeled ambition and hard work. He responded to each additional family responsibility by increasing his workload. It appears that he may have modeled the use of work to decrease feelings of anxiety and loss. With the potential loss of his dealership and the loss of his first daughter, Kristen's father increased his focus on work. Kristen's mother modeled ambition—the desire to give the children the "best of everything." Even family jokes centered around the children achieving degrees of perfection and education beyond their parents. Her parents bragged about the children's achievement to family friends. When father's business was threatened, excessive work by both parents was the family solution. The family atmosphere was one of constant achievement and emotional distance. Both family history and lived experiences would convince Kristen that hard work and achievement was a fundamental coping device.

Kristen's father modeled emotional distance and appeared to use work as a method to reduce anxiety and loss. These are coping mechanisms on which Kristen appears to rely. Kristen's mother supported achievements associated with high socioeconomic status (tennis, ballet) and encouraged academic success. Kristen's maternal grandmother stressed the value of physical beauty, setting Kristen's mother and sister (Sissy) into competition around this value. Kristen's mother lost that competition to Sissy. This historical tension and concern with beauty may be contributing to Kristen's body image issues.

The lifestyle inventory would achieve more depth regarding the nature of the Kristen's relationship with each parent. We suspect that Kristen may be trying to achieve closeness with an emotionally distant father by joining his values. We suspect that Kristen may have absorbed her mother's ambivalence regarding beauty and overemphasizes it as a factor in the breakup of the engagement with Joe.

The fact that a school nurse first recognized Kristen's anorexia suggests that Kristen's parents are confused, neglectful, or in denial regarding Kristen's health issues.

The nature of the parental relationship, which sets up patterns of belief regarding female/male relations, appears both distant and ultimately tumultuous. Kristen's father is absorbed with work, while her mother supports the achievements of the children. The destruction of the family dealership brings her parents together, but only for the purpose of working side by side to rebuild the business. Kristen's father is unfaithful; her mother views separation as the only solution to the infidelity; the marriage ends. The emotional qualities and style of this relationship parallel Kristen's relationship with Joe.

We lack early information regarding Kristen's perceptions of her physical development, feelings about her body, and her sexuality. Her high school experience with the basketball star points out insecurities regarding physical appearance and a sexual reluctance.

While we have no information regarding elementary school achievement, excessive school achievement surfaces in high school. The external focus regarding achievement and appearances influenced her choice of friends. She attempted to belong to a fast, popular, drinking crowd. It seems that she begins her use of dieting and exercise to perfect her body and secure a place with this group. But the group was not emotionally satisfying. Rejected by her boyfriend for a more sexually active girl, Kristen intensified diet and exercise to perfect her body.

We have no information regarding Kristen's childhood friendships, but we suspect she focused on lessons and activities while relationships went underdeveloped. We suspect Kristen struggled with and ultimately avoided attempts to find a place with peers.

Regarding early preferences, Kristen's choice of ballet as a favorite activity suggests an interest in physical expression and may be one key area to begin to explore the world of inner feelings. Ballet may also have, consciously or unconsciously, suggested a rigid standard of thinness and perfectionism.

While there are no *Early Recollections* present in the case study, we assume that these narratives would offer summary which includes a self-image of trying to please, never feeling good enough, and needing to be in control. In terms of world view, life is seen as a struggle—as hard work. She views relationships as desirable, impossible to trust, and out of her reach. In terms of a dominant goal, or self-ideal, she feels that she needs to be perfect just to be acceptable. She believes that she needs to be in control of her feelings and that feelings disable her. In terms of favored mode of operation, Kristen believes in hard work. When faced with a challenge, she relieves anxiety through perfectionistic striving—often redoubling her efforts. She fears feelings and relationships because she does not know how to control or manage them.

Regarding *Interfering Attitudes, Beliefs, and Behaviors*, Kristen's cognition is characterized by rigidly held beliefs and assumptions about herself and others and how life should be managed. These beliefs are self-defeating and self-perpetuating. They impact both her feelings and her behavior. These attitudes would be assembled from the lifestyle information and summarized using her own language and metaphors, for example.

"I am acceptable only if I am perfect."

"I can never do enough."

"It is dangerous to feel. I need to stuff my feelings and purge them from my experience."

"Women should be beautiful."

"Women need important men. I do not know how to get close to a man."

The case conceptualization based on the lifestyle assembles Kristen's *Assets and Strengths*. These include statements like: Kristen knows how to work hard. She has well-developed capacities for discipline and self-control. She appreciates rules and standards. She desires relationships. These abilities, when turned toward balanced development in the lifestyle areas, support therapeutic change.

Kristen's eating disorder involves three core issues: control, competence, and identity. Kristen grew up interpreting her social environment as one in which she must earn her place by being good, by pleasing, and by conforming. She could not elicit responsiveness, interest, and validation from significant others regarding who she was, but rather she needed to respond to what others expected. Given her adaptable temperament, she was able to fit this role. In addition, she was born a year after her stillborn sister. Given the family's general inability to process and resolve feelings, the unaddressed grief over the death of this child would have complicated the relationship between parents and Kristen from the start. Could parents see her and respond to her as a unique individual or only in reference and relationship to the girl child they had lost? Did Kristen experience a sense of ineffectiveness in getting the world to respond to her uniquely? Kristen's identity formation has been problematic and relatively undifferentiated. She has developed a belief that she is acceptable and worthwhile if she meets externally determined standards. During adolescence, when she might have had an opportunity to question family standards and explore different definitions of herself, the crisis of parental divorce caused Kristen to abort self-exploration. The parental crisis encouraged Kristen to rely on her main coping tool and redouble self-control. At the same time, the intensification of the socialization pressures which occur for females at adolescence provided Kristen with ready-made external standards on which to base identity and acceptability. Relying on values learned in the family constellation—social status and physical appearance—Kristen found a peer group. She would revisit this same pattern, with an even more devastating result, when she went off to college.

Dissatisfaction with her body was Kristen's way to concretize her dissatisfaction with herself. It was a method that suggested that she could solve the dilemma of self-acceptance through control of her body—a test of self-control. Focusing on her body and exerting control over it became a way for Kristen to affirm competence. She could accept the general standards for female acceptability, and could judge and determine her success in meeting them. Women with eating disorders are impervious to objective feedback regarding their body image. They become the sole judge. Thus the dilemma of whether the self or others judge acceptability is solved. Kristen complied with the standards, but became sole judge of whether she met these standards. Kristen could express both her desire to conform and to excel, her desire to meet others' expectations, and her need to be self-determined. Body shape became the concrete ideal—the oversimplified perception of a successful woman—an exaggerated version of family perspective regarding female identity. Kristen's eating disorder is an example of competence/mastery and self regulation/control simplified and intensified.

This pattern of self-control and mastery through eating disorders became the major coping pattern associated with peer involvement. Initially Kristen employed the disorder as a way to attain acceptability with peers. After experiencing abusive romantic relationships, she intensified the disorder to avoid experiencing feelings.

The Therapeutic Relationship

Therapeutic Bond

Eating disorders are developmental phenomena, that is, conflicts in growth and mastery of developmental challenges are at the core of eating disorders. The therapeutic relationship, therefore, is of utmost importance. The therapist must provide the interpersonal context in which the individual with an eating disorder can risk growth, and can become active in confronting the challenges of individuation, identity formation, affect regulation, goals selection, and values identification. The client must trust that efforts toward such developmental growth will not result in personal isolation; that the therapist will continue to be involved and supportive of the client's imperfect efforts at growth; that the therapist will be able to tolerate the client's anxiety, conflict, and fears without succumbing to fear or resorting to dogmatism. The therapist-client relationship provides the context in which the eating disordered client can dare to grow with the struggles and mistakes inherent in the growth process. In order to provide such a relationship conducive to growth and development, the therapist must be clear regarding her own history of growth and struggle, her own identity and body image, and her own reaction to socialization pressures.

Transference and countertransference issues will center on issues of power and control. Power and control must be viewed as attempts to counterbalance the intense fears, anxieties, and vulnerabilities which accompany growth. The control/power struggle will be played out in therapy and the therapist will need to be particularly adept at sidestepping power struggles and guarding against adopting a punitive, controlling role which can then be perceived as rejection or as affirmation of the client's negative self-identity.

Early in the relationship, the client may place the therapist into the omnipotent role—all-good, all-giving, all-knowing, in contrast to the client's own perception of herself as all-bad. The therapist will need to be cognizant of this idealization and insist on a collaborative relationship with direct feedback to the client that both therapist and client will struggle side by side to master the challenges presented. Although both therapist and client may wish for someone to take on the strong, reassuring, powerful stance which will "cure" the client of this complex disorder, the therapist must provide a model for the client in which anxieties and uncertainties are embraced and managed in a way that allows the struggle toward health to continue.

The therapist must guard against too much self-disclosure, especially during the early part of therapy. Such disclosure may present a tempting, false solution to the challenge of identity formation. Rather than building one's own identity, the eating disordered client can overidentify with the therapist and assume the identity offered by the therapist. There is a significant difference between utilizing the therapist as *a* role model and adopting the therapist as *the* role model.

The major countertransference issues with which the therapist will be confronted parallel the issues with which the client is struggling. Does the therapist give in and adopt the reassuring, powerful, directive role or choose to tolerate her own anxiety, uncertainties, and concerns regarding the client's faltering steps toward health? Can the therapist manage her own emotional reactions? Can she maintain her sense of competence and her identity as an effective person while the client vacillates in her own identity? For female therapists, the issues of body image and acceptability as females in the culture are triggered by working with these clients. In short, the emotional demands, as well as the time demands, on the therapist working with eating disordered clients are intense. The therapist will need to assess her own ability to manage these demands and will need to essentially "practice what she preaches," that is, utilize her own skills for self-care and social support as the eating disordered client is working to establish her own self-care and social support resources.

Finally, the issues of boundaries and limit-setting are foremost in working with clients engaged in self-destructive behavior such as eating disorders. As mentioned in the goals section, the therapist must anticipate and articulate the consequences of the client's failure to adhere to medically prescribed regimens. The therapist must engage in collaborative discussion with the client and support team and establish the consequences, often hospitalization, of the failure to follow through with health promoting practices. Client collaboration is essential in anticipating and creating these logical consequences. Collaboration removes the punitive aspects of the consequences while sidestepping a power struggle with clients. This modeling of firm, fair, caring boundaries empowers the entire support team and places responsibility for choice on the client.

Roles in the Therapeutic Relationship

For Adlerian therapists, the establishment of the therapeutic bond is of critical importance to the clinical relationship. Truth, honesty, and encouragement form the foundation for this bond. While Adlerian therapy is directive by nature, the directiveness occurs around the therapist's desire to encourage the client to formulate his or her own point of view; to challenge interfering beliefs; and to attempt to creatively assemble and "try out" client-driven solutions to current problems. Movement is encouraged as a way to test options, to experiment and to learn from life.

Adlerians place an encouraging emphasis on creativity of the client—the client's ability to consider, generate, and try new creative choices. The directive focus is often on creating client-preferred movement—movement toward—rather than focusing on historically unsatisfying movement—movement away from. The therapist's role is to encourage and help the client anticipate the consequences of specific choices. Adlerians urge clients to expect imperfection with new choices and to work to revise these choices with an eye toward personal satisfaction and belonging.

Adlerian therapists are directive in framing questions that address and encourage clients to establish social interest in each of the life task areas. Adlerian therapists ask clients to consider issues and effects of issues on relationships within the life task areas: work, family, friendship, self-care, and spirituality.

Adlerian therapy is highly collaborative, encouraging the client to employ additional resources in the course of therapeutic change. Any processes or materials that may support client movement are encouraged.

Treatment Implementation and Outcome

Techniques and Methods of Working

One of the first therapeutic tasks would be to establish a medical support team. This means requesting medical collaboration and a medical case plan with professionals who are knowledgeable and interested in eating disorders. The plan should be done in collaboration with Kristen, her parents, medical team personnel, and the primary therapist. This collaborative plan would inform, clarify, and establish treatment parameters in the following areas: Kristen's current health status and current medical and nutritional treatment needs; medical boundaries regarding weight loss parameters; Kristen's mental health status and needs; guidelines regarding potential hospitalization; establishment of a backup hospitalization plan (with secured authorization for treatment at a facility with a reputable program in eating disorders). This systemic conversation allows all parties, most especially Kristen, to collaborate on the creation of a medical support plan. It also empowers all team members with firm, clear limits and decision parameters regarding weight loss and disordered behavior. Kristen's issues with control will require firm, value-based leadership from those who are invested in her recovery. Periodic systemic meetings would help encourage Kristen regarding her progress as well as revise treatment parameters. The systemic focus brings Kristen out of isolation and reintroduces her to the experience of trusting, boundaries, and relationships.

Whether Kristen is hospitalized or not, initial therapy would involve the establishment of rapport through the lifestyle assessment. Intermittent sessions with selected or all family members would begin the systemic family conversations designed to buttress the work of individual therapy. Choices regarding the balance between individual and systemic work will rest with Kristen's issues and her comfort level with systemic work.

While initial conversations will investigate and identify the purposes served by the eating disorder and the effects of the disorder on her life tasks, these sessions will have the ultimate goal of revisiting Kristen's past flirtations with self-awareness. Kristen has a history of benefiting from therapy. Prior therapeutic understandings allowed her to achieve short periods of more balanced investment in the life tasks. Therapeutic conversations would encourage a return to these helpful understandings and patterns of behavior. Conversations would mine, in great detail, the patterns in her life (in each life task area) during these periods of recovery. Conversations and journal assignments would have Kristen "work hard" to pick out the positive patterns in prior periods of freedom from eating disorders. This hard work would entail the analysis of the effect of these patterns on her life and the beliefs about herself and others associated with preferred patterns. Sessions would stress her creative role in making these alternative choices as well as an understanding of how these alternative patterns affected the quality of her life.

Journal assignments would help her investigate her own feelings regarding patterns of behavior. The journal, if secured as a totally private tool for Kristen's eyes only, will become the one safe place for Kristen to tell herself the truth about her own feelings. Kristen would be encouraged to share this awareness when she is ready. The journal is also a good place to have Kristen begin the work of dismantling perfection. In the journal she can begin to dialogue with perfection and to identify the messages and movements encouraged by perfection. The journal will also be a powerful tool in allowing Kristen to challenge perfection by learning how to keep tasks simple—how to slice tasks down to mini-steps.

Since Kristen would benefit from a group experience, we would encourage her to join a support group like AlAnon. While an eating disorders group may well be of value in establishing a community of support, we would want Kristen to join such a recovery group when she has established a clear identity outside of the eating disorder. We would be concerned that early group involvement might serve to reinforce the eating disorder. The AlAnon group experience would offer a perspective on Peter's alcohol addiction and the issues of codependence which are features of Kristen's family. The 12-step model offers an introduction to issues of spirituality as well as introduces cognitive "thought interruption" tools to help Kristen restructure her thoughts and recognize her feelings. This community would offer an economical, nonjudgmental arena for Kristen to experiment with honesty, budding identity formation, social skill development, and assertiveness skills. This community experience combined with therapy could help Kristen learn how to be a member of a group without excessive striving and self-focus.

After Kristen stabilizes and experiences some success in social relationships, therapy may address the resolution of the trauma associated with her college rape. While it is difficult to predict when this issue will surface, it certainly belongs with the set of beliefs and patterns associated with gender roles. As her ideas about her identity shift, so will her perceptions about relationships with the opposite sex. The goal will be to begin to establish mutually satisfying, honest, intimate, collaborative relationships with men.

The following techniques and methods form the core of our Adlerian approach to this case:

1. *PSYCHOEDUCATION*: The therapist adopts an active role with strong elements of teaching, mentoring, study, and coaching. Kristen needs to be educated regarding the meaning and purposes of her eating disorder. She needs to become aware of the impact of socialization, media, and advertising images which influence women in this culture in terms of their own self-acceptance, body image, and expectations. Reading would be encouraged to promote ongoing exploration of these issues (e.g., Gloria Steinem's *The Revolution from Within*, 1993). Kristen also requires education regarding health, nutrition, and fitness issues. When she is ready to deal with the rape trauma, she would benefit from both discussion and readings regarding the impact of trauma (e.g., Jon Allen's *Coping with Trauma: A Guide to Self Understanding*, 1995). Throughout therapy, the therapist will engage in psychoeducation as an integral part of the therapeutic process.

2. *MONITORING AND JOURNALING*: Monitoring and journaling will be encouraged as a means to enhance self-awareness, self-valuing, and self-acceptance. Monitoring and charting of moods, emotions, thinking, behavior, and environmental triggers will assist Kristen in establishing honesty, self-control, and healthier eating behavior.

3. *SELF-CALMING SKILLS*: Kristen needs to learn to manage her internal feeling states. Early on in therapy, Kristen and the therapist will develop a written list of concrete patterns, activities, and thoughts that Kristen can begin utilizing to replace bingeing/purging/food deprivation/overexercising as a way to regulate affect and to self-soothe. It is important that Kristen

is not handed a list of self-calming strategies. She must actively work to identify and experiment with strategies that have been effective in the past and experiment with the creation of new helpful strategies. The therapist can assist Kristen in this process, but Kristen needs to take responsibility for her own creation and use of internal regulation approaches. This is generally an ongoing process and the goal would be for Kristen to expand her list of self-calming and self-care behaviors as she progresses in therapy. Not only does this provide alternative coping skills to replace eating disordered behavior, but it also improves Kristen's ability to treat herself in a caring way that reinforces self-worth.

4. *ASSERTIVENESS TRAINING:* Assertiveness training can occur within sessions and through reading on her own, with in-session practice, and planned practice in daily life functioning. Kristen may even decide to take a class through the local community college.

5. *COGNITIVE TECHNIQUES:* Kristen has a need for increased cognitive competence. The therapist will incorporate cognitive therapy techniques that include active analysis of thinking patterns, identification, and replacement of cognitive distortions, and a focus on organized problem solving and decision making. The intent is to increase Kristen's ability to function in a more thoughtful, proactive manner rather than being pushed into unhealthy or pleasing responses by impulsive reactions to her emotions. Kristen tends to think and behave in highly dichotomized ways. An ongoing focus in therapy will encourage Kristen to aim for more balance in all aspects of her functioning. This is best accomplished through cognitive awareness and monitoring.

6. *SOCIAL ENGAGEMENT:* Kristen will be encouraged to expand her social connections and involvement. Increased social interaction will serve a number of purposes. Increased self-esteem, the establishment of a stronger sense of identity, an expanded repertoire of social support, and opportunities to establish trust in others would all be impacted through increased social engagement.

7. *SOCIAL INTEREST/MAKING A DIFFERENCE:* One of the hallmarks of the Adlerian approach is to view healthy individuals

as having social interest, that is, a commitment to contribute to the good of humankind. Kristen is exceedingly self-focused and self-protective. As she discovers an authentic sense of self, she will find ways to contribute to the well-being of others. In addition, many believe that when one has been the victim of trauma, resolution cannot be achieved until the individual is able to find a way to utilize the traumatic experience in a way that makes a positive contribution, a difference in the world. By finding a way to contribute to the social good, Kristen will be empowering herself in a positive way and will achieve many of the goals she is currently pursuing in an unhealthy, useless way through her eating disorder.

8. *SYSTEMIC or FAMILY THERAPY:* Systemic and family therapy, which will begin at the onset of therapy with the establishment of a team approach, will be revisited throughout Kristen's recovery and growth process. Addressing issues of family grief and establishing more satisfying interaction patterns would be some of the goals of family therapy. If the family system rigidly resists change, Kristen may have to find support outside of her family of origin.

9. *GROUP WORK:* As mentioned in the section on treatment goals, we would help establish and seek collaboration with the medical team that is working with Kristen: we would want to engage Kristen's family in systemic work; we would be open to systemic work with any significant others in Kristen's life; we would encourage Kristen to join a support group for individuals dealing with eating disorders. ANAD (National Association of Anorexia Nervosa and Associated Disorders) is a resource to help locate such a support group. As her interests emerge, we would encourage Kristen to join specific courses and interest groups, and to actively seek mentoring in areas that anchor and encourage the development of her new identity. If Kristen would benefit from spiritual resources, we would delight in working with a spiritual advisor.

Medical and Nutritional Issues

Medical complications of eating disorders can be severe, even fatal. It is estimated that 5% to 20% of all anorexics will eventually die from the disorder and its complications (Zerbe, 1993). Eating disorders affect every organ, every body system, and the body as a whole. A coordinated approach between therapist and medical personnel is crucial for the successful treatment of eating disordered clients. A holistic, systemic approach in this case will involve individuals in each of Kristen's life task areas: family, friends, work associates, spiritual advisors. In addition, medical personnel are essential treatment team participants, attending to medical history, attuned to medical symptoms and side effects of the disorder, and providing information and education regarding the medical consequences and mortality associated with the disorder. A holistic, integrated approach should be embraced by all involved with Kristen. While medical personnel are focused on eliminating bulimic behavior, establishing good nutrition and regular eating patterns, and addressing physical symptoms due to the eating disorder, their efforts must be incorporated within a context that recognizes the psychological meaning of the eating disorder. While the therapist focuses on increasing skills of self-awareness, self-care, and revision of unhealthy thinking patterns, the therapist must align with medical personnel to confront the client regarding medical status. The therapist must convey acceptance of Kristen and an understanding of the struggle in which she is engaged while at the same time remaining consistently confrontive regarding medical issues. The therapist must take a strong stand in setting limits and establishing expectations that Kristen will adhere to the health regimen prescribed by medical personnel as well as the backup hospitalization plan.

As mentioned in the section on goals, collaboration and ongoing consultation with medical personnel who specialize in eating disorders are critical aspects of the treatment plan for Kristen. The complexity and complications of eating disorders require medical personnel who have expertise in this area. It will not suffice to rely on the family practitioner, no matter how skilled. Issues of hospitalization and medication management for accompanying depression are particularly difficult in the case of eating disordered clients. Therapeutic response to medication and side effects of medication are complicated when the body has been impacted by an eating disorder. The role of the medical specialists in the treatment of eating disordered clients, then, is critical.

Potential Pitfalls in Therapy

The major pitfall in working with eating disordered clients lies within the nature of the disorder itself. Eating disorders have a strong addictive component so that models of addictive disorders offer relevant guidelines and suggest obstacles which may be encountered in treatment of the disorder. In general, addictive behaviors are highly resistant to change because they have a strong history as a coping mechanism. Behaviors which become addictive are those behaviors which serve to alleviate anxiety immediately and quickly despite delayed and long-term negative consequences. Anxiety reduction is the most powerful enabler of behavior. Eating disordered behavior has served the purpose of reduction of anxiety associated with emotional dysregulation. Thus, eating disordered behavior has been powerfully reinforced. Giving up this anxiety-reducing behavior will be a major step for the client in that she will have to accept, tolerate, and learn to manage anxiety that she has been avoiding for a significant period of time. The eating disordered client must trade in the quick-fix, destructive strategies for dealing with anxiety. The client must learn more thoughtful and productive ways to cope with anxiety.

Often an individual will give up a form of addictive coping behavior but replace it with another unhealthy addiction. This is a potential obstacle in treating the eating disordered client. Kristen may give up her bulimic behavior, but replace it with another unhealthy compulsive behavior such as alcohol usage. Kristen already has a history of using exercise and work excessively as alternate methods of avoiding and reducing anxiety.

Learning to tolerate and manage affective states rather than "run from them" is a challenge for many clients but particularly for eating disordered clients. From an early age, these individuals have not developed strategies for tolerating and managing feelings. The therapist will need to be patient and persistent in helping the client identify the small, effective prior successes and current successes in dealing with the disorder. The client will expect large, dramatic, perfect change and may discourage the therapist from appropriate focus on small successful steps.

Termination and Relapse Prevention

Due to the established, addictive, complex nature of Kristen's disorder, termination and relapse prevention require special attention. Kristen needs to consider that she will not arrive at a point where she is "finished" or "cured." She will need to view her work as ongoing.

Termination will be a gradual process with sessions decreasing in frequency over a lengthy period of time—6 months or more—until it is clear that Kristen has consolidated her gains adequately to maintain herself. Kristen will need to commit to ongoing self-monitoring and evaluation of her behavior and coping.

During the termination phase, Kristen would be asked to develop, in writing, a specific plan for self-monitoring and support. The plan would involve looking ahead at the start of each day to plan, to anticipate stressful interactions, and to remind herself of goals for functioning well. At the end of the day, a brief review of functioning with problem solving and "troubleshooting" aimed at improvement would be done. These two monitoring sessions would be brief, only a few minutes in most cases. Gradually, Kristen may be able to move to less frequent and less deliberate monitoring of her functioning. The goals of this monitoring are twofold—to catch signs of relapse early so that measures can be taken to "get back on track" and to reinforce the patterns of these relatively new healthy behaviors. Ongoing social support and support group involvement would be of great benefit in preventing relapse.

Kristen would include in her written plan a list of signs of relapse. She would also need to identify stressors to which she is particularly vulnerable so that she may more effectively anticipate future challenges and prepare to handle them.

Kristen may need to contact her therapist for occasional "booster sessions" at stressful points in her life or when she experiences the need to problem solve regarding an anticipated challenge in her life. Kristen needs to give herself permission to reenter therapy for brief periods, when needed, without viewing this as failure. Kristen will not have eliminated her vulnerabilities but will continue to carry them with her through life. Now, however, she will be cognizant of them and will have gained skills in managing them.

Mechanisms of Change

The quality and depth of the therapeutic bond will be a critical element in Kristen's progress. The relationship requires a structured, encouraging female therapist who is capable of deep empathy and clear boundaries. While initially testing the relationship, Kristen will come to trust in it. Within the relationship—even before Kristen trusts the relationship—she will experience the cognitive understanding and support of the lifestyle process. This process situates both client and therapist in the client's personal narrative. The process invites Kristen to tell her story. It is both through the telling of the story and the careful reflection on the story that the roots of the relationship will take hold. For the client, the telling of her story enhances intimacy. Understanding is developed to the extent that the therapist carefully works within the client's narrative, deeply considering the client's point of view.

For Kristen, the experience of authoring her story and having that authorship taken seriously will be encouraging and anxiety producing. But the process of self-understanding will lead Kristen to the narrative material that will allow her to form her preferred identity. The identity formation process requires that the therapist carefully and slowly introduce support tools and techniques discussed earlier in this chapter. The therapist will need to attend to Kristen's readiness level for each new skill. The therapist will need to modulate both resistance and workaholic approaches to recovery.

REFERENCES

Adler, A. (1998, 1931). *What life could mean to you*. (Colin Brett, Trans.). Center City, MN: Hazelden .

Adler, A. (1998, 1927). *Understanding human nature*. (Colin Brett, Trans.). Center City, MN: Hazelden.

Allen, J. (1995). *Coping with trauma: A guide to self understanding*. Washington, DC: American Psychiatric Press, Inc.

Dreikurs, R. (1989, 1935). *Fundamentals of Adlerian Psychology*. Chicago: Adler School of Professional Psychology.

Dreikurs, R., & Mosak, H. H. (1967). The tasks of life. II. The fourth life task. *Individual Psychologist, 4*, 51–55.

Millon, T., Millon, C., & Davis, R. D. (1994). *Millon clinical multiaxial inventory-III*. Minneapolis: National Computer System.

Mosak, H. H. (1995). Adlerian psychotherapy. In Raymond J. Corsini (Ed.), *Current psychotherapies* (pp. 51–94). Itasca, IL: F. E. Peacock Publishers, Inc.

Mosak, H. H., & Shulman, B. H. (1988). *Life style inventory*. Levittown, PA: Accelerated Development.

Powers, R. L., & Griffith, J. *Understanding life-style: The psycho-clarity process*. Chicago: The Americas Institute of Adlerian Studies, LTD.

Schneider, M. F., & Stone, M. (1998). Process and techniques of journal writing in Adlerian Therapy. *Journal of Individual Psychology, 54*(4), 511–534.

Schneider, S., & Mosak, L. E. (1993). *Life style: A workbook*. Chicago, IL: Adler School of Professional Psychology.

Shulman, B. H., & Mosak, H. H. (1988). *Manual for life style assessment*. Levittown, PA: Accelerated Development.

Steinem, G. (1993). *The revolution from within: A book of self-esteem*. Boston: Little, Brown & Co.

Zerbe, K. (1993). *The body betrayed: Women, eating disorders, & treatment*. Washington, D.C.: American Psychiatric Press, Inc.

9

The Elementary Pragmatic Model

Piero De Giacomo and Antonietta Santoni Rugiu

TREATMENT MODEL

General Theory of the Elementary Pragmatic Model

The Elementary Pragmatic Model grew out of a movement to mobilize mental health care outside of mental institutions in Italy during the 1960s and '70s (De Giacomo, 1993). The movement required a strong focus on family participation and brief interventions in order to meet the needs of the patients and families. An interdisciplinary work group on general systems theory evolved the basic language underlying the Elementary Pragmatic Model (Lefons, Pazienza, Silvestri, Tangorra, Corfiati et al., 1978).

In applying the Elementary Pragmatic Model to eating disorders, we currently adopt two fundamental approaches: one based on family therapy, the other on intensive, multidisciplinary Day Hospital treatment, embracing psycho-education on eating problems, group interaction, diet guidance, creativity groups, and physical rehabilitation.

Both in family therapy and in some of the group activities in the Day Hospital, human interactions and their change are understood according to a model which we have defined as the Elementary Pragmatic Model. This model deals with the "pragmatics" of human relationships, that is, with the practical effect of communication in terms of how it alters behavior. The term "elementary" is derived from the fact that it is built on basic units of interaction, based on an interactionist philosophy that sees the mind as developing within the course of interaction. The triad on which the approach is based is general systems theory, communication theory, and cybernetics, principally derived from the work of Gregory Bateson (1980). Bateson's thought is also the starting point of other models of family therapy, such as the strategic and structural models, those of Milan and Palo Alto (Gurman & Kniskern, 1981). These latter differ from our model to the degree that their theoretical systems are less formal in the mathematical sense, less linked to process, less exclusively relational. The Elementary Pragmatic Model, on the other hand, developed from a close collaboration between psychiatrists, psychologists, information scientists, physicians, and mathematicians expert in the general theory of systems. Not only is the understanding of interactions based on the model, but also the planning of interventions. The model is described in detail in a volume entitled *Finite Systems and Infinite Interactions: the Logic of Human Interaction and its Applications to Psychotherapy* (De Giacomo, 1993).

The Elementary Pragmatic Model is based on four possible patterns that derive, for instance, from subject A's (husband) and subject B's (wife) interaction (De Giacomo, L'Abate, & De Giacomo, 1997). The elements that are used in the construction of the model are (1) one's world, (2) the other's world, (3) whatever is common between the two, and (4) what is external to the two. Thus, the two major dimensions of this model are internality versus externality and common versus uncommon. In the interaction there is a triad: proposal of the first subject, proposal of the second subject, and the result of the interaction (see Figure 9.1). For example, the husband invites his wife to go horseback riding with him (his proposal), she refuses to go (her proposal), and they stay home (result). Four major patterns, or coordinates, may emerge between a pair, illustrating the process of change as the result of mutually coming together.

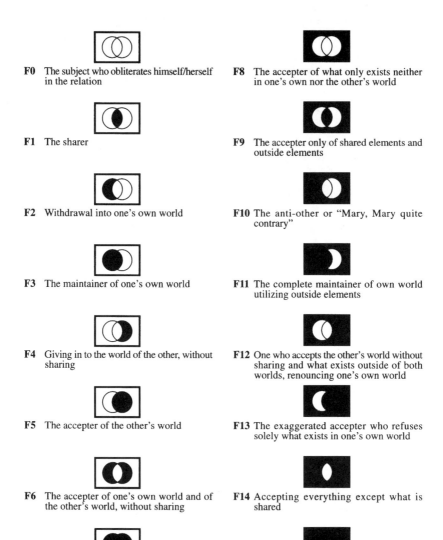

F0 The subject who obliterates himself/herself in the relation

F1 The sharer

F2 Withdrawal into one's own world

F3 The maintainer of one's own world

F4 Giving in to the world of the other, without sharing

F5 The accepter of the other's world

F6 The accepter of one's own world and of the other's world, without sharing

F7 The accepter of one's own and of the other's world, including sharing

F8 The accepter of what only exists neither in one's own nor the other's world

F9 The accepter only of shared elements and outside elements

F10 The anti-other or "Mary, Mary quite contrary"

F11 The complete maintainer of own world utilizing outside elements

F12 One who accepts the other's world without sharing and what exists outside of both worlds, renouncing one's own world

F13 The exaggerated accepter who refuses solely what exists in one's own world

F14 Accepting everything except what is shared

F15 The total acceptance

Shaded areas show how the world of the first subject has changed as a result of the interaction with the other. The left circle represents the first subject's world and the right circle, the world of the other. The overlap represents the shared elements. The area outside of the circles represents everything outside of the two worlds.

FIGURE 9.1   The 16 interactive styles of the Elementary Pragmatic Model.

(1) Something that did not exist in the husband's world but which existed in the wife's world is accepted in the interaction. For instance, when the husband says "I don't want to watch TV," the wife replies: "Come on, in a little while a great program will be on." As a result the husband acquiesces to his wife's proposal, and he watches TV. Symbolically, the interaction is represented as: $0\ 1 \to 1$, representing acceptance.

(2) Maintenance of one's own world, occurring when something that existed in the husband's world but did not exist in the wife's world is accepted. For instance, he suggests: "I want to watch TV"; and the wife replies instead: "I want to go out," but she nevertheless then acquiesces and watches TV. Symbolically: $1\ 0 \to 1$ = maintenance.

(3) Sharing of one's own world with another, when something existing in both the wife and the husband's world is accepted. For instance, he says "Tonight I want to watch TV" and the wife replies: "Me too, dear," and they both watch TV. Symbolically: $1\ 1 \to 1$ = sharing.

(4) Anti-function which represents acceptance of a proposal that is neither in one's own nor in the other's world. For instance, when the husband says "I do not want to watch TV," the wife replies "Neither do I," but they both nevertheless end up watching TV. Symbolically: $0\ 0 \to 1$ = anti-function.

This model not only addresses individual interactions, but also can be extrapolated to groups of individuals who have certain characteristics in common, such as a family, social aggregate, or institution.

From the merging of these four coordinates by composition derive 16 relational styles, or functions, that make up a taxonomy of human interactions and their change (F stands for function; see Figure 9.1):

F0. Emptiness of mind, when nothing is accepted and there is no acceptance of one's world, the world of the other, nor of external elements, as in a comatose person or in an individual who during an interaction loses contact with the other by going blank.

F1. Sharing part of one's world with another, when only what is common to both worlds is accepted. An example is two coworkers who work on something they have to do at work, but who then go their separate ways; or two sex addicts who have a one-night stand without even knowing anything about each other and do not plan to meet again.

F2. Exclusive acceptance of one's world but not of the other, nor whatever the two may have in common. A self-centered individual ignores, dismisses, and discounts the proposal of the other and of whatever they may have in common in the relationship. For instance, in spite of a partner's lack of interest in computers, the individual gives the partner one as a gift, ignoring the partner's lack of interest and following his or her own interest exclusively.

F3. Maintenance of one's own world through the acceptance not only of one's own world but also acceptance of whatever is common with the world of the other. This is seen in extremely selfish and rigidly unbending individuals who take from the other what is already in their world. For instance, these individuals do whatever they want, regardless of the desires of the others.

F4. Accepting the world of another without sharing it. For instance, passive individuals yield uncritically and flexibly to the other's world, surrendering their world to the world of the other, as in the case of a partner who is willing to accede to the other partner's sexual wishes or practices, no matter how extreme these wishes or practices may be.

F5. Accepting only the other's world and what is common to both worlds as, for instance, individuals who altruistically and actively accept the proposals of the other. One example is extreme identification in which an individual is transformed by taking on the characteristics of the partner.

F6. Accepting one's own and the other's world, without sharing it. So-called selfish altruists ambivalently hesitate in sharing either world, oscillating between accepting and refusing their own world or the world of the other without connecting either world. In another case, the individual cannot make up his or her mind one way or another, because there is an underlying agenda that has not been faced by either partner. When a girl has been raped and her family, who knows about it, does not talk about it, it produces a great deal of oscillation that may show itself in conflicts over decisions. In another case, one partner has had an affair of which both partners are aware but do not talk about, producing a distortion in the relationship.

F7. Accepting one's own and the other's world, and harmoniously mediating both worlds without getting lost in the other's world. This is the case with a very close couple, where each partner is available to the other in any possible way, without losing his and her world.

F8. Acceptance only of what does not exist in one's own and in the other's world, but acceptance of external elements of the outside world, which were not previously present in the interaction and which were not common to both worlds. This includes words or acts that are irrelevant or outside the context of what is going on in an interaction, such as asking about the price of eggs in China during sexual intercourse.

F9. Accepting only what exists and what does not exist in one's own and the other's world, such as unquestioning and uncritical sharing of what one has in common in the internal and external worlds. For example, a couple who love animals precisely because they are the supreme creations of nature go out and buy a mechanical one.

F10. Accepting only either what exists in one's internal world as well as the external world, but not what exists in the other's world or whatever is shared, as in "Mary, Mary, quite contrary." This is the active, systematic opposer and spiteful negativist and obstructionist, as seen in individuals who do exactly the opposite of what is proposed by others.

F11. Accepting one's own world, including whatever is shared with the other's world, as well as whatever is foreign to one's own and the other's world. This is seen in an exaggeration in sticking to one's own world while attempting to expand towards the world of others. If there is opposition, however, these individuals become confused, as seen in bullies, dictators, and arrogant egotists when they are faced by strong opposition that they cannot control or dominate.

F12. Accepting only what is in the other's world without sharing it but accepting whatever does not exist in one's own world nor in the other's world. This occurs in pseudo-altruists who appear to accept the other's world but in reality maintain their own world, also in martyrs who make sacrifices for their own sake and not for the sake of others, or in those who receive pleasure vicariously after giving pleasure to others.

F13. Acceptance of the other's world and whatever there is in common that does not exist in one's own and the other's world, but not of what is part of one's own world. This is the amplification of the world of the other while refusing to accept one's own world. For example, if one likes dogs, the partner gives the other a magnificent thoroughbred, well beyond his/her expectations.

F14. Total acceptance of one's own, the other's, and the external world of both without accepting shared elements. This is seen in individuals who cannot focus directly or who cannot complete interactions successfully, as in premature ejaculation or individuals who cannot address issues directly and speak in metaphors, as seen in the language of mobsters.

F15. Total acceptance of whatever exists in one's own and the other's world internally and externally, as seen in individuals who unselectively and inconclusively accept whatever exists and who accept both extremes of any situation without any boundaries.

Psychotherapy

This model predicts what kind of interaction will take place as a consequence of two people interacting using similar or different styles of the 16. From the matrix of the 16 interactive styles, there are 256 theoretically possible interactions. Understanding these interactions allows the therapist to organize specific guidelines for specific interventions. Considering all of the possible combinations and permutations of styles between individuals or members of a family, a therapist can follow certain designated routes that may be possible and that have already been written in a computer program (available from the authors). For instance, if an individual with an F10 style needs to be changed to an F3 style, the therapist or a member of the family, acting according to the therapist's indications, may use an F12 style. That is, if a contrary person needs to learn to maintain his or her own world, the therapist and family may act in a pseudo-altruistic, accepting manner, rendering the designated patient capable of maintaining his/her own world. By the same token, a partner in a couple interacting with an F14 style, accepting but unable to share, can be changed to follow an F3 style when the other partner follows an F12 style. In this case, the first partner talks without focusing on any shared aspect and the other assumes a pseudo-altruistic manner to encourage the maintaining of the first one's own world. When an individual with an F6 style interacts with another individual with an F5 style, the former may follow an F3 style; for example, when the partner becomes ambivalent and the other goes towards his or her world, the ambivalent partner would be rendered more sure of himself or herself.

Regarding anorexia nervosa, an intervention which has raised much interest and discussion is that of the "trip with the father" (De Giacomo, Margari, Santoni Rugiu, 1989a; De Giacomo et al., 1989b; De Giacomo, Renna, & Santoni Rugiu, 1992; Santoni Rugiu, Calò, Caramatti, Catucci, Manca et al., 1999). In brief, in families with an anorectic girl we often observe that the father has far fewer interactions with the daughter than does the mother. Furthermore, the quality of the interactive style he uses is distant, characterized by a tendency to seldom enter her world. The therapeutic strategy, then, consists in greatly increasing the number of interactions between father and daughter and making sure such interactions take place with a specific relational style of acceptance. The prescription is for the father and daughter to take a 3-week trip together and for the father to spend that time trying to understand and accept her world.

The key to success in this intervention, therefore, is that of increasing significantly the closeness between father and daughter. In cases where the father is absent, all members of the family available are involved in therapy, again in accordance with the Elementary Pragmatic Model. The formula is that all available members of the family interact with the patient according to a relational style which leads to desired change. For example, should one wish to modify a tendency toward ambivalence, the family will adopt the style of going towards her world. This means that all of the family members present at the session will use the relational style (the function) that the father would have adopted had he been present, in accordance with the aforementioned prescription of the "trip with the father."

In the case of bulimia, a general scheme which might be adopted is that of opposing purging and fasting. When, as a result, the girl becomes uncertain, doubtful, and ambivalent, one should go towards her world and enter it, by means of a committed search for and understanding of her true self.

THE THERAPIST'S SKILLS AND ATTRIBUTES

The therapist must be an expert in family therapy with at least 4 years of training in accordance with the canons of the Italian School of Psychotherapy (recognized by the Italian Ministry of Health). The aforementioned training consists of 500 hours of theoretical and practical activity aimed at achieving a profound understanding of both the normal and the pathological family, the latter having one or more members affected by mental disturbance. The trainee therapist must learn to work with such families in order to improve the functionality and ameliorate the pathological condition of the designated patient.

The specific characteristic of our group is a theoretical and practical acquaintanceship with the Elementary Pragmatic Model. But the therapist must also possess those gifts of empathy for and interest in the family which are so indispensable for those working in this field.

What distinguishes the method of a therapist from our group from that of therapists from other schools of family therapy is the translation of his or her perceptions and experience of the family into the terms of the Elementary Pragmatic Model. This understanding is transformed into therapeutic maneuvers and prescriptions for the family marked by a sharp sense of strategy aimed at problem solving. It should be emphasized that our approach differs from the structural and strategic approaches by virtue of an altogether different method and way of thinking. The therapist must be able to work with the elements and interactions which emerge during the session. Once read on the grid of the Elementary Pragmatic Model, these are translated into operative terms by means of appropriate strategies: phrases, forms of behavior adopted by the therapist, and prescriptions for patient and family, all of which are aimed at rendering functional the family system and allowing greater liberty to the designated patient. The general scheme is to part from the reality presented by the family, introduce the Elementary Pragmatic Model, place the former in relation with the latter, solicit new ideas, and use them to transform the mental constructs and dysfunctional rules of the family.

THE CASE OF KRISTEN

Assessment, Conceptualization, and Treatment Planning

Assessment

A personal interview with the patient and with her family is necessary in order to codify their manner of communication and to identify the relational styles adopted by the various members of the family. The additional advantage of the direct interview, in Kristen's case, will be that of measuring the degree of commitment of each member of the family to solving Kristen's problem. It should be remembered that, for us, the figure of the father is particularly important in the treatment of anorexia and, in part, bulimia.

A test derived from our model is the SISCI-1, which consists in sequential presentation of 90 ink-blot tables (90 slides, a table each). These tables are administered in an interactive fashion, showing them in slides to singles or groups of subjects. First, subjects view each slide and have to choose which slides of the 90 they prefer. They can choose as many as they like. Then 40 slides, chosen at random from the 90, are shown again with the information (set) that these were the ones chosen by most subjects. In the second presentation, subjects are asked to reselect which slides they liked best. In a third presentation, subjects have to choose again from the original 90 slides, without any set. From these choices, it is possible to find out how much each subject accepts the world of the other (acceptance coordinate), how much one maintains his or her own world (maintenance coordinate), how much one shares his or her own world (sharing coordinate), and how much one accepts whatever was not in the first and second presentations (anti-function coordinate) (De Giacomo, L'Abate, & De Giacomo, 1997; De Giacomo, Silvestri, Pierri, Lefons, Corfiati, & Tangorra, 1986; Pierri & Corfiati, 1990; Silvestri, Lefons, De Giacomo, & Corfiati, 1988).

Another test is the Self-View Questionnaire (SVQ) (L'Abate, 1998), which permits an evaluation of the subject's relational capacity through the subject's recognizing the self and/or the other in the following 16 pairs of adjectives, establishing a preference list from maximum to minimum recognition: empty/absent, participating/ sharing, solitary/reserved, tenacious/egocentric, docile/surrendering, altruist/involved, mysterious/ambiguous, collaborative/ mediator, abstract/unpredictable, sharing/innovative, rebel/antagonist, dominant/dictatorial, double-faced/false-altruist, unpredictable/altruist, inconclusive/disorganized, confused/chaotic. The choice of adjectives forms a continuum, or preference list, which gives first place to the pair of adjectives which most correspond to the patient's personal characteristics (or to those of their partner, if the test is interactive), second to those slightly less appropriate, and so on to the sixteenth place given to the adjectives which least conform to the patient's way of being.

These tests are important, once again, in evaluating Kristen's relational styles and her family's, to provide a basis for programming the relational styles of the therapist and the future behavior of the various members of the family.

Therapeutic Goals

Our primary objectives for Kristen are a reduction of bulimic behavior and the development of a stable base in various aspects of her life. This would involve combating the ambivalence that causes Kristen to oscillate between the "licentious" (the eating binge) and the "saintly" (vomiting). Initially the increase in her capacity to uphold her own world would require the help of others, that is, the therapist, the family, and the therapeutic team as a whole. A fundamental objective would be to enhance Kristen's ability to uphold her own world on a stable basis.

Timeline for Therapy

If this operation of moving towards Kristen's world, amplifying it, can be performed in the presence of her family, and especially of her father, therapy will run more smoothly. If therapy is conducted exclusively by the therapist following an individual approach, much more time will be required.

In family therapy, the schedule which we normally employ is that of 10 weekly hour-long sessions, with expert supervision during the fifth and tenth—an average of 10 weekly sessions lasting around 2 months. Individual psychotherapy, albeit theoretically compatible with the Elementary Pragmatic Model, is rarely employed by our team. An alternative to family therapy is Day Hospital treatment, covering a period of 6 weeks, 7 hours a day for 7 days every other day, reaching a total of 126 hours.

Our experience indicates that if the result is positive, the effects of family therapy are consolidated down the years. Our outcome research demonstrates an improvement with the passing of time (De Giacomo, Margari, & Santoni Rugiu, 1992; De Giacomo, Margari, & Rutigliano, 1997).

Case Conceptualization

It seems evident from Kristen's history that she has enjoyed periods of satisfactory equilibrium, relatively free of eating disorder symptoms. The periods in which her condition worsens are ones of existential difficulty. During these negative periods Kristen becomes incapable of maintaining her own world and turns oscillating and ambivalent, as evidenced by her eating binges and vomiting. During the positive periods, on the other hand, she imposes on herself excessively rigid norms of behavior, a relational style consisting of an exaggerated maintenance of her own proposals, which amounts to a species of internal dictatorship. It is difficult to deal effectively with Kristen in these periods of great determination, insofar as questioning her behavior could drive her into a state of mental confusion. During the periods of ambivalence and oscillation, it is easier to help her.

Kristen is an intelligent and capable individual, as frequently occurs in such cases. In the end she accepted treatment, which undoubtedly is a highly positive result. Kristen seems to possess a rather refined and self-reflective mind, capable of deepening its own world, as long as it is guided in this internal voyage by experts.

According to our case survey, a case of this type has a chance in four of being completely cured (Santoni Rugiu et al., 1999).

The Therapeutic Relationship

The Therapeutic Bond

Our approach to therapy is based on an underlying philosophy of finding new solutions to the patient's problem and, even more, of providing the instruments necessary for the patient to construct solutions with her own mind. The therapist, therefore, presents himself or herself as an expert who is extremely interested in helping Kristen to isolate and solve her problem. The therapist must communicate warmth and demonstrate an ability to establish closeness with her, not as would a friend, relative, or lover, but as a professional, versed in human nature and with superior competence deriving from specialized training based on original and sophisticated mental models. The therapist's aim is that of getting to know Kristen's world, furnishing her with a cognitive framework destined to modify her point of view on certain modes of thought and action.

While this is the general attitude, it should be borne in mind that we privilege the family approach, and hence what has been said regarding Kristen and her relational style is valid also for the other members of the family. In other words, the systemic vision and model that we employ, the Elementary Pragmatic Model of interaction and change, is the vital point of reference. In family therapy, the modification of the relationships existing between the members of the family obviously takes precedence over the relationship between the therapist and Kristen. Essential to our organization of family therapy sessions is the presence of an expert supervisor behind a one-way mirror during the fifth and tenth sessions. In certain cases, the supervisor is either perceived or explicitly presented as a *Deus ex machina* capable of providing that degree of decisive impetus which shall render therapy a success. The therapist creates *ad arte* an expectation on the part of the family regarding the supervisor's involvement in the fifth and tenth sessions, either behind the mirror or in person actively.

In the case of Day Hospital therapy, the setup is obviously entirely different insofar as multiple transferences of varying types are established, according to the species of intervention the Day Hospital provides: group interaction between patients, guided diet, psycho-educative groups, and interaction in creative groups. Thus, Kristen is guaranteed a variety of differing forms of contact with those she encounters during treatment and in the particular setting formed by the various components of the Day Hospital program. The Day Hospital is a sort of gym in which Kristen would need to interact with a wide range of relational styles, a fact inducing her to use differing styles herself. In this way, she would experiment and play a multiplicity of roles.

Roles in the Therapeutic Relationship

The roles in the therapeutic relationship may be understood more specifically in terms of the Elementary Pragmatic Model. The model foresees 16 relational styles as pictured in Figure 9.1: annulment, sharing, withdrawal into one's own world, maintenance of one's own world, passive acceptance of the other's world, active acceptance, oscillation between one's own world and the world of the other, mediation, acceptance of that which previously did not exist in the worlds of the interacting subjects (creativity, paradox, pure divergent thought), creative pursuit of an end, obstinate resistance, exaggerated maintenance of one's own world (dictators, for instance), pseudo-altruism (moving apparently towards the world of the other while in reality maintaining one's own), moving towards the world of the other in a paradoxical manner, accepting everything except a shared central point (metaphorical thought), and finally total acceptance (the loss of all selectivity, of all boundaries, as described in Zen philosophy, classified as mental confusion in Western terms). The most frequent pattern of styles, encompassing all 16, each with its individual percentage from most used to least used, establishes the characteristic role of each interacting subject.

The therapist's role would be that of de-codifying Kristen's family members' roles, clarifying which they are exactly, comparing them, predicting how they will modify in the interaction, and then verifying the prediction and the effective success of the interaction. A vital part of our work is that these complex ideas should be rendered simple and adapted to the powers of understanding of the users. The conceptual background differs from other, better-known once as, for example, Berne, who focuses on the three roles of adult, parent, and child (Berne, 1967). It is our hope, however, that the greater complexity of the Elementary Pragmatic Model allows also for a greater richness and a wider range of possible interventions.

Regarding roles within the family system, when working with the family we find it useful to apply the structural approach of Minuchin, which defines the boundaries between the various subsystems of the family (Minuchin, 1974), modified by the therapist in accordance with the specific situation in hand.

In other words, in the case of Kristen, the family approach may be adopted and what has been said above regarding relational styles and structural approach is pertinent. Should one opt instead for an individual approach, the therapist's role will be that of a warm, humane, and competent expert, willing to embark with the patient on a quest for new solutions.

If Day Hospital treatment is chosen, Kristen will find herself face-to-face with professionals performing various roles within the overall structure and, as previously said, will have to assume differing roles herself, depending on the components of the program which are offered to her.

Treatment Implementation and Outcome

Techniques and Methods of Working

With regard to the use of drugs, whereas in the case of anorexia no result is achieved, in that of bulimia improvement is observed. Hence, a combination of drugs and psychotherapy is to be taken into consideration, the most useful drugs being selective serotonine reuptake inhibitors (SSRIs).

Should we decide for family therapy, it is preferable that during the cycle of sessions no outside professionals should be involved. Even in the case that administration of psychotropic drugs is required, in our group, which includes psychiatrists, normally the family therapist deals with the psychopharmacological aspect.

We would adopt an approach—simple as a formula but neither that simple to explain or implement—which entails employing the relational style classified as "going towards her world." The latter requires a profound understanding of Kristen's world, that she probably lacks herself, a probability which is actually of use to the therapist in the sense that he or she may provide her with the instruments, "containers," or paths by which this understanding will be reached. Once Kristen's world has been recognized by the patient herself, by the therapist, and eventually by her family, the next step is to move in the direction of this world. The therapist would seek to drive beyond the limits of Kristen's own vision, adopting the relational style classified as "going towards the world of the patient amplifying it paradoxically." The main aim of therapy is to increase Kristen's ability to uphold her own world. The general technique employed to obtain this simple result is, as mentioned, that of using a *relational style which moves towards the world of the patient or one which moves towards the world of the patient amplifying it paradoxically.*

On the level of psychotherapy, prescriptions will be given for tasks to be performed at home. In Kristen's case, the father would be assigned the general task of entering into his daughter's world, understanding her constructs and mental processes, and studying her problems with her. He would be given other specific tasks also, such as taking lunch and dinner with her or of taking a trip with her. During these times, he would be expected to prevent her eating-binges and vomiting or, at other times, to assist without interfering.

Another more simple prescription for Kristen herself would be that in her moments of tension she should follow an audiovisual program of ours, to be found in a CD-ROM in Italian and English attached to the volume inspired by the Elementary Pragmatic Model (De Giacomo, 1999) which presents 16 styles of art against a background of Baroque music. The patient must simultaneously concentrate on the images and music, and on the thoughts which cause her the greatest anguish. Other computer programs are available (De Giacomo, 1999). Their aim is to make the mind more flexible and capable of solving problems—in short, to induce cerebral reprocessing.

Other possible suggestions are: reading self-help books, learning to appreciate the taste of the food and the sensation of feeling her stomach, making the patient change something, for example, eating with chopsticks rather than using the hands or knife and fork, using a portable barbecue placed on the table to prepare her food, paying the utmost attention so that every single bit is cooked well, and modifying the rhythm of the vicious circle, for instance, by checking her weight before each meal. These suggestions are valuable only to the extent that the therapeutic relationship is a valid and strong one (De Giacomo, Morgari, & Rutigliano, 1997).

The situation is obviously entirely different in the Day Hospital where a number of professionals are involved, in particular the dietician, who runs a fully-fledged course on eating disorders. There is also the rehabilitation expert, who works with techniques of rehabilitation and reappropriation of body image, which in such cases is normally distorted. Dance forms an important part of this treatment, whereas the art therapist brings to bear the therapeutic power of artistic activity (in accordance with style F9 of the Elementary Pragmatic Model, pursuing an objective creatively, reinforced by exposure to contexts largely conditioned by chance, as in style F15. The art therapist often behaves according to style F9, bringing the patient to adopt it also). Kristen will be asked to draw and paint, and to explain the significance of her work. To all of this is added group interaction which provides anorexic or bulimic patients the vital possibility of expressing their problems, experience, and moods.

Medical and Nutritional Issues

In the case of Kristen, it seems that no emergency medical procedure is required, while haematological and urinary tests can be managed by the family therapy team (which, it has been said, includes psychiatrists with adequate knowledge of the biological characteristics of these patients), availing of public or private laboratories.

In the case of using the aforementioned technique of "Taking a trip with the father," it is foreseen that prior to departure Kristen should dictate to her father the kind of diet that she would prefer, a menu which he will copy out on a piece of paper. Dictation takes place in the presence of the psychiatrist (either a physician or family therapist), thus ensuring that the menu will be suitable to the dietary requirements of the patient. If Kristen is undergoing Day Hospital treatment, obviously the hospital will see to it that an adequate diet is provided. In any case, prior to family therapy or Day Hospital treatment Kristen's physical condition must be checked in order to decide whether dietary integration is required or administration of SSRIs as pharmacological support. Should such substances be employed it will be necessary to monitor some haematic parameters such as transaminase. The medical part of treatment, in our group, is dealt with by a psychiatrist expert enough to manage the physical aspects of the case.

Potential Pitfalls

In the case of Kristen, we foresee no risk of suicide, to the extent that she has always demonstrated having the resources necessary to face the problems of life. Our records over a 20-year period register a zero incidence of suicide. The risk of serious physical problems, such as heart attack, for instance, is extremely low. This notwithstanding, it is our practice to mention such risks to Kristen in order to make her understand that when dealing with eating disorders, one is dealing with problems of life or death. Thus she is indirectly solicited to commit herself completely.

From our point of view, the main problem is precisely this, that Kristen should commit herself entirely to the quest for cure. To this end, we employ specific techniques, such as the "pact with the devil" or the "empty box" (De Giacomo, Pierri, & Margari, 1987; De Giacomo, Margari, & Santoni Rugiu, 1992; De Giacomo, Margari, & Rutigliano, 1997). The former consists of asking the patient and her family whether they are willing to do absolutely anything to solve the problem, making it clear that a decisively positive response is necessary. In the rare event that this is not forthcoming, and the response is uncertain, we resort to the so-called "empty box," which consists in the therapist's declaring that he or she possesses the solution to the problem but that neither patient or family are yet ready to receive it. When they are, the therapist will be available (De Giacomo, Pierri, & Margari, 1987). If we manage to obtain the total agreement of the patient, a positive result is all but guaranteed. The only pitfall resides in the potential failure of therapy, that is, that Kristen should not gain advantage from psychotherapy. However, Kristen has already passed the threshold and sought professional help. Hence, the case presentation leads us to think that she is ready to commit herself to therapy. The issue now is to make her accept a "binding" contract. To this end, the techniques of the "pact with the devil" and the "empty box," besides making her see the mortal danger she is facing, also induce her to accept, as it were, writing a "blank check" to her therapist. The rest depends on the capacity of the therapist to enter her world without provoking her to withdraw entirely into that world. The problem is one of the human capacity and training of the therapist.

The risk of relapse is always present, although with time results tend to improve. Resistance is overcome by means of the relational styles that are established between the therapist, the patient, and her family. One form of resistance could be Kristen's adopting a contrary attitude, which could be overcome by counter-opposition from the therapist. Another form could be produced by an ambivalent attitude, which would be overcome by entering her world, that is, going towards her world. Should Kristen resist by means of passive acceptance, the therapist's response would be that of unflinching maintenance of their own world. A final example of resistance would be a metaphorical tendency on the part of Kristen, which could be overcome by the therapist adopting a markedly goal-directed stance.

Termination and Relapse Prevention

Our work method pre-programs termination of the sessions. As previously mentioned, therapy consists of 10 weekly hour-long sessions, the fifth and tenth supervised by an expert who functions as a catalyst. It is extremely rare that the patient should reach the tenth session without undergoing improvement. Should this occur, one may propose a new cycle or alter the setup of therapy, sending the patient to the Day Hospital.

Once the cycle is complete, the patient returns for a check-up session after certain lapses of time, such as after 3 months, 6 months, a year, and 2 years. In this way, Kristen will know that she is being monitored and may always call the therapist, although we tend to emphasize that she should call only when dealing with something very important.

The alternative to family therapy, as mentioned, is the Day Hospital. Here also treatment is scheduled and hence the termination of therapy is programmed in advance. Part of this treatment is open encounters between ex-patients and multifamily encounters, both held monthly.

Mechanisms of Change

We maintain that change occurs through the modification of the various modalities of the subject's relational styles which, it should be remembered, are 16, with 256 possible modalities of change. Theoretical predictions are possible, such as those we have made for schizophrenia, in which we have simulated the relational styles which lead to the onset of the disturbance and to its cure (De Giacomo, Pierri, Lefons et al., 1990; De Giacomo, Margari, & Rutigliano, 1997). It is our opinion that, at times, change is to be attributed to the fact that patient and family organize their mind in such a way as to be susceptible to cure by means of any kind of intervention. There are, therefore, patients who can be cured by any therapist. In this particular case, there is a tendency towards spontaneous positive evolution which corresponds, for example, to style F12 of the Elementary Pragmatic Model. There are other patients who cannot be cured by any therapist or any form of therapy, due to a mental organization oriented towards a total maintenance of their own constructs, or either to a tendency to annul their minds or an inability to choose, leading to mental confusion. The influence of the outside world is more or less important, depending on the case in hand. In the case of Kristen, it is beyond doubt that the modality of entering the patient's world, amplifying it, would be the most useful, and that the internal dictator who holds her in his grip is not 100% dominant, in which case there would be no exit. Indeed, Kristen seems to us to demonstrate an ability to share creatively, and the capacity to doubt, which is a positive factor of change, as likewise her ability to resist. A third aspect of flexibility, and hence of therapeutic utility, is her ability to identify with others. These three functions will prove favorable to change.

REFERENCES

Bateson, G. (1980). *Mind and nature. A necessary unit.* Toronto: Bantam Books.

Berne, E. (1967). *Games people play: The psychology of human relationships.* New York: Grove Press.

De Giacomo, P. (1993). *Finite systems and infinite interactions: The logic of human interaction and its application to psychotherapy.* Norfork, CT: Bramble Books.

De Giacomo, P. (1999). *Mente e creatività: Il Modello Pragmatico Elementare quale strumento per sviluppare la creatività in campo medico, psicologico e manageriale, artistico e di ricerca* (Mind and Creativity: The Elementary Pragmatic Model as an instrument for developing creativity in the fields of medicine, psychology, management, art and research). Milan: Franco Angeli.

De Giacomo, P., L'Abate, L., & De Giacomo, A. (1997). Integrating models of human interaction: Three models, one reality? *Italian Journal of Psychiatry and Behavioral Science, 7,* 18–23.

De Giacomo, P., Margari, F., & Rutigliano, G. (1997). *Ottimizzazione della visita psichiatrica. Ovvero dell'arte modulare dello psichiatra* (Optimization of the psychiatric visit. Or: Of the modular art of the psychiatrist). Milan: Franco Angeli.

De Giacomo, P., Margari, F., & Santoni Rugiu, A. (1989a). Short-term interactional therapy of anorexia nervosa. *International Journal of Family Psychiatry, 10,* 111–122.

De Giacomo, P., Margari, F., & Santoni Rugiu, A. (1989b). Successful one-session treatments of anorexia nervosa. *International Journal of Family Psychiatry, 10,* 123–132.

De Giacomo, P., Margari, F., & Santoni Rugiu, A. (1992). *Psicoterapie interattive brevi* (Brief interactive psychotherapy). Rome: NIS.

De Giacomo, P., Pierri, G., & Margari, F. (1987). The empty box. *International Journal of Family Psychiatry, 8,* 143–150.

De Giacomo, P., Renna, C., & Santoni Rugiu, A. (1992). *Anoressia e bulimia* (Anorexia and bulimia). Padua: Piccin.

De Giacomo, P., Silvestri, A., Pierri, G., Lefons, E., Corfiati, L., & Tangorra, F. (1986). Research on the effects of psychodrugs on human interaction. *Acta Psychiatrica Scandinavica, 74,* 417–424.

Gurman, S. D., & Kniskern, D. P. (Eds.) (1981). *Handbook of family therapy.* New York: Brunner/Mazel.

L'Abate, L. (1998). Discovery of the family: From the inside to the outside. *American Journal of Family Therapy, 26,* 265–280.

Minuchin, S. (1974). *Families and Family Therapy.* Cambridge, MA: Harvard University Press.

Pierri, G., & Corfiati, L. (1990). The tests based on the Elementary Pragmatic Model. In P. De Giacomo (Ed.), *An Elementary Pragmatic Model: Theory and clinical applications.* Reprinted from the proceedings of the 8th World Congress of Psychiatry, Athens, 13–19 October 1989, pp. 12–20. Amsterdam: Elsevier Science Publishers.

Santoni Rugiu, A., Calò, P., Caramatti, M. V., Catucci, A., Manca, R., Sapone, R., Verrastro, G., & De Giacomo, P. (1999). Anoressia e bulimia: Trattamento in day hospital e ambulatoriale: Risultati (Anorexia and bulimia: day hospital and out-patient treatment: Outcome). In P. De Giacomo, M. Storelli, O. Todarello, F. Scapati, & F. Vadruccio (Eds.), *Psichiatria, 99* (pp. 307–311). Rome: CIC Edizioni internaziondi.

Silvestri, A., Lefons, A., De Giacomo, P., & Corfiati, L. (1988). Evaluation of interactional behavior with age: A theoretical/experimental approach. *Cybernetics and Systems: An International Journal, 19*, 15–39.

10

Integrative Cognitive Therapy for Bulimic Behavior

Stephen A. Wonderlich, Carol B. Peterson, James E. Mitchell, and Scott J. Crow

TREATMENT MODEL

Integrative cognitive therapy (ICT) is a new treatment for individuals with eating disturbances that includes dietary restriction, binge eating, and purging behaviors. While the treatment retains many elements of contemporary cognitive behavior therapy (CBT) approaches for bulimia nervosa (e.g., Fairburn, Marcus, & Wilson, 1993; Mitchell, Pyle, Eckert, Hatsukami, Pomeroy, & Zimmerman, 1990), it is based on a broader model of cause and maintenance of bulimia nervosa which, consequently, places a greater clinical focus on other factors, such as cultural variables, cognitions reflecting self discrepancy, interpersonal schemas, interpersonal relationship patterns, and affect regulation. ICT has been developed for the treatment of bulimic symptoms in normal weight individuals; however, it may be appropriate for the treatment of other types of eating disorders including anorexia nervosa and binge eating disorder.

Presently, ICT is in the relatively early stages of development. We have written a clinician manual and a patient workbook that are currently being pilot tested at the University of North Dakota and the University of Minnesota. Our goal is to test the general and differential effectiveness of ICT in randomized, controlled treatment studies. Hopefully, by retaining elements of CBT which we think are most effective, and adding techniques which have been discussed by feminist (Kearney-Cooke & Streigel-Moore, 1997), interpersonal (Benjamin, 1993), and emotion (Greenberg & Safran, 1987) theorists, we hope to enhance the long-term outcome for treatment of bulimia nervosa. Additionally, recent work on motivational interviewing with alcoholic individuals (Miller & Rollnick, 1991) and modified for the treatment of eating disordered individuals (Vitousek, Watson, & Wilson, 1998) has influenced ICT.

Model of Bulimic Behavior

The model of etiology and maintenance of bulimia nervosa which underlies this approach to treatment is multifactorial and attempts to integrate a broad array of interpersonal, cognitive-affective, cultural, and biological factors thought to increase the risk of developing and maintaining behaviors associated with bulimia nervosa. It is different from other cognitive or interpersonal models of bulimia nervosa (e.g., Fairburn et al., 1993) in that there is a greater emphasis on cultural factors, self-oriented cognition, interpersonal schemas, interpersonal relationship styles, and emotional experiences.

In its simplest form, the model (see Figure 10.1) posits that life experiences (e.g., criticism, rejection, loss) interact with temperamental predispositions (e.g., harm avoidance) to create mental representations of the self and others which are thought to organize and guide future interpersonal perceptions and behavior. Furthermore, representations of the self are characterized by a perceived sense of deficit or inadequacy, which can be specifically operationalized as a *discrepancy* between the individual's perception of the actual self and the standards for evaluating the actual self. This perceived self discrepancy is emotionally significant to the individual because of the perception of threat that it poses for evolving attachment relationships (e.g., I will not be acceptable to others because of my deficiencies.). Largely due to cultural factors, the self discrepancy becomes focused on appearance deficits. Various interpersonal fac-

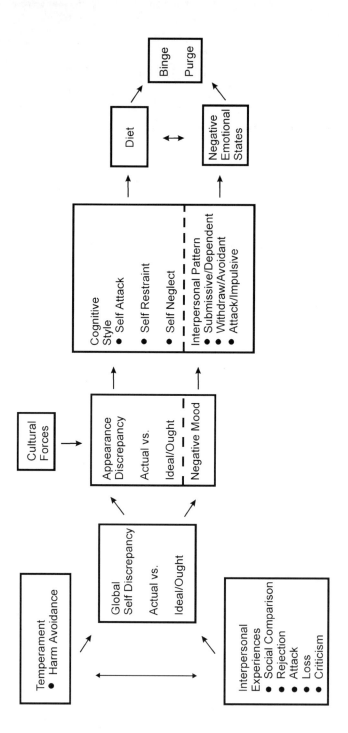

FIGURE 10.1 Model of bulimia nervosa.

tors (e.g., family and peer relationships) interfere with effective cognitive processing and coping with negative affect associated with the self discrepancy. In a continued effort to cope with negative affect associated with self discrepancy, the individual develops maladaptive interpersonal patterns (i.e., submission, walling off, attack), as well as intrapersonal patterns, or cognitive styles (i.e., self-control, self attack, self neglect).

Unfortunately, the interpersonal patterns and cognitive styles that the bulimic individual develops typically heighten negative emotions. Furthermore, as interpersonal and cognitive coping strategies fail to resolve the self discrepancy, cultural messages continue to suggest that dieting and appearance-based solutions may enhance the individual's perception of her actual self. Such a solution is negatively reinforcing because it reduces the degree of discrepancy between perceptions of their actual self and the individual's evaluative standards.

Physiological and nutritional factors associated with dieting may initially precipitate binge behaviors. However, bingeing becomes highly reinforcing behavior because it not only relieves physiologically based distress associated with dieting, but also promotes a psychological experience of escape from negative emotions. Purging reduces the fear of weight gain, and thus serves as a means of reducing self discrepancy. Also, dysregulation in physiological and neurochemical mechanisms and systems, as a result of dieting, bingeing, and vomiting, may serve to maintain eating disorder symptoms.

Temperament

The model posits that bulimic individuals display a temperament that is characterized by propensity to avoid change and generally avoid situations which are perceived as threatening or harmful to their self-esteem. The model relies heavily on the theoretical work of psychobiological personality theorists (e.g., Cloninger, 1987; Tellegen, 1985), some of which has been previously applied to the eating disorders (e.g., Brewerton, Hand, & Bishop, 1993; Bulik, Sullivan, Weltzin, & Walter, 1995). For example, empirical reports have consistently revealed that bulimic individuals show elevated harm avoidance scores (e.g., Brewerton et al., 1993), but novelty seeking and reward dependence have not been consistently shown to be associated with bulimia nervosa (e.g., Bulik et al., 1995; Berg, Crosby, Wonderlich, & Hawley, in press).

Environmental Experience

The model posits that bulimic individuals are likely to experience a broad array of events or circumstances in their life which threaten or interfere with attachment processes (i.e., increase risk of harm). For example, bulimic individuals are more likely to have been adopted (Holden, 1991), experienced child physical or sexual abuse (Welch & Fairburn, 1994; Wonderlich, Brewerton, Jocic, Dansky, & Abbott, 1997) and have parental histories of psychopathology, including depression and substance abuse (Fairburn, Welch, Doll, Davies, & O'Connor, 1997). Also, there is considerable research indicating that bulimic adolescents and adults perceive their relationships with their parents and their overall family environments as conflictual, disengaged, and non-nurturant (Kendler, MacLean, Neale, Kessler, Health, & Eaves, 1991; Strober & Humphrey, 1987; Wonderlich, 1992). Supporting these descriptions, observational studies of bulimic individuals' families in the laboratory suggest that their relationships are best described as disengaged, conflictual, and lacking in effective communication (Humphrey, 1989). Furthermore, recent evidence suggests that individuals with eating related disturbances display unstable attachments as measured by Main's Adult Attachment Interview (Cole-Detke & Kobak, 1996). Interestingly, eating disordered individuals were much more likely than depressed individuals to show a "dismissive" attachment style, implying an emotionally restricted set of mental representations of early relationships. The present model implies that such experiences, along with any other experience that threatens their feelings of interpersonal security and self-esteem (e.g., criticism, teasing, social comparison), will be emotionally significant for the bulimic individual, given their previously described temperamental sensitivity to harm.

Self-Discrepancy

Consistent with recent risk-factor studies (e.g., Fairburn et al., 1997), the model posits that negative self-evaluation is associated with bulimia nervosa and is the consequence of the previously described problematic interpersonal-attachment experiences. However, the model predicts that it is not simply negative self-evaluation (i.e., negative self representation) that is most precisely causal in bulimic individuals, but instead, bulimic individuals perceive a deficit in themselves that reflects a discrepancy between their perceived actual self and a comparative standard that they apply to themselves, or they believe others apply to them (i.e., ideal self, ought self). These ideas are derived from Self Discrepancy Theory (Higgins, 1987) and its application to depression (Higgins, Bond, & Strauman, 1986) and to eating disordered behaviors (Strauman & Glenberg, 1994; Strauman, Vookles, Barenstein, Chaiken, & Higgins, 1991). Specifically, Self-Discrepancy Theory postulates various domains of the self, including the *actual* self (i.e., a mental representation of the attributes or features the individual believes he or she actually possesses), the *ideal* self (i.e., a representation of the attributes that the individual or significant other would ideally like him or her to possess), and the *ought* self (i.e., a representation of the attributes that the individual or a significant other believes it is his or her obligation or duty to possess) (Strauman et al., 1991).

Central to the current theory are Strauman's and colleagues' findings (Strauman et al., 1991; Strauman & Glenberg, 1994), suggesting that actual self-ideal self discrepancies are related to negative mood and, importantly, body dissatisfaction, body size overestimation, and bulimic symptoms. It is further hypothesized that such body dissatisfaction, as a specific facet of self-concept, may exacerbate negative affective states, including depression (Joiner, Wonderlich, Metalsky, & Schmidt, 1995). Furthermore, Altabe and Thompson (1996) conducted a series of experiments which suggest that actual versus ideal discrepancy *in terms of appearance* appears to function as a true underlying cognitive schema that can influence information processing and affect negative mood. Together, these findings suggest that discrepancies between the actual self and ideal self elicit negative affect, body dissatisfaction, and body size overestimation, which in turn interact with one another.

In this model, it is important to emphasize that self-discrepancies are significant not only as cognitive phenomena, but also as interpersonal phenomena. That is, failure to meet ideal or ought standards is considered significant to the individual because of the implications it poses for her level of interpersonal security. The evaluative standards (e.g., ideal self, ought self) that the person holds represent the internalization of external behavioral standards modeled or reinforced by others (e.g., family, friends, culture). Thus, the presence of self-discrepancy and associated affective states is expected to be a motivational stimulus for interpersonal and intrapsychic behavior in the individual. In other words, reducing discrepancy is reinforcing because it implies increased interpersonal security.

Negative Mood

There is considerable evidence to suggest that bulimic individuals experience exaggerated states of aversive self-awareness and a propensity for negative affectivity (e.g., Johnson & Larson, 1982). The present model posits that such negative affectivity and aversive self-awareness is precipitated by the previously described self-related discrepancy and its associated perceived risk of attachment difficulties. Consistent with Escape Theory (Heatherton & Baumeister, 1991), it is predicted that bulimic individuals experience prolonged states of aversive, self-oriented preoccupation with their perceived self-deficits and the implication of such deficits for their interpersonal security. Prolonged states of such negative affectivity may be associated with the high levels of mood and anxiety problems that bulimic individuals report (Strober & Katz, 1988; Wonderlich & Mitchell, 1997) particularly, atypical depression characterized by high levels of anxiety, rumination, and guilt (Cooper & Fairburn, 1986). It is predicted in the model that the magnitude of such negative mood will be positively correlated with a magnitude of self-oriented discrepancies.

Interpersonal Factors and Cognitive Styles

Bowlby (1969) and emotion theorists (e.g., Buck, 1980; Greenberg & Safran, 1987) have described the motivational relationship between emotional states and action dispositions. Recent cognitive behavioral accounts of bulimia nervosa have placed less emphasis on emotional factors than on cognitive factors in the onset and maintenance of bulimia nervosa (e.g., Fairburn et al., 1993; Wilson & Fairburn, 1993).

There are two broad categories of behavior in the model which are thought to occur in bulimic individuals in an effort to regulate negative emotional experience related to self-discrepancy. These are specific interpersonal patterns *and* intrapersonal patterns, or cognitive styles.

Importantly, numerous empirical studies have found that bulimic individuals exhibit problematic interpersonal relationships (Johnson & Larson, 1982) and long-term social adjustment problems (Norman & Herzog, 1984). Bulimic individuals have also reported experiencing less support from existing interpersonal relationships than do non-eating disordered individuals and also perceive themselves as having higher degrees of social conflict and less social competence than controls (Grisset & Norvell, 1992). Furthermore, bulimic individuals reportedly form more dependent relationships (Jacobson & Robbins, 1989) and insecure attachments (Cole-Detke & Kobak, 1996) and experience problems with intimacy (Pruit, Kappins, & Gorman, 1992).

In an effort to reduce negative affect related to self-discrepancy, the model posits that bulimic individuals will emit specific repetitive interpersonal patterns in key relationships. There is some evidence to suggest that interpersonal patterns seen in bulimic individuals are strongly related to negative mood (Wonderlich & Swift, 1990), suggesting that such relationship styles may be an effort to manage negative affect. Influenced heavily by Benjamin's (1993) model of social behavior, the present model implies that these interpersonal patterns are oriented toward avoiding interpersonal rejection or abandonment. The two primary patterns posited to be associated with bulimia nervosa in the model are a *submission* pattern and a *wall-off* pattern, that parallel Bowlby's (1969) original thinking about two forms of "anxious attachment": ambivalent and avoidant. In the submission pattern, the bulimic individual is likely to appease and satisfy key attachment figures in an effort to avoid rejection and associated negative emotional experience. For similar reasons, the high degree of interpersonal withdrawal seen in the wall-off pattern may develop when relationships are perceived as threatening to attachment status and associated self-esteem, and the individual sees no way to reduce the relational problem through engagement in relationships. An additional interpersonal pattern, *attack*, is also hypothesized to be present in some individuals with eating disorders, and may occur when these individuals perceive attachment figures as withdrawing or being unavailable to them. The pattern is based on the fundamental interpersonal idea that some individuals will engage in hostile control behaviors in an effort to prevent the withdrawal of significant others (Benjamin, 1993).

In addition to these interpersonal patterns, the present model highlights intrapersonal patterns, or specific cognitive styles, as another means of attempting to regulate negative affect associated with self-discrepancy. Three specific cognitive styles are predicted: *self-control, self-blame,* and *self-neglect.* Some bulimic individuals may engage in extreme efforts to control the self and attain perfection in order to reduce their self-discrepancy and associated negative affects (i.e., self-control). Others may rely on a more hostile pattern of self-control in which they blame themselves for their self-discrepancy (i.e., self-blame). Still others may attempt to avoid the discrepancy through self-neglect and engage in more reckless unpredictable behaviors (i.e., self-neglect). It is important to note that such cognitive styles are used by the bulimic individual in an effort to manage the underlying negative affect that is ultimately linked to their fundamental self-discrepancy.

Dieting and Negative Emotional States

The model posits that the interpersonal patterns and cognitive styles adopted by the bulimic individual are predicted to have two particular effects. First, the extreme interpersonal patterns (i.e., submission, wall-off, and attack) are likely to result in heightened interpersonal distress, which only intensifies existing negative affect. Furthermore, the cognitive style that the bulimic individual develops (i.e., self-blame, self-control, self-neglect) regarding appearance may increase the likelihood of attempting to reduce appearance-related discrepancy through the pursuit of thinness and dieting. For example, extreme dieting reflects an ironic amalgam of self-control and self-neglect as the bulimic individual attempts to perfect the self (self-control) while simultaneously neglecting fundamental nutritional needs (self-neglect).

The combination of extreme dieting and its associated psychological and physiological dysregulatory effects, in conjunction with the heightened negative emotional states produced by the interpersonal patterns, is posited to increase the likelihood of binge/purge behavior. Consistent with Heatherton and Baumeister's (1991) Escape Theory, binge eating and purging behaviors are posited to provide a transitory avoidance of the bulimic individual's increasing negative affective states. Furthermore, by focusing on more immediate issues such as food consumption and purging, the individual is able to avoid more meaningful underlying issues related to self-discrepancy and the negative effects of interpersonal and cognitive coping styles.

The Therapist's Skills and Attributes

ICT therapists need to adopt an approach to treatment which incorporates two competing perspectives: an ability to *focus* the treatment in a clinically useful manner, while simultaneously assessing *multiple* aspects of the patient's functioning (e.g., eating behavior, cognition, affect, interpersonal patterns, interpersonal schemas). ICT therapists should be comfortable with the basic components of cognitive behavior therapy such as self-monitoring, structured treatment protocols, behavioral and cognitive techniques, and the use of homework assignments. Additionally, the ICT therapists should be able to address recurring interpersonal patterns and the underlying set of "cognitive maps" or "scripts" which guide these interpersonal transactions.

The therapist's style in ICT should be characterized by interpersonal warmth and expression of interest in, and curiosity about, the patient's behavior, thoughts, and feelings. At the same time, it is important for the therapist to remain well differentiated in his or her relationship to the patient, with an expectation that the treatment will be most effective if the patient *collaboratively* engages in the treatment with the therapist. Therapists should not attempt to force the treatment on the patient in any way and should validate the patient's ambivalence about pursuing behavioral change. ICT therapists should be very sensitive to the patient's emotional responding, and attempt to place such affective responses, and other behaviors (binge eating, purge, etc.), into a larger pattern that emphasizes the patient's effort at emotional regulation.

THE CASE OF KRISTEN

Assessment, Conceptualization, and Treatment Planning

Assessment

Before beginning ICT, the patient should be thoroughly evaluated with a thorough psychiatric interview (i.e., clinical or semi-structured) that assesses the full range of eating behaviors and associated psychopathology. In a typical research setting, this may include the Eating Disorder Examination (Fairburn et al., 1993) and the Structured Clinical Interview for DSM-IV (First, Spitzer, Gibbon, & Williams, 1995). Additionally, interpersonally oriented personality measures such as the Wisconsin Personality Inventory (Klein, Benjamin, Rosenfeld, Treece, Husted, & Greist, 1993) or the Differential Assessment of Personality Pathology (Livesley & Jackson, in press) may be administered to clarify personality traits which may be of significance in the overall treatment.

Several additional approaches to assessment would be utilized in ICT. The patient workbook contains several types of assessment. For example, a modification of the Selves Questionnaire (Higgins et al., 1986) and a variation of this questionnaire entitled the Physical Appearance Questionnaire (Altabe & Thompson, 1996) are included in the workbook to attempt to clarify discrepancy between perceptions of the actual self and the ideal or ought-self. Identifying the most salient areas of such self-discrepancy is an important aspect of the early assessments contained in the patient workbook. Second, the patient workbook contains several forms of self-monitoring logs, including a log fashioned after the one developed by Fairburn et al. (1993), on which subjects monitor all food and liquid consumed. Additionally, patients are asked to monitor interpersonal transactions on an "Interpersonal Pattern Worksheet." Here, the patient will carefully monitor specific interpersonal transactions noting the behavior of others, and the associated responses by the patient. These assessments become critical in terms of identifying the fundamental interpersonal behavior patterns.

Therapeutic Goals

ICT pursues several nutritional, cognitive, and interpersonal goals. A primary goal for Kristen would be normalization of meal consumption and weight restoration, which would be a focus in the early phases of ICT. Another major goal for treatment would be reducing self-discrepancy. Specifically, assisting Kristen to more accurately perceive positive aspects of her actual self and modify her unrealistic or rigid evaluative standards (i.e., ideal or ought-self) comprises a major goal for the treatment. Finally, in the latter phases of therapy, modifying interpersonal patterns becomes a primary goal for treatments. Particularly, reducing submissive or walled-off interpersonal patterns and increasing assertive behavior is a goal for ICT. Additionally, reducing potentially destructive cognitive styles such as self-neglect, self-attack, or excessive self-control while simultaneously increasing self-acceptance is a primary intrapersonal goal.

Time Line for Therapy

We are pilot testing ICT to determine if it can be practiced within a structured 20-session protocol, similar to existing CBT protocols for bulimia nervosa. It could also be modified for a less structured and unstandardized length of treatment. In the 20-session protocol, sessions are held twice a week for the first 4 weeks and weekly thereafter. Phase I of treatment (1 to 3 sessions) emphasizes psycho-education regarding cultural issues frequently thought to be relevant to eating disorders (e.g., cultural pressure for thinness, risks of dieting). Also, Phase I relies heavily on techniques from motivational interviewing (Miller & Rollnick, 1991), and these early sessions are utilized to explore and enhance patients' motivation for treatment. Several specific goals would be established for Phase I of treatment. They are: (a) establish a treatment relationship which includes Kristen as a significant collaborator; (b) in order to enhance motivation, begin to develop an awareness of the discrepancy between Kristen's actual level of functioning and her desired level of functioning; (c) remain highly sensitive to Kristen's emotional states and make efforts to identify emotional reactions that the patient experiences during therapy; (d) emphasize how cultural factors may influence Kristen's decisions about dieting and begin to educate the patient about realistic and healthy weight goals; (e) examine self-discrepancy, particularly in terms of perceptions of Kristen's perceived actual appearance and associated evaluative standards; and (6) begin self-monitoring of food intake.

Phase II of treatment (4 to 6 sessions) focuses on meal planning and learning coping skills to assist the patient in managing emotional distress associated with modifying her meal plans. Specific goals established in Phase II include: (a) continue self-monitoring of food intake; (b) continue to identify cognitions regarding self-discrepancy, particularly in terms of appearance; (c) begin formal meal planning with an emphasis on organization of nutritionally adequate meals and snacks; (d) encourage the identification and expression of Kristen's emotional state and teach coping skills to assist the patient in managing emotional distress.

Phase III of treatment (9 to 11 sessions) represents a clear shift towards a focus on interpersonal factors and cognitive styles that are thought to precipitate and/or maintain dietary restriction and bulimic behaviors. The patient is encouraged to identify maladaptive interpersonal patterns and cognitive styles that the model posits evolved to assist the patient in coping with his or her underlying self-discrepancy. Self-monitoring of interpersonal behavior will allow a functional analysis of the relationship between various interpersonal situations and eating disorder symptoms. Several goals are pursued in Phase III of treatment: (a) identify Kristen's repetitive interpersonal behavior patterns and cognitive styles; (b) identify the connection between Kristen's emotional states and interpersonal patterns or cognitive styles; (c) learn to identify underlying interpersonal schemas or rules that govern Kristen's interpersonal behavior; (d) increase assertive interpersonal behavior; and (e) increase Kristen's levels of self-acceptance and decrease self-attack, self-neglect, and excessive self-control patterns.

Finally, Phase IV (1 to 3 sessions) focuses explicitly on relapse prevention and lifestyle management. The following goals are pursued in this phase of treatment: (a) educate Kristen about the nature of relapse; (b) identify Kristen's risk factors for relapse and coping strategies if symptoms worsen; (c) highlight progress made in treatment; (d) develop a maintenance plan for continued improvement and healthy lifestyle management over time; and (e) discuss thoughts and feelings about ending treatment.

Case Conceptualization

We will highlight four selected concepts that the ICT model emphasizes as significant in the development of bulimic symptoms and also specifically targets in treatment. However, it is important to point out that ICT also would underscore the importance of several other problems, such as Kristen's extreme nutritional deficits and associated compromised physiological functioning, as critical elements to correct in her treatment.

The first factor that appears instrumental in Kristen's eating disorder and overall psychopathology is her marked level of self-discrepancy. Here we are referring to the discrepancy between Kristen's perception of her *actual* self (i.e., as is) and her *wished* for self (i.e., ideal self) or the self she feels she *must* be in order to avoid negative outcome (i.e., ought-self). An example of the discrepancy between the actual and ought-selves is seen in her statement, "I think about all the calories I'm burning when I exercise and how thin and in control I'll feel when I lose a few pounds." Similarly, Kristen acknowledges that she "went all out for everything" in a seeming effort to cope with the shame and/or embarrassment of her parents' marital conflict. Her marked actual/ought discrepancy was also seen when she learned that her fiancé was having an affair and she terminated the engagement. She states, "I felt like such a failure. If I'd looked better maybe Joe wouldn't have left me. I just wanted to be invisible or disappear."

Given her extreme self-evaluative standards, the ICT therapist may need to examine the developmental origins of the standards. For example, the family history reveals that Kristen's maternal grandmother focused much of her energy on physical appearances and was a beautiful debutante. Similarly, her maternal aunt was "the beautiful one" while her mother was "the smart one." These values and standards were highly reinforced in Kristen's family, as was an extreme devotion to work, which was also modeled by her father. She was accustomed to hearing her grandparents complain that her cousins may be "out of control" which will bring "shame" to the family. Perhaps the development of her ought-standards can be most clearly seen as she reflects on her parents' relationship to her as a child. She recalls them saying, "Look how well she is doing. She gets A's, she is a prima ballerina, so pretty, so polite, everybody loves her." She reflects "that was all that mattered, like that meant everything was alright."

Second, we must consider Kristen's cognitive style. The ICT model specifies that self-neglect, self-blame, and excessive self-control are problematic self-regulatory cognitive styles. Related to her excessive ought-standards is her high degree of self-control. This finding is apparent in her excessive exercise and tendency to push herself physically to extreme levels. Periods of exaggerated self-control alternate with another cognitive style characterized by self-neglect. For example, her extreme self-discipline would be countered by periods of drunkenness and reckless exposure to risky social situations. Her self-neglect can be seen most clearly when she stated, "I did my best when I was really busy, always on the go. I didn't worry that much about food, and I had a good excuse if friends wanted to go out—I always had homework, projects, presentations."

The third critical area in this conceptualization is her interpersonal patterns. Although there is not a substantial amount of information about her interpersonal patterns, there is some evidence that she engages in highly withdrawn or submissive patterns with other people. For example, her tendency to withdraw into her work or eating disorder may reflect the walling-off pattern identified in ICT. Similarly, her relationship to her fiancé reflected what may be a significant degree of submissive behavior. For example, she reportedly was trying to be good and pleasing when with her boyfriend, and she found it difficult to tolerate his absence when he was on the road. She made every effort to please him and satisfy him, hoping that it would in some way alter his drinking problem.

Finally, the interpersonal schema ties many of these interpersonal and cognitive concepts together. In Kristen's case, we may speculate that the turmoil of her early family life left her feeling interpersonally insecure and personally inadequate (actual-ought discrepancy). In spite of the family's extreme deficits, behavioral standards for the pursuit of perfection seemed to be communicated and reinforced by the family. Beauty, intelligence, and extreme success were indications of acceptability, perhaps to overcome the family's frequent behavioral excesses and deficits. It may be that Kristen then developed a self-regulatory style characterized by high degrees of self-control and self-blame in an effort to regulate herself and meet her (and her family's) excessive self-evaluative ought standard. Furthermore, she may have developed highly submissive or withdrawn interpersonal patterns because she viewed herself as unacceptable to others. In order for someone to care about her, she believes that she must do what they want (submit), given her "obvious" deficits and inadequacies. Formulation of an interpersonal script or map of interpersonal relations is often a useful aid in conceptualizing the case.

The Therapeutic Relationship

The Therapeutic Bond

The relationship between the therapist and patient should be highly collaborative, with the therapist making every effort to attune himself or herself to the subjective and emotional experience of the patient. The therapist should communicate an interest in understanding the patient's subjective experiences while simultaneously introducing opportunities for changes in behavioral patterns. The therapeutic relationship remains reality based, and classical transference exploration is not emphasized. However, if a particular interpersonal pattern is clearly enacted between the patient and therapist which threatens the productivity of the treatment, or provides "data" that can be used to understand patterns or underlying schemas, this should be addressed within the sessions.

In spite of the high degree of collaboration and empathy seen in the therapeutic relationship, therapist and patient must remain interpersonally differentiated. That is, the therapist must be aware of the interpersonal boundaries and autonomy of both therapist and patient, which implies that his or her boundaries will be respected and the therapist simultaneously respects the right of the patient to make decisions about her life in a self-determined manner. The therapist will not exhibit a highly authoritative stance in relationship to the patient, unless the patient exhibits a high degree of risk for self-harm or harm of others, in which case the therapist will shift to a crisis mode and intervene in an appropriate manner.

Roles in the Therapeutic Relationship

The therapist's role in the therapeutic relationship is significantly influenced by the presence of the patient workbook and associated homework assignments. These psychoeducational materials will provide opportunities for the therapist and patient to remain highly focused on problems and issues that are relevant to the treatment. The therapist needs to balance a sensitivity for empathizing and validating various aspects of the patient's experience with a more directive approach for behavioral change. Typically, therapists must first attempt to gain some awareness and appreciation of the patient's subjective emotional experience before direct behavioral change is likely to occur. Therefore, when patients describe various aspects of their interpersonal or cognitive experiences, these are first clarified, understood, validated, and then opportunities for change are explored with the patient. Behavioral change is never expected, but the patient is invited to consider behavioral alternatives to her current eating disturbance, as well as cognitive and interpersonal functioning.

The patient is expected to be an active collaborator in treatment, which means making every effort to complete homework assignments and actively discuss the workbook material and relevant situations that arise during the course of the therapy. When the patient is noncollaborative, this should be discussed and every effort should be made to clarify and remove sources of noncollaboration between patient and therapist.

Treatment Implementation and Outcome

Techniques and Methods of Working

The technical interventions in ICT depend heavily on the phase of treatment. Phase I emphasizes motivational interviewing strategies (Miller & Rollnick, 1991) and psychoeducation regarding cultural factors associated with eating disorders. Motivational interviewing hinges on identifying and focusing on the patient's *ambivalence*: that is, acknowledging that the patient is motivated to continue the problematic behavior because of certain desirable consequences it provides and simultaneously wants to stop the behavior because of negative consequences. There is a high degree of reflective listening on the part of the therapist in this phase of treatment as the therapist identifies themes regarding wishes for change versus fear of changing. The therapist also promotes self-efficacy and avoids confrontation in order to enhance motivation for change.

Following an initial phase of motivational interviewing, there is a more directive phase of the treatment that relies heavily on homework exercises in the patient workbook and attempts to identify evidence of self-discrepancy, particularly in terms of body shape and weight. Additionally, the developmental factors associated with their evaluative standards for appearance, including cultural messages, are examined. During this phase, the therapist, using examples in the workbook, introduces specific strategies to increase self-acceptance and modify maladaptive self-evaluative standards.

After the completion of Phase I of treatment, the patient hopefully shows an increase in motivation for behavioral change and greater knowledge about cultural factors associated with her eating disorder. As the patient moves into Phase II, there is a clear and decisive emphasis placed upon meal planning. Throughout all of Phase II, the therapy focuses on implementing a more normalized approach to eating that is considered essential in alleviating the starvation related nutritional and physiological conditions which may figure prominently in the elicitation of bingeing and purging behavior, as well as facilitating weight stabilization for individuals who need to gain weight. Patients are told that healthy eating involves choosing and consuming foods for the purpose of nourishing the body and eventually responding appropriately to hunger and satiety cues. They are encouraged to eat three meals per day with at least one entree per meal. Patients are highly encouraged to eat regular foods and avoid diet or "light" foods. Most importantly, patients are strongly encouraged to avoid any food restrictions or dieting behavior.

In conjunction with this behavioral intervention, patients in Phase II are also introduced to a series of coping skills that are taught to help the patient manage anxiety or distress associated with changes in eating patterns. Patient and therapist may together choose from a number of strategies to help manage anxiety. Typical skills training procedures included in the protocol are: monitoring and modifying maladaptive thoughts about eating, behavioral shaping and graduated approximations of an adequate meal plan, self-reinforcement, self-regulation skills such as relaxation and breathing techniques, stimulus control procedures such as avoiding problematic stimuli, and gradual exposure to a hierarchy of feared foods.

In Phase III, the therapy techniques include a careful functional analysis of the relationship between interpersonal and eating disorder behaviors. Phase III includes the interpersonal pattern analysis, in which the therapist and patient use exercises from the workbook, as well as samples of everyday behavior, to identify the patient's most typical interpersonal patterns. After carefully reviewing specific samples of interpersonal behavior, the therapist should help the patient to identify the interpersonal pattern that they exhibit in the transaction, as well as the pattern of the other person involved. Frequently identified patterns in such an analysis include: control, blame, ignore, wall-off, submit, and sulk. The clinician manual contains numerous examples of these interpersonal patterns to facilitate accurate recognition. The therapist and patient will collaboratively identify one or two key interpersonal patterns as a goal for change in the therapy. At the same time, the therapist will begin to attempt to identify the underlying interpersonal schema which guides this pattern. The therapist will identify historical antecedents of the pattern in order to help the patient to better understand and confront the pattern and introduce interpersonal change. Specific interpersonal change depends heavily on the interpersonal pattern that the patient exhibits. For example, highly submissive patients may be encouraged to pursue assertive interpersonal patterns which are described by the therapist or modeled in role plays. On the other hand, extremely walled-off individuals may be encouraged to pursue interpersonal patterns characterized by trust and intimacy.

Additionally, in Phase III of treatment the therapist and patient will attempt to identify the typical cognitive style of the patient. Similar to Kristen, many eating disordered patients will show a cognitive style characterized by a high degree of self-control and perhaps self-blame. The therapist attempts to assist the patient in identifying her prototypic cognitive style, and actively encourages alternative self-regulatory styles, which are described in detail in the patient workbook. In some circumstances, historical exploration of the development of the cognitive style becomes a focus of the psychotherapy. Furthermore, a variety of homework assignments in the patient workbook address this topic.

Medical and Nutritional Issues

Attention to possible medical instability and/or nutritional insufficiency are key factors in ICT. Patients need to be assessed for evidence of medical instability and must agree to be monitored medically while they are in treatment. Similarly, although the patient workbook includes a significant amount of information regarding nutritional issues, and the ICT therapist must be familiar with the basic ideas of meal planning, a referral to a dietician may facilitate phase II of treatment as the patient is attempting to develop a healthy meal plan.

Potential Pitfalls

A major concern about Kristen's therapy relates to her high degree of actual/ought self-discrepancy and associated self-blaming cognitive style. That is, her extremely high standards and self-punitiveness may make the therapy process extremely difficult for her to tolerate because acknowledging her eating disorder behaviors, expressing emotions, developing a sense of trust, and experiencing a sense of interpersonal vulnerability may be associated with feelings of shame or failure. Similarly, if she does not make quick and prompt progress she may view herself as inadequate or a failure. On the other hand, given her propensity to please people, she may show a "flight into health" in which she shows a reduction in her eating disorder symptoms without any change in underlying self-discrepancy and interpersonal patterns. Furthermore, submissiveness in the therapy relationship may be associated with indirect or inauthentic communications which minimize problems or feelings.

The therapist working with Kristen should focus carefully on her emotional responding and display a high degree of empathy, patience, and tolerance as she addresses her thoughts of inadequacy or personal insufficiency. The therapist should acknowledge that discussing these issues in therapy is difficult for her, given her high standards. At the same time, the therapist needs to point out how this is precisely the problem: her extreme standards and inability to accept herself as anything but perfect are her major vulnerabilities.

Another possible problem that may arise in her treatment has to do with any decision to pursue the historical origins of her interpersonal patterns, or her self-evaluative standards. She may experience guilt or shame in discussing her family's past. She may feel as if she is betraying the family by talking about them. She may also think that she is blaming her family for her problems and feel guilty. She should be actively reassured that historical exploration of her behavior is conducted simply to provide greater insight into the conditions that shaped her behavioral patterns. In no way is anyone blamed for her behavior and she should be assured that her behavior is ultimately *her* responsibility and choice.

Termination and Relapse Prevention

Phase IV of ICT is devoted to preventing relapse and maintaining a healthy lifestyle. Several sessions focus on identifying potential risks of slip or relapse and developing behavioral plans to avoid such a consequence. Perhaps different from other relapse prevention plans is the continued focus on the role of excessive self-evaluative standards (i.e., ideal, ought) and maladaptive interpersonal patterns and schemas. However, similar to other cognitive behavioral relapse prevention strategies, there is an explicit emphasis placed on developing a personalized plan for slip management and relapse prevention. Also, this work is supplemented in the workbook by numerous homework assignments in which the patient concretely outlines specific plans and interventions.

Mechanisms of Change

Undoubtedly, there are a multitude of mechanisms of change in a multifaceted treatment like ICT. We will comment on three specific mechanisms which we believe are instrumental in recovery from disorders in the bulimic spectrum. First, ICT rests on the assumption that before meaningful interpersonal and cognitive change will occur, there needs to be clear behavioral change in the domain of food consumption, meal planning, and correcting nutritional deficiencies. To the extent that the bulimic individual continues to eat restrictively, additional change is unlikely. Therefore, a primary mechanism is learning about the maladaptive nature of dieting, the cultural forces which promote it, and provision of a concrete alternative to meal consumption which the patient can attempt to incorporate into her lifestyle. We believe that it is important that the meal plan be simple, but comprehensive. Providing numerous samples of possible meals or snacks is essential, and avoiding highly technical language about nutrition and food exchanges is recommended.

Second, a primary mechanism for change is in the modification of the perception of the actual self and the associated evaluative standards, that is, a reduction in self-discrepancy. By highlighting positive aspects of the self previously unrecognized and simultaneously helping the patient to modify her extreme evaluative self-standards, change in a number of domains is facilitated. Once the patient begins to see the unrealistic nature of her standards for herself, and incorporate more flexible standards, such change may occur. Frequently, historical exploration of the development of these standards and beginning to challenge the sources of information associated with these developments allows for meaningful cognitive change.

Third, as the patient's self-discrepancy decreases she may be more amenable to make changes in interpersonal patterns and cognitive styles. Helping the patient to adopt an interpersonal stance that allows her to be interpersonally attached to others, but very much aware of boundaries and limits, is considered optimal. Helping the patient to identify and express her thoughts and feelings in relationships is considered an essential element to the healthy functioning of an autonomous self. Furthermore, helping the patient to identify and change unhealthy relationships in which the patient exhibits recurrent destructive patterns, such as submission, hostile withdrawal, or attack, is a key focus of the treatment. Additionally, helping the patient to develop new cognitive styles, that is, changing the way she treats herself, is a corollary of such interpersonal change. Helping the patient to develop a flexible pattern of relationship to the self in which she is relatively accepting while striving to meet reasonable evaluative standards is optimal.

REFERENCES

Altabe, M., & Thompson, K. (1996). Body image: A cognitive self-schema construct? *Cognitive Therapy and Research, 20*(2), 171–193.

Benjamin, L. S. (1993). *Interpersonal treatment of personality disorders.* New York: Guilford Press.

Berg, M. L., Crosby, R. D., Wonderlich, S. A., & Hawley, D. (in press). The relationship of temperament and perceptions of nonshared environment in bulimia nervosa. *International Journal of Eating Disorders.*

Bowlby, J. (1969). *Attachment and loss: Vol. 1. attachment.* New York: Basic Books.

Brewerton, T. D., Hand, L. D., & Bishop, Jr., E. R. (1993). The tridimensional personality questionnaire in eating disorder patients. *International Journal of Eating Disorders, 14,* 213–218.

Buck, R. (1980). Nonverbal behavior and the theory of emotion: The facial feedback hypothesis. *Journal of Personality and Social Psychology, 38,* 811–824.

Bulik, C. M., Sullivan, P. F., Weltzin, T. E., & Walter, K. H. (1995). Temperament in eating disorders. *International Journal of Eating Disorders, 17,* 251–261.

Cloninger, C. R. (1987). A systematic method for clinical description and classification of personality variants. *Archives of General Psychiatry, 44,* 573–588.

Cole-Detke, H., & Kobak, R. (1996). Attachment processes in eating disorder and depression. *Journal of Consulting and Clinical Psychology, 64,* 282–290.

Cooper, P. J., & Fairburn, C. G. (1986). The depressive symptoms of bulimia nervosa. *British Journal of Psychiatry, 148,* 268–274.

Fairburn, C. G., & Cooper, Z. (1993). The eating disorders examination (12th ed.). In C. G. Fairburn & G. T. Wilson (Eds.), *Binge eating: Nature, assessment, and treatment* (pp. 317–360). New York: Guilford Press.

Fairburn, C. G., Marcus, M. D., & Wilson, G. T. (1993). Cognitive-behavioral therapy for binge eating and bulimia nervosa: A comprehensive treatment manual. In C. G. Fairburn & G. T. Wilson (Eds.), *Binge eating: Nature, assessment, and treatment* (pp. 361–404). New York: Guilford Press.

Fairburn, C. G., Welch, S. L., Doll, H. A., Davies, B. A., & O'Connor, M. E. (1997). Risk factors for bulimia nervosa: A community based case-control study. *Archives of General Psychiatry, 54,* 509–517.

First, M. B., Spitzer, R. L., Gibbon, M., & Williams, J. B. (1995). *Structured Clinical Interview for DSM-IV Axis I Disorders-Patient Edition.* New York: Biometrics Research.

Greenberg, L. S., & Safran, J. D. (1987). *Emotion in psychotherapy.* New York: Guilford Press.

Grisset, N. I., & Norvell, N. K. (1992). Perceived social support, social skills, and quality of relationships in bulimic women. *Journal of Consulting and Clinical Psychology, 60,* 293–299.

Heatherton, T. F., & Baumeister, R. F. (1991). Binge eating as escape from self awareness. *Psychological Bulletin, 110,* 86–108.

Higgins, E. T. (1987). Self-discrepancy: A theory relating self and affect. *Psychological Review, 94,* 319–340.

Higgins, E. T., Bond, R., & Strauman, T. (1986). Self-discrepancies and emotional vulnerability: How magnitude, accessibility and type of discrepancy influence affect. *Journal of Personality and Social Psychology, 51*, 5–15.

Holden, N. L. (1991). Adoption and eating disorders: A high risk group. *British Journal of Psychiatry, 158*, 829–833.

Humphrey, L. L. (1989). Observed family interactions among subtypes of eating disorders using structural analysis of social behavior. *Journal of Consulting and Clinical Psychology, 57*, 206–214.

Jacobsin, R., & Robbins, C. J. (1989). Social dependency and social support in bulimic and nonbulimic women. *International Journal of Eating Disorders, 8*, 665–670.

Johnson, C., & Larson, R. (1982). An analysis of moods and behavior. *Psychosomatic Medicine, 44*, 341–351.

Joiner, Jr., T. E., Wonderlich, S. A., Metalsky, G. I., & Schmidt, N. B. (1995). Body satisfaction: A feature of bulimia, depression, or both? *Journal of Social and Clinical Psychology, 14*(4), 339–355.

Kearney-Cooke, A., & Striegel-Moore, R. (1997). The etiology and treatment of body image disturbance. In D. M. Garner & R. E. Garfinkel (Eds.), *Handbook of treatment for eating disorders*, 2nd ed. (pp. 295–306). New York: Guilford Press.

Kendler, K. S., MacLean, C., Neale, M., Kessler, R., Health, A., & Eaves, L. (1991). The genetic epidemiology of bulimia nervosa. *American Journal of Psychiatry, 148*, 1627–1637.

Klein, M., Benjamin, L., Rosenfeld, R., Treece, C., Husted, J., & Greist, J. (1993). The Wisconsin personality disorders inventory: Development and psychometric characteristics. *Journal of Personality Disorders, 7*, 285–303.

Livesley, W. J., & Jackson, D. N. (in press). *Manual for the Dimensional Assessment of Personality Pathology*. Port Huron, MI: Sigma Press.

Miller, W. R., & Rollnick, S. (1991). *Motivational interviewing: Preparing people to change addictive behavior*. New York: Guilford Press.

Mitchell, J. E., Pyle, R. L., Eckert, E. D., Hatsukami, D., Pomeroy, C., & Zimmerman, R. (1990). A comparison study of antidepressants and structured intensive group psychotherapy in the treatment of bulimia nervosa. *Archives of General Psychiatry, 47*, 149–157.

Norman, D. K., & Herzog, D. B. (1984). Persistent social maladjustment in bulimia: A one-year follow-up. *American Journal of Psychiatry, 143*, 444–446.

Pruitt, J. A., Kappins, R. E., & Gorman, P. W. (1992). Bulimia and fear of intimacy. *Journal of Clinical Psychology, 48*, 472–476.

Strauman, T. J., & Glenberg, A. M. (1994). Self-concept and body-image disturbance: Which self-beliefs predict body size overestimation? *Cognitive Therapy and Research, 18*(2), 105–125.

Strauman, T. J., Vookles, J., Barenstein, V., Chaiken, S., & Higgins, E. T. (1991). Self discrepancies and vulnerability to body dissatisfaction and disordered eating. *Journal of Personality and Social Psychology, 61,* 946–956.

Strober, M., & Humphrey, L. L. (1984). Familial contributions to the etiology and course of anorexia nervosa and bulimia. *Journal of Consulting & Clinical Psychology, 55,* 654–659.

Strober, M., & Katz, J. L. (1988). Depression in eating disorders: A review and analysis of descriptive, family, and biological findings. In D. M. Garner & P. E. Garfinkel (Eds.), *Diagnostic issues in anorexia nervosa and bulimia nervosa* (pp. 80–111). New York: Brunner/Mazel.

Tellegen, A. (1985). Structures of mood and personality and their relevance to assessing anxiety, with an emphasis on self-report. In A. H. Tuma & J. D. Maser (Eds.), *Anxiety and the anxiety disorders* (pp. 681–706). Hilsdale, NJ: Erlbaum.

Vitousek, K., Watson, S., & Wilson, G. T. (1998). Enhancing motivation for change in treatment resistant eating disorders. *Clinical Psychology Review, 18,* 391–420.

Welch, S. L., & Fairburn, C. G. (1994). Sexual abuse and bulimia nervosa: Three integrated case control comparisons. *American Journal of Psychiatry, 151,* 402–407.

Wilson, G. T., & Fairburn, C. G. (1993). Cognitive treatments for eating disorders. *Journal of Consulting and Clinical Psychology, 61*(2), 261–269.

Wonderlich, S. A. (1992). Relationship of family and personality factors in bulimia nervosa. In J. H. Crowther, D. L. Tannenbaum, S. E. Hobfoll, & M. A. P. Stephens (Eds.), *The etiology of bulimia nervosa: The individual and familial context* (pp. 170–196). Washington, DC: Hemisphere Publishing.

Wonderlich, S. A., Brewerton, T. D., Jocic, Z., Dansky, B. S., & Abbott, D. W. (1997). Relationship of childhood sexual abuse and eating disorders. *Journal of the American Academy of Child and Adolescent Psychiatry, 36,* 1107–1115.

Wonderlich, S. A., & Mitchell, J. E. (1997). Eating disorders and comorbidity: Empirical, conceptual, and clinical implications. *Psychopharmacology Bulletin, 33*(3), 381–390.

Wonderlich, S. A., & Swift, W. J. (1990). Perception of parental relationships in eating disorder subtypes. *Journal of Abnormal Psychology, 99,* 353–360.

11

Cognitive Analytic Therapy and the Transtheoretical Framework

Janet L. Treasure, Ulrike H. Schmidt, and Nicholas A. Troop

TREATMENT MODEL

We were trained by Gerald Russell and have been influenced by his conceptualization of anorexia nervosa not merely as a dieting disorder but as a form of stress response: "The patient avoids food and induces weight loss by virtue of a range of psychosocial conflicts whose resolution she perceives to be within her reach through the achievement of thinness and/or the avoidance of fatness. These conflicts will still include the dread of fatness but may need to embrace the fear of sexuality and fertility, or the reluctance to acquire independence from the family, or some other as yet unrecognised factor" (Russell, 1995, pp. 10). Our research backs up this conceptualization. Anorexia nervosa is usually triggered by severe life events or difficulties (Schmidt, Tiller, Blanchard, Andrews, & Treasure, 1997; Troop, Schmidt, & Treasure, 1999) which the individual attempts to cognitively avoid (Troop & Treasure, 1997a). This may result from a developmental trajectory in which helplessness and low levels of mastery are present from childhood (Troop & Treasure, 1997b). The anorexic symptomatology maintains this avoidant response as it serves to suppress awareness of underlying conflicts and the attendant negative emotions (Wolff & Serpell, 1998). The illness is also perceived by the sufferer to provide many benefits such as allowing her to feel safe, special, and protected (Serpell et al., 1999).

Our approach to treatment is not based on a single theoretical perspective or treatment model. Rather, we integrate cognitive and analytic techniques that reflect our conceptualization of the development and maintenance of eating disorders. In addition, we employ stage models developed in health psychology to provide a framework for sequencing interventions.

The Transtheoretical Model of Change

In the early phase of treatment we find it helpful to structure our thinking about the patient using the *Transtheoretical Model of Change* (Prochaska, 1979; Prochaska & DiClemente, 1982; Prochaska & Norcross, 1994) and the therapeutic style of *Motivational Interviewing* (Miller & Rollnick, 1991) as combined in *Motivational Enhancement Therapy* (Miller, Zwebeen, DiClemente, & Rychtarik, 1992). This allows us to address the questions of "Where is the patient at; where is she coming from and how can we help her move in the direction of sustained change?" This approach strongly informs our patient manual (Treasure, 1997) and the accompanying workbook (Treasure, 1998) which are given to patients and their families at the time of the first assessment and provide a blueprint for the structure of therapy.

To describe this approach briefly, the transtheoretical model proposes that in recovering from a disorder, individuals pass through a number of stages. Initially, they are in precontemplation where they either fail to perceive they have a problem or else perceive it but have no intention of changing. In contemplation, individuals realize they have a problem and think they might like to do something about it. In action, individuals are taking active steps to tackle their problem behavior while in maintenance they seek to maintain the improvements they have made. Individuals can rotate through this cycle of change a number of times before finally recovering and exiting the cycle. In addition, the model proposes that different processes are more or less important at different stages of recovery. For example, cognitive and emotion-oriented techniques are more useful at earlier stages, while behavioral techniques are more useful in the later stages.

In terms of the transtheoretical model, patients with anorexia nervosa presenting for treatment are at best in the *contemplation* stage, that is, ambivalent about change (Ward, Troop, Todd, & Treasure, 1996; Blake, Turnbull, & Treasure, 1997) but often they are in the *precontemplation* stage with their anorexia being highly valued and ego syntonic (Serpell, Treasure, Teasdale, & Sullivan, 1999; Vitousek, Watson, & Wilson, 1998) and the need for change vigorously denied. Patients in *contemplation*, on the other hand, may recognize that their anorexia is a problem but may perceive that they do not have the coping resources to overcome this problem (or other problems that help perpetuate what they now perceive to be a problem). In helping people move from contemplation to action, it is essential, therefore, to increase the patient's feeling of self-efficacy and confidence in solving their problem.

We are particularly struck with the way in which this conceptualization does away with the rather static notion that anorexic patients are in *denial*. The transtheoretical model implies that the pre-contemplating patient is not in denial but simply resistant to change currently. As we describe below, it also provides a prescription of necessary strategies and therapist behaviors to encourage patients to move on. Overall, the transtheoretical model is a more optimistic approach to the treatment of anorexia nervosa than simply resigning oneself to a relentless wall of denial.

Cognitive Analytic Therapy

Motivational Enhancement Therapy is designed specifically to in-crease motivation but does not necessarily equip patients with the specific tools necessary for recovery. We find that the theory and tools of cognitive analytical therapy (CAT) are very helpful in this task (Ryle, 1990, 1995). CAT combines the techniques and skills of cognitive therapy with (a) a prominent focus on interpersonal relationships, in particular that of the therapist and patient, and (b) an understanding of the patient's current maladaptive patterns of thinking and behavior in the context of earlier attachment and peer relationships. Thus, aspects usually considered to be the province of psychodynamic therapies are discussed vis-a-vis past and present relationships and the change process (Treasure, Todd, Brolly, Tiller, Nehmed et al., 1995; Treasure & Ward, 1997a). However, the trans-theoretical model is still valuable in monitoring change, describing various levels at which change needs to occur: these include behavioral, cognitive/emotional, intrapersonal and interpersonal aspects. Anorexia nervosa frequently involves dysfunction at all levels, some of which may be merely a consequence of the illness interfering with normal development while others may have greater aetiological significance. The CAT formulation links these various levels of dysfunction with problems in everyday living.

We have found that a simple cognitive model of anorexia nervosa in which weight and shape concerns attach themselves to low self-esteem and lead to dieting is inadequate to describe the complexity of anorexia nervosa. We feel that anorexia involves a more fundamental disturbance in the development of self. The development of a sense of self is thought to be made up of several schemata which are deep-seated beliefs forming an internalized working model by which meaning is given to the outside world and on which predictions are based, especially in terms of relationships with others. The quality of an individual's relationship with her attachment figures during early development often lays the foundation for the development of maladaptive core schemata in the areas of care eliciting or caregiving, whereas problematic relationships with peers vary along the dimensions of cooperation or competitiveness.

Space does not permit detailed discussion of these dimensions of interaction. However, they will be described briefly.

Care Eliciting

This behavior develops in response to a schema which says that close others will ignore you or abandon you and cannot be trusted to provide security. The compensatory schema to this is that it is essential to make yourself noticed by the close other to avoid being abandoned or ignored. Overclose relationships with dependent, clingy behaviors can solve the problem but frequently the other person becomes overwhelmed and suffocated by this dependence. The relationship breaks down leaving the person abandoned yet again and strengthening his/her belief (schema maintenance). Anorexia nervosa provides an alternative mechanism for eliciting care. As people with anorexia nervosa appear so fragile and shockingly ill, they elicit strong caregiving responses from others. Parents who may have become distant from each other are often drawn back together to nurture and protect their child. On the other hand, some parents are so upset, angry, and puzzled by the behavior that they withdraw. This may perpetuate the problem as it is perceived as further abandonment and reinforces the need to elicit even more care. Often there is a history of loss or abandonment from an attachment figure.

The flip side of the schemata relating to frantic care eliciting behavior is a group of schemata where the underlying theme is that of "care avoidance." These schemata involve a fear and distrust of close relationships. There is a terror of being rejected, judged, or controlled by another who may be seen as unpredictable. There is a tendency to be shy, to fear new relationships, and avoid social interactions. Such people will have few friends. The compensatory schema to this is to be very controlling, demanding, and jealous with rigid expectations and standards. It may be difficult to separate physical intimacy from other aspects of the relationship and there is a tendency to be competitive and to struggle for power. The background to this sort of thinking and behavior lies in attachment figures in childhood who were intolerant and critical of the individual's needs and distress. Thus, rather than the attachment figure providing any security in the face of distress they compounded the distress by being angry, critical, or rejecting of the child for being tearful, weak, and inferior. The social isolation and lack of sexuality typically encountered in anorexia nervosa signal and stabilize this care avoidance.

Caregiving

A setting condition for the development of maladaptive schemata in this area is that close others are perceived as vulnerable and in need of care, as is the case if an individual has to act as a parental figure in childhood to an ill or single parent or to a sibling. Having to ignore and suppress one's own needs out of necessity often is coupled with the belief that if the person did anything for themselves or attended to their own needs they would be selfish. Individuals with these schemata often make overwhelming efforts to try to please and care for others. At times when the compensatory schema is activated it can lead to the individual riding roughshod over the feelings of others, behaving in an almost psychopathic manner. Individuals with anorexia nervosa often behave as if they have no personal needs and therefore they are available to care wholeheartedly for others.

Competitive Interpersonal Relationships

Problems in this domain result from maladaptive core schemata relating to personal weakness and inferiority (self as powerless). This extreme pole has as its opposite (schema compensation) being powerful or superior. Individuals with strongly developed schemata in this domain will have a tendency in relationships with others to quickly fall into a competitive relationship and either to be critical and contemptuous if the other is judged to be weak or cringing, or humiliated and shamed if the other is appraised as powerful. Anorexia nervosa is a pseudo-solution for this "self as weak" schema as it gives the impression of exemplary control and power. Exam situations in the broadest sense tend to act as critical events which activate this group of schemata. A relationship with caregivers which gives the impression of conditional acceptance with comparisons made between siblings and others can lead to the development of this schema.

Cooperative Relationships

Setting conditions for problems in this area all involve situations in which individuals perceive themselves as somehow different or defective. They may have had a handicap such as dyslexia or a chronic disease like coeliac disease. There is frequently a history of bullying at school because they were alienated from their peers in some way. Shameful experiences that can result from this type of history are so distressing that they can have long-lasting effects. Physical and sexual abuse can lead to the experience of shame about the body (Andrews, 1997a, 1997b). People with little value of their own worth or who regard themselves as flawed or disgusting in some way have difficulty accepting that they merit a place in society. The compensatory pole of this schema is the idea that if they were special in some way they could be accepted. This leads to perfectionism and the tendency to try to please others. Relationships with others tend to be judgmental and polarized into despising or admiring. Anorexia nervosa can offer a compensation for a defectiveness schema as it gives the feeling of specialness—as someone who can exist almost without eating.

THERAPIST SKILLS AND ATTRIBUTES

Therapists in our unit are trained in motivational interviewing (Miller & Rollnick, 1991), a directive, client-centered counseling style that aims to help patients explore and resolve their ambivalence about behavior change. It combines elements of therapeutic style (warmth and empathy) with technique (e.g., key questions and focused reflective listening). One of the principles of this approach is that head-to-head conflict is unhelpful. What is more helpful is a collaborative, shoulder-to-shoulder relationship in which therapist and patient tackle the problem together. The patient's motivation to change is enhanced if there is a gentle process of negotiation in which the patient, not the practitioner, articulates the benefits and costs involved in change.

Rollnick and Miller (1995) were able to define specific and trainable therapist behaviors that they felt led to a better therapeutic alliance and better outcome. We train all our therapists to use these: (1) Try to understand the other person's frame of reference; (2) Express acceptance and affirmation; (3) Filter the patient's thoughts so that motivational statements are amplified and nonmotivational statements dampened; (4) Elicit the patient's self-motivational statements, expressions of problem recognition, concern, intention to change, and ability to change: (5) Monitor the level of readiness to change and ensure that they (the therapists) do not jump ahead of the patient; (6) Affirm the patient's freedom of choice and self direction.

Additionally, all our therapists have a good grounding in cognitive-analytical therapy (Ryle, 1990) and receive ongoing supervision in this model, which in terms of therapist's skills and attributes combines the stance of Beck's "collaborative empiricism" with the ability to reflect on transference and countertransference issues. The two approaches complement each other well and aid the development of a solid therapeutic alliance. This requires the therapist to avoid resistance by working at the correct stage of change by developing accurate empathy and by not entering into a dysfunctional role driven by the patient's core schemata.

THE CASE OF KRISTEN

Assessment, Conceptualization, and Treatment Planning

Assessment

Kristen has experienced many of the negative features of an eating disorder such as poor physical health (tiredness, dizziness, sensitivity to cold, weakness and lack stamina, amenorrhoea, swollen parotids, hypotension, dental enamel erosion, dehydration, low potassium) as well as problems in her psychological (poor concentration, irritability, low mood), work (lateness, problematic interpersonal relationships), and social life (social isolation). She has also experienced shame and misery associated with binges and has compulsive exercise regimes. The temptation for an inexperienced therapist might be to focus prematurely on trying to resolve her work crisis, as Kristen reports being especially concerned about this and would presumably be very motivated to work on this particular aspect of her problem. Alternatively, the therapist, motivated by his or her own concerns, might be drawn into lecturing Kristen about the seriousness of her health problems and the physical danger she is in.

Although both of these approaches would be well meant, neither of these is appropriate. Instead, and perhaps paradoxically, we must pay attention to the positive features of the anorexia nervosa. We can assume these positive features to be very strong, given the chronicity of Kristen's eating disorder. This may sound like a potentially dangerous thing to do, perhaps reinforcing patients' pro-anorexia beliefs. However, recall that this helps to engage the patient in treatment and can often even surprise the patient. It is also done in the first phase of treatment, after which the therapist can attempt to elicit the patient's perceived cons when she is engaged in treatment. We can only speculate about Kristen's meta-beliefs about her anorexia nervosa, but our working hypothesis is that these are:

To avoid negative emotions of sadness, shame, and disgust;

To give direction and security after a negative life event or ongoing difficulties;

To attain standards of beauty and attractiveness that hold the key to acceptance;

To fill empty time and reduce the sense of loneliness.

Once we have looked at the pros and cons of anorexia nervosa in Kristen's life, we will be a lot clearer about her stage of change. We suspect that, while she is in action vis-a-vis her work problems, and perhaps also her binge eating, she remains in *contemplation* or even *precontemplation* in other aspects of her disorder such as her health problems and relationships.

Therapeutic Goals

The goal in the early stages of treatment is to shift the decisional balance so that the "cons" of anorexia nervosa outweigh the "pros," the situation usually found in people in the *preparation* or *action* phase. This involves making the cons of the illness more salient and trying to decrease the power of positive reinforcers. If the patient is in the *precontemplation stage* or early *contemplation stage* (i.e., alternating between precontemplation and contemplation) then the approach should be to raise awareness by giving feedback about the illness and its consequences. Self-treatment books (Crisp, 1980; Treasure, 1997), books by ex-sufferers (Claude-Pierre, 1998; Hornbacher-Beard, 1998; MacLeod, 1982; Shelley, 1997), and videos or electronic media can be useful in this context. There are many other techniques that can be used for shifting the balance between the pros and cons of anorexia nervosa (Treasure & Ward, 1997b). It is important to ensure that great attention is also paid to self-esteem throughout this process as motivation to change can only occur if there is enough self efficacy to make a start. Hopelessness, helplessness, and despair are very near the surface and may lead to a retreat to the security of anorexia nervosa. After all, to the extent that anorexia provides a solution to other problems, patients have already demonstrated their tremendous efficacy in this strategy. This first phase of treatment usually takes 4 to 8 weeks; however, it may take longer to develop enough trust to overcome avoidance of shameful and difficult issues.

Another key goal is to develop a good therapeutic alliance. This is not going to be easy as Kristen has a history of breaking off treatment and has in the past not been open with her therapist about her ongoing bulimic symptomatology. Within a relationship of trust it may be possible to build up a picture of the relevant details necessary to develop a clear conceptualization of her case. This would also allow a candid discussion of Kristen's therapeutic options. A limited goal might be to help Kristen back to a level of weight at which she can function safely at work. Kristen has managed to achieve this once before with very little therapeutic input when she went to see the nutritionist. A more ambitious goal of therapy would be for Kristen to understand the role that her eating disorder plays in her life, to be less dependent on it both as a support and an emotion regulator, and to become able to use alternative strategies to fulfill these important functions. This would mean that change would need to occur at all levels of difficulties defined in the transtheoretical model.

The core schemata that Kristen has developed date back to her childhood and will be very difficult to shift. In part, this may be because she is unaware of them as problems, but also such habitual patterns involving others will be difficult to change unilaterally. Hopefully, with time, Kristen would become increasingly able to notice when maladaptive schemata are activated and monitor their appearance. With time and experience, Kristen will be able to build up a network of people who can offer support and security without such relationships becoming polarized by the operation of any of her core schemata. Also Kristen will be able to build up more cooperative relationships with friends and colleagues at work without the element of competition or her need to be special causing difficulties.

Given the long-standing nature of Kristen's difficulties and Kristen's stage of change, it may be sensible to offer her a course of therapy with relatively limited goals with the option of having a second bout of therapy once the first is completed. The decision to embark on the second phase of therapy should not be made until a few months have passed after the initial treatment is over. We frequently find that a great deal of positive change occurs in the first few months after finishing treatment. Additional treatment might be seen, falsely, to lead to greater benefits when in fact these might have been achieved anyway. For the patient to observe for herself the changes that she makes independently of the therapist, this will increase even further her self-efficacy beliefs. It also means that, if and when additional therapy does begin, it does not simply start where the previous therapy left off. It can build upon the gains (or even losses) that have been made since the end of the first treatment.

Timeline for Therapy

Kristen would be offered a course of 20 sessions of weekly therapy (50 minutes) followed by 5 monthly sessions.

Case Conceptualization

Parental Core Schemata and Experiences. **Charlotte** (Kristen's mother): In her own childhood, Charlotte's family placed great emphasis on competition between the children. This may have led her to develop a strong competitive schema. Charlotte had been considered weak on beauty with the compensatory pathway of intellectualization and academic success. It is possible that she experienced abandonment and rejection from her mother because she was different from her, that is, not a beauty. Her father was unable to compensate for this as he had emotionally abandoned the family and obtained his security from his work, church, and social life. Comparison and competition between the grandchildren and sons-in-law is still a strong organizer in the maternal grandparents.

James (Kristen's father): James was thrust into the role of a parentified child from the age of 12 when his father died. It is probable that this led to the development of a powerful caregiving schema. He would have been made aware of the importance of financial security as his mother had to attain this as a priority, neglecting the care of her children and delegating it to him.

James and Charlotte: Their whirlwind marriage may have been precipitated by each trying to compensate for their maladaptive attachment relationships. James may have been seduced by attaining care for himself, escaping the responsibilities of his family of origin. Charlotte may have craved for a relationship in which she attained fused care without any need for conditional approval. Both of them were able to shake off the necessity of completing their education. James was able to be irresponsible, childlike, and impulsive for once. Charlotte found that she was not valued just in terms of academic success. Once married, particularly following the birth of his children and the loss of his first daughter, James had his caregiving schema activated. This took the form of providing practical care, that is, earning enough money to give security. However, this may have re-created in Charlotte the sense of abandonment she had experienced as a child. Charlotte may not have been able to grieve adequately over the stillbirth as she was not given emotional support by James. James may have appeared to have abandoned her in order to focus on his traditional male role. It is possible that Charlotte had an abnormal adjustment reaction with depressive features at the time of Kristen's birth which would have impaired her ability to respond to her child. This may have set the scene for Kristen's insecure or avoidant pattern of interaction with her mother, with her father being unavailable to moderate this effect.

The loss of safety and security caused by the fire would have been threatening for both parents. James lost all his achievements as a practical provider. Charlotte was thrust back into a weak position in comparison to her sister. However, both parents were able to cope with this loss by practical effort. Charlotte's competitive schema would also have been activated when her husband had an affair with another woman. This may explain the severity and bitterness of her reaction. She felt catastrophically let down by this. She was unable to forgive James and forced him to go. The continuing parental battles were a manifestation of the failure to process the cognitive and emotional sequelae of this event.

Kristen: It is possible that Charlotte may have had a slightly unusual relationship with Kristen from her birth. Kristen may have been special (i.e., replacement for stillbirth) and yet also defective—

perhaps because she was not the baby who died or even because she was also vulnerable and could also die. Charlotte had her role of being a good mother threatened by the stillbirth and it is probable that James was not able to give Charlotte the emotional support she needed at this time. Charlotte may not have been able to respond to Kristen's needs at this time as she herself would have been insecure and vulnerable. After the fire, not only did Kristen have many losses to her lifestyle but she was abandoned by both parents. She was looked after by a grandmother who appears to be somewhat narcissistic and overly interested in appearances, and Kristen experienced a period of conditional acceptance. She was only noticed and given attention if she achieved, for example, by being a perfect dancer. It is probable that her parents were unable to respond to her and were intolerant of her emotional needs as they were overstretched themselves. Kristen then experienced abandonment by her father while in high school, although this was in part caused by her mother's extreme reaction. This would have led to very mixed emotions with the loss of her parents as a source of security, disgust that adult sexuality had caused these problems, and anger at both parents for their selfishness.

These experiences appear to have led to the development of attachment schemata in which close others may not be trusted to give security or else are seen as abandoning. In terms of relationships with peers, Kristen appears to have developed a strong competitive schema from a sense of weakness as the youngest of three and in the context of a maternal family in which competition was fostered. She also had a somewhat impaired self-esteem which made cooperative behavior weaker and so she was unable to respond to support from her peers and at many stages in her life felt alienated or rejected by them.

The strong competitive schema fueled her academic success. However, her somewhat insecure and avoidant attachment schema led to difficulties in close relationships. Her avoidant pattern meant that she allowed herself few experiences of close relationships. She eventually chose someone who probably also shared this trait and who had difficulty with intimacy and loyalty. She shows a pattern of being drawn to men who, on the surface, appear exciting, special, and powerful, and who offer the potential to compensate for her experience of herself as weak and defective. It is likely that these men have core schemata similar to hers but use their sexuality to attain power. The lack of close attachment figures meant that she was vulnerable in the face of stressful life events. In writing this, of course, without the opportunity to probe further, this is largely speculation, but this is the line of thinking that would inform our initial understanding of schema formation. In talking further with Kristen, we would amend this conceptualization as new information and insights emerged.

In our therapeutic approach, the prominent patterns of thinking about the self in relation to others as well as hypotheses about the origins of these beliefs and critical life events activating these schemata are written into the formulation. This is shared with the patient in the form of a letter which uses, as much as possible, the patient's own expressions rather than any technical or medical language. This letter forms the basis for future therapeutic work. Below is an example of the kind of letter we might send to Kristen.

Dear Kristen,

I have attempted to summarize the content of our meeting and to develop an understanding of your difficulties. This is a first draft and I would welcome feedback from you about it at our next session.

You came to the eating disorder clinic because you were concerned that your eating disorder had begun to impinge on your work. You had a warning at your appraisal because you had become more irritable and that you were not showing the team skills that were required. This has shocked and terrified you because your career development is one aspect of life that you feel has been successful following your MBA *cum laude*.

You have been able to put many of the other consequences of your eating disorder to the back of your mind. You have impressive stoicism. For example, you have been able to override any concerns you may have had about the damage to your teeth and the severe electrolyte imbalance with low potassium and magnesium that you know can be dangerous to your heart and kidneys. You have been able to keep going despite the weakness and fatigue that you have experienced.

Your eating disorder has also sheltered you from the narrowness of your social life and from meeting with your family as it takes up most of your leisure time and a good portion of your other resources.

Your eating problem began at high school in the context of disappointment at the loss of your first boyfriend. Your loss was tinged with disgust and shame or embarrassment as he left you because of your sexual reservations. Your parents were not able to give you the sense of security and support you needed at that time as they were experiencing their own losses and difficulties. You also had problems accepting help from friends. You have experienced relapses of your eating disorder as a result of further losses in your life. You lost your trust in your college friends after the traumatic incident there and more recently with the breakup of your relationship. These incidents have led you to experience a mixture of emotions such as misery, shame, and disgust. You have not been able to turn to your family for support and comfort and you have tended to turn to work rather than to friends for solace. It is as if your eating disorder has provided you with a sense of security during these times of difficulties. The certainty and clarity you have about the rules around eating may have led you to feel control. The metabolic haze and distractions caused by food and hunger may have helped you block off the negative emotions and to limit your focus to work and academic achievement. You had learned at your grandmother's knee how shape, weight, and appearance were of critical importance, and your weight control measures allowed you to achieve the special cachet of thinness. The sense of mastery that you were able to attain by shifting your focus to weight and work have helped you attain a sense of power and strength which compensated for the vulnerability you felt inside. At the same time, your physical vulnerability at times did signal to others your sense of distress, and your parents became drawn into helping you during your first episode of illness.

You may have become sensitized to losses and disappointments in your life by the series of losses that your family experienced during your childhood. The danger to your family and the unavailability of your parents could have impaired the development of your own sense of security. You may have had difficulty developing cooperative relationships with peers because there was a culture of competition and rivalry within your extended family.

It is apparent that you never had the opportunity to appreciate that close others could be available to offer support when you were distressed. Rather you learned that others may rely on you to be perfect and self-sufficient. You quickly took on board that it was important to please significant others in order to keep them close.

We know that one of the dangers for you will be your wish to please your therapist rather than addressing your real needs. Also, it will be difficult for you to trust anyone enough to work on some of the issues we discussed. Either of these might lead you to want to leave therapy. However, you are determined to make a change as you fear that your problems are now closing in on you and threatening your job, an important aspect of security and mastery that you had.

Kristen, you have immense persistence and resilience and have been able to fight back from several setbacks and these will be immense strengths for you to draw upon in therapy.

I have given you a book which details information that might be of help to you and a workbook that we will use as the basis of therapy.

The issues which I think we will need to work on in therapy will be:

(1) how your eating disorder symptoms help you to deal with emotional distress, loneliness, and difficulties with others and yourself

(2) what alternative ways there might be for you of dealing with emotional distress

(3) how you might improve your relationships with your colleagues

(4) and last but not least, how you might improve your relationships with close others

I look forward to seeing you at our next session.
With best wishes,

Additionally, the patterns by which thoughts, feelings, and behaviors interact and the way in which behaviors manifest themselves either as maintenance, compensatory, or avoidance behaviors are traced onto a diagram (sequential diagrammatic reformulation: Ryle & Marlowe, 1995). Kristen will also be given the following diagrams (see Figures 11.1, 11.2, and 11.3) which the therapist uses to illustrate her patterns of relating to others.

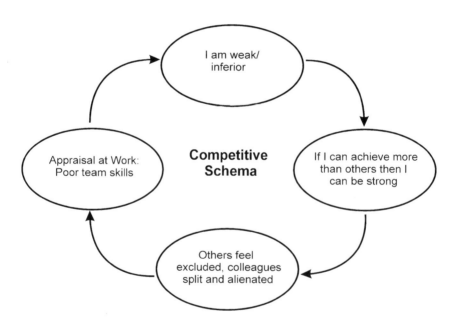

FIGURE 11.1   Peers/work colleagues.

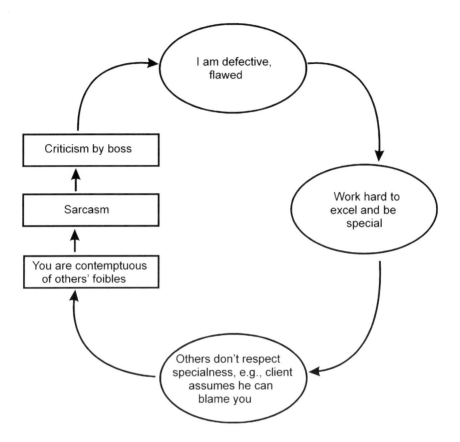

FIGURE 11.2

The Therapeutic Relationship

The Therapeutic Bond

The essence of the form of therapy that we use is to develop a very open collaborative relationship. The therapist will need to pay a great deal of attention to try to bolster self-esteem and self efficacy as it is obvious that these are core difficulties for Kristen. The therapist must avoid getting drawn into any hint of criticism or disappoint-

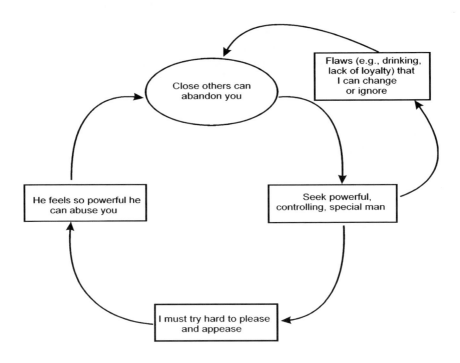

FIGURE 11.3   Close attachment.

ment as these will trigger the relevant schemata. On the other hand, the therapist will need to provide clear boundaries. The time, duration and setting of therapy need to be clearly defined. There need to be clear rules about disruptions to therapy such as missing sessions, losing weight, or metabolic crises.

Roles in the Therapeutic Relationship

The therapist should use as many objective and subjective markers to direct therapy as possible. We discuss below the role of regular weighing and measurement of electrolytes to assess the therapeutic relationship and the readiness to change.

Whenever possible, a diagram outlining the pattern of the therapeutic relationship should be drawn. This will probably be very similar to many of the other patterns of Kristen's other interpersonal relationships. It is probable that the most common pattern of the therapeutic relationship will resemble other important attachment patterns. In this case, the therapist may be treated as if special and powerful. Any flaws and doubts will be suppressed but will act as important roadblocks unless they are addressed. In Kristen's case, the experience with the previous therapist is an important warning about what might happen in this therapy unless the therapist is on her guard. It is likely that the previous therapist was placated by Kristen and, unable to read Kristen's mind, failed to realize that Kristen's bulimic problems were still present. The therapist should anticipate getting things wrong, making occasional mistakes, and should constantly check with the patient that she has understood her correctly or is making herself clear. The therapist should try to take a one-down position as much as possible to avoid getting into competitive power struggles. The therapist should invite help and constructive criticism. There is no need for self-disclosure on the part of the therapist although the use of stories and examples when suitable may be helpful.

Supervision is essential as this allows the therapist to take a meta perspective on the therapeutic process and to reflect upon the various forms of relationship in which the patient and therapist are engaged.

Treatment Implementation and Outcome

Techniques and Methods of Working

In the initial phase of therapy, to develop trust, and to explore any ambivalence about change the therapist would use the techniques of motivational interviewing.

There are five basic motivational principles:

(1) Express empathy
(2) Develop discrepancy
(3) Avoid argumentation
(4) Roll with resistance
(5) Support self-efficacy

Exploring the patient's meta beliefs about the anorexia nervosa, that is, the attitudes and assumptions she holds about the illness itself, gives important insights into the function of the symptomatology, its reinforcers, the kind of "solutions" it provides in helping her to cope with underlying problems and difficulties. These beliefs can be elicited by asking the patient about the good things that anorexia nervosa provides. This can be done by getting the patient to draw up a list of the advantages ("pros") of the anorexia nervosa, or to write a letter to the anorexia nervosa as a friend, or to depict the positive benefits of the anorexia in a collage or painting. Once a patient feels that her therapist has taken on board the positive aspects of the anorexia nervosa, she will be much more willing to divulge some of the not so good things about anorexia nervosa. She may be asked to draw up a list of the "cons" of anorexia nervosa or to write a letter to anorexia nervosa, the enemy. If the patient is in *contemplation* then there is an equal balance between the pros and the cons of the illness, whereas in *precontemplation* the pros outweigh the cons.

Once the formulation and the diagrams have been agreed upon, therapist and patient would come to an agreement about which goals should be the focus of therapy. Problem behaviors, such as weight loss or self-induced vomiting with resulting changes in potassium levels, are monitored during therapy and are used to gauge successful engagement and the stage of change. It is common for the patient to be at a different level of motivation to change for each of her problem behaviors and core schemata. The therapist may need to oscillate between the therapeutic stance and processes appropriate for the *precontemplation phase* and those for the *action phase*. It is common for many people with maladaptive schemata to be unaware of them and the problems they evoke. Therefore, having introduced the patient to the concepts, an important therapeutic task is to help the patient to become increasingly aware of her particular maladaptive schemata and the effect these beliefs have on her life. The simple loop diagrams (linking thoughts, feelings, and behaviors, Figures 11.1–11.3) are an invaluable form of shorthand. Important interactions occurring in day-to-day life are traced on these diagrams, providing the patient with an increasingly richer understanding of their maladaptive schema. Over time, the patient will become increasingly able to identify situations that activate her core schemata. A variety of techniques of cognitive restructuring, emotional processing, and behavioral experiments which challenge the schemata are used during this phase of treatment.

We would offer additional sessions with significant others if this was agreed on. The therapist would ask Kristen who she would like to bring who might be able to help in the change process. She could bring several members of her family individually or together. In meetings with the significant other, the therapist would focus on ways in which they might be able to help Kristen move on. The significant other would also be encouraged to develop some of the skills of motivational interviewing. Further sessions could be arranged if this appeared to be of help. The patient would be offered our structured homework book (Treasure, 1998) but this should be used with discretion.

Medical and Nutritional Issues

Kristen would have a medical evaluation at her first assessment which includes a basic examination of weight, height, pulse rate, blood pressure, and muscle power. We would plan to measure her weight each week at the beginning of the session. Her urea and electrolytes would be measured weekly until they came into the normal range when they could be measured monthly. An electrocardiogram would be helpful. We would advise Kristen to have a bone scan given the early onset and long duration of her illness and the accompanying acidosis, all of which are associated with osteoporosis.

Weight is a marker of the therapeutic alliance and is a clear indicator of whether the therapist and patient are working together on shared goals. If Kristen's weight falls further in treatment, this is a clear marker that she is in *precontemplation*. If she maintains a low weight this would suggest that she is in contemplation. Weight gain is usually a sign that the patient is in action. However, based on Kristen's previous experience in therapy, the therapist should be aware of the possibility that weight gain may simply reflect placation rather than unambiguous desire for change. The serum electrolytes can also be used in a similar manner to assess compliance and engagement. Signs of dehydration with postural hypotension, and low blood pressure are additional factors that should be monitored.

Other signs to look out for are:

1. Thigh and muscle weakness which makes climbing stairs or brushing hair difficult;
2. Faints or dizziness on getting up suddenly;
3. Fits;
4. Episodes of lightheadedness or panic with palpitations;
5. A measles-like rash;
6. Breathlessness;
7. Severe exhaustion;
8. Extremely cold and blue toes.

If there is continuing weight loss, it is important to monitor the medical condition regularly and to consider using a higher intensity care such as day patient or inpatient treatment.

The therapist would discuss with Kristen whether she wants to discuss nutritional matters. It may be helpful to suggest that there should not be any emphasis on this until Kristen has completed the first phase of therapy and is in *action* to move on this. On the other hand, the therapist should make it clear what would happen if further weight loss occurred and should discuss strategies for maintenance. There are worksheets in our Clinician's Guide and the self-help manual (Treasure, 1997; 1998) which cover nutritional issues, and the patient can use these when she is ready. Once the therapist is certain that Kristen is in *action*, she can go through the relevant calculations in the worksheet with her to work out her calorie requirements and target weight range.

Potential Pitfalls

One of the major pitfalls would be for the therapeutic relationship to become stuck in a maladaptive loop, such as the therapist acting as a powerful and critical other who has to be appeased (or, indeed, any of the other maladaptive forms of attachment relationships). Supervision and the use of diagrams to map patterns of interaction can be of great value in preventing this from happening. Another problem is that the therapist may become impatient or feel that she isn't doing enough for Kristen if she keeps dipping back into the *precontemplation* stage vis-a-vis some of her schemata. Usually therapists want to move into *action* and to see change but this can be counterproductive. The more the therapist pushes for this to happen, the more resistant the patient will become. One of the tasks of supervision is to soothe this desire for results and action. It can be very frustrating for the therapist to see her patient enter into a relationship with the outside world with all the hallmarks of dysfunction upon it. The therapist must sit on her hands at this point as too active a stance will merely serve to stoke resistance.

Termination and Relapse Prevention

In our unit, therapy (as opposed to continued contact for monitoring or support) is always time limited. This does not mean that the number of sessions is rigidly adhered to. If a patient uses her therapy well and, over the course of treatment, it becomes clear that certain issues need more time than initially planned for, extensions to therapy can be negotiated. The concept of time-limited therapy does, however, imply that throughout therapy the focus is on ending. The process of termination often powerfully reactivates maladaptive schemata and, therefore, needs careful thought and supervision. The work of ending requires both the patient and the therapist to review the therapy and to address the failures and the successes.

The therapist will remind Kristen about the number of sessions and the procedure involved in ending from the tenth session on. Given the number of losses and disappointments in Kristen's life, we would predict that she will find the loss of therapy difficult. She may be tempted not to attend some of the last sessions so that she can avoid dealing with the painful emotions that ending will evoke. The therapist must anticipate and preempt such a flight.

It is necessary to appraise accurately what has been lost through the ending and to experience the emotions of anger and sadness so that it is possible to move on to a new phase. In our unit, part of the process of ending therapy involves both the patient and therapist writing good-bye letters to each other summarizing and acknowledging what has been done in therapy and addressing what will happen in the future.

Mechanisms of Change

The aim of therapy is twofold: Firstly, for Kristen to be able to reflect upon her mind and the working models of self-others and world that it contains. We will want her to develop a meta view of all the procedures and processes that she uses in relationships with others. Secondly, for Kristen to become able to experience, express, process, and resolve avoided conflict. Only the combination of the two will bring sustained change and will enable Kristen to move away from the rigid patterns laid down by her schemata and away from the limited and false solution provided by her chronic eating disorder.

REFERENCES

Andrews, B. (1997a). Bodily shame as a mediator between abusive experiences and depression. *Journal of Abnormal Psychology, 104*, 277–285.

Andrews, B. (1997b). Bodily shame in relation to abuse in childhood and bulimia: A preliminary investigation. *British Journal of Clinical Psychology, 36*, 41–49.

Blake, W., Turnbull, S. J., & Treasure, J. L. (1997). Stages and processes of change in eating disorders: Implications for therapy. *Clinical Psychology and Psychotherapy, 4*, 186–191.

Claude-Pierre, P. (1998). *The secret language of eating disorders.* London: Doubleday.

Crisp, A. H. (1980). *Anorexia nervosa: "Let me be."* London: Academic Press.

Hornbacher-Beard, M. (1998). *Wasted.* Harper Collins.

MacLeod, S. (1982). *The art of starvation: A story of anorexia and survival.* Harmondsworth, UK: Virago.

Miller, W., & Rollnick, S. (1991). *Motivational interviewing. Preparing people to change addictive behaviors.* New York: Guilford Press.

Miller, W. R., Zwebeen, A., DiClemente, C. C., & Rychtarik, R. G. (1992). *Motivational enhancement therapy manual: A clinical research guide for therapists treating individuals with alcohol abuse and dependence.* Rockville, MD: National Institute on Alcohol Abuse and Alcoholism.

Prochaska, J. O. (1979). *Systems of psychotherapy: A transtheoretical analysis.* Chicago: Dorsey.

Prochaska, J. O., & DiClemente, C. C. (1982). Transtheoretical therapy: Toward a more integrative model of change. *Psychotherapy: Theory, Research and Practice, 19*, 276–288.

Prochaska, J. O., & Norcross, J. C. (1994). *Systems of psychotherapy: A transtheoretical analysis (3rd ed.).* Pacific Grove, CA: Brooks/Cole Publishing Company.

Rollnick, S., & Miller, W. R. (1995). What is motivational interviewing? *Behavioral and Cognitive Psychotherapy, 23*, 325–334.

Russell, G. F. M. (1995). Anorexia nervosa through time. In G. Szmukler, C. Dare, & J. Treasure (Eds.) *Handbook of eating disorders: Theory, treatment and research* (pp. 5–17). Chichester: John Wiley and Sons.

Ryle, A. (1990). *Cognitive analytical therapy: Active participation in change.* Chichester: Wiley.

Ryle, A. (1995). *Cognitive analytic therapy: Developments in theory and practice.* Chichester: Wiley.

Ryle, A., & Marlowe, M. J. (1995). Cognitive analytic therapy of borderline personality disorder: Theory and practice and the clinical and research uses of the self states sequential diagram. *International Journal of Short Term Psychotherapy, 10,* 21–34.

Schmidt, U. H., Tiller, J. M., Blanchard, M., Andrews, B., & Treasure, J. L. (1997). Is there a specific trauma precipitating anorexia nervosa? *Psychological Medicine, 27,* 523–530.

Serpell, L., Treasure, J. L., Teasdale, J., & Sullivan, V. (1999). Anorexia nervosa: Friend or foe? *International Journal of Eating Disorders, 25,* 177–186.

Shelley, R. (1997) *Anorexics on anorexia.* London: Jessica Kingsley Publishers Ltd.

Treasure, J. L. (1997). *Anorexia nervosa: A survival guide for families, friends and sufferers.* Hove: Psychology Press.

Treasure, J. L. (1998). *A clinician's guide to anorexia nervosa.* Hove: Psychology Press.

Treasure, J. L., Todd, G., Brolly, M., Tiller, J. M., Nehmed, A., & Denman, F. (1995). A pilot study of a randomised trial of cognitive analytical therapy vs. educational behavioral therapy for adult anorexia nervosa. *Behavior Research and Therapy, 33,* 363–367.

Treasure, J. L., & Ward, A. (1997a). Cognitive analytical therapy (CAT) in eating disorders. *Clinical Psychology and Psychotherapy, 4,* 62–71.

Treasure, J. L., & Ward, A. (1997b). A practical guide to the use of motivational interviewing in anorexia nervosa. *European Eating Disorders Review, 5,* 102–114.

Troop, N. A., Schmidt, U. H., & Treasure, J. L. (1999). A review of life events, difficulties and the onset of eating disorders. Manuscript submitted for publication.

Troop, N. A., & Treasure, J. L. (1997a). Psychosocial factors in the onset of eating disorders: Responses to life-events and difficulties. *British Journal of Medical Psychology, 70,* 373–385.

Troop, N. A., & Treasure, J. L. (1997b). Setting the scene for eating disorders II: Childhood helplessness and mastery. *Psychological Medicine, 27,* 531–538.

Vitousek, K., Watson, S., & Wilson, G. T. (1998). Enhancing motivation for change in treatment-resistant eating disorders. *Clinical Psychology Review, 18*, 391–420.

Ward, A., Troop, N. A., Todd, G., & Treasure, J. L. (1996). To change or not to change—"How" is the question? *British Journal of Medical Psychology, 69*, 139–146.

Wolff, G., & Serpell, L. (1998). A cognitive model and treatment strategies for anorexia nervosa. In H. W. Hoek, J. L. Treasure, & M. A. Katzman (Eds.), *Neurobiology in the treatment of eating disorders* (pp. 407–429). Chichester: Wiley.

12

Comparative Treatments: Summary and Conclusions

Katherine J. Miller

The case of Kristen has been comprehensively addressed by authors from nine different approaches who have applied their theories and practices to Kristen's assessment and treatment planning. Three of the models are explicitly integrative—Bryant-Waugh's developmental-systemic-feminist therapy, Wonderlich, Peterson, Mitchell, and Crow's integrative cognitive therapy for bulimic behavior, and Treasure, Schmidt, and Troop's cognitive analytic therapy within the transtheoretical framework. Cognitive-behavior therapy had previously integrated cognitive and behavioral methods, here interpreted by Williamson and Netemeyer. Sands' self psychology approach represents one of the four psychologies of psychoanalysis and is thus closely related to the psychoanalytic psychotherapy chapter by Fallon and Bunce. Interpersonal psychotherapy, described here by Wilfley, Dounchis, and Welch, and Gralewski and Schneider's Adlerian approach also have psychodynamic origins but offer striking differences as well. The only model that begins with family therapy is De Giacomo and Rugiu's elementary pragmatic model, which is based on systems theory and cybernetics.

This chapter will summarize and compare the nine models in each of the 13 areas under consideration, followed by closing comments.

TREATMENT MODEL

The cognitive-behavior model was defined as a multidisciplinary continuum of care with very specific protocols. Kristen would begin inpatient treatment with cognitive-behavioral individual, family, and group therapies running parallel to dietary and medical interventions. The primary aim would be to decrease Kristen's extreme weight control methods and fear of weight gain since the core of the disorder is seen as fear of weight gain, overconcern with body size and shape, and body-image disturbance. The treatment uses exposure and response prevention to normalize eating as well as work on cognitive biases and automatic thoughts about eating and body size and core beliefs regarding worthiness.

Psychoanalytic psychotherapy would follow standard analytic techniques such as focusing on conscious and unconscious motivation, conflicts, defenses, and interpersonal patterns from childhood. Kristen's eating disorder is viewed as symptomatic of the underlying psychological problems and would be seen as serving important functions for her. The therapy would help her to recover the split-off parts of her self contained in her bulimic symptoms. Kristen's bulimia would indicate that her body is poorly integrated into her sense of self, including sexuality, distortions, and delusions about body shape.

The self psychology chapter is also an intensive, long-term model of therapy which focuses more on underlying dynamics than on eating and weight-related behaviors. The eating disorder is used in lieu of other people to help Kristen feel cohesive and alive, and analyzing the transference relationship would be a major part of the work. The therapist would in effect ask Kristen to reexperience early needs and to risk disappointment and shame within the therapeutic relationship. The aim is for Kristen to give people another chance.

The interpersonal psychotherapy model is similar to the psychoanalytic models in terms of focusing on Kristen's problems in interpersonal relationships which are related to the onset and/or maintenance of the eating disorder. The therapy focuses on the relationship between current interpersonal functioning, low self-esteem, negative mood, and eating behaviors. Although early attachment relationships are considered to be a source of current problems, alteration of the present interpersonal context is the strategy here.

The developmental-systemic-feminist model integrates understandings from developmental psychology, systems theory, and feminist ideology. Kristen's eating disorder is understood in relationship to her developmental history and attachment within the family and cultural context. Kristen and the therapist would collaboratively formulate a functional analysis, looking at problematic behaviors, thought patterns, and emotions in the context of life events, emotional responses, social and family circumstances, and personal cognitive style. While minimizing their power differential, the therapist would validate Kristen's responses and enhance her autonomy and self-worth, building on strengths, knowing that messages about womanhood may have been negative.

The Adlerian model emphasizes the socially embedded, creative, responsible, and becoming aspects of being a person. Behavior is seen as social and purposeful, guided by lifestyle beliefs about the self, self-ideal, nature of reality, and methods of movement open to one—all strongly influenced by the family. A unique aspect of this therapy is challenging clients to demonstrate healthy social interest through useful involvement in the world. Kristen would be invited to reflect on her lifestyle, eating-disordered beliefs, and behaviors; challenged to reconsider her values and future options; and helped to "edit" the patterns of her life. Family sessions and group work would most likely be used in addition to individual therapy.

The elementary pragmatic model would initially use family therapy to evaluate Kristen's patterns of interaction, based on a taxonomy of 16 interactional styles. The therapist's interventions would be based on the same taxonomy, designed to facilitate a healthier outcome. With anorexia nervosa, the authors most commonly work toward the distant father entering and accepting the world of the daughter. Multidisciplinary day hospital treatment may also be used if more structure and input is needed.

The last two models purposefully integrate cognitive and psychodynamic concepts and methods. Wonderlich et al.'s integrative cognitive therapy for bulimic behavior is based on a broad model of

contributory factors: cultural variables, life experiences, temperament, representations of self and other, interpersonal schemata,
relationship patterns, and affect regulation. Kristen's perception of
her self as deficient is threatening to relationships and leads to
negative mood; to prevent significant others from withdrawing, she
may submit, wall off, or attack, all related to anxious attachment.
Kristen cognitively controls, blames, and neglects her self, turning
to eating disorder behaviors to feel more worthy and to avoid negative
affect and meaningful issues. In addition to cognitive-behavioral
methods, techniques are incorporated from feminist, interpersonal,
and emotion theorists, and from motivational interviewing.

Cognitive analytic therapy and the transtheoretical framework
emphasize the anorexic person's disturbance in sense of self and
working models about the world, low levels of mastery, and cognitive
avoidance of severe life events or problems as a rigid coping style.
Kristen's maladaptive core schemata from early relationships would
be a focus, particularly in areas of care eliciting, caregiving, and peer
cooperation and competitiveness. Interventions would be chosen
according to Kristen's motivation to change, based on the transtheoretical model of change, and would include motivational interviewing, cognitive therapy techniques, and a great focus on
interpersonal relationship patterns in earlier attachments, current
relationships, and the therapeutic relationship.

To summarize, the treatment models draw on the clinical wisdom
of their own theories and practices. They vary, for example, on
relative emphasis on behavioral methods, work with systems, use of
historical material, and focus on eating and weight-related behaviors
or underlying dynamic issues. They all have some focus on interpersonal relationships, and all attempt to influence the beliefs and
cognitive processes of the patient. The settings of the treatment
range from multilevel care to solo practice.

THE THERAPIST'S SKILLS AND ATTRIBUTES

All approaches require specialized training in their model of therapy,
beyond basic academic degrees. The cognitive-behavioral and interpersonal psychotherapy authors noted that experience in treating
people with eating disorders is also a necessity. Clinical supervision

was advised if the therapist has less than 2 years of experience in treating eating disorders in cognitive-behavior therapy, while cognitive analytic and Adlerian models recommended ongoing supervision and collaboration, consultation, and peer supervision, respectively.

In addition, knowledge of systems, families, and groups is valued by the Adlerian, developmental-systemic-feminist, and elementary pragmatic models. The cognitive-behavior therapists recommended being well-trained in the philosophy of science to increase objectivity and scientific skepticism, and also suggested that Kristen's therapist be female to make the work on the sexual traumas easier.

The personal qualities needed by the therapist which were mentioned for several orientations include warmth and genuineness, empathy, respect, acceptance of the client's emotions and perceptions, collaborativeness, personal awareness of and ability to handle countertransference, and being a good role model about eating habits and body image. Additional desirable qualities mentioned in the psychoanalytic chapter were patience, truthfulness without the need for self-disclosure, cognitive flexibility, and appreciation of the complexity of human nature. The developmental-systemic-feminist model valued creative and spontaneous response to where the client leads, extracting and building on client strengths, being sensitive to the power differential, knowledge of developmental tasks and stages in relation to events and situations, and the abilities to positively reframe and to negotiate around health and safety. Other desired qualities mentioned by various authors were maturity, sensitivity to the client's emotional responding, having good boundaries and a strong sense of responsibility, being well-differentiated, not being perfectionistic, having a present orientation, verbal skillfulness, and having a good memory for details.

There were not strong differences among orientations in ideal therapist characteristics, and none of them were mutually exclusive. There was, however, a difference in relative emphasis on therapist characteristics which varied from very little, as in the elementary pragmatic model, to a great deal, particularly the psychoanalytic and self psychology models.

Listening with an open mind to understand the patient's frame of reference and eliciting self-exploration were emphasized in several models. The cognitive analytic and integrative cognitive methods require skills in motivational interviewing, such as eliciting motivational statements and monitoring the stage of readiness to change. The interpersonal psychotherapy model encourages the patient to take responsibility for the direction of therapy, and the therapist must be skilled in conveying hope and optimism, fostering a safe and supportive working environment, seeing patterns quickly, and formulating and focusing on time-limited goals. Both this model and the Adlerians mentioned helping the client see the relationship between the eating disorder and interpersonal disturbances. The integrative cognitive model emphasized the ability to assess multiple aspects of the client's functioning while keeping the treatment focused and validating ambivalence rather than trying to force treatment, also a cognitive analytic stance.

ASSESSMENT

The primary commonality in assessment was the use of interviews to find out the patient's view of her problems, gather history, identify symptoms and eating patterns, and check on suicidality, self-harm, and substance abuse. Some also used structured interviews regarding eating disorder symptomatology (EDE, IDED-IV) or psychopathology (e.g., SCID). Five models used objective or projective psychological tests to evaluate personality characteristics (MCMI-III, Wisconsin Personality Inventory, MMPI, TAT, Rorschach), depression (BDI), and/or intellectual functioning (WAIS-III). Three used measures particular to their emphasis, for example, Life Style Inventory (Adlerians), Inventory of Interpersonal Problems (interpersonal psychotherapy), or Selves Questionnaire and Physical Appearance Questionnaire to clarify self-discrepancy (integrative cognitive). The developmental-systemic-feminist model used parallel time lines of life events and eating disorder events and a cost-benefit analysis of keeping or giving up the eating disorder.

The preferred modality of the elementary pragmatic model is family sessions, in which interactional styles are appraised at the outset. The developmental-systemic-feminist and Adlerian models incorporated family members into early sessions to learn about early experiences, current coping strategies, and systemic factors. Only the cognitive-behavior and integrative cognitive therapists mentioned body image assessment, body composition measurement, or self-monitoring logs in this section, although self-monitoring was mentioned by other authors in later sections. The self-monitoring regarding food intake included recording situational and emotional events related to eating and purging.

The psychoanalytic and self psychology chapters emphasized the ongoing nature of evaluation, conceptualization, and hypothesis testing. Both are relatively less focused on symptoms and more focused on the patient's inner world and personality structure, and on the interpersonal processes in the sessions.

THERAPEUTIC GOALS

While all methods aimed for alleviation of the eating disorder behaviors, this emphasis was balanced in different ways with concerns about engaging Kristen in the therapeutic process. For example, cognitive-behavior therapy specified an immediate major focus on normalizing eating patterns and weight restoration, but only mentioned the importance of Kristen developing trust. In contrast, other models emphasized an initial primary focus on engaging Kristen's motivation and setting collaborative goals in a variety of areas, not just eating and weight-related behaviors. The latter group was concerned with immediate physical safety, but they described process goals as necessary steps to significant symptom change.

Most authors addressed interpersonal functioning and related interpersonal needs and coping styles to Kristen's eating disorder symptoms. The goal of having Kristen understand the function of her symptoms was an integral part of the process, which required her to recognize patterns and modify her behavior, cognitive style, and underlying schemata. Learning to identify and regulate tension and affective states was also a major theme. Kristen's developing more realistic and flexible evaluative standards, a goal for many, would contribute to improving self-esteem, decreasing depression, and improving relationships.

Only the cognitive-behavior therapists specifically mentioned modifying body-image disturbance. The Adlerians and elementary pragmatic therapists aimed for improving Kristen's family relationships. Resolution of her sexual trauma or posttraumatic stress was mentioned by the Adlerians and cognitive-behavior therapists.

TIME LINE FOR THERAPY

Five of the models are time-limited in nature, with some built-in flexibility. The elementary pragmatic family therapy model involves 10 weekly sessions, with 6 weeks of day hospital treatment as a backup plan. Integrative cognitive therapy involves 20 sessions over 16 weeks, with four flexible phases planned in advance. Cognitive analytic therapy involves 20 weekly sessions followed by 5 monthly sessions. Developmental-systemic-feminist therapy is delivered in five blocks of sessions, each ending with a review session and a break designed to allow reflection and consolidation, enhancing the client's self-reliance; the span of 12 to 18 months includes follow-up sessions. Interpersonal psychotherapy involves three stages of work over 20 sessions at the most, with further sessions allowed only after the client has some months to consolidate gains on her own.

The cognitive-behavior therapists were the only ones to firmly specify the need for hospitalization, and in their continuum of care model, the primary therapist would follow Kristen through all four stages; the maximum amount of time appears to be about 16 months, with follow-up over the next several years.

The self psychologist recommended three sessions per week for Kristen at the outset; length of treatment would be determined by ongoing assessment and the development of the transference. The psychoanalytic approach in general would take between 1 and 5 years, perhaps with multiple sessions per week. The Adlerians estimated 1.5 to 2 years of therapy, with two or three sessions per week (1.5 hours each) at the outset.

CASE CONCEPTUALIZATION

The cognitive-behavior therapy conceptualization identified etiological factors for Kristen's anorexia nervosa as family events and relationships, social pressures toward overconcern with body size and shape, and posttraumatic stress disorder and obsessive-compulsive disorder.

In adolescence, dieting and exercise were used to control anxiety about body and appearance, and there was an interaction of habits, emotions, and overvalued ideas leading to control of eating and body size. The date rape led to depression and binge-eating, and fear of weight gain led to purging. While the eating disorder was controlled for a few years, the relapse related to her fiance's infidelity, binge-purge behavior during travel, and depression. Major depression as well as PTSD and OCD were seen as comorbid disorders.

In the psychoanalytic chapter, Fallon and Bunce observed that Kristen's family emphasized beauty, competition, and perfection, and Kristen grew up with a sense that there was never enough emotional nurturance or other essentials. She tried to manage her emptiness through achievement, relationships, and food, all of which had failed her at the time she entered therapy. She was ashamed of having physical or emotional needs, and she purged or restricted to rid herself of them and her sense of shame. Kristen's need for nurturance complicated her love relationship with Joe and worked against her seeing his shortcomings. Kristen managed anxiety through somatization, isolation of affect, and acting out, avoiding dealing with her inner life; she held in anger until she exploded periodically. She was not completely differentiated from her mother, whom she protected from angry and rivalrous feelings, a source of some control issues and difficulties in intimate relationships. The four sexual traumas Kristen experienced (father's affair, abandonment of her high school boyfriend, rape, and Joe's cheating on her) were sources of depression and eating disorder symptoms, which symbolized both her feelings and an attempt at coping with them.

The interpersonal psychotherapists conceptualized Kristen's dilemma as centering around social isolation and chronically unfulfilling relationships. While they focused primarily on current patterns, they indicated that painful events in the past (e.g., parents' separation, her rape) shed light on current interpersonal problems. Restricting, bingeing, purging, and over-exercise have been a way for Kristen to disconnect from her feelings, and she has used food and restraint to comfort herself or feel in control.

Kristen's strengths as a resource for change were noted in the developmental-systemic-feminist model: hard-working, committed, and determined. In her family, Kristen was expected to fulfill her parents' wishes and aspirations, to do everything right, and not to displease. Consequently, she is accommodating to others, minimizes her own needs and distress, and is self-doubting and self-critical. Her all-or-nothing thinking leads to viewing her present crisis as catastrophic, to doing things full-time or not at all, and to ending relationships if she cannot be good, pleasing, and successful. The "crisis" involved Kristen's eating behavior being out of control and her falling behind in work commitments.

The self psychology formulation characterized Kristen as having a self disorder—anxious, unaware of physical and emotional needs and desires, and trying to create an appearance of perfection with disregard for her limitations. Her early developmental needs for comfort, protection, admiration, and responsiveness had not been adequately met, and Kristen had not internalized the ability to soothe herself. She was rewarded for being pleasing, attractive, and accomplished, but not seen in her uniqueness. Her symptoms were attempts not to experience a need for others, and she turned to bulimia and food restriction for regulation of affect and self-esteem during vulnerable times. A number of traumas betrayed Kristen's trust in others, including her father's business being lost, his affair, her rape, and her fiance's affair. After the first two she tried to become self-sufficient; after the second two, she turned to her eating disorder. Nevertheless, Kristen may have experienced survivor guilt for her degree of success, eliciting self-defeating behaviors out of family loyalty. This conceptualization also included a list of Kristen's considerable strengths, such as competence, persistence, and creativity.

The Adlerian therapists mapped Kristen's basic beliefs and lifestyle strategies through a careful review of her history. They identified her core issues as control, competence, and identity. Kristen's early needs for nurturing and validation were not adequately met, and she felt she had to conform and be perfect to be acceptable and get what she needed from others. In adolescence, self-exploration was aborted by her parents' divorce; she retained her family's values of social status and beauty, which were reinforced by peer standards. Kristen's dissatisfaction with herself was concretized in body dissatisfaction, and she tried to gain control of her body both to meet others' standards and to be self-determined. Like her parents, she coped with anxiety by hard work and achievement, valuing high socioeconomic status, academic success, and competition. Holding these values may have been an effort to become close to her distant father; in fact, Kristen's primary model for marriage was distant, tumultuous, and rigid. Kristen has strengths to support therapeutic change, such as being hard-working, self-controlled, and wanting relationships.

The elementary pragmatic model credited Kristen with periods of satisfactory equilibrium in which she treats herself in a rigid, perfectionistic way—"the internal dictator." In negative periods, she is oscillating and ambivalent, "incapable of maintaining her own world" and managing by binge-eating and vomiting. Kristen is intelligent, capable, and self-reflective, and through seeking treatment will be able to deepen her own world.

The integrative cognitive model underscored the importance of Kristen's nutritional deficits and compromised physiological functioning and addressed four major etiological factors that guided the goals for treatment. The discrepancy between Kristen's perception of her actual self and her ideal self or ought-self is marked in many areas, including her body image. Her standards evolved from family focus on physical appearance, devotion to work, and appearing in control and superior. Kristen's cognitive style of excessive self-control, self-blame, and self-neglect led to risky behaviors in her search for self-regulation and perfection. Kristen's early family life most likely left her feeling insecure and inadequate, and she tends to withdraw (into work or her eating disorder) or be submissive in interpersonal relationships. This seems based on her belief that, because of her inadequacies, others could only care about her if she does what they want.

The cognitive analytic formulation noted intergenerational themes of competition, caregiving, and maladaptive attachment relationships. Difficult events were not processed adequately in Kristen's family, such as the stillbirth and the fire, and Kristen's mother did not have adequate support or closeness from her husband. This probably affected her ability to be nurturing and responsive to Kristen, contributing to Kristen's sense of insecurity. Kristen felt abandoned by her father in high school and became a confidant for her mother. The competitive schema from being youngest, having a competitive family, and having low self-esteem probably made cooperation with peers more difficult for Kristen, losing potential peer support through difficult times. She was successful academically but had difficulties in close relationships, tending to avoid them. Dating special and powerful men served as compensation for her experience of herself as weak and defective but left her vulnerable to overlooking their flaws and feeling less powerful in the relationship. Being competitive and disconnected at work led to negative feedback which fed her sense of being defective and needing to try harder. Hard work and her eating disorder symptoms were ways that Kristen tried to feel special, strong, and secure.

A number of themes recur throughout these conceptualizations. Kristen's difficult life events affected her anxiety level and her view of the world and herself, and decreased the amount of support she received. Early family attachments were lacking in validation and security, which affected her self-esteem, sense of self, and future relationships. Kristen had a pattern of unfulfilling relationships in which she tried to be perfect and pleasing or else withdrew and denied her needs. Eating disorder symptoms were used to regulate her emotions: to disconnect from her feelings, to soothe herself, and to regain a sense of control. Other themes in the case conceptualizations were competitiveness, competence, and cultural emphasis on thinness and appearance.

THE THERAPEUTIC BOND

Almost all of the models described risks in the therapy relationship stemming from Kristen's transferring expectations, fears, and maladaptive interpersonal styles from earlier relationships. The psychoanalytic, self psychology, and interpersonal models emphasized transference in the therapeutic bond as a potential source of rupture and of healing. All models described Kristen's need to experience a new kind of relationship in which she could be understood, accepted, and nurtured in a reliable way. The therapist must provide empathic understanding, warmth, compassion, predictability, and firm boundaries, such as limiting self-disclosure. As the bond evolves and Kristen feels safe, she will be able to change her beliefs about relationships, experience herself and others in new ways, and learn to stay connected rather than withdrawing when she has needs and feelings.

The collaborative nature of the therapeutic bond was emphasized by several models, partly to encourage self-reliance and differentiation. In the family therapy of the elementary pragmatic model, the therapist takes a somewhat more authoritative stance in facilitating healthier interactions between the family members.

The potential ruptures to the therapeutic bond come not only from Kristen's lack of trust and fear of revealing her true self, but also from potential countertransference of the therapist. For example, getting pulled into power struggles with Kristen, being too directive rather than collaborative, becoming bored with her compliance, and being too pushy or overly protective are potential errors.

ROLES IN THE THERAPEUTIC RELATIONSHIP

All models made some reference to indicate that Kristen is in charge of her recovery—the therapist collaborates, elucidates, and even suggests, but Kristen must choose what changes she will make. Some models noted the therapist's role in mobilizing Kristen's motivation for change, such as using motivational interviewing techniques or the Decision Analysis Form. The therapist also educates the client about the particular form of therapy and about eating disorders, but goal-setting and movement through the tasks of therapy are done collaboratively. The therapist needs to frequently check that communications are accurate. The cognitive-behavioral and cognitive analytic authors referred to "collaborative empiricism" in which the therapist collaborates with the client to evaluate beliefs and interpretations of events.

The therapist's role in all cases included raising Kristen's awareness about her cognitions, emotions, and/or behavior, particularly in regard to her eating disorder symptoms and interpersonal relationships. This requires the therapist to create a safe and supportive environment in which Kristen could be honest without experiencing an overwhelming sense of shame. In many models, the therapist's role also includes monitoring transference and countertransference, and discussing with the client the parallels between the therapy relationship and others. In general, the therapist is responsible for ongoing assessment of Kristen and of the therapy relationship, maintaining clear boundaries, attending to safety issues such as weight and dehydration, avoiding control struggles, and fostering collaboration toward goals.

There were differences among the models in how the therapist would structure sessions. For example, in the psychoanalytic and self psychology approaches, Kristen would be expected to say what came to mind and the therapist would conduct "sustained empathic inquiry," with the analysis of the transference being a major piece of the work. Other methods use more active ways of eliciting feelings, beliefs, and behaviors, and working toward alternatives. This was particularly true for the more time-limited models such as cognitive-behavioral, interpersonal, developmental-systemic-feminist, integrative cognitive, and cognitive-analytic models. Nevertheless, facilitating exploration was common to all forms of therapy.

The family therapist of the elementary pragmatic model works to define boundaries between family subsystems and improve the interactions between family members. The patient and family members would be expected to carry out interactional tasks outside of the sessions. The Adlerian model involves encouraging social interest in each life task area and encourages using outside resources such as groups to support movement.

TECHNIQUES AND METHODS OF WORKING

Three models were explicitly integrative in nature—developmental-systemic-feminist, integrative cognitive, and cognitive analytic within a transtheoretical framework. Others used techniques and methods that were directly from their model but often incorporated methods associated with other models.

The developmental-systemic-feminist model flexibly draws techniques from many schools of therapy to meet the four tasks of the therapy: for therapist and client to explore, understand, accept, and experiment. The initial formulation is written in the form of a letter to Kristen to gain clarity and to use in negotiating treatment goals. The dietician does much of the work on eating patterns so that the therapy time can be used on other areas. The format of having blocks of sessions followed by review and a 1-month break encourages focus. The collaborative style of planning and evaluation is paced toward Kristen doing more and more of the work on her own, perhaps with the help of a support group in the last stage.

Both the integrative cognitive and cognitive analytic approaches use motivational interviewing, cognitive-behavioral techniques, and psychodynamic methods. Integrative cognitive therapy for bulimic behavior begins with psychoeducation about the eating disorder, using a workbook to help keep the focus. There is homework on the origins of Kristen's self-discrepancy and appearance standards, and she would be taught strategies for increasing self-acceptance and modifying her perfectionistic standards. In the second stage of therapy, the focus would be on normalizing her eating and Kristen learning coping skills. Thirdly, Kristen would work toward a functional analysis of her interpersonal and eating disordered behaviors and work on her interpersonal schemas, historical antecedents, cognitive style, and alternatives.

The cognitive analytic model also begins by exploring attitudes and assumptions about anorexia nervosa, perhaps by listing the pros and cons of the disorder or writing a letter to the anorexia. Kristen would monitor her problem behaviors throughout, and weight gain would be seen as a measure of the therapy work. The therapist would foster awareness of her maladaptive schemata, triggers, and effects of the eating disorder on her life, using loop diagrams to help her see the patterns. The work would include cognitive restructuring, emotional processing, and behavioral experiments, perhaps using a structured homework book. In addition, significant others may be invited to sessions to learn how to best support Kristen.

The cognitive-behavioral model was the only one that definitely recommended hospitalization as the first of four stages of care. They have an initial emphasis on weight gain, using the exchange system, nutritional education, self-monitoring, behavioral contracting, highly structured days, and homework. The therapist would help Kristen identify and change her automatic thoughts related to eating and weight and develop new ways of coping with stress. In addition, they would work on identity issues and general schemata about self-worth, healthy relationships, and perfectionism. The body image therapy would include education, cognitive restructuring, and behavioral exposure. Family education about eating disorders and the recovery process would be offered.

Both the psychoanalytic and self psychology models use standard psychoanalytic methods to foster the working alliance, helping Kristen to identify and articulate feelings, interpreting defenses, and looking at patterns of behavior, resistance to treatment, and transference. Both involve working through the transference and seeing parallels between early experiences, current relationships, and the therapeutic relationship, and both might help Kristen with problem solving, behavioral ideas, or information as necessary. The psychoanalytic authors mentioned highlighting inconsistencies between Kristen's behavior and goals to help develop introspection, a method also used in motivational interviewing. They would inquire about Kristen's feelings before and after binge-eating or purging to help her understand the use of her eating disorder. The self psychology emphasis is on helping Kristen understand her needs and defenses in relation to food and eating, gradually transferring her needs to the therapist.

The Adlerians would help Kristen assess the patterns in her life, looking at past difficulties and successes and analyzing current patterns and beliefs. They would use cognitive techniques, such as work on cognitive distortions, problem solving, and decision making. They would teach Kristen self-calming skills and assertiveness and help her become less impulsive and less intent on pleasing others. Journaling, family work, group work, and social relationships of other kinds are significant methods of change also.

The elementary pragmatic model would use family sessions to help Kristen and her family understand her better. The therapist would amplify her world paradoxically, most likely with family tasks in the session and at home or by asking Kristen to change something (e.g., eat with chopsticks). The father-daughter interaction would be a major focus to help Kristen's father become closer to her, but a special computer program for tension reduction and self-help books might also be used. If the day hospital were needed, Kristen would receive a course on eating disorders, do body-image work, and participate in group therapy, dance therapy, and art therapy.

All therapists would educate Kristen about the treatment process and make sure she got information about her eating disorder in terms of medical and nutritional needs. There were different configurations for delivery of service among the chapters which made a difference in the therapist's role, but most models involved collaboration with medical personnel and a nutritionist. Most would consider the use of an antidepressant (usually a selective serotonin reuptake inhibitor, SSRI), and most would help Kristen find better ways of tension reduction and self-soothing.

Some of the basic differences among approaches are the amount of explicit focus on the therapy relationship, the directiveness in influencing behavioral changes, and the inclusion or exclusion of family therapy and group therapy. The inclusion of day treatment or hospitalization also varied.

The cognitive behavioral, integrative cognitive, and cognitive analytic approaches advocated working directly on eating behaviors and actively monitoring weight and eating behaviors. The developmental-systemic-feminist approach allowed for this as a possible goal, and the elementary pragmatic model recommended tasks for Kristen and her family related to eating. The other four models primarily left monitoring of weight and food intake to physician and nutritionist, focusing in therapy on their meaning and function.

MEDICAL AND NUTRITIONAL ISSUES

All of the authors recommended that Kristen be evaluated and monitored by a physician who is knowledgeable about eating disorders and that the therapist collaborate with the physician on an ongoing basis. There were divergent opinions about who should weigh Kristen and monitor her food intake and eating behaviors. The psychoanalytic, Adlerian, and interpersonal writers recommended that someone other than the therapist weigh Kristen; Bryant-Waugh suggested negotiating with Kristen about whether the therapist or nurse would weigh her; and Treasure et al. believed the therapist should weigh her. The Adlerians recommended that medical personnel explain the potential dangers of eating-disordered behaviors, lab results, and the need for monitoring, while Bryant-Waugh recommended that the therapist do this. The Adlerians, nonetheless, said the therapist may need to confront Kristen on her medical status, while being empathic toward her struggles in this area.

The cognitive-behavior therapists recommended starting with inpatient treatment, while others acknowledge that inpatient or day treatment may be needed if Kristen continues to lose weight, if starvation compromises psychotherapy, or if she fails to maintain a specified weight.

Slow refeeding is an essential element in the cognitive-behavior treatment model, starting in the first phase, and these authors noted the need to check on edema, fluid overload, gastric motility, and bowel function. They noted that Kristen may need multivitamins, gastric motility agents or fiber, and/or a dietary supplement, and that withdrawal symptoms should be explained in advance. Kristen may also need a dental consult and a bone scan, which could demonstrate the need for calcium supplements or estrogen replacement therapy to lower the risk of osteoporosis.

Everyone mentioned the possible need for psychotropic medication, generally an SSRI, with psychiatric evaluation. Fallon and Bunce specified consults with a psychodynamically minded psychiatrist who would be aware of the meanings of the medicine and the use to which the patient put them.

Some therapists recommended immediate referral to a nutritionist or dietician, while others believed in evaluating Kristen's readiness first. Sands evaluates the patient's amount of knowledge, fear, and interest regarding the nutritional information. Both Wonderlich et al. and Treasure et al. recommended a nutritional consult in the *second* phase of therapy. The elementary pragmatic family therapy model relies on the therapist to help the family formulate reasonable eating patterns as a part of the assigned tasks, except in the day hospital where a dietician is involved.

POTENTIAL PITFALLS

The primary issues that may jeopardize Kristen's therapy relate to her staying in treatment, her fear and lack of trust, her motivation for change, and inappropriate therapist responses. The responses regarding potential pitfalls are integrated here, while contributions of individual models are listed in Appendix A.

Kristen may drop out of treatment due to the method being ungratifying, because of feelings of shame and failure, or because of ambivalence about taking time off work. She may even make a "flight into health" or decide she failed if not progressing quickly.

On the other hand, Kristen may be reluctant to end therapy at the agreed-upon time.

Another set of possible difficulties has to do with Kristen's lack of trust and fear of closeness, having a sense of vulnerability and fear of her own emotions. Kristen is very vulnerable to feeling a sense of shame and failure due to her self-perceived deficiencies. She may withhold information, use deceit, or simply be superficial and intellectualized in order to appear perfect; she has difficulty reaching out for help and becoming fully engaged, as demonstrated by her earlier therapy experiences, and she may appease the therapist instead of acknowledging her true feelings and thoughts. Talking about her family may lead to guilt-feelings and shame for Kristen. She also may act out her feelings through the eating disorder symptoms rather than expressing them in the therapy, or focus solely on eating and weight issues in her sessions. Having difficulty identifying her emotions to begin with could also slow the therapy process, especially since many models of therapy work on relating feelings to eating disorder symptoms. A related problem which could arise is Kristen's feeling shamed, exposed, or disarmed when the therapist interprets her fears.

Kristen may find it too difficult to give up her eating disorder symptoms after losing her fiancé and having job difficulties, at least before developing new coping strategies. She has been coping with anxiety through her eating disorder and work and, if forced to change, could replace the eating disorder with other unhealthy methods of managing her affective states. Kristen also may not work on her goals, perhaps by forgetting, and she may not, in fact, see severe restraint as a problem. Other difficulties with motivation to change are that Kristen has not acknowledged the seriousness of her condition and may not commit herself to the goals or process of healing.

Countertransference may be evoked around control issues, with the therapist put in the role of the powerful and critical other. The therapist may become impatient and push in an inappropriate way when Kristen regresses to precontemplation in an area of previous progress.

Kristen's traumatic feelings about the rape may surface and require concentrated work. A final danger is relapse after a period of freedom from her symptoms, a subject to which we turn in the next section.

TERMINATION AND RELAPSE PREVENTION

The decision when to terminate the therapy is somewhat preplanned in the interpersonal, developmental-systemic-feminist, integrative cognitive, cognitive analytic, and elementary pragmatic models. Treasure et al. would remind Kristen of the termination date each week from the tenth session on. Bryant-Waugh writes that there is no termination phase in the developmental-systemic-feminist model because of the careful emphasis on empowering the client. In several models, there is a tapering off with longer times in between the final sessions.

The psychoanalytic model has three criteria for termination: amelioration of symptoms, substantial resolution of the transference, and Kristen having developed the capacity for self-observation. When the patient wants to leave therapy before achieving the goals, the therapist must weigh her chances of relapse against damaging her sense of autonomy in making such a decision. The Adlerian approach recommends preparing for termination when Kristen has consolidated her gains adequately to maintain herself, using ongoing self-monitoring and evaluation of her own behavior and coping.

The preparation for termination was emphasized by the psychoanalytic, self psychology, cognitive analytic, and Adlerian models, who set the date well in advance to allow time to work on separation-individuation issues and feelings about ending. The therapist must help Kristen to process the accomplishments of therapy and explore her fears and disappointments. The cognitive analytic therapists discussed the need to preempt Kristen's flight once the date has been set, helping her to experience the anger and sadness over the loss of therapy. They sometimes have client and therapist write good-bye letters to each other summarizing therapy and plans for the future.

Planning for the future is essential in the termination process, and the cognitive-behavior and Adlerian therapists specifically mentioned teaching Kristen that recovery is a lifelong process. Several models used relapse prevention techniques such as identifying risks for a slip or relapse and developing behavioral plans to avoid and, when necessary, to manage them. Identifying outside supports and when further therapy sessions are needed are other important steps in planning, conveying that returning is not a defeat. Most models build in "booster sessions" or follow-up sessions over several months or years.

MECHANISMS OF CHANGE

Just as the problems of eating disorders build on one another and develop powerful cycles, so can the positive factors leading to recovery. The models we have presented address links among thoughts, feelings, and behaviors which, when shifted, allow for a new set of connections and an elimination of the need for the eating disorder.

Most models identified the therapist's relationship with Kristen as an essential precursor to change, with emphases on the therapist's provision of empathy, safety, guidance, insight, and support tools. In psychoanalytic psychotherapy and self psychology therapy, Kristen would be seen as internalizing aspects of the therapeutic relationship—the abilities to self-soothe, to contain her own feelings, to experience her own needs and desires, and to value and care for herself.

Another element shared by most models is the belief that Kristen needs a cognitive understanding of how her thoughts, feelings, and behaviors are related to her eating disorder. The etiological model of each type of therapy is applied to help Kristen make sense of her experience. The cognitive-behavior therapists see the primary mechanisms of change as cognitive, such as altering Kristen's overvalued ideas about thinness and her core beliefs, but they believe change also comes about by breaking the connections between distorted thinking, negative emotions, and disturbed eating behaviors. The interpersonal psychotherapists focus on the interpersonal problem most associated with the onset and/or maintenance of Kristen's eating disorder.

Both Sands and Wilfley et al. mentioned that reinstating developmental processes were mechanisms of change. The integrative cognitive authors stated that behavioral change in eating patterns would have to occur before interpersonal and cognitive change. Then it is essential to modify Kristen's cognitive style; working models of self, others, and the world; core beliefs; the self-ideal discrepancy; overvalued ideas about thinness; and/or self-undermining cognitions.

The elementary pragmatic model noted some of Kristen's strengths as mechanisms of change—her ability to share creatively, her capacity to doubt, and her ability to identify with others' help. Bryant-Waugh emphasized Kristen's discovery of a capacity to make better choices for herself. The integrative cognitive approach would situate Kristen's problems in relation to cultural forces and help her consider the maladaptiveness of dieting and more positive alternatives.

All approaches saw improvements in Kristen's interpersonal relationships as essential for her growth, related to her self-esteem and eating disorder symptoms.

CONCLUSION

The evidence of integrative thinking, albeit in varying degrees, is striking within this volume. While this is probably not a surprise to therapists who work in the field of eating disorders, the increasing sophistication of multidimensional models of eating disorders and their application is notable.

Fundamental themes across orientations are interpersonal relationships, underlying beliefs about the self and others, and cognitive patterns or styles. The authors varied in relative emphasis on cognition, emotion, and behavior, but each one has some way of connecting these aspects of the person to the eating disorder and each other.

All models saw a therapeutic alliance as essential to treatment and Kristen's motivation as critical to the success of psychotherapy. However, there were differences in the degree of the therapist's directiveness about behavioral changes, explicit discussion about the therapeutic relationship, and conceptualization about matching Kristen's readiness to change with intervention strategies. All authors agreed that an SSRI may be advisable, but there were differences in who would handle various aspects of Kristen's medical and nutritional care.

The use of time in a shorter-term, time-limited structure and a longer-term therapy of undefined length was a major difference in the ways of working. Time-limited models generally used more assessment tools and more structured goal-setting, and were more likely to use homework, including ongoing self-monitoring and workbooks. All models specified preparations for the ending of therapy that recognized the high relapse rate among eating disorders, but several also emphasized the continuing improvement after therapy and the potential sense of self-efficacy that Kristen may gain from this.

In addition, there seemed to be a big difference in the resources available to different therapists and clients. Having multiple levels of care and many kinds of therapists available provides options that the private practitioner cannot provide, and being in a rural setting or a system with few resources limits the way of working. The authors of these chapters were clearly speaking from their own available resources, and there were many differences among them, ranging from multilevel programs to solo practice.

It is difficult to tell what remains unsaid in these chapters, what we might observe about these therapies if watching the work directly. For example, would the family therapy of the cognitive-behavior therapists resemble the Adlerians' use of family sessions? Is the work on interpersonal relationships in interpersonal psychotherapy very different from cognitive analytic work? Since it is not possible to be comprehensive in a chapter, there may be more similarities, or differences, than we have seen so far.

Lastly, it is interesting that some authors referred to Kristen as anorexic while others saw her as bulimic, yet the label did not seem to be the determining factor in treatment recommendations. Anorexia nervosa and bulimia nervosa share a number of diagnostic criteria, especially the bulimic subtype of anorexia, and it is common in clinical practice to see clients who alternate between the two diagnoses. These authors have addressed multiple relationships between eating disorder symptomatology and Kristen's inner world and interpersonal relationships, and at this point in time it seems that this is the most useful approach for clinicians.

The contributions of theoreticians and clinicians from many branches of psychotherapy have enriched our clinical understanding of the eating disorders. Research has demonstrated significant risk factors, characteristics of persons with eating disorders, and diverse efficacious methods of treatment, but there is a great deal yet to be learned about processes of change. Sophisticated clinicians are continuing to search for approaches that address the multidimensional nature of eating disorders and the individualized nature of psychotherapy.

Appendix

	Treatment Model
Cognitive-Behavioral	Continuum of care (4 levels) depending on severity. Specific protocol, multidisciplinary, including CBT individual, family, group, and pharmacotherapy, dietary, and medical interventions. Core of disorder: fear of weight gain, overconcern with body size and shape, body-image disturbance. Aim: decrease fear of weight gain and extreme weight control methods. Exposure to foods, prevention of purging, and work on cognitive biases, automatic thoughts, and core beliefs regarding worthiness.
Psychoanalytic	Dynamic unconscious; focus on motivations, conflicting mental processes, use of defenses to make compromises, influence of interpersonal patterns from childhood. Bulimic symptoms reflect different conflicts, compromises, relational history. Bulimics don't care for their own needs—body is poorly integrated into the sense of self, including sexuality, distortions, delusions about body shape.
Interpersonal	Focus on disturbances in social functioning related to onset and/or maintenance of disorder in 4 domains: grief, interpersonal role disputes, role transitions, interpersonal deficits; based on the relationship between interpersonal functioning, low self-esteem, negative mood, and eating behaviors.
Dev.-Systemic-Feminist	Integrates developmental psychology, systems theory's application to therapy, and feminist ideology. Explores developmental history, maintenance of problems within family context. Based on right to equality between men and women; validates enhancement of autonomy and self-worth, building on strengths. Requires collaborative relationship, validation, identification of factors maintaining or perpetuating problems or inhibiting progress. Broadly nondirective, but structured; uses functional analysis for formulation.
Self Psychology	Intensive, long-term therapy focused on underlying dynamics via the transference relationship rather than on symptoms or activities. Therapist has empathic/introspective stance, fo-

cuses on client's self experience (cohesiveness, vitality), self-object experience, and self-object transference. ED is used to meet selfobject needs, avoid disappointment and shame. Early needs reexperienced in therapeutic relationship. Aim: patient will give people another chance.

Adlerian	Sees individual as socially embedded, creative, responsible, and becoming. All behavior is social, purposeful (conscious or unconscious); basis for movement is subjectively held beliefs about the self, self-ideal, nature of reality, and methods of movement open to one. Family influences values, social interest, meaning. Individuals are challenged to demonstrate healthy social interest within the life tasks. Three stages of therapy: reflective, re-creative, and creative-constructive; client sees ED as "sideshow" in personal story, edits patterns.
Elementary Pragmatic	Family therapy or intensive, multidisciplinary day hospital treatment. Interactions evaluated and interventions planned according to taxonomy of 16 interactional styles. With AN, usually work toward distant father entering and accepting her world.
Integrative Cognitive	Broad model of cause and maintenance—cultural variables, life experiences, temperament, representations of self and other, interpersonal schemas, relationship patterns, affect regulation. Techniques from CBT; feminist, interpersonal, and emotion theorists; motivational interviewing. Self perceived to be deficient, threatening relationships, and leading to negative mood. Person develops *submission, wall-off,* anxious attachment, *attack* styles to prevent withdrawal of significant others. Cognitive styles: *self-control, self blame,* and *self neglect.* Person turns to ED symptoms to resolve self discrepancy, avoid negative affect and more meaningful issues.
Cognitive Analytic	By AN, the person tries to cognitively avoid severe life events or problems; disturbance in sense of self and working models about the world; low levels of mastery. Maladaptive core schemata from early relationships in areas of care eliciting, caregiving, with peers varying in cooperation, competitiveness. Sequence interventions by transtheoretical model of change, using motivational interviewing, cognitive therapy techniques, and prominent focus on interpersonal relationship patterns in earlier attachments, current relationships, and therapeutic relationship. Four levels of change.

The Therapist's Skills and Attributes

Cognitive-Behavioral	Case manager is primary therapist through all levels of care. Female therapist is better because of sexual trauma. CBT train-

ing + 2 years of full-time ED treatment experience (or intensive supervision). Healthy model for flexible eating habits, no over-concern about weight and shape. Sensitive to client's overvalued ideas. Good boundaries, strong sense of responsibility, not perfectionistic. Well-trained in the philosophy of science.

Psychoanalytic — One- or 2-year postdoctoral program that includes theory, supervised therapy, and psychoanalysis to do psychoanalytic psychotherapy. To do psychoanalysis: 5–6 years of courses, 8–12 years total study. Need personal warmth, genuineness, truthfulness without a need for self-disclosure, empathy, patience, self-awareness, appreciation of complexity of human nature, ability to tolerate and contain intense transference, cognitive flexibility, ingenuity in eliciting self-exploration, and the ability to be intensely involved without losing judgment.

Interpersonal — Reading, training, and tape supervision in IPT; familiar with eating disorders; professional degree + 2 years of psychotherapy experience. Present orientation, intensive interpersonal focus; able to relate interpersonal and eating disturbances, quickly see patterns, maintain focus, encourage patient responsibility, offer hope, foster safe and supportive working environment.

Dev.-Systemic-Feminist — Genuineness, empathy, respect, acceptance of individual differences. Knowledge of developmental stages and tasks, impact of events. Able to address power differential, extract and build on client's strengths, positively reframe, be creative and spontaneous, firm, and negotiate therapeutic objectives, especially around health and safety.

Self Psychology — Capacity to empathize deeply is most important. Intellectual acumen, verbal skill, sensitivity, tact to formulate interpretations that make the patient feel deeply understood. Warm, human, resonating with patient's experience rather than being "neutral."

Adlerian — Rapport, empathy, self-awareness in interaction, maturity, open-mindedness. Skilled in listening, reflective focusing with families, Socratic questioning, lifestyle assessment. Knowledge of systems, including families and groups. Collaborative with other professionals; gets peer supervision and consultation.

Elementary Pragmatic — Expert in family therapy, minimum of 4 years training, with 500 hours of theory and practice. Knowledge of Elementary Pragmatic Model. Empathy, interest in the family. Able to strategize changing rules of the family, their perceptions of reality.

Integrative Cognitive	Incorporate 2 competing perspectives: *focus* the treatment in a clinically useful manner and assess *multiple aspects* of patient's functioning. Comfortable with basic CBT components, able to address recurring interpersonal patterns and cognitive maps. Warm, curious, well-differentiated, collaborative. Sensitive to patient's emotional responding and able to see patterns of emotional regulation. Validates ambivalence about change, doesn't force treatment in any way.
Cognitive Analytic	Trained in motivational interviewing, cognitive analytic therapy; on-going supervision. Directive, client-centered style. Warm, empathic, accepting, affirming. Develops collaborative relationships, affirms patient's freedom of choice, self-direction. Able to reflect on transference and countertransference to help form solid therapeutic alliance.

Assessment	
Cognitive-Behavioral	Three- to 4-hour outpatient assessment session. Psychological assessment: IDED-IV, EAT, Bulimia Test—Revised, BDI, SCID, Body Image Assessment; interview for PTSD and maybe OCPD and Major Depression. Psychiatric assessment: diagnose opinion, family history of psychiatric problems, biological and psychosocial determinants, need for medication follow-up and meds.; get medical history. Dietary assessment: dietary history, current nutrient intake, determination of normal weight range; teach self-monitoring if outpatient. Body composition evaluation: bioelectric impedance and skinfold measurement for body composition to obtain BMI, estimate of body fat, lean body mass, and body fluids. May order medical evaluation and lab studies, have follow-up(s) with patient and family
Psychoanalytic	Usually requires several sessions initially, and assessment, conceptualization, hypothesis testing, and reevaluation continue throughout treatment. WAIS-III, Rorschach, TAT, and MMPI may be used for speed or when the patient is unwilling or unable to provide accurate information. *Object relations evaluation:* fears about early relationships? Quality of intimate rel.? Sexual history? Variable or distant? How do they end? Etcetera. Affects therapeutic relationship and her ability to use it. *Introspection:* How aware is she toward self and others? Experiences what feelings? Sees relationship between feelings and behavior? Between events and eating symptoms? Can she use interpretations to become more aware or increase her flexibility of response? *Ego strength:* How does she handle daily anxieties, pressures, serious disappointments? Reality testing? Judg-

ment? Regulation of emotion and impulses? Defenses to contain emotions and maintain self esteem? *Other symptomatology:* evaluate self-esteem, guilt, depression, anger, interpersonal sensitivity, quality of relationships, fear of loss of control, impulsivity (substance abuse, self-mutilation included), sequelae of sexual assault and PTSD, suicidality, potential for other abuse, personality disorders. *Motivation for treatment:* Motivation depends on ego strength, level of discomfort, desire for health, willingness to assume responsibility, stamina to endure emotional pain. Infer from previous therapies her response to frustrating life circumstances, willingness to make sessions a priority.

Interpersonal	Eating Disorders Examination, SCID for alcohol abuse/dependence, Inventory of Interpersonal Problems, Social Adjustment Scale, UCLA Loneliness Scale—Revised, Beck Depression Inventory, SCL-90-R, Emotional Eating Scale, Rosenberg Self-Esteem Scale, Interpersonal Inventory. Generate hypotheses about interpersonal problems.
Dev.-Systemic-Feminist	Detailed history, general mental state examination, risk assessment, Eating Disorders Examination. Two parallel time lines: key life events and weight history, eating difficulties, weight and shape concerns. Meet with Kristen and family member(s) to learn more about early experiences and responses with current dysfunctional coping strategies, developmental and systemic factors. Do cost-benefit analysis of keeping or giving up ED.
Self Psychology	Assess family history of mental disorders, EDs, extent of depression, suicidablity, early sexual trauma. Learn about Kristen's inner world by how she chooses to reveal herself. Ongoing evaluation of Kristen's self-experience, shown in thinking, affect, behavior; degree of cohesiveness and vitality, how easily narcissistically injured; how flexible or rigid boundaries are between self states; self-object transference; how quickly she can recover after a rupture; self states before and during bingeing, purging, and exercising; functions of ED (comfort, punishment, dissociation?)
Adlerian	Assess suicidal thoughts, behavior; secure medical team collaboration. Lifestyle assessment, MCMI III, Life Style Inventory (family constellation, early recollections, interfering attitudes and beliefs, behaviors, assets, strengths). Interview on siblings, physical development, school, meaning given to life, gender and sexual information, social and parental relationships, demographics, models, 6–8 early memories.
Elementary	Interview with patient and family to identify relational styles,

Pragmatic	assess commitment to solving the problem. Tests: SISCI-1, Self-View Questionnaire.
Integrative Cognitive	Psychiatric interview to assess eating behaviors and associated psychopathology, for example, EDE, SCID; may use Wisconsin Personality Inventory of Differential Assessment of Personality Pathology to clarify personality traits. Patient workbook: modification of the Selves Questionnaire and Physical Appearance Questionnaire to clarify self- discrepancy (actual vs. ideal or ought self). Self monitoring logs for food and liquids; Interpersonal Pattern Worksheet.
Cognitive Analytic	Look at Kristen's meta-beliefs about her anorexia—how it has helped her. Don't focus prematurely on her work crisis or lecture her on dangers to her health.

Therapeutic Goals

Cognitive-Behavioral	Initial goals: adequate nutrition to increase weight; 3 meals and 2 snacks/day without purging; decrease depression. Long-term goals: decrease anxiety related to eating, modify body-image disturbances, increase interpersonal trust, improve PTSD and OCPD symptoms.
Psychoanalytic	Relief of emotional distress, reduction of bulimic symptoms, acquisition of solutions to deal with life problems, especially work. Short-term: development of a therapeutic alliance, development of an observing ego, awareness of affective states, recognition of consistent patterns of behavior incongruent with Kristen's goals. Long-term: altering personality characteristics and interpersonal behavior patterns, understanding functions of bulimic symptoms, improving self-esteem, increasing degree of self-differentiation, ameliorating bulimic symptomatology, improving social functioning.
Interpersonal	Reduce interpersonal deficits; write individualized goals which help reduce isolation and encourage emotionally intimate friendships, reducing the need to turn to food. Identify ways ED is used to substitute for relationships.
Dev.-Systemic-Feminist	Generate goals together, related to ED or other areas. Accept putting job first, but make clear that other priorities may emerge. Aim for client to gain awareness, become more in control of emotional and behavioral responses, find alternative coping mechanisms. Goals usually include staying out of the hospital, improving relationships, deriving satisfaction in some aspects of her life.
Self Psychology	Symptomatic and underlying structural change, mainly

strengthening the self through integrating unfulfilled self-object longings of childhood; includes better tension and affect regulation, vitality, self-esteem, relationships. Kristen must decide on behavioral goals.

Adlerian	Understand function of ED and make choices in line with life goals. Reduce social isolation, improve interpersonal relationships; revise self-defeating goal, beliefs, values; manage feeling states. Resolve sexual trauma, family issues.
Elementary Pragmatic	Reduction of bulimic behavior and ambivalence, increase in capacity to uphold her own world on a stable basis.
Integrative Cognitive	Normalization of meal consumption and weight restoration. Reduction of self-discrepancy. Modify interpersonal patterns and cognitive styles, increase self-acceptance.
Cognitive Analytic	Help Kristen move to the action phase. Develop a good therapeutic alliance. Safe weight level. Understand role of ED, learn alternative coping strategies, alter maladaptive schemata. Improve relationships.

Timeline for Therapy

Cognitive-Behavioral	Inpatient: 2–3 weeks to stabilize medical condition, begin refeeding, perhaps begin antidepressant. Partial day hospital program: 7 days/week for 6–8 weeks, moving to 3–4 days/week. Intensive outpatient therapy: 3–5 hours/day for 3–5 days/week, fading to once/week over 3–4 weeks. Outpatient: once/week individual and group therapy; fading over 6–12 months. Follow-up for several years.
Psychoanalytic	If psychoanalysis, 4–5 sessions/week. Psychoanalytic psychotherapy: frequency depends on client's ego strength and on the therapist's orientation (time-limited vs. open-ended). Length: 1–5 years, until personality patterns are resolved, not just till symptoms remit.
Interpersonal	Typically 12–20 sessions of individual therapy or 16–20 for group treatment. Three stages: identifying the problem area, working on it, and consolidating work, and preparing Kristen for work on her own.
Dev.-Systemic-Feminist	Time-limited therapy delivered in blocks of sessions, each ending with review session, spanning 12–18 months. Package includes 2 assessment sessions, around 18 individual therapy sessions, 3 review sessions, and 5 individual support sessions.
Self Psychology	See 3 times/week if Kristen is willing because of level of distress

and severity of ED. Can't predict length of therapy without knowing her or how the transference will develop.

Adlerian

One-and-one-half to 2 years of ongoing, intensive work. Phase 1: 2–3 sessions/week, perhaps 1.5 hours each. Terminate individual and family sessions over 6 months, stay in group 6–8 months longer.

Elementary
Pragmatic

Ten weekly 1-hour sessions of family therapy, with expert supervision during 5th and 10th. Day hospital: 6 weeks, 7 hours/day.

Integrative
Cognitive

Twenty-session protocol: twice/week for 4 weeks, weekly thereafter. Phase I, 1–3 sessions; Phase II, 4–6 sessions; Phase III, 9–11 sessions; Phase IV, 1–3 sessions.

Cognitive Analytic

Twenty sessions of weekly therapy (50 minutes) followed by 5 monthly sessions.

Case Conceptualization

Cognitive-
Behavioral

PTSD and OCD are comorbid to Anorexia Nervosa and Major Depression, and played an etiological role as well. ED is from life stressors starting at age 8 (business crisis) into adolescence (isolation from parents, parental conflict, and separation), and from overconcern with body size and shape (social pressures from grandmother, gymnastics). In adolescence, dieting and exercise were used to control anxiety about body and appearance; there was an interaction of habits, emotions, and overvalued ideas leading to Kristen's secret of success as control of eating and body size, leading to anorexia. Date rape led to depression and binge-eating, which led to purging. ED was controlled for a few years, with relapse related to fiancé's infidelity, binge/purge behavior in travel, and depression.

Psychoanalytic

A full conceptualization would evolve over time. Kristen's family emphasized beauty, competition, and perfection. Charlotte's failure to meet her family's expectations may have lowered her self-esteem, making it hard to be attuned to Kristen's needs. Themes of need, emptiness, consumption, greed, and satiety in family; Kristen tries to repair emptiness through achievement, use of relationships, and food. Kristen's accomplishments gratified her mother but placed her in competition or painful contrast; she had to quell some of her own initiatives and negative emotions. Kristen was very close to her mother and has had few same-sex relationships and poor heterosexual relationships. Kristen binged to feel full but feared fatness; she hides needs and problems out of shame. Defenses: uses somatization, isolation of affect, and acting out (work, exercise, binge/purge, alcohol) to avoid her tumultuous inner life and not become overwhelmed by feelings. Kristen holds in anger until she "vomits" it destructively; at work she was angry when she couldn't control the client's reaction or get approval. She can't allow herself joy or contentment when her mother is unhappy for fear of destroying her, and thus can't individuate. Restricting relates to control issues; bingeing is symbolically emotional nurturance, while vomiting frees her of the unwanted aspects. Four sexual traumas: father's affair, high school boyfriend's abandonment, rape, and fiancé cheating on her.

Interpersonal	Kristen's problem area is interpersonal deficits—social isolation and chronically unfulfilling relationships.
Dev.-Systemic-Feminist	Strengths: works hard, committed, determined, under pressure to live up to expectations. Family role: receptacle for parents' wishes and aspirations, increasingly impossible to fulfill; need to do things right, not to displease, and to be good at all she does. Personality traits: accommodating to others, minimizes own needs and distress, self-critical, self- doubting; all-or-nothing patterns; for example, if she can't be good, pleasing and successful, she can't continue in relationships. Work crisis experienced as catastrophic. Now she's highly anxious, confused, out of control, failing to keep work commitments. "Slapping on a smile" isn't working.
Self Psychology	Split-off need for others, physical and psychological needs, desires; disregards her limitations, seeks to appear perfect. Grandiose, omnipotent sector of personality is defense against emptiness and longings; closed system of self- sufficiency and perfectionism; ED is selfobject substitute arising out of aloneness. Consciously identifies with grandiose sector of personality, bulimia shows the other side. ED is the behavioral component of a separate self state with its own set of needs, feelings, perceptions, identity, and behavior—healthy longings. "Since I don't have needs, you are not failing to meet them." Trouble with affect regulation, self-esteem; couldn't idealize figures and merge; also mirroring deficits—mirrored false self. Gratified parents' emphasis on appearance. Trauma of betrayal—fire, father's affair, rape, fiancé's affair. With first two, turned to self; second two, to ED. Shame and rage probably shattered self experience. "Survivor guilt"—doing the best in her family. Strengths: intelligent, attractive, talented in dance, music, sports; hard-working, competent, persistent, creative, productive; social skills.

Adlerian	Core issues: control, competence, identity. Had to please, conform to get what she needed. Undifferentiated identity possibly related to unaddressed grief over sister. Crisis of parents' divorce aborted self-exploration; looked to peer standards for identity and acceptability, based on family's values (social status, physical appearance). Dissatisfaction with self concretized in body dissatisfaction. Control of her body promised self-acceptance, competence, with Kristen as the sole judge; could both confirm and excel, meet others' expectations, and be self-determined. Coped with peer involvement through ED; abusive romantic relationships.
Elementary Pragmatic	Positive periods: excessively rigid norms of behavior; hard to help her. Negative periods: she can't maintain her own world; oscillating and ambivalent; acceptance of treatment a positive sign. Intelligent, capable, refined, and self-reflective mind, capable of deepening its own world with expert guidance.
Integrative Cognitive	Kristen's marked self-discrepancy is instrumental in her ED and psychopathology. Relates to family's focus on physical appearance, extreme devotion to work; fear of being out of control produces shame. Cognitive style: great self-control relates to ought-standards, as does self-neglect. Interpersonal patterns: withdrawn or submissive; early family life perhaps left her feeling insecure and inadequate.
Cognitive Analytic	Kristen's mother's family had powerful emphasis on competition; father was parentified child, with powerful caregiving schema. Parents' marriage was effort to compensate for maladaptive attachment relationships, but it didn't work; fire and affair were particularly hard, neither processed adequately. Mother insecure after Kristen's birth, threatened by stillbirth, unsupported by husband. Abandoned by both parents after the fire; conditional acceptance by grandmother. Abandonment by father in high school, partly because of mother's extreme reaction. Attachment schemata: others can't be trusted to give security, or are abandoning. Strong competitive schema from being youngest, having competitive family, and impaired self-esteem made cooperative behavior weaker, couldn't respond to peer support. Fueled academic success but insecure; avoidant attachment led to relationship problems. Drawn to exciting, special, powerful men to compensate. Formulation shared with client by letter with diagrams, asking for feedback.

The Therapeutic Bond

Cognitive-Behavioral	Encourage Kristen to use rationality and intellect to change feelings and behavior, while giving encouragement, support,

	and reassurance. Use interpersonal processes in psychotherapy to understand and modify dysfunctional beliefs about relationships. Transference: Kristen believes she can't have mutually fulfilling relationships, that trying produces pain; she will test the therapist's trustworthiness and acceptance.
Psychoanalytic	Alliance fostered by therapist's empathy. Therapist needs to be consistent, predictable, have good boundaries. Kristen fears abandonment and rejection, or that she'll destroy the relationship with anger or imperfection. Need strong, collaborative bond for Kristen to overcome mistrust, fear of being controlled. Countertransference: anger, protectiveness, or helplessness; compliance and false self can lead to boredom, frustration, or pushing, with Kristen distancing or trying to control the therapy.
Interpersonal	Therapist conveys supportive and strong working alliance through genuine regard for Kristen and respect for the relationship; creates safe environment for feedback, experimentation, and experience of being esteemed.
Dev.-Systemic-Feminist	Therapist shows respect, acceptance, reliability, positive sense of separateness, clear boundaries, no self-disclosure; helps Kristen address difficulties by working together, not by having the answers; self-reliance is encouraged. Transference and countertransference may occur in relationship; dialogue furthers self-understanding.
Self Psychology	Relational needs experienced in relationship to therapist; structural change occurs through working through of the transference, analyzing disruptions. Needs have been detoured to food—this relationship has to be understood first. Firm boundaries and empathy create safety to explore; keep self-disclosure to a minimum.
Adlerian	Kristen needs safety to risk, know the therapist will stay with her even if imperfect, tolerating anxiety, conflict, and fears without becoming afraid or dogmatic. Requires that therapist be clear on own issues around power, competence, identity, body image, and gender. Kristen may treat therapist as omnipotent; therapist must insist on a collaborative relationship, modeling tolerance of anxiety and uncertainty. Must sidestep power struggles, avoid self-disclosure, set boundaries; in limit-setting, use collaborative approach and logical consequences.
Elementary Pragmatic	Therapist presents self as expert interested in helping Kristen understand and solve her problem. Warm, able to establish closeness, well-trained; seeks to know the world of the patient and modify her cognitive framework. Supervisor is *Deus ex machina*. Day hospital: multiple relationships, transferences, and experiments with roles.

Integrative Cognitive	Highly collaborative relationship, with therapist very attuned to Kristen's subjective experience; communicate interest in understanding and introduce opportunities for behavior change. Relationship is reality based, but if transference threatens treatment or gives data, discuss. Therapist keeps boundaries, respects Kristen's right to self- determination, isn't highly authoritative. If high degree of risk, therapist will shift to crisis mode.
Cognitive Analytic	Open, collaborative relationship. Therapist needs to try to bolster self-esteem and self-efficacy, avoid hint of criticism or disappointment. Also, provide clear boundaries, as about time, duration, and setting of therapy, rules about disruptions such as missing sessions, losing weight, metabolic crises.

Roles in the Therapeutic Relationship

Cognitive-Behavior	Therapist engages Kristen's active participation in "collaborative empiricism." Therapist constantly tests own hypotheses. Clarify roles early—the therapist isn't going to "fix it" or force her to change; written contract. May use Decision Analysis Form to increase motivation. Have Kristen make pie charts on actual and desired amount of time spent on fears and habits related to weight gain.
Psychoanalytic	Therapist is nondirective and rarely structures sessions, makes specific suggestions, or gives homework. Work with patient's current concerns, helping her understand the implications of her verbalizations. Transference is identified, explored, and interpreted by therapist who is neutral, not controlling, or disengaged. Being Kristen's superego would allow her to disown hers, rebel, then acquiesce out of fear of retaliation and disapproval. Countertransference shows issues that need exploring.
Interpersonal	The relationship enacts the social microcosm, so the therapist relates interpersonal patterns in the session to the patient's social life. The therapist is not distant, passive, or interpretative, but in a relationship with Kristen working collaboratively based on agreed-upon goals.
Dev.-Systemic-Feminist	Collaborators with a shared focus. Therapist sets out basic tenets of the working relationship—will inform, reflect, and advise where appropriate, but rarely issue instructions. Therapist expects Kristen to work on what they've agreed on, at her own speed. Only directive if client has lost ability to take care of herself, making clear this is time-limited.

Self Psychology	Therapist's central role: sustained empathic inquiry, neutral enough to allow transference. Warm, human, interpersonally responsive. Kristen must say what comes to mind, observe certain boundaries, and try to be honest. Collaborative process with reciprocal, mutual influence. Therapist notes patient's unconscious communications, monitors personal reactions; if enactments occur, both sort them out.
Adlerian	Bond founded on honesty and encouragement. Directive in getting client to formulate own point of view, challenge beliefs, try new solutions. Encourages Kristen to generate and try creative choices, anticipating possible consequences, tolerating imperfection; frames questions encouraging social interest in each life task area; encourages use of outside resources that support movement.
Elementary Pragmatic	Therapist explains roles according to Elementary Pragmatic Model, defines boundaries between family subsystems. Individual treatment: therapist is warm, humane, competent expert helping patient find new solutions. Day hospital: many roles for Kristen in relation to multiple professionals.
Integrative Cognitive	Therapist first gains awareness and appreciation of Kristen's subjective emotional experiences, validates them, then explores possibilities for change in eating behaviors, cognitive, and interpersonal functioning. Patient is collaborator (homework, active discussion of workbook, relevant situations); if not, discuss to remove sources of noncollaboration.
Cognitive Analytic	Therapist uses many objective and subjective markers to direct therapy, assess therapeutic relationship and readiness to change. Draws diagram of therapeutic relationship, noting parallels to other important attachment patterns. Therapist constantly checks on accuracy of communication, avoids power struggles, invites Kristen's help and constructive criticism, and gets supervision.

Techniques and Methods of Working

Cognitive-Behavioral	Continuum of care. Seek weight gain of 1–2 lbs./wk. Exchange system, nutritional education, self-monitoring, behavioral contracting, highly structured days, homework. Work on "automatic thoughts" about eating and weight, alternative ways of coping with stress, identity, general schemata about self-worth, healthy relationships, perfectionism. Body image therapy includes education, cognitive restructuring, behavioral exposure. Family education about eating disorders and the recovery process. May use anxiolytic or SSRI.

Psychoanalytic	Foster working alliance, educate about treatment process, support development of observing ego, active participation in treatment. If needed, promote hope, reality testing, and problem solving initially. Explore thoughts and feelings before and after bingeing or purging. Highlight inconsistencies between behavior and goals to help develop introspection. Techniques include: informative comments or clarifications, identification and articulation of feelings, and interpretations of defenses, patterns of behavior, resistance to treatment, transference. "Work through" transference, identify parallels in current life, therapeutic relationship, and early relationships.
Interpersonal	Relate ED symptoms to interpersonal issues by encouragement of affect, communication analysis, identifying 1–2 people from whom to get feedback, clarification, exploratory techniques. Sessions 1–5: evaluate interpersonal history, ED, past therapy; educate about ED, IPT; reach consensus on problem, goals, and steps. Sessions 6–15: work on problems including outside practice, review week's difficult interactions and feelings of isolation, look at patterns in therapeutic relationship, relate ED symptoms to isolation. Sessions 16–20: review, consolidation, planning.
Dev.-Systemic-Feminist	Main tasks: explore (genograms, life journeys, diaries), understand (reflective listening, art therapy, psychoeducation, cognitive analytic techniques), accept, experiment (cognitive-behavioral, problem solving, and solution focused strategies, homework). Have at least 1 collaborator (dietician, relaxation trainer, co-therapist for family sessions). Write letter to Kristen with proposed initial formulation to discuss. Three blocks of sessions with month in between (readings, support network, phone contacts possible), plus follow-up.
Self Psychology	Standard psychoanalytic techniques. Work with internist to ensure Kristen's physical safety, perhaps nutritionist. No involvement of significant others or homework. Share useful behavioral ideas (e.g., monitoring) and information. Help Kristen understand needs, defenses transferred to food and eating. Arouse the bulimic self state in the session so her observing self can communicate it. Affirm the assertion and punishment of self. Then needs can be slowly transferred to therapist, with fears of retraumatization addressed over and over, and her bulimia respected.
Adlerian	Establish medical plan with Kristen, parents, and medical team; set parameters on weight loss, hospitalization, etcetera. Establish rapport through lifestyle assessment. Look at what she previously learned from therapy, positive patterns during

	periods of recovery, analyze effects of patterns on her life, beliefs, and self and others associated with them. Family work; journaling; teach self-calming skills, assertiveness; cognitive techniques—work on cognitive distortions, problem solving, decision making, decrease pleasing or impulsive behavior. Social engagement, groups.
Elementary Pragmatic	May use SSRI. Family therapy with relational style "going towards her world," helping Kristen understand it better. Then therapist amplifies her world paradoxically. Father will be given tasks to do with her at home or on trip. May prescribe CD-ROM program to reduce tension, self-help books, having Kristen change something (e.g., eat with chopsticks). Day hospital: course on EDs, body-image work, dance and art therapy, group therapy.
Integrative Cognitive	Motivational interviewing strategies; psychoeducation; homework exercises to identify origins of self discrepancy and appearance standards. Introduce strategies for increasing self-acceptance, modifying maladaptive self-evaluative standards. Implement normalized approach to eating, with coping skills to manage attendant anxiety. Functional analysis of relationship between interpersonal and ED behaviors; goal to change 1–2 patterns. Work on interpersonal schemas, historical antecedents, cognitive style, and alternatives.
Cognitive Analytic	Motivational interviewing; explore meta-beliefs about AN (have Kristen write letter to AN as a friend, make collage or painting, list pros and cons). Using formulation, agree on therapy goals. Monitor problem behaviors. Foster awareness of maladaptive schemata, triggers, effects on her life (loop diagrams link thoughts, feelings, behaviors). Use cognitive restructuring, emotional processing, and behavioral experiments. May add sessions with significant others; focus on how they might help her, develop motivational interviewing skills. May use structured homework book.

Medical and Nutritional Issues

Cognitive-Behavioral	Refeed slowly, checking for edema, fluid overload, adequate gastric motility, and bowel function. May need gastric motility agents and bulk fiber. Predict temporary bloating and constipation. Dietary supplement, multivitamins if needed. Bone scan; calcium supplement and/or hormone replacement therapy. Dental consult.
Psychoanalytic	Talk directly with physician, set minimum weight to stay out of hospital. Someone other than the therapist should recom-

mend nutritionist, monitor weight, food intake, and eating behaviors to avoid control dynamics and allow focus on deeper issues. If psychotropic meds, use dynamically minded psychiatrist, since there are inevitable reactions.

Interpersonal

Starvation effects may compromise ability to benefit from psychotherapy. Therapist consults weekly with internist and dietitian. Kristen must reach and stay at 90% of recommended weight to continue in therapy; if condition worsens, medical treatment takes priority over psychological treatment.

Dev.-Systemic-
Feminist

Bone scan. Explain potential dangers of Kristen's behaviors, need for monitoring of physical well-being, and lab results. Clearly agree on who will provide medical backup care, get permission for therapist to collaborate. Will need regular blood tests and physical checks. Clearly agree if clinic nurse or therapist will weigh her.

Self Psychology

Collaborate with internist as condition of treatment. If Kristen's depressed, get psychiatric consult for medication. Use nutritionist, depending on Kristen's amount of knowledge, fear, and interest.

Adlerian

Medical personnel (expert in EDs) get medical history, symptoms, and side-effects, give information on medical consequences of EDs, focus on eliminating bulimic behavior, establishing good nutrition and eating patterns, address ED symptoms. Therapist confronts Kristen on medical status, sets limits yet is accepting of her struggle.

Elementary
Pragmatic

Physical exam; if SSRI, monitor transaminase. Blood and urinary tests, medications handled by psychiatrist on family therapy team. If trip with father, type of diet planned ahead of time with therapist. Day hospital: adequate diet provided.

Integrative
Cognitive

Assess for evidence of medical instability; patient must agree to be monitored medically while in treatment. Referral dietician may help in Phase II.

Cognitive Analytic

Initial medical evaluation. Measure urea and electrolytes weekly till normal, then monthly. EKG and bone scan best. Weigh each session. Monitor dehydration, blood pressure. If weight lost, may need day patient or inpatient treatment. Don't emphasize nutrition in first phase of therapy; worksheets then useful.

Potential Pitfalls

Cognitive-
Behavioral

Kristen doesn't fully acknowledge the seriousness of her ED, only motivated by decreased functioning at work. Previously not fully engaged in therapy. Could take "flight into health," relapsing quickly after inpatient treatment. May try to appear perfect instead of discussing feelings and fears. May not invest in the therapeutic relationship but remain superficial and intellectual.

Psychoanalytic	Mistrusting the therapist may lead to withholding information, deceit. Termination because method isn't gratifying. Lack of psychological-mindedness may create frustration, rather than verbal expression. Countertransference about issues, projective identifications, pseudo-compliance. Defensive independence instead of true individuation.
Interpersonal	Kristen has trouble identifying her emotions, connections to use of food. May fear being overpowered by emotions. May not work on goals due to lack of coping strategies, fear she'll get bigger and be less liked. May want to focus on eating and weight issues instead of the related feelings and impact of people on her mood. May fail to see severe restraint as a problem. Traumatic feelings about the rape resurface. May feel unable to reach out to anyone. May want to prolong treatment.
Dev.-Systemic-Feminist	Loss of Joe and concern about losing job increase Kristen's reliance on ED, and she may not feel able to lose her ED as well initially. Ambivalence about attending therapy because of taking time off work.
Self Psychology	Kristen may not be able to tolerate analytic therapy because of anxiety, fear of closeness, and revelation of needs, fantasies, and raw feelings. Therapist's interpretations of her fears and needs may shame, expose, or disarm her.
Adlerian	ED resistant to change because it's a coping mechanism to alleviate anxiety quickly. Could replace ED with unhealthy ways of coping, for example, alcohol, overwork, exercise. Discouragement.
Elementary Pragmatic	Uncommitted to quest for cure. Resistance. Relapse.
Integrative Cognitive	Self-discrepancy and self-blaming may make it hard to tolerate therapy because of shame or failure. Could see herself as a failure if she doesn't progress quickly, decrease ED symptoms without changing underlying patterns, minimize problems or feelings in session, or feel guilt or shame in discussing family's past, as if she's betraying or blaming them.
Cognitive Analytic	Therapist could get into role of powerful and critical other who has to be appeased. Therapist may become impatient or feel she's not doing enough for Kristen when she dips back into precontemplation, become pushy.

Termination and Relapse Prevention	
Cognitive-Behavioral	Teach recovery as a lifelong process. Teach to identify and practice adaptive responses to high-risk situations. Practice active coping skills and recovering quickly from lapses.
Psychoanalytic	Ideal criteria for termination: amelioration of symptoms, substantial resolution of the transference, capacity for self-observation. If patient pushes for termination after symptoms improve, therapist must weigh chances of relapse against damaging her sense of autonomy. Set date well in advance for work on separation-individuation issues; review and process accomplishments of therapy, explore fears, disappointments. Convey that return to treatment later isn't defeat.
Interpersonal	Collaborate on areas of difficulty, warning signs warranting further treatment. Relate fears about termination to past endings; encourage expression of feelings, grieving. Identify changes and successes. If client wants more sessions now, explore feelings of aloneness, ask her to work on her own a few weeks first. 8 monthly booster sessions.
Dev.-Systemic-Feminist	From the start, the therapist works with Kristen to bring out and build upon her strengths and inner resources, restart the developmental process, with the therapist's presence becoming less and less central. Further outside support is planned. Kristen has increased responsibility to assess her need for support and to obtain it.
Self Psychology	Termination date is determined months before, and therapist keeps it in awareness of both. Explore and work through feelings related to endings.
Adlerian	Kristen needs to see her work as ongoing, not being "cured." Decrease frequency over 6 months when Kristen has consolidated gains adequately to maintain herself. Develop specific plan for ongoing self-monitoring, evaluation of her behavior, coping, and support. Needs ongoing support group, booster sessions at stressful times.
Elementary Pragmatic	Preprogrammed termination. If no progress in family therapy, start new cycle or day hospital. Follow-up sessions after 3, 6, 12, and 24 months.
Integrative Cognitive	Phase IV: identify risks of slip or relapse, develop personalized behavioral plans to avoid them. Include focus on role of excessive self-evaluative standards and maladaptive interpersonal patterns and schemas.
Cognitive Analytic	Time-limited therapy keeps a focus on ending. Remind about

number of sessions and procedure involved in ending from 10th session on. Ending may reactivate maladaptive schemata, and therapist must preempt flight. Review the therapy, address failures and successes. Appraise what's been lost through the ending, experience anger and sadness. May write good-bye letters to each other summarizing therapy, addressing what will happen in the future.

	Mechanisms of Change
Cognitive-Behavioral	Primary mechanisms are cognitive: alter overvalued ideas about thinness, overcome fears, modify core beliefs. Break connections between distorted thinking, negative emotions, and disturbed patterns of eating.
Psychoanalytic	Corrective emotional experiences, making the unconscious conscious, the acquisition of insight, and internalization. Therapist provides safety, security, and experienced guidance; respects her and her right to be who she is. Kristen will borrow the therapist's good judgment until she internalizes self-care, self-valuing.
Interpersonal	Focus on interpersonal problem most associated with onset and/or maintenance of ED. Therapeutic bond of trust, collaboration, and advocacy. Milestones of social development improve her general functioning. Improved interpersonal functioning increases self-esteem, decreases isolation and ED symptoms. Better mood and self-esteem decrease dieting, weight, and shape concerns. Changes in long-term problems improve sense of efficacy.
Dev.-Systemic-Feminist	Better understanding of how and why she developed her pattern of responses to conflict, stress, and difficult emotions. Discovery of capacity to make personal choices to better her life, including reducing self-destructive ED behaviors and unaccepting, self-undermining cognitions. Collaborative process of exploring, understanding, reframing, accepting, and experimenting.
Self Psychology	Transmuting internalization process, reinstatement of developmental processes, integration of disowned domains of the self, and desomaticizing process. Allowed by therapist's empathic stance, holding Kristen's disowned parts simultaneously.
Adlerian	Quality and depth of therapeutic bond. Experiencing understanding and support in lifestyle assessment, then trust and intimacy. Therapist works with Kristen's point of view, slowly

introduces support tools and techniques, attends to her readiness for each, and modulates resistance and workaholic approaches to recovery.

Elementary
Pragmatic

Entering patient's world, amplifying it. Kristen's ability to share creatively, capacity to doubt, and ability to identify with others' help.

Integrative
Cognitive

Behavioral change in eating patterns before interpersonal and cognitive change. Learning about maladaptiveness of dieting, cultural forces, concrete alternatives. Modification of self-discrepancy, cognitive style. Learning to attach with awareness of boundaries and limits, express thoughts and feelings in relationships, change destructive patterns.

Cognitive Analytic

Helping Kristen to reflect upon her working models of self, others, and world, and her procedures and processes in relationships with others. Helping her become able to experience, express, process, and resolve avoided conflict so she can move away from her rigid patterns and limited, false solution provided by ED.

Index